Critical Thinking

Critical Thinking
An Introduction to the Basic Skills
5TH EDITION

William Hughes
Jonathan Lavery

broadview press

LIBRARY AND ARCHIVES CANADA CATALOGUING IN PUBLICATION

Lavery, Jonathan Allen, 1965–
      Critical thinking : an introduction to the basic skills / Jonathan Lavery. — 5th ed.

Includes index.
Fourth ed. written by: William Hughes, Jonathan Lavery.
ISBN 978-1-55111-884-0

      1. Critical thinking—Textbooks. 2. Logic—Textbooks. I. Title.

BC177.L39 2008   160   C2008-901415-4

BROADVIEW PRESS is an independent, international publishing house, incorporated in 1985. Broadview believes in shared ownership, both with its employees and with the general public; since the year 2000 Broadview shares have traded publicly on the Toronto Venture Exchange under the symbol BDP.

NORTH AMERICA
Post Office Box 1243,
Peterborough, Ontario,
Canada K9J 7H5

2215 Kenmore Ave.,
Buffalo, New York, USA 14207
TEL: (705) 743-8990
FAX: (705) 743-8353

customerservice@broadviewpress.com

UK, IRELAND, & CONTINENTAL EUROPE
NBN International, Estover Road,
Plymouth, UK PL6 7PY
TEL: 44 (0) 1752 202300
FAX: 44 (0) 1752 202330
enquiries@nbninternational.com

AUSTRALIA & NEW ZEALAND
UNIREPS, University of New South Wales
Sydney, NSW Australia 2052
TEL: 61 2 96640999
FAX: 61 2 96645420
infopress@unsw.edu.au

We welcome comments and suggestions regarding any aspect of our publications—please feel free to contact us at the addresses above or at broadview@broadview press.com/www.broadviewpress.com.

Broadview Press acknowledges the financial support of the Government of Canada through the Book Publishing Industry Development Program (BPIDP) for our publishing activities.

Cover design and interior by Em Dash Design

 This book is printed on paper containing 100% post-consumer fibre.

Printed in Canada

Contents

Acknowledgements   13

PART I: INTRODUCTION

Chapter 1:   Reasoning and Critical Thinking   17

1.1 Reasoning   17
1.2 The Concept of Logical Strength   19
1.3 Truth, Logical Strength, and Soundness   21
1.4 Critical Thinking Skills   22
1.5 Critical Thinking and the Science of Logic   24
1.6 Self-Test No. 1   25
1.7 Questions for Discussion   27

PART II: MEANING

Chapter 2:   Meaning and Definition   31

2.1 The Complexity of Language   31
2.2 The Meaning of Language   33
    2.2.1 The Reference Theory of Meaning   33
    2.2.2 The Idea Theory of Meaning   34
    2.2.3 Meaning As Use   34
2.3 The Main Functions of Language   36
2.4 Self-Test No. 2   40
2.5 Questions for Discussion   41
2.6 Definition   42

2.7 The Purposes of Definition   43
   2.7.1 Reportive Definitions   43
   2.7.2 Stipulative Definitions   43
   2.7.3 Essentialist Definitions   44

2.8 Methods of Definition   44
   2.8.1 Genus-Species   44
   2.8.2 Ostensive   45
   2.8.3 By Synonymn   46
   2.8.4 Operational   46
   2.8.5 Contextual   46

2.9 Assessing Reportive Definitions   46
   2.9.1 Too Broad   47
   2.9.2 Too Narrow   47
   2.9.3 Too Broad and Too Narrow   48
   2.9.4 Circular   48
   2.9.5 Obscure   49

2.10 Assessing Stipulative and Essentialist Definitions   49

2.11 A Warning   51

2.12 Self-Test No. 3   52

2.13 Questions for Discussion   53

Chapter 3:   Clarifying Meaning   55

3.1 The Principle of Charity   55

3.2 Linguistic Ambiguity   56
   3.2.1 Ambiguity and Vagueness   56
   3.2.2 Referential Ambiguity   58
   3.2.3 Grammatical Ambiguity   59
   3.2.4 Use and Mention   60

3.3 Self-Test No. 4   61

3.4 Analytic, Contradictory, and Synthetic Statements   61

3.5 Self-Test No. 5   63

3.6 Descriptive and Evaluative Meaning   64

3.7 Self-Test No. 6   65

3.8 Necessary and Sufficient Conditions   66

3.9 Self-Test No. 7   69

3.10 Questions for Discussion   70

Chapter 4:   Reconstructing Arguments   73

4.1 Reconstruction   73

4.2 Missing Premises and Conclusions   74

4.3 Self-Test No. 8   77

4.4 Special Cases   78
    4.4.1 Reports of Arguments   78
    4.4.2 Explanations   79

4.5 Self-Test No. 9   82

4.6 The Structure of Arguments   83
    4.6.1 Simple Arguments   83
    4.6.2 T Arguments   84
    4.6.3 V Arguments   85
    4.6.4 Complex Arguments   86

4.7 Self-Test No. 10   88

4.8 Another Warning   89

4.9 Questions for Discussion   90

PART III: ASSESSING ARGUMENTS

Chapter 5:   Strategies for Assessing Arguments   95

5.1 The Fallacies Approach   96

5.2 The Criterial Approach   96
    5.2.1 The Three Criteria of a Sound Argument   97

5.3 Seven Rules for Assessing Arguments   98

Chapter 6:   Assessing Truth-Claims   101

6.1 Theories of Truth   101
    6.1.1 The Correspondence Theory   101
    6.1.2 The Coherence Theory   102
    6.1.3 The Pragmatic Theory   104

6.2 Types of Truth Claims   105
    6.2.1 Empirical Truth-Claims   106
    6.2.2 Non-Empirical Truth-Claims   108

6.3 Acceptability   110

6.4 Self-Test No. 11   113

6.5 Questions for Discussion   114

6.6 Assessing the Acceptability of Premises   114

6.7 Some Particular Fallacies   115
    6.7.1 Begging the Question   116
    6.7.2 Inconsistency   117
    6.7.3 Equivocation   120
    6.7.4 False Dichotomy   121

6.8 Self-Test No. 12   122

6.9 Questions for Discussion   123

Chapter 7:   Assessing Relevance   125

7.1 The Criterion of Relevance   125

7.2 Recognizing Irrelevant Premises   126

7.3 Appeals to Authority (1)   129

7.4 Some Particular Fallacies   130
    7.4.1 Ad Hominem   131
    7.4.2 Tu Quoque   132
    7.4.3 Straw Man   133

7.5 Self-Test No. 13   135

7.6 Questions for Discussion   136

Chapter 8:   Assessing Adequacy   139

8.1 The Criterion of Adequacy   139

8.2 Appeals to Authority (2)   142

8.3 Appeals to Ignorance   143

8.4 The Slippery Slope Fallacy   144

8.5 Causal Fallacies   147
    8.5.1 Post Hoc   147
    8.5.2 Confusing Cause and Effect   148
    8.5.3 Common Cause   149

8.6 Self-Test No. 14   150

8.7 Questions for Discussion   152

Chapter 9:   Deductive Reasoning   155

9.1 The Nature of Deductive Reasoning   155

9.2 Truth-Functional Statements   157

9.3 Formal Validity and Soundness   161

9.4 Valid Argument Forms   162

9.5 Formal Invalidity   165

9.6 Self-Test No. 15   167

9.7 Questions for Discussion   168

Chapter 10: Inductive Reasoning   171

10.1 The Nature of Inductive Reasoning   171

10.2 Inductive Generalization   172

10.3 Statistical Syllogism   174

10.4 Induction By Confirmation   175

10.5 Analogical Reasoning   179

10.6 Self-Test No. 16   184

10.7 Questions for Discussion   185

PART IV: APPLICATIONS

Chapter 11: Scientific Reasoning   191

11.1 Causation/Correlation   192

11.2 Mill's Methods   194
  11.2.1 Method of Agreement   194
  11.2.2 Method of Difference   197
  11.2.3 Joint Method of Agreement and Difference   199
  11.2.4 Method of Concomitant Variations   202
  11.2.5 Method of Residue   203

11.3 Self-Test No. 17   205

11.4 Argument to the Best Explanation   207
  11.4.1 Choosing between Rival Restricted Hypotheses   208
  11.4.2 Choosing between Rival Unrestricted Hypotheses   211

11.5 Case for Discussion: Semmelweis's Discovery of Antisepsis   214

Chapter 12: Moral Reasoning   219

12.1 Moral Judgements and Judgements of Taste   219

12.2 Moral Justification   221

12.3 Appeals to Principles of Right and Wrong   222

12.4 Self-Test No. 18   226

12.5 Questions for Discussion   226

12.6 Appeals to Consequences   227

12.7 Self-Test No. 19   230

12.8 Questions for Discussion   230

12.9 Rational Agreement   231

12.10 Moral Maturity   232

12.11 Questions for Discussion   234

Chapter 13: Arguing Back   237

13.1 Explaining the Weakness   237

13.2 Counter-examples   238

13.3 Absurd Examples   240

13.4 Counter-arguments   242

13.5 Self-Test No. 20   243

13.6 Questions for Discussion   244

Chapter 14: Irrational Techniques of Persuasion   247

14.1 Loaded Terms   247

14.2 Vague Terms   248

14.3 Loaded Questions   249

14.4 False Confidence   251

14.5 Selectivity   252

14.6 Misleading Statistics   253

14.7 Humour   255

14.8 Red Herring   256

14.9 Guilt By Association   257

14.10 Persuasive Redefinition   257

14.11 Self-Test No. 21   258

14.12 Questions for Discussion   260

Chapter 15: Critiquing the Media   263

15.1 Determining Bias   264

15.2 Is Objective Reporting Possible?   266

15.3 How to Assess News Reports   270
    15.3.1 Assessing Factual Claims   270
    15.3.2 Assessing Interpretive Frameworks   271

15.4 Another Warning   272

15.5 Questions for Discussion   274

Chapter 16: Writing and Assessing Argumentative Essays   291

16.1 Writing Argumentative Essays: Structure   292

16.2 Writing Argumentative Essays: Style   294

16.3 Assessing Argumentative Essays   295

16.4 Assessment of a Sample Argumentative Essay   297

16.5 Question for Discussion   306

Chapter 17: Strategies for Organizing an Argumentative Essay   309

17.1 Advocate's Strategy   312

17.2 Critic's Strategy   316

17.3 Impartial Adjudicator's Strategy   320

17.4 Questions for Discussion   323

APPENDICES

Appendix I: Paradoxes and Puzzles   325

1. Logical Paradoxes   325
2. Puzzles   329
3. Solutions to the Puzzles   332

Appendix II: Answers to Self-Tests   335

Self-Test No. 1   335
Self-Test No. 2   338
Self-Test No. 3   339
Self-Test No. 4   340
Self-Test No. 5   341
Self-Test No. 6   342
Self-Test No. 7   343
Self-Test No. 8   345
Self-Test No. 9   345
Self-Test No. 10   347
Self-Test No. 11   349
Self-Test No. 12   351
Self-Test No. 13   352
Self-Test No. 14   354
Self-Test No. 15   356
Self-Test No. 16   358
Self-Test No. 17   361
Self-Test No. 18   363
Self-Test No. 19   364
Self-Test No. 20   367
Self-Test No. 21   368

Glossary   369
Index   385

Acknowledgements

Many people have helped me during the process of writing and revising this book. I am grateful to Dr. Jack Macdonald, Vice President Academic of the University of Guelph, for support from the New Initiatives Fund, which enabled me to produce the first draft of this book. I am also grateful to all the University of Guelph students in 74–210 who, through their questions and comments, gave me a better understanding of what is (and what is not) needed in a critical thinking course. I am especially grateful to those students who have changed my mind about so many matters by successfully arguing back (see Chapter 13), thereby demonstrating directly that there is something of practical importance to be learned from mastering critical thinking skills.

The following colleagues and students deserve special mention for their generosity with their time and their helpful suggestions: John-Paul Boyd, Brian Calvert, Tobias Chapman, Paul Genest, Jeff Hurdman, Susan-Judith Hoffmann, Hugh Lehman, Neil MacGill, Stella Ostick, Rob Ridley, and Brian Wetstein.

Finally, I want to acknowledge a special debt of gratitude to my family: to my wife, Daphne, for her general support as well as her efforts to clean up my prose and help me achieve a measure of clarity; and to my children, Miranda, Jeremy, Jonathan, and Anna, for putting up with so much over the years while providing grist for the mill. To them all, I dedicate this book.

—Bill Hughes, 3rd Edition

Broadview has kindly allowed me to add a new chapter to the 5th edition, and I have taken advantage of this opportunity to offer some advice to students in *writing* argumentative essays. Usually, critical thinking texts books concentrate on the analysis and assessment of arguments that students will come across in other university courses, the mass media, and other venues. But I have always made writing, even essay writing, a central component in my own critical thinking courses, because the skills and concepts are readily applied in the construction of arguments as much as in the analysis of them. Bill Hughes made "Writing and Assessing Argumentative Essays" the capstone chapter of earlier editions of this book, and I recommend students read it even if their instructor does not get to that chapter in their course. Now I have added chapter 17, "Strategies for Organizing an Argumentative Essay" as an expansion of the final chapter of the 4th edition. Whereas chapter 16 summarizes a procedure for the step-by-step construction of an argumentative essay from its conception to its final state, chapter 17 outlines three strategies for organizing the macro-structure of an argumentative essay. These are not the only macro-structural forms available for use, but they have very broad applications and after students become familiar with these three strategies they may discover innumerable ways in which they can be modified and adapted.

A second change in the 5th edition is less noticeable at first glance. I have gone through the self-tests, the examples and the text, and improved the material as much as possible. Most of these things remain unchanged, but instructors who have used the 4th edition of the text are warned to check carefully before they make use of a particular example in class or in a test.

A third change is at the end of chapter 15 on critiquing the media. The long examples in the 15.5 have been updated and slightly expanded.

And finally, Broadview has generously agreed to provide electronic support for this text, which will supplement it and include more examples. Part of the challenge of working on a book such as this is providing a sufficient number of exercises and examples without adding extra pages (and thereby making it more expensive). The electronic resources that accompany the 5th edition should prove to be beneficial to both students and instructors.

The most difficult challenge in completing this edition was working on my own most of the time. Bill Hughes died in August 2003, just as changes were completed on the 4th edition. I had consulted Bill extensively over plans for alterations to that edition, and his guidance saved me from making numerous mistakes. He was able to provide some of the new material for that edition, too, and for that I was also grateful. This time, however, I had to plan and carry out the revisions myself. I was aided considerably by insightful criticism from several anonymous readers, whose contributions must be acknowledged. But the greatest help came, in the final stages, from Robert Martin. Bob read the entire manuscript and made *countless* improvements. Not only has his excellent judgement improved the text immeasurably, but his good humour and sharp eye for detail made it fun to work through the final draft.

Thanks are owed, also, to Stephen Haller, Louis Groarke, and Michael Crawford, all good friends who gave timely advice about Chapter 11. I am also grateful to Daphne Hughes for her cheerful co-operation in getting the 5th edition off the ground, and to my family—Julie, Sadie and Tamsen—for their ongoing support. And finally, I want to thank Catherine Hundleby's Logic and Argumentation class at the University of Windsor for alerting me about numerous problems that they discovered in the 4th edition, and my own student-assistant, Evan Habrik.

My work on this edition is, once again, dedicated to Bill.

— Jonathan Lavery, 5th edition

part one
INTRODUCTION

1. Reasoning and Critical Thinking

1.1 Reasoning

The ability to reason is the fundamental characteristic of human beings. It has long been held that the capacity to reason is unique to human beings, but even if it is not—if it turns out, for example, that reasoning is a quality we share with dolphins or apes or even computers—the capacity to reason is nevertheless central to what we are and how we think of ourselves. Virtually every conscious human activity involves reasoning; we reason whenever we solve problems, make decisions, assess character, explain events, write poems, balance chequebooks, predict elections, make discoveries, interpret works of art, or repair carburetors. We reason about everything from the meaning of life to what to have for dinner.

Of course, much of the time we are not engaged in conscious reasoning; often we simply listen to what others say, take note of things around us, experience feelings, daydream, listen to concerts, tell stories, or watch television. These activities need not involve conscious reasoning, but to the extent that we understand what is going on around or inside us we are not entirely passive. Some reasoning must be taking place even if it is at a pre-conscious level. To understand reasoning properly, however, we need to understand how it differs from mere thinking. When we are merely thinking, our thoughts simply come to us, one after another; when we reason, we actively link thoughts together in such a way that we believe one thought provides support for another thought. This active process of reasoning is termed *inference*. INFERENCE involves a special relationship between different thoughts: when we infer B from A, we move from A to B because we believe that A *supports* or *justifies* or *makes it reasonable to believe* in the truth of B.

The difference between mere thinking and reasoning or inference is easy to understand through examples. Consider the following pairs of sentences:

Alan is broke, and he is unhappy.
Alan is broke, therefore he is unhappy.

Anne was in a car accident last week, and she deserves an extension on her essay.
Anne was in a car accident last week, so she deserves an extension on her essay.

This triangle has equal sides and equal angles.
This triangle has equal sides; hence it has equal angles.

Notice that the first sentence in each pair simply asserts two thoughts but says nothing about any relationship between them, while the second sentence asserts a relationship between two thoughts. This relationship is signalled by the words *therefore*, *so*, and *hence*. These are called INFERENCE INDICATORS: words that indicate that one thought is intended to support (i.e., to justify, provide a reason for, provide evidence for, or entail) another thought. Other common inference indicators are:

since
thus
implies
consequently
because
it follows that
given that

It is important to note that sometimes the inference indicator is missing; this can occur when a speaker thinks the inference is quite obvious. For example:

It's raining; I'd better take my umbrella.

The actual presence of an inference indicator is not important. What is important is the relationship of support between the thoughts of the speaker. This relationship is a defining condition of an inference: if two thoughts are linked by such a relationship they constitute an inference, otherwise they do not.

When we express an inference in words, we do so by means of statements. A STATEMENT is a sentence (i.e., a set of words) that is used to make a claim that is capable of being true or false. If a sentence is not capable of being true or false, then it is not a statement. Questions (*Are you awake?*) and commands (*Wake up!*) are not capable of being true or false and, hence, are not statements. Only statements can be true or false. When an inference is expressed in statements, it is called an argument. An ARGUMENT is a set of statements that claims that one or more of those statements, called the PREMISES, support another of them, called the CONCLUSION. Thus, every argument claims that its premises support its conclusion.

1.2 The Concept of Logical Strength

Since a statement makes a claim that can be true or false, any statement can be assessed by asking whether it is true or false. Is Alan really unhappy? Was Anne actually in a car accident? When we assess the truth or falsity of a statement, it makes no difference whether or not it is part of an argument. A statement that is part of an argument is assessed in the same way as one that is not. The truth or falsity of the statement that Alan is unhappy does not depend upon whether or not it is part of an argument. To discover the truth or falsity of statements we examine the statement itself and look for evidence that will show us whether it is true or false.

Assessing an argument is more complex than assessing an isolated statement. Since an argument always includes a claim that its premises support its conclusion, assessing an argument means assessing this claim. Do the premises really support the conclusion, and if so, how much support do they provide? In other words, how *strong* is the inference from the premise(s) to the conclusion? We say that an argument has LOGICAL STRENGTH when its premises, *if true*, actually provide support for its conclusion.

The concept of logical strength is central in critical thinking and has two important features that need to be stressed. First, the logical strength of an argument is independent of the truth or falsity of its premises: we do not need to know that the premises of an argument are true in order to assess its logical strength. When we assess the logical strength of an argument, we are really asking, *If the premises are true would we be justified in accepting the conclusion?* and we can answer this question without knowing whether or not the premises actually are true. Consider the following example:

> The population of Chatham is 27,000.
> The population of Orillia is 26,000.
> Therefore, Chatham has a larger population than Orillia.

Even if we don't know the populations of Chatham and Orillia, we can still see that the inference in this argument is a strong one. If both premises are true, then obviously the conclusion would have to be true as well. The fact that either or both premises might be false does not affect the logical strength of the argument. For similar reasons, an argument with premises and conclusion that are known to be true may be a very weak argument. For example:

> Toronto is the capital of Ontario.
> Ottawa is in Ontario.
> Therefore, Ottawa is the capital of Canada.

In this example, the premises and the conclusion are all true, but the facts that Toronto is the capital of Ontario and that Ottawa is in Ontario provide no support for the statement that Ottawa is the capital of Canada. The inference is therefore a bad or weak one. Only if the information contained in the premises really provides a good reason for holding that the conclusion is true can we say the inference is a strong one.

Second, the logical strength of an argument is often a matter of degree. Some arguments are so strong that the truth of the premises guarantees the truth of the conclusion. Such arguments are called DEDUCTIVE ARGUMENTS, and they constitute strict proofs. But most arguments are not as strong as this; usually, the truth of the premises makes it reasonable to hold that the conclusion is also true, but does not provide an absolute guarantee. Such arguments are called INDUCTIVE ARGUMENTS. For example:

Arthur has been a moderate social drinker for twenty years.
No one has ever known him to get drunk.
Therefore, he won't get drunk at the party tonight.

This is a strong argument, since if the premises are true it is reasonable to conclude that the conclusion will also be true. Nevertheless, Arthur might get drunk tonight. Given the truth of the premises this might astonish us, but it is not impossible.

Understanding the concept of logical strength is the key to developing critical thinking skills. The fact that the logical strength of an argument is independent of the truth of its premises means that in order to assess an argument we must do more than merely determine whether its premises are true. And the fact that logical strength may be a matter of degree means that we must be sensitive to the various features of arguments that affect its degree of strength. If we lack critical thinking skills, we can easily be fooled into thinking that an argument is strong when the premises actually provide little or no support for the conclusion. Consider the following inferences:

The Liberals won a majority of seats in the last election.
So, they must have received more votes than any other party.

My sister always got better grades in school than I did.
That proves that she's smarter than I am.

Eighty per cent of those who tried Painaway said they would take it the next time they had a headache.
Therefore, Painaway is a better headache remedy.

The city council is unfair to city employees.
Jones is a city councillor.
Hence, Jones is unfair to city employees.

A majority of the union members voted in favour of the contract.
Consequently, these people must be in favour of the 1% pay reduction in the contract.

Whenever there is high unemployment interest rates increase.
So, high unemployment causes high interest rates.

These are all weak arguments: the conclusions are not adequately supported by their premises. This does not mean that the conclusions are false or even likely to be false. It only means that the evidence presented in the premises, even if true, does not entitle us to draw the conclusion. The premises do not, in other words, adequately support the conclusion.

1.3 Truth, Logical Strength, and Soundness

In section 1.2 we drew a distinction between assessing the truth or falsity of a statement and assessing the logical strength of an inference. Although these are quite different tasks, both are important if we want to arrive at the truth. Remember that a strong argument is one whose premises really do support its conclusion. In other words, its premises, *if true*, provide a justification for believing the conclusion to be true. But a logically strong argument, as we saw, may have false premises. So, if we want to know whether the conclusion of an argument is likely to be true, we need to know *both* that the argument is a strong one *and* that its premises are true. What we want, in other words, are logically strong arguments with true premises. An argument that has both logical strength and true premises is called a SOUND ARGUMENT.

It is very important to be aware of the differences among these three properties. *Truth* is a property of statements and never of inferences. *Logical strength* is a property of inferences and never of statements. Logical strength refers to the inferential connection between the premises and conclusion of an argument. *Soundness* is a property of an argument as a whole. Always keep the question of strength separate from the question of truth when dealing with any argument. Never ask simply, *Is this a good argument?* Ask two questions instead:

(1) Is this a logically strong argument? and
(2) Are its premises true?

The order in which these questions are asked is not important. What is crucial is that they be asked separately. Only when both have been answered are we in a position to know whether an argument is sound—whether we have a good reason to accept its conclusion.

Sometimes, however, it is inappropriate to ask whether the premises are true. We may, for example, want to explore the consequences of an assumption whose truth or falsity we cannot determine. For example:

No one knows for certain whether Martin Bormann died in 1945. If he did not, then he probably escaped through Switzerland and Italy to South America. That is what Adolf Eichmann and a number of other high-ranking Nazis did.

There are even times when we want to develop an argument with premises that we know or assume to be false. Such arguments are called COUNTERFACTUAL ARGUMENTS because at least one premise is a *counterfactual statement*. For instance, we may want to explore the consequences of the supposition that some historical event never happened. For example:

> If Hitler had invaded Britain in 1940 he would have succeeded, because at that time the Germans had military superiority.

Or we may want to explore the consequences of the occurrence of some hypothetical situation. For example:

> If the provincial sales tax were reduced to 5 per cent, there would not be a corresponding decrease in government revenues. This is because part of the decrease would be offset by an increase in sales as a result of the sales tax reduction.

We should also note a special kind of counterfactual argument called the REDUCTIO AD ABSURDUM. In a reductio argument, a statement is proven to be true by assuming it to be false and then deriving a contradiction from that assumption. For example:

> It is preposterous to claim, as some people have, that Gorbachev engineered the August 1991 coup attempt by Communist hard-liners in order to strengthen his position and stop the secessionist movements in the republics. If he engineered the coup then we would have to conclude that he is an exceptionally stupid man, for not only did the coup weaken his personal position and strengthen the position of Yeltsin, his chief rival, but it unleashed a wave of secessionism that destroyed the Soviet Union. Gorbachev may not be the smartest man in the world, but no one could have become political leader of the Soviet Union and been that stupid.

In all these kinds of cases we want our arguments to be strong, but we cannot even pretend that these arguments are sound, since we know or assume that at least one of the premises is false.

Counterfactual arguments, however, are the exception to the rule. In almost all cases our main concern is with sound arguments. If we start with true premises, and use only logically strong arguments, we are entitled to rely on the conclusions we reach. Sound arguments expand our knowledge and increase our understanding. This is why developing the ability to recognize sound arguments is so important.

1.4 Critical Thinking Skills

The primary focus of critical thinking skills is on determining whether arguments are sound, i.e., whether they have true premises and logical strength. But determining the soundness of arguments is not a simple matter, for three reasons.

First, before we can assess an argument we must determine its precise meaning. It would be convenient if the meaning of arguments were always clear, but unfortunately this is often not so. An argument may be unclear because the meaning of one or more of its statements is unclear or because the nature of the connection that is being asserted between the premises and conclusion is unclear. This means we have to learn how to interpret statements and arguments in a way that makes their meaning as clear as possible. The skills needed for this task are interpretive skills. Chapters 2 to 4 are aimed at developing these skills.

Second, determining the truth or falsity of statements is often a difficult task. Even when we are sure we know precisely what a statement means, we may be unsure about its truth and may even be unsure how to go about determining whether it is true or false. As we shall see, there are several different types of statements, and each type has its own method for determining truth and falsity. The skills needed for this task are verification skills. We shall deal with these skills in Chapter 6.

Third, assessing arguments is complex because there are several different types of inferences, and each type requires a different kind of assessment. It is necessary to learn how to recognize these different types of inferences and to become familiar with these different methods of assessment. For this purpose reasoning skills are needed. These skills are dealt with in Chapters 7 to 15.

These three types of skills—interpretive skills, verification skills, and reasoning skills—constitute what are usually referred to as critical thinking skills. Developing a mastery of them is important for several practical reasons.

First, we are inundated with information of all sorts, but this information is useless unless we know how to use it in our thinking to draw out its implications and consequences. Much of it is incomplete and one-sided in ways that are often not apparent, and if we are not on our guard, we may be misled.

Second, we are constantly presented with arguments designed to get us to accept some conclusion that we would otherwise not accept. Politicians, preachers, advertisers, editorial writers, and special-interest groups of all sorts spend a great deal of time, thought, and money attempting to persuade us to believe the things they want us to believe, and it is important to be on guard against arguments that fail to meet the appropriate logical criteria. This is partly a matter of our own self-interest. When others seek to make us believe things that are in *their* interests, it is possible, or even likely, that our interests are not being well served.

Third, mastering critical thinking skills is also a matter of intellectual self-respect. We all have the capacity to learn how to distinguish good arguments from bad ones and to work out for ourselves what we ought and ought not to believe, and it diminishes us as persons if we let others do our thinking for us. If we are not prepared to think for ourselves, and to make the effort to learn how to do this well, we will always be in danger of becoming slaves to the ideas and values of others due to our own ignorance.

And finally, critical thinking skills can make it easier for us to persuade others to change their beliefs. Many beliefs are based more on emotion than on reason, although those holding them usually believe they are based on reason. In fact, it is rare to find a person, even a complete bigot, who does not believe that his or her beliefs have a rational basis. Critical thinking skills can be effective in dislodging such beliefs and persuading others to change their views.

This last point raises a number of moral questions. Like any skill, critical thinking skills can be used for good or ill. There are many ways in which they can be abused. They can be used to make a bad argument look much stronger than it really is and to make an opponent's position look much weaker than it really is. They can be used to make ourselves look wise and to make others look foolish. They can be used to avoid having to respond to legitimate criticisms and to persuade others to change their beliefs for inadequate reasons. Every day we find ourselves in situations in which we could use our critical thinking skills for such purposes, and sometimes we may be tempted to do so. Yielding to the temptation, however, is dishonest and hypocritical. It is analogous to a medical doctor who uses his or her medical training not to help people but to torture them more effectively.

There are other, more difficult, moral questions that can arise. How far should we go in revealing the weaknesses we see in our arguments to our opponents? Is it always right to attack the weaknesses in the views of others? How are we to be fair to those who disagree with us? How far should we go in our attempts not to distort others' views when discussing them? How forceful should we be in attempting to persuade others to agree with our views? As we shall see, there are no easy answers to such questions. They need to be approached with an equal regard for the truth and for the feelings of others and with a proper sense of our own fallibility.

1.5 Critical Thinking and the Science of Logic

Reasoning skills involve the application of principles of logic. Logic is the science that studies the relationships between premises and conclusions with a view to determining when and to what extent the premises actually support the conclusion. Logic was first recognized as a science in the fourth century BCE by Aristotle, who described what he believed were the basic principles of correct reasoning. These principles were elaborated and developed by a number of medieval logicians, but the basic nature of logic remained essentially Aristotelian until the late nineteenth century. About a hundred years ago, logic entered a period of radical change when mathematicians began using logic to solve certain problems regarding the foundations of mathematics. More recently, computer science and artificial intelligence have contributed to further developments in logic. As a result, logic has become a highly complex and sophisticated discipline of considerable theoretical importance. The power and sophistication of modern logic, however, have been purchased at the price of increasing abstractness. The principles of modern logic have been abstracted from ordinary language and are considered as purely formal principles, devoid of content.

Many of the critical thinking skills described in this book are drawn from logic. Our interest in them, however, is not in their theoretical foundations or theoretical significance but in their practical application. In particular, we are interested in the way in which the principles of logic function when used in natural language (that is, the languages such as English, French or Mandarin that have evolved organically and continue to evolve as people use them in everyday life, as opposed to artificial languages such as the symbolic logic covered in chapter 9 in which all the elements have fixed rules for usage). When any logical principle is used in a real-life setting, we face a host of special problems that take us beyond the domain of formal logic. These problems of practical application will engage most of our attention here. The principles of formal logic have their own interest and intellectual challenge, but they lie beyond the scope of this book.

There is, however, one underlying commitment that we want to preserve from the science of logic. This is something that Aristotle, the medieval logicians who followed his lead, and modern logicians who work on mathematical logic all seem to agree upon: it is that logic, as a science, is a study of *normative* principles, it does not merely *describe* its subject. Normative principles function as standards for assessment or guides for action, whereas descriptions merely attempt to accurately represent something. Henry Gray's *Anatomy* is a great work of physiology because it *describes* its subject accurately and comprehensively. Logic, however, does not simply discover how people do happen to reason in this descriptive manner. It explores the *norms* of reasoning and discovers how people *ought to* reason. Patterns of reasoning that have been identified as inductively deductively strong are reliable for anyone to use. But once a pattern of reasoning is discovered to be faulty or fallacious, we ought to avoid this pattern as unreliable. This is why the critical thinking skills outlined in 1.4 are so useful. There are reliable and unreliable ways of drawing implications and consequences out of information. There are reliable and unreliable ways in which other people attempt to persuade us to accept their positions. Conversely, there are reliable and unreliable ways in which we may persuade other to accept our reasoning. Most importantly, by becoming more aware of the principles of good reasoning we *earn* our own intellectual self-respect by thinking in ways that measure up to the normative standards of good reasoning.

1.6 Self-Test No. 1

I. Which of the following passages are arguments? For those that are arguments, identify the premise(s) and the conclusion.

1. You should go home next weekend because you promised your parents you would.

2. You should go home next weekend and have a good time with your friends.

3. Ted won the Intercollegiate 10,000 metres last year and has been training hard ever since, so he should win easily this year.

4. I will be able to visit you next month after all. The doctor just told me that a second operation won't be necessary and that I'll be able to go home this Friday.

5. His car skidded on the ice and hit a van in the middle of the intersection. The car was a write-off, and the van suffered $3,000 in damage.

6. It is obvious that no great leader ever suffered from low self-esteem.

7. The company laid off 250 assembly line workers last week. I think they were justified because their sales had declined by 23 per cent in the past three months.

8. Many people think that thunder is caused by lightning. This is a mistake.

9. Most evenings I go for a walk after dinner. Usually, I walk to the park and back, which is about three kilometres, but last night I only went as far as the library.

10. You're crazy if you think you can take a full course load while working 20 hours a week and pass your semester. You should remember what happened to Van and Patti when they tried to do that last year.

11. My purse with several hundred dollars in cash, my watch, and my necklace have gone missing from my hotel room. The door was locked while I was out, and there's no sign of forced entry. It looks like someone on staff at this hotel is a thief.

12. We drove to Moncton to visit Sally in the morning, spent the afternoon in Sackville with Roopen and his family, then stopped at Betty's for dinner in Amherst. By the time we finally arrived in Halifax last night, we were happy about visiting friends but tired from all the driving.

II. When you know enough to judge the truth or falsity of the premises, indicate which of the following arguments are sound.

1. Winnipeg is in Manitoba. Manitoba is in Canada. Therefore, Winnipeg is in Canada.

2. Montreal is larger than Beaver Creek. Beaver Creek is larger than Vancouver. Therefore, Montreal is larger than Vancouver.

3. Shaquille O'Neil is taller than Steve Nash. Steve Nash is taller than Tom Cruise. Therefore, Tom Cruise is shorter than Shaquille O'Neil.

4. No one under the age of 18 is legally an adult. Katherine is only 15 years old. Katherine is not legally an adult.

5. Hockey is Canada's national sport. A country's national sport is likely to be very popular in that country. Therefore, hockey is likely to be very popular in Canada.

6. Fez is north of Casablanca. Tangier is north of Fez. Therefore, Tangier is north of Casablanca.

7. A cat makes a good house pet. A tiger is a cat. Therefore, a tiger makes a good house pet.

8. No human being is immortal. Even the prime minister is a human being. Therefore, the prime minister is not immortal.

9. Everybody loves a winner. The New York Yankees have won more games than any other baseball team since its inception. Therefore, everybody loves the Yankees.

10. At this moment, I am reading a book. If I am reading a book, I must be awake. Therefore, I must be awake.

11. The HMS Pinafore is a faster vessel than the SS Minnow. The SS Minnow is faster than the Yellow Submarine. Therefore, the Yellow Submarine is the slowest of the three vessels.

12. Dogs make excellent companions. Cerberus is a dog. Therefore, Cerberus is an excellent companion.

1.7 Questions for Discussion

In section 1.1, an argument was defined as a set of statements that *claims* that its premises support its conclusion. Sometimes it is not clear whether a speaker intends to make such a claim. In these cases we have to rely upon whatever clues the context provides to decide whether it is reasonable to interpret what the speaker has said as being an argument rather than something else. For each of the following passages, briefly describe a context that makes it reasonable to interpret it as either an argument or not an argument.

1. The expressway was closed for three hours this afternoon because of the train derailment on the overpass.

2. When George finished speaking, Frances sat quietly for several minutes, her brow furrowed in intense concentration. Suddenly, she leapt up and ran to her room, rummaged through her desk, found a sheet of paper, and scrawled a few words on it. She crammed it in an envelope, addressed and stamped the enve-

lope, ran out of the house, and thrust it into the mailbox. "That's done," she said. "Now I am committed, and my life will never be the same again."

3. The company laid off 250 assembly line workers last week because their sales had declined by 23 per cent in the past three months. The company seems to have had no choice.

4. Mike refuses to vote because he thinks all political parties are the same.

5. I went for a walk last evening, but when I got to London Road it started to rain, so I turned around and came home.

6. Hey, it's seven o'clock; it's time to go.

7. To get rid of hiccoughs, breathe into a paper bag for a few minutes.

8. By the end of the war in 1945, Churchill realized that, although Britain had won the war against the Axis powers, it was an economically devastated nation that would need massive foreign aid if it was to recover.

9. This is an important decision, obviously, and I don't want to decide in haste. I suppose, all things considered, that the best thing to do would be to resign, but I would like to have until tomorrow to think about it.

10. It is a beautiful day out, and a walk in the park will make you feel better.

part two
MEANING

2. Meaning and Definition

Reasoning, we have said, involves thinking. Thinking, in turn, involves language, for without language we could not express (and probably not even have) any thoughts. In order to understand reasoning, therefore, it is necessary to pay careful attention to the relationship between thought and language. The relationship seems to be straightforward: thought is expressed in and through language. But this claim, while true, is an oversimplification. People often fail to say what they mean. Everyone has had the experience of having their words misunderstood by others. And we all use words not merely to express our thoughts but also to shape them. Developing our critical thinking skills, therefore, requires an understanding of the ways in which words can (and can fail to) express our thoughts.

2.1 The Complexity of Language

Language is an extremely complex phenomenon. The number of different words in any language is finite, but these words can be used to generate an infinite number of different sentences with different meanings. Many of the ordinary things we say or write have never been said before by anyone. For example:

> *Professor Sutherland reminds me of my Uncle Tony; they both have the habit of running their fingers through their hair when they are thinking hard.*

It is likely that when this sentence was first said or written, it had never been said before. And it is not just the precise wording that is unique: it is unlikely that anyone has ever had the same thought. In fact, there is no limit to the number of new sentences with new meanings that could be created. Conversely, there are often different ways of saying the same thing. For example:

> *Anne is older than everyone else in the room.*

Everyone else in the room is younger than Anne.

In addition, there are often many different sentences that mean more or less the same thing. One lexicographer has recorded over 2,200 synonyms for the word *drunk*.

Written and spoken language, although closely connected, are nevertheless not identical: spoken language is more flexible (and hence more complex) than written language, for we can change the meaning of words and sentences through our gestures, tone of voice, and facial expressions. Note the different meanings that arise when the underlined word is emphasized in the following sentences:

> <u>You</u> *shouldn't steal library books.* (But it may be acceptable for others to do so.)
> *You <u>shouldn't</u> steal library books.* (But I won't be surprised if you do.)
> *You shouldn't <u>steal</u> library books.* (But defacing books is acceptable.)
> *You shouldn't steal <u>library</u> books.* (But stealing books from the bookstore is acceptable.)
> *You shouldn't steal library <u>books</u>.* (But stealing magazines from the library is acceptable.)

Understanding spoken language, therefore, requires much more than knowing the written language. In fact, the close connection between written and spoken language that exists in European languages is sometimes absent in other languages. Chinese spoken dialects (which are as different from one another as English and German) all use the same written language, so that people who speak different dialects can communicate through writing even though they may not understand each other's speech.

Language is always in a state of gradual change, in ways that are in large part unpredictable. A single language can, in a few centuries, evolve into two languages so different from one another that those who speak one will find the other incomprehensible. Given the complexity of language, it is astonishing that we learn almost everything we will ever know about language before we are old enough to go to school. We are all intimately familiar with at least one language, and we therefore understand what language is, at least in the sense of knowing how to use language. But at a deeper level most of us have only the most elementary understanding of what language is and how it works. Even linguistic theorists are uncertain about many features of language. They do not know, for example, whether the basic structure of language (i.e., its underlying grammar) reflects certain characteristics of the human mind or is merely conventional in nature. Nor do they fully understand the relationship between language and thinking: we normally use a language when we think, but is language necessary for human thought? And if it is, do people who think in different languages think differently? When we translate a speech from Russian into English, can we be sure that we understand exactly what it meant to the original speaker or what it means to a Russian audience? The relationship between language and reality is also problematic. Does language describe the world as it really is, or do we use language to impose a structure on our experience, experience that would otherwise be chaotic and meaningless?

2.2 The Meaning of Language

Usually it is not difficult to explain what a particular word or sentence means. But there is much that is puzzling about the nature of meaning itself. How do words get their meaning, and how do meanings change? Is the meaning that words have different from the meaning of sentences? In order to enhance our understanding of the nature and complexity of meaning, we will look briefly at three theories of meaning. The first two are common-sense views that have been held by many people, including many philosophers and linguistic theorists. Unfortunately, both are open to serious objections, and many philosophers now regard them as untenable. The third theory avoids the weakness of the first two and is the one we will rely upon in this book.

2.2.1 THE REFERENCE THEORY OF MEANING

The reference theory of meaning was first expounded by Aristotle in the fourth century BCE. According to this view, the meaning of a word consists in what it refers to. The word *dog* refers to all the dogs in the world, so it seems plausible to hold that the meaning of *dog* is all the dogs in the world. After all, if we know what *dog* refers to, we obviously know what the word means. Similarly, the meaning of *tree* is every tree in the world, the meaning of *automobile* is every automobile, the meaning of *joke* is every joke, and so on. The meaning of a term thus consists of its reference class, that is, the class of objects to which the word refers. At first glance, the reference theory is a plausible account of meaning, and its plausibility is enhanced by the fact that pointing to the reference class is often a good way of explaining the meaning of a word. If you don't know what *antimacassar* means, I can easily explain its meaning by pointing to an antimacassar and explaining that other antimacassars vary in size and design but have the same function as this one.

There are, however, serious difficulties with the reference theory. At the heart of the theory there seems to be a confusion between understanding the meaning of a word and having knowledge of what the word refers to. When we understand the meaning of the word *dog*, we usually have knowledge of only a small proportion of the dogs that exist, and this is puzzling if the meaning of *dog* is the reference class of the term. The fact that even small children can understand the meaning of *dog* on the basis of direct knowledge of only a few dogs cannot be explained by the reference theory. The theory encounters even more serious difficulties, however, when we consider words that have no reference class. What do the following words refer to: *unless, after, yes, unlikely, the, nevertheless, was, if, where*? Does it even make sense to suggest that the meaning of *unless* is the class of unlesses? In addition, there are certain phrases whose meaning is easily understood but whose reference is unknown. For example, we all understand the meaning of the phrase *the oldest man in the world*, even when we don't know to whom it refers. If the meaning is the reference, then we shouldn't be able to understand what the phrase means unless we know who is the oldest man in the world. The reference theory of meaning, therefore, has to be rejected. As we shall see in 2.6, it is important to distinguish meaning and reference.

2.2.2 THE IDEA THEORY OF MEANING

The idea theory of meaning was developed by John Locke in the seventeenth century. He held that the meaning of a word consists of the idea or mental image that is associated with the word. When we think of the word *dog*, it seems that we have a mental image we associate with the word, and it is plausible to hold that the meaning of *dog* is this image in our minds. This theory seems to be able to deal with phrases like *the oldest man in the world*, since it is plausible to suggest that we have a mental image we associate with this phrase.

But the idea theory also encounters several difficulties. Just as the class of unlesses seems to make no sense, the mental image of unless also seems to make no sense. But in addition, the image or idea we associate with a word like *dog* turns out on reflection to be very unclear. If we attempt to describe our image of a dog, we might describe an ordinary particular dog: one that is black, short-haired, about 18 inches high, with a short tail, etc. Of course, we know that many dogs are not black, that some are long-haired, that some are very small and some are very large, and so forth. But we cannot have an image of a dog which is both black and not black, both long-haired and short-haired, and both tall and short. It is impossible for our image of a dog to include all those characteristics that we know dogs have. How, then, can our image *be* the meaning of the word?

A final difficulty with the idea theory is that it has the consequence that we can never know what another person means by certain words. You can never see my mental images, and I can never see yours. If the mental image is the meaning, how can I know what you mean by *dog*, and how can you know what I mean by *dog*? So the idea theory is problematic for several reasons.

2.2.3 MEANING AS USE

A new approach to meaning was developed more recently by Ludwig Wittgenstein (1889–1951) and John Austin (1911–60). They recognized that many words do refer to things and that many words have a mental image or idea associated with them, but they held that the primary bearers of meaning are not words but sentences. Words have meaning only when they are used in sentences: without such a context they have no meaning. When we ask what some particular word means, we seem to be asking for *the* meaning of the word itself, as if it had a meaning apart from the way it is used in sentences. In fact, the only meaning a word can have is the meaning it gains from the meanings of the sentences in which the word is typically used. Notice how the different meanings of a word are expressed by using that word in different sentences:

I gave him a <u>hand</u> with his baggage. (i.e., help)
The crowd gave him a <u>hand</u>. (i.e., applause)
Please <u>hand</u> me the scissors. (i.e., give)

She is a <u>green</u> lawyer. (i.e., inexperienced)
He is looking <u>green</u>. (i.e., nauseous)

We had a <u>green</u> Christmas last year. (i.e., without snow)

Don't <u>strike</u> that child. (i.e., hit)
The <u>strike</u> was over wages. (i.e., refusal to work)
<u>Strike</u> three! (i.e., the batter is "out")

But if the meaning of sentences is primary and the meaning of words is derivative—if we cannot derive the meaning of a sentence from the meanings of the words it contains—how are we to account for the meaning of sentences? Wittgenstein and Austin held that the meaning of sentences is to be found in their use. Language is a tool, and just as we don't really know what a hammer is until we know what its use is, so we don't know what a sentence means until we know what it is being used to do. In order to know what a particular sentence means we need to ask, *What is this speaker, talking to this audience in this particular context, using this sentence to do?* If someone says *Hold it*, we cannot know what the sentence means until we know what the speaker intends to accomplish by saying it, what conventions apply in the situation, and how the audience reacts to the sentence. Did the speaker say *Hold it* to get someone to stop doing something or to instruct someone to grasp hold of an object? Only when we have answered this question will we know what the sentence means.

It is important to pay attention to the context, for the context typically gives us the clues we need to determine what the speaker is using a sentence to do and thus what the sentence means. There are various contextual features we can make use of, such as the social setting, the speaker's personal goals, the nature and expectations of the audience, and what has just been said by other speakers. Changing the context of a sentence can sometimes dramatically affect its meaning. For example:

The queen is in a vulnerable position: (a) when said by a spectator at a chess match and (b) when said by a teacher in a lecture on the role of the monarchy in Britain.

The President has been shot and died a few minutes ago: (a) when said by a character in a film and (b) when said by a radio announcer in a news broadcast.

Let me go: (a) when said by a person whose arm has been grabbed by someone and (b) when said by a child whose teacher has asked for a volunteer to run an errand.

More commonly, however, context affects meaning in less dramatic but equally important ways. Usually, there are only a few possible uses of a sentence in any particular context, and we can make a reasonable judgement of its primary or intended use. It is important, therefore, to understand the various uses or functions of language.

2.3 The Main Functions of Language

Whenever we use language we do so for some purpose, and if we consider these purposes, we can see that there are several different types. Language, in other words, has several functions. Language is often characterized as a means of communication, and although this view is correct, it is not very informative. When we use language we almost always communicate something to someone, but usually our purpose is much more specific, and frequently we are not primarily concerned with communicating information at all. Our purpose is usually not merely to communicate, but to communicate for a specific purpose. What we mean often reflects these purposes. Consequently, how we interpret, and therefore react to, what others say depends upon what we take their purpose to be. It is therefore important to be aware of the main purposes for which language is used and how these purposes affect meaning. Each of these purposes reflects a different function of language. These purposes are not mutually exclusive, but it is helpful to keep them distinct from each other.

1. DESCRIPTIVE: One very important function of language is to describe (i.e., to convey factual information about) something. Whenever we describe something—an object, a situation, or a feeling—we are stating facts, or what we believe to be facts. For example:

> This coffee is cold.
> I don't have any change for the coffee machine.
> A cup of coffee would calm my nerves.

Almost every time we use language we convey factual information, even though this may not be our primary purpose.

2. EVALUATIVE: Often we use language not (or not merely) to describe something but to make a value judgement about it, that is, to evaluate it. For example:

> Julie is the best student in the class.

This is different from a mere factual description, for it presents a value judgement about Julie. There are several different types of evaluations: aesthetic, moral, economic, technological, and even scientific. For example:

> That was the worst movie I've seen in years.
> He is an irresponsible person.
> The best way to get rich is by investing in real estate.
> The safest way of disposing of uranium waste is to bury it in old coal mines.
> The theory of evolution provides the best account of the origin of biological species.

3. EMOTIVE: Language is sometimes used to express emotions and thus has an emotive function. When you hit your thumb with a hammer, you probably say something. If you say, *My thumb hurts*, you are describing your feelings. If you say, *This is a terrible hammer*, you are evaluating the hammer. But if, like most people, you say, *Damn!* (or worse), you are not describing or evaluating anything but are simply expressing your feelings or emotions. Almost any emotion can be expressed in words. For example:

> *I love you.*
> *You are a loathsome creature; go away.*
> *I shall die of unrequited love.*
> *Thank heavens that's over.*

Note that these sentences also convey factual information about the speakers' feelings, but in most contexts this function would be secondary.

4. EVOCATIVE: Language can also be used for the purpose of evoking certain emotions in an audience. If we want someone to feel sad about something, we can try to evoke that emotion through the careful choice of words and images. Poets are especially concerned with this function of language. Consider, for example, the line from T.S. Eliot's "The Love Song of J. Alfred Prufrock," which beautifully evokes the feeling of a meaningless life:

> *I have measured out my life with coffee spoons.*

Again, W.B. Yeats, in "The Lake Isle of Innisfree," evokes a feeling of peacefulness:

> *And I shall have some peace there, for peace comes dropping slow.*

Advertisers frequently use language to evoke certain feelings. For example:

> *At Speedy you're a Somebody.*

And everyone from time to time wants to evoke certain emotions in their audience. We want others to feel pity for someone, to feel anger at some situation, or to approve of something, and we use language for this purpose. Threats are usually intended to evoke fear in the victim. Political speeches are often aimed at making voters feel that a government is trustworthy or untrustworthy. Sermons often are designed to make us feel ashamed of the mean things we do.

5. PERSUASIVE: One of the most widespread uses of language is to persuade people to accept something or to act in a certain way. For example:

> *You shouldn't take astrology seriously. There is no scientific basis for it.*

I know you don't like parties, but I hope you'll come anyway. There will be several people there that you have been wanting to meet. I know you will enjoy yourself once you get there.

We try to persuade people to recycle waste, that the government's budget is likely to increase unemployment, that the police officer should not give us a speeding ticket, or that lotteries are a waste of money. Every argument is an example of the persuasive use of language. There are two ways language can be used to persuade. Sometimes our purpose is to persuade by means of rational arguments, even if we often fail to achieve our purpose. But often we abandon this restriction and use anything we think might succeed in persuading our audience. This is the case with propaganda and most advertising.

6. INTERROGATIVE: In order to elicit information we usually need to ask for it. Most often this is done by asking a question. For example:

What is the due date for the essay?

But asking questions is not the only way to elicit information. For example:

Tell me your age.
I won't lend you $20.00 unless you explain why you need it.

Whatever form of words we use, we are not describing, evaluating, expressing, or evoking anything, or attempting to persuade, but seeking to gain information.

7. DIRECTIVE: We sometimes use language to command others to do something or to provide advice. For example:

Go to the principal's office immediately.
Take these pills twice a day.

These sentences would normally be used to tell someone to do something. They do not describe or evaluate anything, express or evoke an emotion, seek information, nor, usually, do they attempt to persuade us of anything. They simply tell us what to do. The directive use of language covers ordering, commanding, directing, advising, requesting, and similar types of actions.

8. PERFORMATIVE: There is an interesting class of sentences that are known as performative utterances, i.e., utterances that are not descriptions, evaluations, directives, and so on, but are themselves to be regarded as actions. They are actions that consist of saying certain words; that is, in uttering a performative, the speaker performs some action *in addition to* merely saying a sentence. If a question arises of whether someone actually performed such an action, the only relevant evidence would consist of showing that the person uttered certain words under appropriate circumstances. For example:

I find the accused guilty of murder.

If these words are uttered by Judge Bean at the conclusion of a trial, they constitute the action of finding someone guilty of murder. If someone asks for proof that Judge Bean found the accused guilty of murder, it would be sufficient to quote the judge's words. It would make no sense to suggest that Judge Bean might have been mistaken or lying. If he said the words at the conclusion of the trial then he did find the accused guilty of murder. On the other hand, if I say,

Judge Bean found the accused guilty of murder,

I could not appeal to the fact that I said it as proof that it is true, since I might be mistaken or lying. It is not a performative utterance, but a description: it is true only if it correctly states or describes a fact. Similarly, if after the trial Judge Bean says,

I found the accused guilty of murder,

this would not be a performative utterance, for we could not appeal to the fact that Judge Bean uttered this sentence as proof that it is true, since he might be mistaken or lying. Here are two more examples of performative utterances:

I now pronounce you husband and wife.
I resign, here and now.

When uttered under the appropriate circumstances, each would constitute an action.

9. RECREATIONAL: Finally, we should not overlook the fact that language is often used to amuse ourselves and others. We tell jokes and stories, write novels, invent puns, do crossword puzzles, play guessing games, make up limericks, sing nursery rhymes, and write rude things on washroom walls. When language is used in any of these ways it serves a recreational function. People who tell jokes, write stories, or sing nursery rhymes usually do so out of simple enjoyment.

There are other functions of language, but these are the main ones, and all others can be fitted into at least one of the above categories. For example, we sometimes use language to hurt others' feelings, but this can be regarded as an evocative use of language. It is important to understand that these categories are not mutually exclusive: most of the time language serves more than one function. Often we intend to use a sentence for two or more purposes. We tell a joke in order to make someone relax (i.e., we amuse in order to evoke a feeling). We describe an automobile accident in hopes of persuading someone to drive more carefully. We evaluate a murder so as to express our abhorrence. We order someone to do something in order to evoke in them a feeling of respect for our authority.

The functions of language can be viewed from both a subjective and an objective point of view. From the subjective point of view, we regard the speaker's intention or purpose as primary. Did Sally intend to express her feelings or to convey information? Did Todd really intend to say something funny or was he just trying to be helpful? Was the doctor just describing the options or was she trying to persuade me to have the operation? From this point of view what is important is the speaker's intentions. From the objective point of view, on the other hand, we disregard the speaker's intentions and consider how the audience is affected by what is said. From the objective point of view every utterance always has several functions, even when the speaker has only one purpose. The other functions go beyond what the speaker intends. For example, we always convey some information to our audience whenever we speak, even when conveying information is not our purpose. Again, it is sometimes difficult, or even impossible, to describe certain things in a way that avoids expressing our emotions. (Try to describe a rape in a way that expresses nothing of your feelings.) Sometimes when we intend to describe something we inadvertently amuse others, as in *We had chork pops for dinner*. Frequently, there is an unacknowledged persuasive or evaluative function in what people say. From the objective point of view, we can often draw out levels of meaning in what someone says of which the speaker is not only unaware but may even refuse to admit are present.

The difference between these two points of view is important. To understand the meaning of what someone says, we must give priority to the subjective point of view. As we shall see later, when we assess an argument it is important to pay careful attention to what the speaker means, i.e., to the subjective meaning.

2.4 Self-Test No. 2

Using the contextual clues provided, which of the nine functions listed in 2.3 is the most likely primary purpose for each of the following sentences?

1. If you want to succeed in life you need a good education. (Said by a father to his 17-year-old daughter who has just told him she wants to drop out of school.)

2. Retail clothing stores can increase sales by about 30 per cent through advertising in local media. (Said by a teacher in a business class at a community college.)

3. You can increase your sales by 30 per cent through advertising in local media. (Said by an advertising salesperson from a local TV station when talking to the manager of a clothing store.)

4. I love you more than anyone else I've ever known. (Said by a young woman to a young man.)

5. She loves him more than anyone she's ever known. (Said by a father about his daughter and her boyfriend.)

6. Peter Piper picked a peck of pickled peppers. (Said by a father to his four-year-old daughter.)

7. Your essay must be at least 1,500 words and must include a full bibliography. (Said by a professor to a class.)

8. I now declare this building officially open. (Said by a politician when cutting the ribbon at the opening of a new school building.)

9. Pedestrians Cross Here. (A sign at a crosswalk.)

10. Reading an old copy of a Dickens novel is like spending an afternoon in the attic of an old house: the feel of the old paper, the look of the dated typeface, and the musty smell all take you back to the days when even your grandparents were still children. (From an article by a literary critic entitled *Why Reading Literature is Important*.)

11. Cloven Pickard, stop, in the name of the law. (Said by a police officer to a fleeing suspect.)

12. Cloven Pickard, you are under arrest and being charged for the murder of Oma Sage. (Said by a police officer to Cloven Pickard.)

2.5 Questions for Discussion

Unlike the self-test questions above, the contextual clues provided here allow more than one reasonable answer. Suggest additional contextual details that would support attributing at least two plausible purposes to the speakers.

1. Why can't you pay attention? (Said by a Grade 6 teacher to a student who frequently daydreams.)

2. The next car I buy will definitely be a Volvo. (Said by someone in a TV ad for Volvo.)

3. Military intelligence is a contradiction in terms. (Said by a historian in a course on the history of World War II.)

4. Frankly, Scarlett, I don't give a damn. (Said by Clark Gable in the film *Gone With The Wind*.)

5. Like, wow, man, what a blast. (Said by a teenager after a rock concert.)

6. Can you imagine what it must have been like, having to care for two small children in a Nazi concentration camp? (Said by a woman about her grandmother.)

7. Your time is now up. (Said by a teacher at the end of an examination.)

8. Most of the time he's a real jerk. (Said by a girl about her brother.)

9. I have often wondered what became of him. (Said by a middle-aged woman about a childhood friend.)

10. The best way to remove chewing gum from a carpet is to rub it with an ice cube for a minute or so. (An excerpt from a book of household hints.)

11. You've just proven that billboard advertising works! (Written on a billboard.)

12. Read me another story, grandma. (Said by a child at bedtime.)

2.6 Definition

In section 2.2.3 we noted that words often have more than one use or meaning. It is important to understand that not all the different uses of a word need have anything in common; for some words there may be a common element, but for many there is not. As long as we know how to use a word for some particular purpose, we know what the word means when used in that sense. Indeed, it is often difficult to enumerate all the different accepted uses of a word. But this is not a problem for the meaning-as-use theory, for it denies that words must have a single meaning. Since words typically have several different uses, it follows that there will be several different meanings, and as long as we understand a particular use (i.e., know how to use the word for that purpose) we understand the meaning of the word when used in that way.

We have seen that the meaning of language depends upon its use and context, and that it is often very difficult to say precisely what a word means if we ignore its use and context. Normally this is not a serious difficulty, for we can usually get by with a rough idea of what words mean as long as they are being used in ordinary contexts. But sometimes this casual approach is inadequate, and it becomes important to focus on the precise meanings of a word. When a lawyer explains what constitutes an assault, or a sales clerk says the microwave oven is warranteed, or a scientist talks about energy, we run the risk of misunderstanding if we fail to pay careful attention to the precise meanings of their words. These are the kinds of occasion when definitions are important; without them we may misunderstand what is being said. Of course, we also need definitions when we come across a word we are unfamiliar with or when a familiar word is being used in an unfamiliar way. In these cases, it is not misunderstanding that we want to avoid but not understanding at all.

To understand how definitions work we need to note the distinction between the *sense* of a term (sometimes called its *connotation* or *intension*) and its *reference* (or *denotation* or *extension*). The SENSE of a word is that which we understand when we understand its meaning, and the REFERENCE is the class of things to which the word refers. The sense of the term *bachelor*, for example, is the concept of an unmarried male, and the reference of the term is the class of all bachelors in the universe, not only those who now exist but those who have existed in the past and will exist in the future. All words must have a sense, although some words, as we saw in section 2.2.1, have no reference.

2.7 The Purposes of Definition

In order to understand how definitions work, we need to be aware of the different purposes for which definitions may be put forward. There are three main types.

2.7.1 REPORTIVE DEFINITIONS

The most common purpose of definitions is to convey the information needed to use a word correctly. The correct use of a word consists of its standard usage—how the word is in fact used by those who make regular use of it. When we want to know the meaning of a word in its standard usage, we need a reportive definition, i.e., one that reports its standard usage. Standard, desktop dictionaries give reportive definitions.

Reportive definitions can sometimes be troublesome because it may not be clear whether or not a particular use can be regarded as part of the standard usage. For example, 50 years ago the word *cohort* was standardly used only to refer to a group of persons banded together. (This reflected its original meaning in Latin, where it referred to a military unit roughly akin to a platoon.) Now, however, it is usually used to refer to a friend or associate. The sentence *Fred arrived with his cohort*, if used to mean that Fred arrived with his friend, would have been incorrect 50 years ago, but is now usually accepted as correct. This shift in meaning was probably brought about by people who did not understand the old usage and who were therefore using the word incorrectly, but the mistake has become so widespread that it is no longer regarded as incorrect. Only dedicated linguistic reactionaries continue to regard the new usage as incorrect. Except for cases where a meaning shift has not yet been accepted as standard usage, however, reportive definitions are usually quite straightforward.

2.7.2 STIPULATIVE DEFINITIONS

Sometimes it is useful to be able to create a new precise meaning. For example, a report on land use in Ontario would find it necessary to define the categories of land use that are being employed. The report would therefore stipulate how the words *agricultural, residential, industrial, recreational*, and so forth are being used. When we do this we are not attempting to report the standard usage, although it would clearly be foolish to depart radically from it. For many specific purposes, such as doing research or enacting legislation, it makes good sense to stipulate the precise meaning that is to be attached to key words. As long as this stipulated meaning is explicitly stated, there is no risk of misunderstanding, and there is an obvious gain in clarity and precision.

There is nothing to prevent us from inventing a new word by using a stipulative definition. For example, we might invent the word *spinge* to refer to the deposit that builds up between the bristles on a toothbrush, or the word *tele-rape* to refer to obscene telephone calls. We can also stipulate a new meaning for an old word: for example, using *bubble* to refer to a promise made by a politician. There is, however, no guarantee that these new words or uses will become part of the standard usage. This is likely to happen only when there is a need (or a perceived need) for the new term. If enough people think it is important to be able to talk about a new object or phenomenon or to refer to something in a new way, then a new word will usually be forthcoming, and will soon become part of standard usage. Until this happens, however, new words depend for their meaning upon stipulative definitions.

2.7.3 ESSENTIALIST DEFINITIONS

Some words—such as *justice, truth, love, religion, freedom, deity, death, law, peace, health,* and *science*—refer to things or qualities that have considerable importance. When we ask *What is justice?* we are not asking for a reportive definition, since such a definition might reflect a widespread misconception about the essential nature of justice. Nor would we be asking for a stipulative definition, since we can invent these for ourselves as easily as the next person. We are asking for a definition that reveals the essential nature of justice.

The correctness of an essentialist definition cannot be determined merely by an appeal to standard usage, like a reportive definition, nor by an appeal to its usefulness, like a stipulative definition. Essentialist definitions really need to be understood as compressed theories; they attempt to express in succinct form a theory about the nature of what is being defined. Thus, assessing an essentialist definition involves assessing a theory, and this goes far beyond questions about the meaning of words.

These three purposes of definition are important since when we want to determine whether a definition is acceptable we must first decide its purpose. Good stipulative definitions and good essentialist definitions are usually inadequate reportive definitions, and good reportive definitions are usually unsatisfactory essentialist definitions.

2.8 Methods of Definition

There are several different methods that can be used to define words. These methods can be used for reportive, stipulative, and essentialist definitions.

2.8.1 GENUS-SPECIES

A common method of defining a word referring to a kind of thing is to mention a larger category (a genus) to which that kind of thing belongs, and then to specify what makes that particular kind (that species) different from the other species in that genus. (Note that this is not the more particular meaning of the words genus and species in biology.) For example:

> A *sea-plane is an airplane that is adapted for landing on and taking off from a body of water.*

The definition states that a sea-plane is a member of the class of airplanes (i.e., it is a type of airplane) that is distinguished from other airplanes by being adapted for landing on and taking off from a body of water.

Most words can be defined using the genus-species method. Some, however, cannot because they lack a genus of which they are a member. A sea-plane is a member of the class of airplanes; an airplane is a member of the class of machines; a machine is a member of the class of...? At this point we have to look hard to find an appropriate class. We might use the class of systems:

> A *machine is a system of interacting parts.*

But then what is the appropriate class for systems? At some point, the process of finding a genus-class must end, and at this point we can no longer use the genus-species method.

2.8.2 OSTENSIVE

Sometimes the meaning of a word can easily be conveyed by giving examples, either verbally or by pointing. If someone wants to know what a bassoon is, it may be sufficient to hold one up and say,

> *Here is a bassoon.*

Or we may point one out by saying,

> *The bald guy in the third row of the orchestra is playing a bassoon.*

Sometimes it is necessary to give several examples in order to ensure that the meaning is clear. If we try to define *vehicle* ostensively, we will need to point to more than cars: we will also need to point to vans, trucks, buses, tractors, motorcycles, bicycles, and so on. If the range of examples given is too limited, we will have conveyed only part of the meaning of the term.

Using ostensive definitions for general terms can be problematic. If we attempt to define ostensively terms such as *fairness* or *truth*, it may be difficult for someone to grasp what the different examples have in common. It is difficult to point to or give examples for some words: for example, *neutron, space,* or *history.* And words that have no reference (for example, *very, where,* and *forever*) simply cannot be defined ostensively because there is nothing to point to.

2.8.3 BY SYNONYM

Often all that is needed to define a word is to give a synonym. For example:

Effulgent means the same as radiant.

Obviously, this method only works for words that have more or less exact synonyms. Words that lack a synonym have to be defined using one of the other methods. And, of course, such definitions will only be helpful for someone who understands the meaning of the synonym.

2.8.4 OPERATIONAL

Sometimes a term can be defined very precisely by specifying a rule of operation. In science, for example, it is essential that each concept be defined in a way that specifies exactly when it can be applied and when it cannot. One way of achieving such precision is to establish a rule that the term is to be applied only when a specified test or operation yields a certain result. For example:

A genius is anyone who scores over 140 on a standard I.Q. test.

Operational definitions are commonly used outside science when defining terms that are used to distinguish things that form a continuum, such as the quality of meat, student performance, or degree of drunkenness. Thus we have operational definitions for such terms as *Grade A beef, honours standing,* and *legal intoxication.* Operational definitions often arise initially as stipulative definitions, but may become part of the standard usage.

2.8.5 CONTEXTUAL

Some words can best be defined by using the word in a standard context and providing a different sentence that does not use the word but has the same meaning. For example, the concept of *logical strength* used in this book can be defined as follows:

This argument has logical strength *means the same as* The premises of this argument, if true, provide a justification for believing that its conclusion is true.

2.9 Assessing Reportive Definitions

A good stipulative definition is one that fixes a precise meaning of a term in a way that will be useful for some specific purpose. A good essentialist definition is one that reflects a true or reasonable theory about the essential nature of the phenomenon to which the term refers. But what is a good reportive definition? The short answer to this question is that a good reportive definition of a word is one that tells us what others mean when they use the word and what others will understand us to mean when we use it. In other words, it will accurately describe the actual standard usage of the term. There are several ways in which a reportive definition can fail to be a good definition.

2.9.1 TOO BROAD

A definition is too broad when the defining phrase refers to some things that are not included in the reference of the term being defined. The definition

> *A typewriter is a means of writing*

fails as a definition because the defining phrase (*a means of writing*) refers not only to typewriters but also to chalk, pens, and pencils, among other things. The definition is too broad because it includes more than it should. Here are some other examples of definitions that are too broad:

> *Soccer is a game played with a ball.*
> *A beaver is an amphibious rodent, native to northeastern North America.*
> *A sofa is a piece of furniture designed for sitting.*

If we regard these not as definitions, but as statements, they are all true. Soccer is, obviously, a game played with a ball. In a sense, therefore, definitions that are too broad do not say anything that is actually false. It is when such statements are put forward as definitions that problems may arise.

2.9.2 TOO NARROW

A definition is too narrow when the defining phrase fails to refer to some things that are included in the reference of the term being defined. The definition

> *A school is an institution that aims at teaching children how to read and write*

is a bad definition because the defining phrase fails to refer to schools that do not aim at teaching children how to read and write, such as medical schools and dance schools. It is too narrow; it excludes these other kinds of schools. Here are some other examples of definitions that are too narrow:

> *A parent is a person's biological mother or father.*
> *A farm is a place where crops are grown.*
> *A bigamist is a man who is married to two women at the same time.*

As with definitions that are too broad, definitions that are too narrow do not say anything that is obviously false. What they say may be true for a large portion of the class of things being defined, but because they are not true for *all* of the things being defined each is a bad definition.

2.9.3 TOO BROAD AND TOO NARROW

A definition can sometimes be too broad and too narrow at the same time. This happens when the defining phrase refers to some things to which the term does not (too broad) and also fails to refer to some things to which the term does (too narrow). For example:

> *A pen is an instrument designed for writing words.*

This definition is too broad because it includes pencils and typewriters as well as pens, and it is too narrow because it fails to include pens that are designed for drawing pictures.

In order to determine whether a definition is too broad or too narrow, it is necessary to compare the reference of the term being defined with the reference of the defining phrase. Two questions need to be asked: (1) does the reference of the defining phrase include things that are not included in the reference of the term being defined? If it does, then the definition is too broad. And (2) does the reference of the defining phrase exclude things that are included in the reference of the term? If it does, then the definition is too narrow.

Here are some examples of definitions that are both too broad and too narrow:

> *Hockey is a game played on ice in Canada.*
> *A doctor is a person who treats physical ailments.*
> *A professor is a teacher who does research.*

2.9.4 CIRCULAR

A circular definition is one that includes the term being defined (or its cognate) in the definition. For example:

> *A golf ball is a small spherical object used in the game of golf.*

The problem here is obvious: anyone who does not already know what golf is, is not going to be enlightened by the definition. Circular definitions are therefore usually useless.

When a definition uses a cognate of the term being defined the circularity may be less obvious. For example:

> *A surgeon is a person who practises surgery.*

This definition is circular because *surgeon* and *surgery* are cognates (i.e., they come from the same root). Circular definitions involving cognates may not always be useless, however, since a person may know the meaning of one and not the other.

People do not often put forward circular definitions that are as blatant as these examples. But sometimes a pair of definitions, neither of which is itself circular, can lead to a kind of circularity when taken together. If someone defines *freedom* as *the absence of coercion*, and then defines *coercion* as *the absence of freedom*, the definitions taken together are circular and therefore likely to be useless.

2.9.5 OBSCURE

A definition can also be useless when it fails, through the use of vague, obscure, or metaphorical language, to express clearly the meaning of the term being defined. Consider the following definitions:

> *A marathon is a long foot-race.*
> *A grampus is a kind of blowing, spouting, blunt-headed, dolphin-like cetacean.*
> *A fact is anything that rubs the corners off our prejudices.*

The first of these definitions uses a vague expression (*long*) that leaves the meaning of the term somewhat obscure, and if we read it charitably as "longer than 1 kilometre," say, that only makes it too broad. The second uses a scientific term (*cetacean*) that is likely to be unenlightening (to non-biologists, at least). The third is likely to be uninformative because it uses a metaphor (*rubs the corners off*). In most circumstances these definitions will be unsatisfactory. However, a definition that uses an obscure technical term may nevertheless be correct (for example, the second of the above definitions); if we want to have a precise understanding of the term, we will have to look for a definition of the obscure term and hope that it is not equally obscure.

2.10 Assessing Stipulative and Essentialist Definitions

The errors in section 2.9 describe five different ways in which a definition can fail to convey adequately the standard usage of a term. Stipulative and essentialist definitions, however, are not intended to convey the standard usage of a term. As we saw in section 2.7.2, stipulative definitions are intended to establish a new or restricted meaning for a term and cannot, therefore, be criticized for failing to convey adequately the standard usage of the term. Essentialist definitions are intended to describe the essential nature of something, and since there is no guarantee that the standard usage of a term will reflect a correct understanding of its essence, we cannot criticize an essentialist definition for failing to convey the standard usage of the term. How, then, are such definitions to be assessed?

Stipulative and essentialist definitions are always put forward for a specific purpose. Whatever their purpose, they must enable the audience to know how to use the term in accordance with its stipulated or essential meaning, and this means that they should not be obscure or circular. For example, if a report defined an offensive weapon as

anything that can be used to inflict harm on another person

we could criticize it for being vague, even though we recognize that it is intended as a stipulative definition. Similarly, the definition

love is essentially a mutual loving dependency between two people

is clearly circular. Except in contexts where a definition has a humorous purpose, obscurity and circularity will be grounds for criticism.

A more serious problem can arise when a stipulative or essentialist definition of a term is significantly different from the standard usage of the term. The fact that the two meanings are different is not by itself a problem, but it can lead to misunderstanding and confusion. It might be reasonable for some purposes to stipulate the meaning of heat wave as a period of at least three successive days in which the high temperature exceeds 30 degrees Celsius. But if the high temperatures over the past week were 29, 35, 35, 29, 35, 35, and 29, we would be puzzled if someone denied we were in a heat wave. Anyone who uses such a stipulative definition should remind us of this fact; for example, by saying, *Technically, this doesn't count as a heat wave.*

The possibilities for misunderstanding are increased when the term being given a stipulative or essentialist definition lacks a clear and precise usage, since the discrepancy between the ordinary usage and the defined meaning may not be immediately apparent. Worse, terms whose ordinary meaning is somewhat vague often stand in the greatest need of a more precise definition; for example, *conflict of interest, sexual harassment, potentially violent offender, dangerous level of PCBs, mental abnormality, pollutant,* and *national security.* For bureaucratic or legal reasons, such terms may need to have a precise meaning assigned, and it is extremely important to be aware of the possible meaning shifts that may deliberately or inadvertently be involved.

These meaning shifts can best be described by reference to the concepts of too broad and too narrow. We have seen that in order to determine whether a reportive definition is too broad or too narrow we compare the reference classes of the defining phrase and the term being defined. This same comparison allows us to determine whether the reference of a stipulative or essentialist definition of a term is broader or narrower than the standard usage of the term. Consider the following stipulative definition, taken from section 2 of the Narcotic Control Act of Canada.

> *"Narcotic addict" means a person who, through the use of narcotics, (a) has developed a desire or need to continue to take a narcotic, or, (b) has developed a psychological or physical dependence on the effect of a narcotic.*

This definition is broader than the standard usage of the term, since it regards a person who has developed a desire to continue to take a narcotic as an addict. We must be careful, however, in making claims about standard usage. Do those who commonly use these terms in fact agree that someone who, through the use of narcotics, has developed a desire to continue to take a narcotic, would not be called a narcotic addict? Most people would probably want to say that such a person is in danger of becoming an addict, but if the desire is not a strong one and is easily and regularly overcome, they would likely deny that such a person is an addict. If this is the standard usage of the term *narcotic addict*, we can conclude that the definition contained in the Narcotic Control Act is a broad one.

If we want to criticize such a definition, however, we must do more than point out that it is broader or narrower than the standard usage. The question is whether the broader or narrower definition has desirable or undesirable consequences. In some cases it may be desirable to broaden or narrow the scope of a term and in other cases not. There is nothing sacred about standard usage, so such questions are always debatable. These debates sometimes raise important questions of social policy. More commonly, however, it is only necessary to remember that a stipulative or essentialist definition of a term gives a *different* (i.e., broader or narrower) meaning than the term has in its standard usage. For example, when the theologian Paul Tillich defines atheist as a person who lacks what he calls *ultimate concern*, it is important for the reader to be aware that Tillich's definition is significantly different from the ordinary usage of the term; he is trying to provide an essentialist definition. And when a piece of legislation defines a terrorist as "anyone who belongs to a terrorist organization, whether or not they commit or plan a terrorist act," it is important to be aware that this definition is much broader than standard usage for reasons that have to do with the enforcement and administration of the law.

What is suggested by these special considerations for stipulative or essentialist is that we must first identify whether a definition is reportive, stipulative or essentialist. Then, if it is stipulative, we must identify the purpose for which the definition is formulated, and assess whether it fulfils this purpose. (Of course, we should think critically about this purpose, too, but for the moment we are concentrating on definitions.) And if it is essentialist, we must do the hard work of understanding the theory within which the definition is set; then we can assess whether all the appropriate essential details are included within the definition as the author has formulated it. (Again, of course, we should think critically about the entire theory, but for the moment we are concentrating on definitions.) In these cases, we cannot appeal to standard usage to assess the definition, but we can assess them on rational grounds according to the purposes associated with stipulative and essentialist definitions.

2.11 A Warning

Defining words is an art. It requires good judgement to know what kind of definition is appropriate in any particular context. Compilers of dictionaries attempt to provide definitions that can serve in a very broad range of contexts, but even they make no claim to give a full and complete account of the meanings of words. They do not, for example, attempt to cover every slang, dialect, or metaphorical use.

Most of us are not writers of dictionaries, and we only attempt to provide definitions when a particular need arises. Sometimes we are asked what a word means. A friend asks what the difference is between *disinterested* and *uninterested*. A German tourist asks what *street* means. A child asks what *obstetrician* means. In such circumstances, there is no need to give a full definition: we need only provide enough information to remove the questioner's ignorance. The friend may only need to be told that *disinterested* means the same as *impartial*. The German tourist only needs to be informed that *street* means *Strasse*. The child will be content if told that *obstetrician* means *a doctor who treats pregnant women*. The appropriate kind of answer is one that meets the needs of the questioner, and this is usually less than a full reportive definition.

Sometimes, however, we need to define a word because we want to increase or deepen our understanding. This is likely to arise with terms that are abstract or stand for a complex object or phenomenon; we often have a general idea of what they mean and can point to examples, but find it very difficult to say precisely what they mean. For most people, the following terms fall into this category: *energy, classical, crime, psychiatry, nation, pornography, religion, imagination, evil, illness, cause*, and *trust*. These are important matters, and if we want to increase our understanding of them we must attempt to ensure that we have a clear understanding of the words. But even here we do not usually want a full reportive definition. Often we are interested in only one sense of the word (for example, *energy* as a scientific term), and sometimes we want only to be able to distinguish between similar things (for example, between *psychiatry* and *psychology*).

2.12 Self-Test No. 3

What errors are committed by the following definitions? (Assume a context in which they have been put forward as reportive definitions.)

1. Parliament is the supreme legislative body of Canada.

2. Poetry is an art form that uses words to communicate ideas and images.

3. A snowplough is an implement designed to remove snow.

4. Restoration is the process or activity of restoring something to its former condition.

5. A tritone is the musical interval of an augmented fourth or a diminished fifth.

6. A stapler is a device for fastening pages together.

7. A nurse is a woman who is trained to look after the sick.

8. A bungalow is a one-storey building.

9. The United Nations is an organization aimed at fostering co-operation and peace between nations.

10. A sport is any activity involving competition between individuals or groups of individuals.

2.13 Questions for Discussion

In light of the purposes and methods of definition covered in this chapter, assess the following definitions:

1. A psychological disorder is any personal way of perceiving or interpreting events which is used repeatedly in spite of its consistent failure (from G.A. Kelly, *Personality Theory and Research* [Toronto: John Wiley and Sons, 1970], p. 240).

2. The term suicide is applied to all cases of death resulting directly or indirectly from a positive or negative act of the victim himself, which he knows will produce his death (from Émile Durkheim, *Suicide: A Study in Sociology*, tr. Spalding and Simpson [New York: Free Press, 1966], p. 44).

3. No person is criminally responsible for an act committed or an omission made while suffering from a mental disorder that rendered the person incapable of appreciating the nature and quality of the act or omission or of knowing that it was wrong (from the *Criminal Code of Canada*, section 16.(1)).

4. SOCIALISM. Principle that individual freedom should be completely subordinated to interests of community, with any deductions that may be correctly or incorrectly drawn from it, e.g. substitution of co-operative for competitive production, national ownership of land & capital, State distribution of produce, free education & feeding of children ... (from *Concise Oxford Dictionary*, 1934 edition).

5. FULL-TIME STUDENT: A full-time student is one who (i) is geographically available and visits the campus regularly, (ii) is not regularly employed, save in the most exceptional circumstances, for more than an average of 10 hours per week during any period in which the student is registered as a full-time graduate student, and (iii) is not employed outside the University except by the Advisor's permission; and in light of the foregoing is designated as a full-time graduate student (from *University of Guelph, Graduate Calendar, 1994-1996*, p. 161).

6. Poetry is the spontaneous overflow of powerful feelings ... recollected in tranquillity (from William Wordsworth, *Preface to Lyrical Ballads*, 1800).

7. A cynic is a person who knows the price of everything and the value of nothing (attributed to Oscar Wilde).

8. Liberty is the right to do whatever the law permits.

9. TERRORISM: an ideologically motivated unlawful act or acts, including but not limited to the use of violence or force or threat of violence or force, committed by or on behalf of any group(s), organization(s) or government(s) for the purpose of influencing any government and/or instilling fear in the public or section of the public. (Widely used home-owner's insurance policy definition for the purpose of a terrorist exclusion clause)

10. A material witness is someone who has information that may be important for a police investigation and, while not being a suspect himself or herself, is believed to pose a flight risk.

3.   Clarifying Meaning

The failure to understand the meaning of what others say, and the failure to understand how others can misunderstand the meaning of what we say, are the seeds of much frustration, resentment, and discord. In this chapter we examine some of the ways in which misunderstanding can result from a lack of clarity in the language we use. Our purpose here is to develop the ability to recognize obscurity in what others say and to learn how to say clearly what we mean.

3.1 The Principle of Charity

Often we are confronted by a choice between two or more interpretations of what someone has said, and sometimes these interpretations have different degrees of plausibility. If we adopt the least plausible interpretation, it is often easy to show that the statement is false. On the other hand, if we adopt the most plausible interpretation, it is usually more difficult to show that the statement is false. It is tempting, therefore, when faced with a statement we disagree with, to adopt the least plausible interpretation of it. After all, if we can get away with foisting an implausible view on our opponents it makes it easier to show that they are wrong (or stupid, irrational, foolish, etc.) It is especially tempting to do this when the most implausible interpretation is the literal one. For example:

> *The worst thing that can happen to a worker in this province is to fall into the clutches of the Workers' Compensation Board.*

> *The only difference between an amateur and a professional musician is that the amateur performs for personal satisfaction while the professional performs for money.*

> *Doctors who perform abortions are guilty of first-degree murder.*

We all recognize that the literal interpretation of such statements is unlikely to be what the speaker intended. They are exaggerations or overstatements. If the speaker is present we may want to have a bit of fun by pointing out the absurdity of what was actually said. Sometimes this is legitimate; for example, when debating in parliament. However, when there is an important issue at stake, we should not let our desire to poke fun at our opponents prevent us from listening to what they are really trying to say. When our opponents are not present and cannot clarify what they have said, we ought to be prepared to do so on their behalf. It is up to us to find the fairest interpretation of their words that is available, the one that best represents their presumed intentions.

Thus, in any discussion we have a moral obligation to treat our opponents fairly. When they are present, we ought to give them the opportunity to clarify what they have said. When they are not present, we have a moral obligation to follow the PRINCIPLE OF CHARITY, that is, to adopt the most charitable interpretation of their words among the possible interpretations suggested by the context. The most charitable interpretation is the one that makes our opponent's views as reasonable, plausible, or defensible as possible. According to the principle of charity, whenever two interpretations are possible, we should always adopt the more reasonable one (unless something in the context suggests that another interpretation is what the person meant).

Why should we be charitable to our opponents? After all, it might be argued that if the purpose of engaging in a debate is to win, the principle of charity will make our task more difficult. But winning is not the primary purpose of rational discussion. The primary purpose should always be to discover the truth and to develop views and positions that are as reasonable and defensible as they can be. It is always possible that our opponents are right and we are wrong, or that our opponents are partly right and our position needs to be amended in some way; in either case, we stand to benefit from discussion. Even if our opponents are totally wrong, it is a useful test of the strength of our own position to be able to show their errors. In any case, we owe it to our opponents to interpret their words in a reasonable manner. Anyone who has ever been involved in a discussion with an opponent who persistently violates the principle of charity will understand the unfairness of such treatment and will appreciate the importance of observing the principle.

The principle of charity should be followed not only when we are interpreting single statements, but also when we are interpreting longer passages and even entire books. Throughout this book we shall often find it necessary to invoke the principle of charity. Being charitable to our opponents should eventually become second nature.

3.2 Linguistic Ambiguity

3.2.1 AMBIGUITY AND VAGUENESS

Some sentences are ambiguous. Some sentences are vague. But ambiguity and vagueness are not the same. An AMBIGUOUS SENTENCE is one that has two or more different but possibly quite precise meanings. A VAGUE SENTENCE is one that lacks a precise meaning. Ambiguous sentences should be avoided whenever there is a risk of misinterpretation—whenever there is a risk that the hearer will select the wrong meaning. Except in jokes and when it serves a clear literary purpose, ambiguity is something we must avoid. Vague sentences, however, are necessary if we are trying to express a vague thought or feeling. For example:

> *I don't care much for Beethoven's early string quartets.*
> *That was a noisy party they had last night, and it went on until all hours.*
> *Lots of people own two television sets.*
> *Margaret Laurence's novels have a disquieting effect upon the reader.*

These sentences are vague, but they are not ambiguous. In most contexts, there is no need for greater precision about such matters. If challenged, we could easily be a little more precise, but it would be very difficult (and usually pointless) to attempt to remove the vagueness altogether. There is nothing wrong with vagueness when we want to express a vague thought or when there is no need for precision.

In contexts in which precision is needed, however, we sometimes come across sentences that look quite precise, but that turn out to be extremely vague. For example:

> *Applicants must hold a diploma in early childhood education or have equivalent work experience.*

The phrase *equivalent work experience* sounds quite precise, but without further information it is impossible to tell what kinds of work experience are going to count as equivalent. Does raising three children of one's own count? What about occasional baby-sitting over a period of six years? A half-time job as a helper in a nursery school for three years? Two years' experience as a kindergarten teacher? Potential applicants need a precise statement of the minimum qualifications for the position, but the sentence fails to provide it.

Those who use vague sentences when precision is needed, or who use vague sentences that look precise, should be challenged. Sometimes it is quite easy to see precisely what needs to be challenged. For example:

> *The fact that the Liberals won more seats than any other party in the 2004 federal election shows that the voters want a Liberal government.*

The vagueness here arises with the phrase *the voters*. We need to ask *How many voters?* We know that *the voters* cannot refer to all the voters, since other parties also received votes. Does it mean most of the voters? This may well be the speaker's intent, but, if so, the claim is false since in fact fewer than half of the votes cast were for Liberal candidates in that election (not an unusual situation for any federal government in Canada). The Liberal victory resulted from the multi-party system, not from the support of most of the electorate. This example shows the importance of asking for quantifiers: *Do you mean all, most, or just some?* and *Do you mean always, usually, or just sometimes?*

In other cases, however, the vagueness arises from the use of terms that are inherently vague. The cabinet minister who says,

> *My officials are monitoring this situation very closely, and I can promise that we shall take all appropriate measures to ensure that the situation is resolved in a way that is fair to all the parties involved,*

should be challenged on grounds of vagueness. Despite the appearance of having promised to do something specific, the minister has not really promised to do anything at all. What are *appropriate measures*? They could be anything or nothing. What does *fair to all* the parties mean? We have no clear idea. Such phrases are inherently vague and can mean almost anything. People who use them should be challenged to say more precisely what they mean.

It is important to understand that ambiguity and vagueness arise from the use of words within sentences and not properties of the words themselves. This is because, as we saw in section 2.2.3, words typically have more than one meaning, and the context in which they are used usually tells us which meaning is the intended one. It is the context that makes sentences vague, and it is when the context lets us down that sentences become ambiguous. Of course, the ambiguity or vagueness of a sentence often rests upon the meaning of a word or phrase, but the ambiguity or vagueness arises only at the level of the sentence.

Here are some other sentences that should be challenged on grounds of vagueness, at least in normal contexts:

> *Essays for this course should be long enough to deal adequately with the assigned topic.*
> *You should sign our petition to protest against the violation of our rights by the government.*
> *If you persist in this course of action, all hell is going to break loose.*

3.2.2 REFERENTIAL AMBIGUITY

REFERENTIAL AMBIGUITY arises when a word or phrase could, in the context of a particular sentence, refer to two or more properties or things. Usually the context tells us which meaning is intended, but, when it doesn't, we may choose the wrong meaning. If we are not sure which reference is intended by the speaker, we will misunderstand the speaker's meaning if we assign the wrong (i.e., the unintended) meaning to the word. If someone tells you that *Pavarotti was a big opera star*, you will have to guess whether *big* refers to *fat* or to *famous*. Sometimes, however, it is the context that creates the ambiguity. If someone is comparing the merits of two universities and says, *It is quite a good university*, the context may not tell us which university is being referred to.

Referential ambiguities are usually easy to spot and, once recognized, are easily avoided. This is especially true in conversation, since we can ask for clarification: *Do you mean that Pavarotti was fat or famous?* Or, if we select the wrong meaning, it will not be long before we discover our mistake: *Oh, I thought you meant he was famous!* There is, however, one type of referential ambiguity that deserves special mention: that between the collective and the distributive use of a term. Most nouns refer to a class of individual objects: *dog*, for example, refers to the class consisting of all dogs, and *book* refers to the class of all books. Usually when we use such nouns we do so in order to say something about each and every member of the class. When we use a term in this way it is being used DISTRIBUTIVELY. But sometimes we use terms to say something not about each and every member of the class but about the class as such. When we use a term in this way it is being used COLLECTIVELY. Consider the following:

> *Our university has a large wrestling team.*

If we interpret *wrestling team* distributively, the statement means that the individual members of the team are large. If we interpret the term collectively, the statement means that the team has a large number of members. Usually the context makes it clear whether a term should be interpreted distributively or collectively, but sometimes it does not, and we can mistakenly assume the wrong interpretation.

It is useful to develop the ability to recognize referential ambiguities even when they are unlikely to cause misunderstandings, for then we are less likely to assume a wrong interpretation inadvertently. Here are some more examples of sentences containing referential ambiguities:

> *Tom gave Ted's skis to his sister.*
> *Harold told me that he would do it next week.*
> *Americans make more telephone calls than Canadians.*
> *The government has provided constant funding for post-secondary education over the last three years.*

3.2.3 GRAMMATICAL AMBIGUITY

GRAMMATICAL AMBIGUITY arises when the grammatical structure of a sentence allows two interpretations, each of which gives rise to a different meaning. A few years ago a British newspaper reported that

> *Lord Denning spoke against the artificial insemination of women in the House of Lords.*

The grammar makes it unclear whether it was the speech or the insemination that took place in the House of Lords. This is because the phrase *in the House of Lords* could modify either *insemination* or *spoke*. Of course, which meaning applies in this case is clear despite this ambiguity, but that is not always the case.

Here are a few examples:

He promised to pay Stephanie and Michael $50 to clear all the junk out of the basement and take it to the dump.
Ashley strode out of the studio with Nikki following her, saying, "I'll never give him up."
Daphne decided to quit smoking while driving to New Denver.
Jim and I have suffered tremendously; often I wake up in the morning and wish I were dead, and I know Jim does too.
Women with babies who attend university encounter all sorts of exceptional challenges.

3.2.4 USE AND MENTION

Another type of linguistic ambiguity arises through the failure to distinguish between USING a word or phrase and MENTIONING a word or phrase. Consider the following sentences:

Tom said I was angry.
Tom said, "I was angry."

Clearly these sentences have different meanings, even though the words are identical. The difference in meaning arises because the phrase *I was angry* is being *used* in the first sentence but is only *mentioned* in the second. Quotation marks or italics are commonly used to mark the difference. But direct quotation is not the only occasion when we want to mention a word, and in these cases we should also use italics or quotation marks to make our meaning clear. For example:

Paddy is Irish.

As it stands, this sentence means that a particular person, called Paddy, is an Irishman. But if we put quotation marks around "Paddy" it would mean that "Paddy" is an Irish name. Here are some more examples of sentences whose meaning would change if the word or phrase which is mentioned (as indicated by quotation marks) were being used instead:

The word "itself" is hard to define.
"John Smith" was placed on the ballot.

Examples such as these are really only problematic in speech. But the ability to detect linguistic ambiguities is an important skill, for undetected ambiguities can create misunderstandings that lead to those frustrating discussions in which everyone seems to be at cross purposes. On the other hand, people who delight in finding linguistic ambiguities that do not in fact mislead anyone may be amusing for a time but can become extremely annoying. Since our interest is in clarifying meaning, we are concerned only with ambiguities that do or may mislead (which is why it is so important to make use of the writing conventions that are available to help avoid these problems).

3.3 Self-Test No. 4

Identify the kind of ambiguity in each of the following sentences and state the different ways in which each sentence can be interpreted.

1. Billy gave his sisters a box of candy for Christmas.

2. He's a chicken.

3. Melissa only has one dress.

4. The General loses battle with nurses. (A newspaper headline)

5. Conversational German is extremely difficult.

6. Children need discipline to become responsible adults.

7. If, after you think it over, you still decide to drop out of school, I promise I won't say another word to you.

8. In multi-section courses, the instructors should be free to choose the text.

9. Eighty per cent of the stores tested illegally sell cigarettes to minors with no questions asked.

10. She arrived at the theatre in a white limousine with a bright red hood.

11. The apartment superintendent came to our door during the party last night to complain about the noise in his pyjamas.

12. Tell me where she hit you.

3.4 Analytic, Contradictory, and Synthetic Statements

Usually, when we know what a statement means we still do not know whether it is true or false. If I say, *I was born on October 22*, you understand the meaning of what I have said, but you do not know whether what I have said is true or false. The sentence is one of a large class of sentences for which the truth or falsity is not determined by its meaning. There are, however, certain statements whose truth or falsity is determined by their meaning. Consider the following examples:

All bachelors are unmarried adult males.
Some bachelors are married.

Once we understand the meaning of these statements, we know that the first is true and the second is false. They are true, or false, by definition. We do not need to investigate the facts in order to know whether they are true or false. Someone who tries to discover their truth or falsity by sending a questionnaire to a group of bachelors asking whether or not they were married obviously does not understand the meaning of the statements.

A statement that is true by definition is called an ANALYTIC statement. A statement that is false by definition is called a CONTRADICTORY statement. A statement whose truth or falsity is not solely dependent upon the meanings of the words in it is called a SYNTHETIC statement. All statements can be placed in one of these three categories.

These distinctions are useful in clarifying the meaning of certain statements whose meaning is imprecise. When a statement seems false, we can ask whether it is a false synthetic or a contradictory statement. When a statement seems true, we can ask whether it is a true synthetic or an analytic statement. For example, if someone claims that every successful person is wealthy, it is useful to know whether they are interpreting the word successful as meaning financially successful. If so, their claim becomes analytic, for it really means that all wealthy people are wealthy. In a case such as this, it may seem to be a waste of time arguing against an analytic statement, but it is helpful to identify *that* it is analytic rather than synthetic; it helps clarify what is at stake in a disagreement. In practice, people do not usually approach discussions with precise definitions of the key terms. It is when they are challenged—for example, when someone says, *I know several very successful poets and artists who are not wealthy*—that the temptation arises to define words in a way that makes their claim analytic. Since analytic statements are true by definition, such a move seems calculated to ensure victory in the debate.

But such victories are usually hollow, for analytic statements are always in a sense trivial. Obviously, all successful people are wealthy—if, by *successful*, you mean *wealthy*. But why should anyone think it interesting to claim that all wealthy people are wealthy? It is true, but trivially true. The interesting question in such a debate is whether one should regard financial success as the only kind of success, and this cannot be determined merely by defining words. In practice, people who attempt to win a debate by making their claim analytic usually shift back and forth between analytic and synthetic interpretations in the course of the debate. To show that their claim is true they adopt the analytic interpretation; to show that it is important they adopt the synthetic interpretation. In this way they convince themselves that their claim is both true and important, but the true meaning is trivial and the important meaning is unproven and possibly false.

Sometimes a claim is made into an analytic one in ways that are indirect, and it may take some perseverance to uncover these moves. Usually, these indirect moves arise from arguments that are used to defend a claim. The claim that a free-enterprise system is superior to a socialist system, in its most plausible interpretation, is a synthetic statement. But suppose the following argument were put forward to support this claim:

(1) In a free-enterprise system market forces determine how resources are allocated within the society.

(2) It is more efficient to allocate resources through market forces than through decisions by government officials.

(3) An efficient system is superior to an inefficient system.

(4) Therefore, a free-enterprise system is superior to a socialist system.

This is a logically strong argument, in the sense that, if the first three statements are true, then the conclusion must also be true. The danger arises when attempting to show that premises (2) and (3) are true. It is all too easy to assume their truth by regarding them as analytic. Premise (2) becomes analytic if it is assumed that an efficient allocation of resources is by definition one that is produced by market forces. Premise (3) becomes analytic if it is interpreted to mean that an economically efficient system is economically superior to an economically inefficient system. But if the premises are interpreted in this way, then the conclusion needs to be re-interpreted to mean that a system that allocates resources efficiently is more efficient than one that does not allocate resources efficiently. In this way, the conclusion itself becomes analytic. It is true, but trivially so, since its truth depends not on the facts but only on the way the key terms are defined. The real argument will, of course, resurface as an argument about the truth or adequacy of the interpretations of premises (2) and (3).

3.5 Self-Test No. 5

For each of the following sentences, determine whether it is best interpreted as analytic, synthetic, or contradictory.

1. A full deck of playing cards contains 52 cards.

2. A centimetre is longer than a millimetre.

3. It is better to be free and unhappy than to be a contented slave.

4. No one has ever run the marathon in less than two hours.

5. Death comes for us all, sooner or later.

6. I'm not saying that postal workers should not have the legal right to strike, but the postal service is so vital to the economy, and postal strikes cause so much personal inconvenience to so many people, that I think the government should enact legislation banning strikes in the post office.

7. In the southern hemisphere, the sun rises in the west and sets in the east.

8. All parents love their children, when they are new born.

9. A rose by any other name would smell as sweet.

10. A rose is a rose is a rose.

11. You can't fit a square peg into a round hole.

12. My bicycle is in excellent condition, once both wheels are straightened out, the broken frame is welded, the tires are patched, the handlebar gets replaced and a seat is put on it.

3.6 Descriptive and Evaluative Meaning

In section 2.3 we characterized the main uses of language. The first two of these—the descriptive and the evaluative—are probably the most common uses of language and probably also the most fundamental. As a result, we find that many words have come to have meanings that are both descriptive and evaluative. When someone says that Fritz Kreisler was a renowned violinist, the word *renowned* has a double meaning. First, it means that Kreisler was well-known as a violinist. Second, it means that he was an excellent violinist. The first meaning is descriptive, since it refers to the fact that Kreisler was well-known. If there is a disagreement about this fact, it can be settled by looking for historical evidence regarding how widely known he was during his lifetime. The second meaning, however, is evaluative; the speaker is giving his or her opinion that Kreisler was an excellent violinist. This opinion is not factual, since if there is a disagreement over whether Kreisler was an excellent violinist, it cannot be settled by consulting the facts. Someone who thinks that Kreisler was not an excellent violinist would be able to accept the descriptive meaning but would have to reject the evaluative meaning of our statement.

There are many descriptive words and phrases that also have an evaluative meaning. It is common to find two or more words or phrases that have more or less the same descriptive meaning but different evaluative meanings. We have seen that *renowned* and *well-known* have the same descriptive meaning, but the former has a positive evaluative meaning that the latter lacks. The word *notorious* has the same descriptive meaning but has a negative evaluative meaning. The evaluative meanings of *renowned* and *notorious* convey an evaluation of the person as being good or bad, whereas *well-known* conveys nothing about the speaker's evaluation. Notice the shift in the evaluative meanings in the following pairs of sentences while the descriptive meaning remains more or less unchanged:

He is very self-confident.
He is arrogant.

She is sexually liberated.
She is promiscuous.

He is a dedicated conservative.
He is a fanatical conservative.

They are freedom fighters.
They are terrorists.

It is important to be aware of such differences in meaning, since we can sometimes be led to accept a particular evaluation through a failure to distinguish descriptive and evaluative meanings. The facts that would show that someone is very self-confident and the facts that would show that someone is arrogant are very similar, and a skilled arguer can easily create the impression that someone who is self-confident is really arrogant (or vice versa). But the same facts can only be used to justify two statements with different evaluative meanings if the evaluative meaning is ignored and they are regarded as purely descriptive statements. The evaluative part of the meaning requires a separate justification.

3.7 Self-Test No. 6

The italicized word or phrase in each of the following sentences has both a descriptive and an evaluative meaning. Indicate whether its evaluative meaning is positive or negative and briefly paraphrase its descriptive meaning in non-evaluative terms. Suggest a descriptive synonym or equivalent phrase that has a neutral (or no) evaluative meaning but preserves the descriptive meaning of the sentence.

1. There is *vicious* competition among students at the Julliard School of Music.

2. Jennifer is a *compulsively* tidy person.

3. This year Mark has been a very *responsible* student.

4. During the last 30 years the moral standards of ordinary people have *declined*.

5. Simon is one of those people whose main motivation in life is *greed*.

6. The Minister announced that the budget for social services would be *slashed* by 12 per cent over the next three years.

7. I think your doctor is being *excessively* cautious in his approach to treating your illness.

8. Jon was *suckered* by the salesman into buying the car.

9. Beethoven's Ninth Symphony was composed during his *mature* years.

10. So we have a deal, then. I'll get my *girl* to type it up and send it to you for signing.

3.8 Necessary and Sufficient Conditions

A special kind of ambiguity can arise when talking about the conditions that have to be met in order for a claim to be true or for something to occur. We call these conditions ANTECEDENT CONDITIONS, and the outcome or resultant state is called the CONSEQUENT. Referring to such conditions is common when we are talking about the causes (i.e., the causal conditions) of certain events: for example, *Under what conditions would a major economic depression occur again?* It is also common when we are talking about entitlements or justifications for certain actions: for example, *What are the conditions for graduating with distinction?* It seems that all we need to do to answer such questions is to list the conditions that, if they existed, would lead to a depression or to graduating with distinction. Unfortunately, the relationships between conditions and what they are conditions for (the consequent) are often a great deal more complex than they seem, and, in order to clarify these relationships, philosophers and scientists have developed a distinction between two types of conditions, necessary conditions and sufficient conditions. Much confusion and ambiguity can result when these two types of conditions are not clearly distinguished.

To understand the ambiguity that results when the two types of conditions are not distinguished, consider the following:

(1) *Being at least 18 years of age is a condition for being eligible to vote in federal elections in Canada.*

This could mean either of the following:

(2) *Anyone who is at least 18 years of age is eligible to vote in federal elections in Canada, or*

(3) *Anyone who is not at least 18 years of age is not eligible to vote in federal elections in Canada.*

These sentences have different meanings. We can see the difference by asking what each says about a particular case, for example, a 57-year-old electoral officer. According to (2) such a person is eligible to vote, but (3) makes no such guarantee. In fact the correct interpretation of (1) is (3). By law, every eligible voter must be at least 18 years of age—that is, if you are not 18 you can't vote—but the law also states that electoral officers and insane persons are not eligible to vote (and until recently, this list also included prison inmates). So not everyone who is 18 years of age is eligible to vote, which means that (2) is false. Being at least 18 years of age is *a* condition, but it is not the only condition that has to be satisfied for someone to be an eligible voter. To avoid this ambiguity, we should revise (1) to read:

(4) Being at least 18 years of age is a necessary condition for being eligible to vote in federal elections in Canada.

A NECESSARY CONDITION is defined as follows: X is a necessary condition for Y if, and only if, when X is false Y must also be false (or, when X is absent Y cannot occur). In other words, unless the necessary condition X is true, Y will not be true; but the truth of X does not guarantee the truth of Y. This yields a simple test for the truth of a necessary-condition statement: look for an instance of Y that is not also an X. If we can find one such case, then the statement must be false, since we have discovered an instance where X is not a necessary condition for Y. If we cannot find such a case, then we should accept the statement.

A sufficient condition is quite different from a necessary condition. Consider the following:

(1) Holding a BA from the University is a condition for being a member of the University Alumni Association.

This is ambiguous between:

(2) Anyone holding a BA from the University is a member of the University Alumni Association, and
(3) Anyone not holding a BA from the University is not a member of the University Alumni Association.

Obviously, (2) is the most likely interpretation of (1), for someone with a BSc or any other degree from the University is an alumnus. Notice the structural difference from our first example, where (3) was the correct interpretation. This is because here we are dealing with a sufficient condition. A person who holds a BA from the University does not need to meet any additional conditions in order to be a member of the University Alumni Association, although obviously holding a BA is not the only way one can become a member of the University Alumni Association. To remove the ambiguity we need to revise (1) to read:

(4) Holding a BA from the University is a sufficient condition for being a member of the University Alumni Association.

A SUFFICIENT CONDITION is defined as follows: X is a sufficient condition for Y if, and only if, when X is true Y must also be true (or, when X is present Y must occur). In other words, a sufficient condition for Y is something whose truth or presence guarantees Y, but whose falsity or absence does not prevent Y. This yields a simple test for the truth of a sufficient-condition statement: look for an instance of an X that is not also a Y. If we can find one such case, then the statement must be false, since we have discovered an instance where X is not a sufficient condition for Y. If we can find no such case, then we should accept the statement.

The difference between a necessary and a sufficient condition is subtle but important. Essentially, it's a question of what kind of guarantee is being made. When the condition is necessary, the author is asserting that its falsity or absence *guarantees* that the logical consequent won't be true. On the other hand, when the condition is sufficient, the author is asserting that the condition is something whose truth or presence *guarantees* that the logical consequent will be true. Chapter 9 introduces some concepts from deductive logic that will help make this difference clearer, but until then we can focus on the nature of these two guarantees: a necessary condition guarantees that Y (the logical consequent) won't be true unless X (the antecedent conditions) is true, whereas a sufficient condition guarantees that Y will be true if X is true.

Sometimes, a condition can be both necessary and sufficient at the same time. Consider the following:

> *It is a condition for a candidate being declared the winner in an election for the Ontario legislature that the candidate received more votes than any other candidate in the election.*

In this example, receiving more votes than any other candidate is a sufficient condition for being declared the winner (since anyone who receives more votes than any other candidate must be declared the winner), and it is also a necessary condition (since every candidate who is declared the winner must have received more votes than any other candidate). Another example of this sort is the relationship between *Today is Tuesday* and *Tomorrow is Wednesday*. Each of these statements is both a necessary and sufficient condition for the other.

Now, just to make things more complicated, we need to note what can happen when two or more conditions for the same thing are joined together. Being at least 18 years of age is not the only necessary condition for being eligible to vote in federal elections in Canada; we have already noted that one must not be an electoral officer or an insane person, but in addition one must also be a Canadian citizen. We can set out these necessary conditions as follows:

> *The necessary conditions for being eligible to vote in federal elections in Canada are:*
> *(1) being at least 18 years of age,*
> *(2) not being an elections officer or an insane person, and*
> *(3) being a Canadian citizen.*

These constitute all the necessary conditions for being eligible to vote in federal elections in Canada. But notice that these three necessary conditions are, *when taken together*, a sufficient condition. This is because any person who satisfies all three of these conditions is eligible to vote. Whenever we can list all the necessary conditions for something, we will have listed the conditions that are JOINTLY SUFFICIENT conditions. So, in this case, (1), (2), and (3) are individually necessary and jointly sufficient conditions.

In a similar way, we can sometimes find two or more different sufficient conditions for something. For example, according to the *Criminal Code of Canada* section 222.(5), a culpable homicide is committed when someone causes the death of a person:

(a) by means of an unlawful act,
(b) by criminal negligence,
(c) by causing that human being, by threats of fear of violence or by deception, to do anything that causes his death, or
(d) by wilfully frightening that human being, in the case of a child or sick person.

This section states four sufficient conditions for the crime of culpable homicide. If, in a particular case, any one of these conditions is met, the accused person will be found guilty of culpable homicide. If we take all four conditions together, that is, if we take section 222.(5) as a whole, we can say that it states the necessary condition for culpable homicide in the sense that at least one of these conditions must be met by every case of culpable homicide. This is because the absence of all four conditions means that an accused person would not be found guilty of culpable homicide.

So far, all our examples have dealt with criteria or entitlements. When dealing with causes, necessary and sufficient conditions work in the same way. When scientists search for a *full* account of the causes of some phenomenon, they are looking not only for the conditions that are individually sufficient, but also for the conditions that are individually necessary and jointly sufficient. However, if our sole interest is in controlling some phenomenon all we need is a partial account of the causes of that phenomenon. If we want to prevent something from happening we don't need a full account of its causal conditions, since if we can eliminate one necessary condition, then we can prevent the event from occurring. For example, if we want to prevent a disease from spreading all we need to do is find and eliminate one of the necessary conditions for the spread of the disease. On the other hand, if we want to produce a certain effect, all we need to do is to find one (or one set) of its sufficient conditions that we can bring about. For example, if we want to lose 20 pounds, we need to find only one way (for example, exercise) that works (i.e., is sufficient), and can ignore all the other ways (for example, dieting, diet pills). We shall return to reasoning in scientific contexts in Chapter 11.

3.9 Self-Test No. 7

State whether the italicized phrase in each of the following sentences identifies a necessary condition or a sufficient condition or a combination of the two. (*Note*: Once you understand the two different meanings of each sentence, you will have to use your common-sense knowledge to decide which is the more likely meaning.)

1. To bring down a fever, *apply a cloth dampened in cold water to the patient's face, arms, and legs.*

2. *Any student who has not paid his or her tuition fee by the first day of the term, or who has not made arrangements with the bursar's office for delayed payment,* will be automatically required to withdraw from the university.

3. To be admitted as a graduate student, *applicants must have a four-year honours degree with a 75 per cent average on all courses taken in their last two years.*

4. You cannot get an A average unless *you work hard throughout the whole term.*

5. Essays will be returned to the student without being graded, if *they are submitted without a proper bibliography.*

6. The Bruce Prize of $500 will be awarded to *the graduating student who has the highest cumulative average in all his or her philosophy courses.*

7. No one can become prime minister in our system of government unless *he or she is a Member of Parliament.*

8. For the business community to regain confidence in the economy, *interest rates must come down.*

9. *You have to have good physical coordination* to be a good skier.

10. No one can become a university professor these days unless *they have a PhD degree.*

11. You can't watch television tonight, Sarah, until *your homework is done and you've had a bath.*

12. The results of a departmental vote are valid if, and only if, *at least 25 per cent of members are present at the meeting in which the vote took place.*

3.10 Questions for Discussion

In light of the distinctions and concepts outlined in this chapter, discuss the following passages:

1. We hold these truths to be self-evident, that all men are created equal, that they are endowed by their Creator with certain unalienable Rights, that among these are Life, Liberty, and the pursuit of Happiness (from the *Declaration of Independence*).

2. No rational person ever commits suicide.

3. Adding Courses: All course additions to a student's program for a particular semester are to be completed by the end of the six-day add period. The addition of a course after the end of the add period will be considered only in exceptional circumstances and will require the approval of both the instructor for the course and the program counsellor of the program in which the student is registered. The program counsellor's signature should be sought first but does not presume the judgement of the instructor as to the appropriateness of the late addition for his or her particular course (from *University of Guelph Undergraduate Calendar, 1995–1996*, p. 66).

4. *Politician*: As far as we are concerned an impartial dispute-settling mechanism is an essential precondition for any free trade deal between Canada and the United States.
Interviewer: So you are saying, then, that you would support a free trade deal as long as the Americans accept an impartial dispute-settling mechanism.

5. Suppose someone is drowning 20 feet from shore. We throw him 10 feet of rope and he drowns. It would be illogical to conclude: "Rope is useless in the prevention of drowning." But this is the logic of the speech given by the Premier last week to the Chamber of Commerce in which he asserted that most government-funded social assistance programs are "based on the assumption that any social problem can be solved simply by throwing enough tax dollars at it." No one with any understanding of our social problems has ever made such a stupid and simplistic assumption, yet the Premier persists in spreading the myth that only such an assumption can justify social assistance programs.

6. For years, Canadian governments have persisted in lecturing other countries about their racist policies. Last week the Minister of Foreign Affairs continued this tradition by lecturing the Malaysian government about its racist policies. May I pose a question for the Minister and for all those who think the same way: Why should another country pay attention to the carping of foreigners whose own country still follows racist policies and practices? I refer, of course, to the large number of subtle ways in which our government discriminates against our native people. The overall effect of these policies is to bring about a slow cultural genocide.

7. Thou shalt not kill.

8. The Association for the Mentally Retarded recently changed its name to The Association for Community Living. The Association felt that "retarded" was a derogatory term and that dropping the term was an important step in their fight to change public attitudes towards a social group that has often suffered in the past from cruel and hostile treatment at the hands of the more unenlightened members of the community.

9. For many years public opinion polls have shown that about two-thirds of Canadians support capital punishment for premeditated murder. Year after year the fluctuation has never been more than 2 or 3 per cent. Last year, however, a pollster who was surveying public opinion on a range of social issues inadvertently changed the wording of the question about capital punishment and used the term *death penalty* instead. The results were astonishing. Forty-seven per cent of the respondents agreed that the death penalty should be used for premeditated murder while 48 per cent disagreed. It is possible that some people who were asked the old question confused capital punishment with corporal punishment and thought that they were supporting the use of corporal punishment for murderers. It is more likely, however, that the image conjured up in their minds by the term *death penalty* is much more vivid and violent than that of *capital punishment*, which has a much more bureaucratic or clinical connotation. If this is a correct explanation for the difference in the impact of the two terms, then *death penalty* should be the preferred term, for it is surely closer to the reality of what happens. This would mean that the results of the poll are not a fluke, and that public opinion in Canada is actually evenly split on the question.

4.   Reconstructing Arguments

4.1 Reconstruction

Unfortunately, the arguments we encounter in real life do not come with their premises and conclusions neatly labelled. Even worse, they are usually embedded in extraneous material that, although it may aid in interpreting the argument, is not actually part of the argument itself. Before we can critically assess an argument, therefore, we have to determine what the actual argument is. What is its conclusion, what are its premises, and what is the precise relationship between them? The process of eliciting this information is called RECONSTRUCTING THE ARGUMENT. The aim of reconstructing an argument is to produce a set of statements that represents the actual argument—the premises, the conclusion, the relationship between premises and conclusion—the author intended to present. The specific words used in the reconstruction need not be the actual words used by the author, for, as we have seen, it may be necessary to revise the words used in order to clarify the meaning or to remove ambiguities. What is important is to ensure that as far as possible the reconstruction does not violate the author's intent, and where this is unclear, does not violate the principle of charity.

Reconstructing an argument involves two phases. In the first, the premises and the conclusion of the argument must be identified. In the second phase the structure of the argument must be identified. When identifying the premises and conclusion of an argument that is presented in written form we will use the following conventions:

(1) The conclusion is underlined and labelled by C.
(2) Premises are enclosed in brackets and labelled by P1, P2, P3, etc.
(3) A missing premise or conclusion is labelled by MPx or MC.

To see how this works in practice we will reconstruct the following argument:

The most important challenge facing educators today is to teach students how to write decent prose. By "decent prose" I do not mean elegant writing: I mean simple straightforward writing that conforms to the rules of English grammar and clearly conveys its meaning. The ability to write decent prose is important because those who lack it will be unable to understand the great achievements of our cultural heritage—whether of Homer or Hemingway—and, perhaps even more important, will be unable to communicate effectively in today's world.

The first step is to identify the conclusion. What is the author's main point? What is the author trying to get the reader to accept? It seems quite clear that the conclusion is the first sentence: that the most important challenge facing educators today is to teach students how to write decent prose. We should always be careful at this step. It is extremely important that the conclusion be correctly identified, for if we misidentify the conclusion whatever we say about the argument will almost certainly miss the point and be a waste of everyone's time.

The second step is to identify the premises. What reasons does the author present to support the conclusion? There are two: (1) those who lack the ability to write decent prose will be unable to understand the great achievements of our cultural heritage, and (2) those who lack the ability to write decent prose will be unable to communicate effectively in today's world. The second sentence in the passage, it should be noted, is not a premise, since it cannot plausibly be regarded as providing a reason in support of the conclusion. Its function is to explain in more detail the meaning of the conclusion. So in reconstructing the argument within the passage, we can set this sentence aside.

Following the suggested conventions, the passage should now look like this:

<u>*The most important challenge facing educators today is to teach students how*</u> <u>*to write decent prose*</u> *(C). By "decent prose" I do not mean elegant writing: I mean simple straightforward writing that conforms to the rules of English grammar and clearly conveys its meaning. The ability to write decent prose is important because [those who lack it will be unable to understand the great achievements of our cultural heritage](P1)—whether of Homer or Hemingway—and, perhaps even more important, [will be unable to communicate effectively in today's world] (P2).*

Before moving to the second phase in reconstructing an argument, that is, identifying its structure, we need to consider how to deal with missing premises and conclusions.

4.2 Missing Premises and Conclusions

Many of the arguments we encounter in real life are incomplete, in the sense that if we consider only what the author says, we will be forced to assume that the speaker has left something out. Consider:

P. Doug's birthday is tomorrow.

C. Therefore, Bob should buy him a present.

If this is the entire argument, it is quite weak. The mere fact that tomorrow is Doug's birthday is not by itself a good reason for Bob to buy him a present. Either the speaker is quite stupid, or something is missing, such as the fact that Bob and Doug are brothers or are close friends. The principle of charity requires us to consider whether something is missing. If the author is present, we need only ask; once we learn that Doug and Bob are brothers, we have the missing premise that makes sense of the argument:

MP2. Bob is Doug's brother.

If the author is not present, we have to use whatever knowledge we possess and whatever clues the context provides to supply a missing premise that makes the best sense of the argument. If, however, we lack the knowledge that would allow us to supply the missing premise, we can make only a tentative assessment of it. We should say that, unless there is some special relationship between Doug and Bob, the argument is a weak one.

Supplying missing premises is not always as simple as this. Consider the following argument:

P1. High crime rates are caused by the widespread use of probation and suspended sentences.
C. Therefore, we should amend the criminal law to provide for mandatory minimum prison sentences for all crimes.

A fair interpretation of this argument shows that there are two missing premises. The first is the relatively obvious one, that we are experiencing higher crime rates; clearly, this is something the author believes. Thus, we need to add the following:

MP2. Crime rates are high.

The second missing premise is a little less obvious. On reflection, however, it seems likely that the speaker is also assuming the following:

MP3. A policy of mandatory minimum prison sentences for all crimes will lead to a reduction in crime rates.

Supplying these two missing premises increases the strength of the argument. The strength of this reconstructed argument, it should be noted, is its logical strength: if its premises are true, then its conclusion will also be true. (It is probably not a sound argument, however, since it is unlikely that P1 and MP3 are true.)

There is an important difference between the two missing premises. MP2 supplies some missing information that presumably the speaker knows or believes. MP3, on the other hand, is an assumption or PRESUPPOSITION. A presupposition is not simply missing information; it is a statement that is logically required by the argument in order for one of its stated claims to be true. In this case, the argument draws a conclusion about mandatory sentences, even though the premise makes no mention of the practice. What's missing after P1 has been identified and MP2 supplied is not simply something of the argument's factual content; rather, what's missing is something indispensable for its logical strength. In reconstructing the argument, we needed to ask, what must be logically presupposed about mandatory sentences in order for the conclusion to be true? Finding the presuppositions that underlie an argument can often be quite difficult and usually requires considerable care. Such presuppositions are important because frequently they are the real bone of contention between the two sides of an issue.

Let us return to the argument we started to reconstruct in section 4.1. We have already established the premises and conclusion:

> P1. *The ability to write decent prose is important because those who lack it will be unable to understand the great achievements of our cultural heritage.*
> P2. *The ability to write decent prose is important because those who lack it will be unable to communicate effectively in today's world.*
> C. *The most important challenge facing educators today is to teach students how to write decent prose.*

Is there a missing premise in this argument? It is clear that the author is making the following assumption: that educators have a responsibility to give students an understanding of the great achievements of our cultural heritage and to teach students how to communicate effectively. On the basis of what the author has said, it is almost certain that he or she is making this assumption. Otherwise, it is difficult to imagine why the author thinks that the conclusion is supported by the given premises. So we must add the following premise:

> MP3. *Educators have a responsibility to give students an understanding of the great achievements of our cultural heritage and to teach students how to communicate effectively.*

How can we be sure that this is the actual presupposition of the author? If the author is available, we can ask whether he or she accepts this assumption. If the author is not available, there may be other of his or her writings we can consult. Otherwise we will have to follow the principle of charity and attempt to work out the most plausible assumption and add it as a missing premise.

When eliciting assumptions of this sort there are two factors to be considered. We need to find a premise that, if true, actually provides support for the conclusion, and the premise should be as plausible as possible. Often these two factors pull in opposing directions: a premise that gives the argument logical strength may be less plausible than another premise that provides less logical strength to the argument. We might, for example, have tried another version of MP3:

MP4. Educators have the sole responsibility for giving students an understanding of the great achievements of our cultural heritage and for teaching students how to communicate effectively.

This, however, is less plausible than MP3, since it denies that parents, for example, have any responsibility in these matters. But if we use it instead of MP3 in our reconstruction, the argument would have greater logical strength. The choice between MP3 and MP4 should be made on the basis of the principle of charity: which version of the missing premise yields the more reasonable interpretation of the argument? In this case MP3 seems a much more reasonable presupposition than MP4.

Sometimes we encounter an argument with a missing conclusion. Usually it is easy to figure out what the conclusion should be. For example:

People who want to see the death penalty reintroduced in Canada should look at the United States. In the United States the death penalty is routinely applied for first degree murder, yet their murder rate is much higher than the murder rate in Canada.

The most likely interpretation of this passage is: this is an argument whose conclusion is that the death penalty should not be reintroduced in Canada. It is difficult to imagine a context in which the speaker would not intend his or her comment to be a reason for not reintroducing the death penalty. When reconstructing an argument with a missing conclusion, we should follow the guidelines suggested above for dealing with missing premises.

4.3 Self-Test No. 8

Supply the missing premises or conclusions in the following arguments.

1. It is after midnight and the gas stations are all closed, so I won't be able to drive you home.

2. Whenever your car's engine is flooded, you should put the accelerator right to the floor and then try to start it. So floor it and try again.

3. But you are still a Catholic, and Catholics are supposed to make a special effort to attend church at Easter.

4. Living in a large metropolis like Chicago is much more stressful than living in a small town. That must be why Jennifer is more uptight than her sister.

5. Well, it's no wonder he failed his mid-term. He skipped more classes than he attended.

6. I am not surprised. After all, children whose parents are extremely strict usually turn into teenage rebels, and Todd's father was tougher on him than any parent I know.

7. You broke my hearing aid, you clumsy oaf. Now I'll have to get a new one.

8. The high school drop-out rate in our district is about 15 per cent higher than the provincial average. Clearly, the school board ought to introduce programs to persuade students not to drop out, as well as programs designed to make it easier for those who have already dropped out to resume their education.

9. I deserve a much higher grade on my essay than a D+. I worked really hard on it.

10. There ought to be a law prohibiting the use of animals in research. After all, we would not tolerate that kind of treatment of humans.

4.4 Special Cases

The examples we have been considering so far contain arguments in which there is an inference from the premises to the conclusion that attempt to show that the conclusion is true. The truth is transmitted, so to speak, from the premise(s) to the conclusion. But not everything that contains premises and a conclusion follows this pattern, and there are two special cases that we should keep in mind as we go on.

Sometimes we encounter passages which contain arguments but are not arguments themselves. These are called reports of arguments. And sometimes we encounter explanations in which the inference from the premise(s) to the conclusion is not a transmission of truth, because the truth of the conclusion is not at issue; rather, explanations outline the logically prior principles that outline *why* a state of affairs is as the conclusion describes it.

4.4.1 REPORTS OF ARGUMENTS

A report of an argument is a statement that says that so-and-so argued in a certain way. For example:

John refuses to vote in elections because he believes that all politicians are dishonest.

This statement tells us that John refuses to vote in elections and that his reason for not voting is his belief that all politicians are dishonest. But the statement itself is not an argument: it simply tells us that John reasons in a certain way. A report of an argument is no more an argument than a photograph of an accident is itself an accident. Of course, since it is a statement, we can ask whether or not it is true, that is, if it correctly reports some facts about John. It may be false because John's refusal to vote may rest on his belief that despite their promises, all political parties behave the same if they win. Or it may be false because, although he believes all politicians are dishonest, he votes anyway. If the statement is true, however, that does not make it an argument, because its truth consists only in the fact that it reports correctly how John reasons. Here are two more examples of reports of arguments.

> *According to an editorial in* The Chronicle, *standardized, nation-wide scholastic achievement testing will improve the quality of education because it will enable us to learn what works and what doesn't work in the classroom.*

> *In 1851 John Stuart Mill argued that we should never restrict freedom of expression because in the long run complete freedom of expression has beneficial social consequences, even if in some particular cases the consequences are harmful.*

These are both reports of arguments put forward by someone other than the speaker. We may agree that *The Chronicle* and John Stuart Mill did say what the speaker claims they said, but this does not mean that we agree with the arguments that are being reported.

Of course, the arguments that are reported can be considered as arguments in their own right. But to do this we must no longer regard them merely as reports of what others have said: we must view them as arguments that claim to give us good reasons for accepting their conclusions. Now we must ask ourselves whether standardized testing will improve the quality of education and whether complete freedom of expression will in the long run have beneficial social consequences. What *The Chronicle* and John Stuart Mill believe is now irrelevant. What is relevant is only the argument itself.

It is sometimes difficult to know whether a report of an argument is intended by the speaker to be taken as an argument. Some people seem to prefer to take part in discussions by citing other people's arguments; they are inclined to agree with the arguments they report, but if they meet serious criticism they can easily back off by claiming that they don't fully agree with *The Chronicle* or John Stuart Mill. But often people who introduce another person's argument into a discussion clearly do mean to stand by it; they report the argument precisely because they think it is a sound argument. In these cases, we are entitled to interpret a report of an argument as itself an argument. There is no easy test to decide when we should treat a report of an argument as itself an argument. We can only rely upon the context and the principle of charity to help us decide.

4.4.2 EXPLANATIONS

The second kind of special case consists of explanations or explanatory arguments. An explanation is an attempt to show *why* or *how* something happens (or has happened) when there is little reason to doubt the truth of the conclusion. For example:

My car won't start because it is out of gas.

The reason the Liberals lost the last election is that they were perceived by the voters as arrogant and uncaring.

Teachers, who in recent years have become increasingly sensitive to public criticism, are opposed to nation-wide scholastic achievement testing since they fear that the results could be used or misused in attempts to criticize them as poor teachers.

The Canadiens got a penalty because they had too many players on the ice.

There are several different types of explanations. Many explanations are causal: they explain an event by reference to its causes. But some explanations are non-causal. We explain how volleyball is played not by reference to the causes of volleyball, but to the rules of volleyball. We explain how to register as a university student by reference to the university's registration procedures. We explain people's behaviour by reference to their motives and goals. We explain what a hammer is by reference to its function.

The purpose of an explanation is to make explicit why or how some phenomenon occurred or some event happened; as we said above, explanations are appropriate when the event in question is taken for granted and we are seeking to understand *why* it occurred. Thus, when I say that my car won't start because it is out of gas, I am not trying to find support for my belief that my car won't start. I know this already. What I want is an explanation for the fact that it won't start. Is it because the engine is flooded, or because of an electrical fault, or because the car is out of gas? If the gas gauge indicates "empty" and I accept this as accurate, I can say *My car won't start because it is out of gas.* The stated premise *It [my car] is out of gas* and the missing premise *A car without gas will not start* explain why *My car won't start.* In this case, there is no doubt about the truth of the stated premise, nor the missing premise (a presupposition), nor the conclusion. It is not that the mere truth of the premises is transmitted to the conclusions, but their intelligibility; that is, we seek explanations not because the truth of the conclusion is in question, but because our understanding of it is incomplete.

By contrast, with the arguments we have been considering up until now what is at issue is primarily whether the conclusion *is* true; the function of the premises is to supply reasons for believing that the conclusion is true or correct. Because these arguments purport to *prove* that their conclusion is true, they may be described as **probative**. Consider the following argument, which might look at first like an explanation:

Susan, you should visit your parents more often, because it gives them such pleasure when you do.

Here the speaker is trying to persuade Susan to do something she is reluctant to do by providing a reason for doing so. It would make little sense to interpret this passage as an explanation, that is, that the speaker and Susan both agree that she should visit her parents more often and are discussing why this is so. More plausibly, the speaker has some doubt as to whether Susan believes she should visit her parents more often, and this persons offers a reason for Susan to accept it.

When we read a passage that cites evidence in support of a conclusion, we should first ask whether the conclusion is presented as (1) a statement that is true but is more clearly understood in light of the evidence provided in the premise(s) or (2) as a statement whose truth is in question but is purported to be true on the basis of the evidence provided in the premise(s). If the answer to (1) is "yes," then it is an explanation; if the answer to (2) is "yes," then it is an argument in the usual, narrow sense of the word that we have been using in this book—i.e., it is probative.

There are, however, cases where only the context can tell us whether we should treat a passage as an explanation or as an argument in the narrow, probative sense of the word. For example:

Jim's health is good because he has a healthy diet and gets plenty of exercise.

We can imagine a context in which both the speaker and the audience know that Jim's health is good, and the speaker wants to explain why this is so. But we can also imagine a context in which they know that Jim has a healthy diet and gets plenty of exercise, and the speaker wants to argue that Jim is in good health. Usually, the context makes it clear whether it is an argument or an explanation that we are dealing with.

Explanations are of course subject to debate, and there are many disagreements as to what is the correct explanation for some phenomenon or event. This means that sometimes explanations themselves become the subject of an argument. For example:

Women are economically disadvantaged in our society not because they have traditionally been socialized into accepting passive and supporting roles, but because they have been and still are excluded by men from economic power. The effects of the traditional socialization on women's attitudes are still very real in many cases, but it does not account for their economically disadvantaged position, since when women do seek careers in business, which is where the real wealth is to be made, they are systematically excluded by men from the corridors of real power and influence.

This is an argument about what is the correct, or best, explanation of the fact, which is not at issue, that women are economically disadvantaged in our society. The speaker is, however, not merely asserting an explanation, but attempting to argue that his or her explanation is correct. Arguments about explanations, like this one, can sometimes be difficult to distinguish from the explanations themselves. For now, the best we can do is rely upon the context to help us decide, bearing in mind, as always, the principle of charity. In Chapter 11.4, in connection with Scientific Reasoning, we shall return to explanations in more detail, including questions about rival explanations.

4.5 Self-Test No. 9

For each of the following passages, indicate whether it is an argument in the usual, probative sense, an explanation, or a report of an argument.

1. I find it extremely difficult to perform for an audience. When I was a child, my parents used to brag all the time about what a prodigy I was, and they used to get so upset when I played badly that I was always terrified that they would stop loving me if I didn't play well. Consequently, I still imagine all sorts of things going wrong, like having a memory lapse, or dropping my flute.

2. David was so upset at what he had done that he ran all the way home to fetch the first aid kit and tried his best to bandage up the cut on Michael's foot. Then he helped Michael walk home and explained to his mother what had happened. The fact that it was really Michael's fault—as even his mother realized—didn't make any difference to David at all; he felt responsible for his friend.

3. We'd better watch Mary closely for the next 24 hours. She has had a nasty knock on the head, and there could be a concussion. If we see any signs of grogginess or disorientation, then we'll take her to the hospital.

4. There are several reasons why a child's school performance can suddenly deteriorate. Sometimes it is because a physical problem, which may be caused by a virus or a poor diet, affects the child's concentration. Sometimes it is because of a problem at school, such as an inexperienced teacher who has not learned how to recognize when children are only pretending they understand their lessons. Most commonly, it is because of a problem at home, such as the parents getting a divorce.

5. The reason your local taxes go up when you make improvements to your home and property is that the tax rate is based upon the value of your property. The more your property is worth, the higher your local tax. It may not be fair, but that is how the system works.

6. According to a recent Canadian Supreme Court decision, the previous sexual conduct of a woman may be introduced by the defence in sexual assault cases. The court argued that the right of an accused to a fair trial was more important than the right of the victim to avoid possible embarrassment.

7. You should never turn off your computer without following the exit procedure for your software program. This is because you will lose the files you have been working on, unless you save them before you exit.

8. I have consulted my lawyer, and he advised me that unless you refund the entire purchase price, I could take you to court and get my money back. And he says that if I complain to the Ministry of Commercial Relations, you could lose your licence.

9. Using juries in criminal trials is a stupid system. When there is only a judge trying the case, the prosecution has to persuade only one person that the accused is guilty. But when there is a jury, the prosecution has to persuade all 12 members of the jury that the accused is guilty. If only one juror has a grudge against the police, or has sympathy for the accused, or is just too dumb to understand the evidence, then a guilty person will go free. The jury system works to the advantage of criminals. We should abolish it.

10. Americans really don't understand the way political parties operate in Canada, for they fail to realize the tremendous power that the leader of the party has over rank-and-file party members and especially over the elected members of the legislature. In the United States the party leader's power is much more limited, even when the leader becomes president. This is because their constitution is based upon the separation of power between the legislative and administrative branches of government.

4.6 The Structure of Arguments

The structure of an argument is important because it can tell us how the premises are intended to support the conclusion and can give us some of the information we need in order to undertake a critical assessment of the argument. The easiest way to see the structure of an argument is to represent it graphically using what is called a *tree diagram*. A TREE DIAGRAM is a schematic representation of the structure of an argument using letters (P1, P2, MP3, C, etc.) to represent the premises and conclusion, and an arrow to represent *therefore*. There are three basic argument structures.

4.6.1 SIMPLE ARGUMENTS

In section 1.1 we saw that every argument must have a conclusion and at least one premise and that the premises and conclusion are connected by an implicit or explicit *therefore*. The simplest type of argument consists of a single premise and a single conclusion. Such arguments have a structure that we will call a SIMPLE ARGUMENT. For example:

P. *When Jim quit playing the trumpet, he gave it to his younger brother.*
C. *Hence, Jim won't be able to lend his trumpet to Andrew.*

The tree diagram for such simple argument structures is:

4.6.2 T ARGUMENTS

When we consider arguments with two premises, there are two possible structures the argument might have, and it is important to be aware of how they differ. Consider the following argument:

> P1. *Every medical doctor has had to tell someone that a loved one has died.*
> P2. *Beth is a medical doctor.*
> C. *Therefore, Beth has had to tell someone that a loved one has died.*

This argument has the following structure:

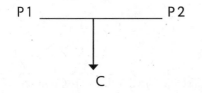

Notice that each premise, considered by itself, provides little or no support for the conclusion. By itself, the fact that every medical doctor has had to tell someone that a loved one has died provides no support for the conclusion. Similarly, the fact that Beth is a medical doctor does not by itself provide any support for the conclusion. If either premise were false, the remaining premise would provide little or no support for the conclusion. It is only when both are true that they provide support. An argument with this structure is called a T ARGUMENT, because the lines joining the premises to the conclusion form a T.

T arguments may sometimes have three or more premises. Consider the following argument:

> P1. *Every physically handicapped person who has tried to find employment knows the anguish of rejection.*
> P2. *Jody is physically handicapped.*
> P3. *Jody has tried to find employment.*
> C. *Therefore, Jody knows the anguish of rejection.*

The tree diagram for this argument is:

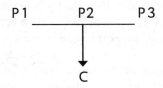

4.6.3 V ARGUMENTS

The third basic structure can be seen in the following argument:

> P1. *Frances is very successful in her career.*
> P2. *Frances has a secure and supportive marriage.*
> C. *Therefore, Frances is a happy person.*

This argument has the following structure:

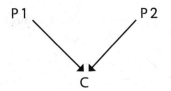

Notice that two separate reasons are offered in support of the conclusion. Each operates independently of the other. If either premise is missing or false, the remaining one still provides support for the conclusion. We shall call arguments with a structure of this sort V ARGUMENTS, because the lines joining the premises to the conclusion form a V.

Like T arguments, V arguments can have three or more premises. For example, the argument above would be strengthened by adding another premise that functions in the same way as the first two:

> P3. *Frances had a stable and secure childhood.*

Our argument now has the following structure:

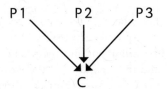

Obviously, the diagram now looks more like a W than a V, but to keep things simple we will continue to call it a V argument.

The distinction between T and V arguments is important because they represent two different ways in which two or more premises can combine to support a conclusion. To distinguish the two types of argument structure, it is necessary to ask whether the premises have to work together in order to provide support for the conclusion or whether they work independently of each other. The premises of a T argument work as a team, and both must be true to provide support for the conclusion; if either premise is false, then the other by itself would provide little or no support for the conclusion. On the other hand, each of the premises of a V argument provides independent support for the conclusion: if either premise is false, the other would still provide independent support for the conclusion. We shall see the importance of the distinction when we come to the assessment of arguments. If one of the premises of a T argument is false, then the argument is weak even if the other premise or premises are true. But if one of the premises of a V argument is false, the argument may still be strong if the other premise or premises are true. It is important, therefore, to pay careful attention to the structure of arguments.

4.6.4 COMPLEX ARGUMENTS

The above are the three basic structures out of which more complex structures are constructed. Consider the following argument:

> P1. *Max was born in Canada to Canadian parents.*
> P2. *This means that Max is a Canadian citizen.*
> C. *Therefore, Max can vote in federal elections.*

This argument has the following structure:

Note that the tree diagram contains two arrows. This is because the second premise is really a sub-conclusion that is supported by the first premise. In reality, there are two arguments here; P2 is the conclusion of the first argument and the premise of the second. The first argument is P1 therefore P2, and the second is P2 therefore C. The combined argument does not, however, present two separate reasons to support the conclusion, but only one. P2 presents a reason for C and P1 presents a reason for P2. We could delete either premise and the remaining one would still support the conclusion.

When reconstructing an argument that has two conclusions, it is necessary to determine which is the main conclusion and which is the subordinate conclusion. Sometimes the argument makes this quite clear. When it does not, we should ask which is best regarded as a premise for the other. Taking account of all the contextual clues and the principle of charity, which of the following makes better sense of the argument?

C1 *therefore* C2, or
C2 *therefore* C1.

Consider the following argument:

City Council should approve the proposed arts centre without delay, for several reasons. The need for a centre has been demonstrated many times; anyone who examines the evidence will agree that existing facilities are woefully inadequate. The financial benefit to the community is harder to pin down precisely, but no one can deny that local merchants and the city's tax base will benefit. The only question is whether the city can afford to make a reasonable contribution to the annual operating costs. It is foolish to expect a consensus on this question: after all no one likes higher taxes, no matter how worthy the cause. But the fact is that Guelph has a lower tax rate than most cities its size and is in excellent financial shape. And the proposed increase in taxes would amount to only $2.00 per year. It is clear, therefore, that the city can afford the arts centre.

This passage has two conclusions. The opening sentence is a conclusion, which the passage goes on to give reasons for. But the final sentence gives another conclusion. We determine which is the main conclusion by asking which of the following makes the best sense of the whole passage:

(1) City Council should approve the proposal for an arts centre. Therefore, the city can afford an arts centre.
(2) The city can afford an arts centre. Therefore, City Council should approve the proposal for an arts centre.

It is obvious that (2) makes good sense while (1) does not. This means that we should regard the opening sentence of the passage as the main conclusion. The other is a sub-conclusion or the conclusion of a subsidiary argument that has been included to support one of the premises of the main argument.

Some arguments, however, are much more complex than these examples suggest. Here is another argument with a complex structure:

P1. When the Meech Lake agreement was negotiated, it had the support of the Prime Minister and all provincial premiers, who represented all the major political parties.
P2. In several provinces the opposition parties voted to ratify the agreement.

P3. So politicians of all political parties all across Canada strongly supported the agreement.
P4. However, the vast majority of Canadians outside Quebec and a significant minority inside Quebec were strongly opposed to the agreement.
C. Therefore, the politicians were out of touch with the views of the people.

In this argument P1 to P3 constitutes a sub-argument: it is a V argument with P1 and P2 as premises and P3 as its conclusion. P3 is then used as a premise in a second argument: it is a T argument with P3 and P4 as premises and C as its conclusion. The tree diagram for this argument is thus a combination of a T and a V structure:

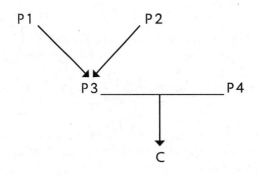

4.7 Self-Test No. 10

Label the premises and conclusion and draw a tree diagram for each of the following arguments. Where appropriate, supply missing premises or conclusions.

1. Anyone who has brains and ambition will go far in this world. Carla has certainly got plenty of both, so she will go far.

2. I have never had any problems with the last four Fords I've bought, so I don't think I'll have any problems this time.

3. The Expos should win the National League pennant this year. They have solid depth in their pitching staff, their hitting has been consistently good this year, their coaching is excellent, and there is a good team spirit.

4. A recent public opinion poll showed that more than two-thirds of Canadians believe that most politicians are dishonest. Clearly, there is a crisis of confidence in Canadian politics.

5. In the last 30 years in Canada, there has been a tremendous increase in the university participation rate (i.e., the percentage of population in the 18- to22-year-old age group that attends university). In 1960, the participation rate in

Canada was only 5 per cent. But by 1990 the participation rate was over 15 per cent.

6. Laura gets pretty good grades, she is the best gymnast in the school, she has a lot of friends, and she organized the campaign last year that forced the school to start a recycling program. I think she will probably win the election for president of the Students' Council.

7. If he tells his teacher he cheated, he will be punished by the principal. But if he doesn't tell his teacher he cheated, he will be punished by his parents. Either way he is going to be punished.

8. Since angle CAB is 60 degrees, and angle ACB is 40 degrees, then angle ABC must be 80 degrees.

9. Any reporter who says that good reporters never slant their stories but simply report the objective facts, must be either stupid or dishonest, since it is obvious that one cannot write anything without an element of interpretation creeping in....

10. ... and that reporter is obviously not stupid. He must be dishonest.

4.8 Another Warning

People talk about all sorts of things for all sorts of reasons. Sometimes we can be fooled into interpreting something as an argument when it really isn't. Sometimes people use language that makes it appear that they are presenting an argument when they are really just expressing a strongly held opinion and not attempting to defend it with reasons. For example:

> The press in this country seems quite uninterested in serious political discussion. Whenever an important political issue arises, such as Aboriginal rights or free trade, the press seems interested only in personalities and whether the issue will hinder this party's chances of re-election, or improve that leader's public image. I think the press should take a good hard look at itself and ask whether a truly responsible press would conduct political discussions at such a juvenile level.

Is this an argument? To answer this question we should ask whether we can, without doing violence to the author's apparent intentions, interpret it as presenting a conclusion accompanied by one or more supporting premises. Clearly, the author wants us to agree with his or her view that the press is irresponsible in its approach to serious political discussion. But it is probably unfair to the author to insist that any of the statements should be regarded as presenting a reason for this view. In fact, what is interesting about this passage is the absence of any real supporting evidence. All we are offered is the suggestion that the press ignores serious political discussion and deals only with peripheral matters, and if we regard this as a premise, it is an extremely weak one. It is much better to interpret this passage as an expression of an opinion. The principle of charity supports this interpretation, since otherwise we would have to regard the argument as a very weak one.

However, since we are sometimes entitled to supply missing premises and missing conclusions, we may be tempted to turn a non-argument into an argument by reading a great deal more into a passage than is really there. When dealing with a doubtful passage we should therefore be careful not to assume that it must be an argument, or we may find ourselves reconstructing an argument that the author never intended. There is no simple way of determining when we are dealing with an argument and when we are not. We should remember that people do many things besides argue: they complain, express opinions, make observations, make accusations, tell stories, give illustrations, bestow praise, and so on. The principle of charity dictates caution. Common sense usually suggests the most plausible interpretation.

4.9 Questions for Discussion

Read carefully each of the following passages, and, if you decide it is an argument, work out the best reconstruction.

1. (BACKGROUND: A father is talking to his 16-year-old son.)

It wouldn't matter if everybody in the school was going to the rock concert. The point is that you know that you shouldn't go. You promised me that if we didn't give you a curfew any more, you would ensure that every school assignment would be submitted on time. And there is no way you can finish your history essay if you go to that concert.

2. (BACKGROUND: A student who has missed a mid-term approaches the instructor to ask for a make-up test.)

I'm sorry I missed the test, but it really wasn't my fault. I went home on the weekend, and didn't get back until midnight. I studied until four in the morning, and as a result I didn't hear my alarm and missed the test. It would be really unfair if I were to be punished for something that is not my fault.

3. (BACKGROUND: A letter to the editor commenting upon a recent US court ruling that teaching scientific creationism in science courses in public schools is unconstitutional. Scientific creationism holds that the biblical account of creation is a legitimate scientific theory that should be taught in science courses along with the theory of evolution.)

Your recent report on scientific creationism was very interesting and I don't disagree with anything it said, but it failed to point out the true nature of these so-called "scientific" creationists. The fact is that they are a bunch of intellectual misfits and misguided crackpots who wouldn't recognize a truly scientific theory if you hit them over the head with it. They are either lamentably ignorant, or bigots, or both.

4. (BACKGROUND: Several students are discussing the US war in Iraq. One, who supported the war, is responding to the objection that the US has no right to act as a world policeman.)

But of course the US has the right to police the world. The US is one of the most powerful nations in the world; surely you don't deny that. Well, that's one of the things world powers can do. If a world power decides to act as a world cop, then it has that right.

5. (BACKGROUND: A lawyer is attempting to persuade a client not to sue his doctor for malpractice.)

I understand why you feel a sense of grievance, but I don't think it is a good idea. First, you have to prove that the doctor was negligent, i.e., that he failed to provide medical care that is up to the accepted standard. And given what you've told me, I don't think we would prove that at all. After all, he did explicitly warn you that there was only a 70 per cent chance of success. Secondly, a trial will be extremely stressful for your wife, since she will have to answer a lot of intimate personal questions which I'm sure she would prefer to avoid.

6. (BACKGROUND: From a talk on student stress given by an educational psychologist to a group of high school teachers.)

Finally, we come to the type of stress that is induced by the learning process itself, for example, stress that results from getting low grades, from not understanding the material, from being late with assignments, or from asking dumb questions in class. Unlike other types of stress, this type is caused by you as teachers. If you want to reduce this type of stress the solution is in your hands: develop better methods of presenting material and motivating the students to master it, make sure students don't get into courses they cannot handle, be more reasonable about accepting late assignments, and be polite to students who ask dumb questions.

7. (BACKGROUND: A university student is talking to a friend about smoking marijuana.)

My mom and dad, and my older sister too, used to warn me about the evils of taking drugs. I remember the first time I went to a party where people were smoking pot; I mean, I thought I was in a den of iniquity and I left as soon as I could. But after a while you realize that there are all sorts of perfectly ordinary people walking around who smoke a bit of pot now and again. So I figure there can't be anything really wrong with it.

8. (BACKGROUND: From an article entitled "Technology: Boon or Doom?")

These astonishing achievements—achievements that earlier generations could only dream of—have produced in many a faith in the limitless capacity of technology to benefit mankind. During the past two decades, however, there has been increasing evidence that this faith is unreasonable. The space shuttle disaster, the Chernobyl and Three Mile Island nuclear accidents, acid rain, and a host of other technological misfortunes have each in their own way shown that there are significant limitations to what technology can do.

9. (BACKGROUND: Gord has gone to seek counsel for work and family trouble from a psychic.)

As your regular psychic, I understand exactly why you have been having a rough time lately, Gord. Your sign is Cancer, and for the last three weeks your moon has been in the house of Scorpio. Because of the tension between your sign, which is ruled by the moon, and Scorpio, which is ruled by Mars and Pluto, your entire universe is in disarray. Hence, all the trouble you're having at work and with your family is entirely predictable.

part three

ASSESSING ARGUMENTS

5.   Strategies for Assessing Arguments

We now come to the assessment of arguments. Before we consider the details of how this should be done, we need to say something about the nature of the task. Every argument, as we saw in section 1.1, supports its conclusion by making a double claim: (a) that its premises are true and (b) that its premises support its conclusion. Whenever we assess an argument, we are really only asking whether these claims are true. An argument makes a kind of promise; assessing an argument is asking whether it can make good on its promise. A good argument is one that does what it claims to do, and a bad argument is one that fails to do what it claims to do. But how are we to tell whether an argument has made good on its promise?

Philosophers have developed two approaches for assessing arguments. The first and more traditional is the FALLACIES approach, in which we identify all the specific fallacies (or mistakes) that an argument can make and then ask whether a given argument commits any of these fallacies. If it commits none of them, it will be a good argument, and if it commits one or more of them, it will be a bad argument. The second is the CRITERIAL approach in which we appeal to the criteria, or standards, that a good argument must satisfy and ask whether a given argument meets these criteria. If it meets them all, it will be a good argument, and if it fails to meet one or more of them, it will be a bad argument.

The fundamental approach of this text is criterial. It has several very important advantages over the fallacies approach, which will be noted below. Nevertheless, the fallacies approach is sometimes useful because it identifies certain common mistakes. In the following chapters we adopt the criterial approach but will introduce specific fallacies when they can help put us on our guard against certain mistakes. But first we need to discuss the two approaches in more detail.

5.1 The Fallacies Approach

The concept of a fallacy presents several theoretical difficulties for logicians that need not detain us here. For our purposes we can define a FALLACY as any error or weakness that detracts from the soundness of an argument, yet somehow manages to disguise this weakness so as to give the argument the appearance of being better than it really is. For example, one traditional fallacy is the appeal to pity, as in:

> *Jane is a widow with three teenage children living in a two-bedroom basement apartment.*
> *Therefore, her employer should promote her to supervisor.*

Whether Jane should be promoted depends upon whether she has the qualifications and experience to be a good supervisor. The fact that she is a widow with three teenage children living in a two-bedroom basement apartment says nothing about her qualifications as a supervisor. But if someone can arouse our sympathies for Jane, we may want her to be promoted for reasons that have nothing to do with the qualifications necessary for the job. Since the pity we naturally feel is irrelevant to the question whether she should be promoted, the appeal to pity is fallacious.

Logicians have long been fascinated by fallacies and have devoted much time and energy to identifying and explaining specific fallacy types. Aristotle listed 13 types, but modern logicians have identified approximately 150 different types. This proliferation of fallacies suggests a misleading picture of a logician as a kind of microbiologist of the intellect searching for new logical viruses.

One problem with the fallacies approach is that there is no limit to the number of ways in which an argument can be weak. The only way to limit the list of fallacies is to restrict ourselves to those errors that occur frequently. However, we still will never have a list of fallacy types that is complete, for there is no simple way to determine what counts as a "frequently" occurring error. Another problem is that as more and more fallacy types are identified, it has become increasingly difficult to use them effectively as the basis for assessing arguments. Not only do we have to memorize a very long list of fallacies, but we often find arguments that clearly contain a weakness but where we have difficulty in deciding which particular fallacy has been committed.

The underlying problem with the fallacies approach is that it is negative in nature. This is an especially serious problem when we are trying to develop good arguments for ourselves, rather than merely criticizing other people's arguments. Rather than telling us what we want to see in a good argument, it only tells what we should try to avoid.

5.2 The Criterial Approach

The criterial approach, unlike the fallacies approach, is positive in nature. It begins by establishing the criteria that a good argument must satisfy and then uses these criteria as the basis for assessing particular arguments. To develop these criteria we rely directly upon the concept of a sound argument. In section 1.1 we defined a logically strong argument as one whose premises, if true, support its conclusion, and a sound argument as a logically strong argument whose premises are true. It is now time to use these concepts to establish the criteria for a sound argument. They give rise to three criteria.

5.2.1 THE THREE CRITERIA OF A SOUND ARGUMENT

The requirement that a sound argument must have true premises is the basis for our first criterion for a sound argument: it should have true premises. Obviously, since premises are offered as support for a conclusion, if a premise is false, then no matter how good the argument is in other respects, the premise provides no support for the conclusion. But there is a problem here. Often we are not able to *prove* that our premises are true: most of us cannot actually prove, for example, that cigarette smoking is a health hazard. However, in most contexts there are reasons that justify the acceptance of such a claim even though we cannot prove it is true. The fact that our government requires all cigarette packages to include the claim as a warning, for example, makes it reasonable for us to accept it, even though such a reason is clearly not a proof. We must therefore expand our first criterion to take account of those contexts where all that we can reasonably demand is that there be good reasons for accepting the premises. Our first criterion, therefore, is that the premises must be ACCEPTABLE. Of course, in some contexts, such as assessing mathematical proofs, the only good reason for accepting the premises will be that they can actually be proven.

Logical strength, the second requirement for a sound argument, gives rise to our second and third criteria. The second is that the premises must be relevant to the conclusion. We noticed in section 1.2 that an argument may have premises that are known to be true but that nevertheless fail to provide any support for its conclusion. This is what happens when the premises are not relevant to the conclusion. Clearly, if the premises of an argument are to support its conclusion, they must supply us with information that is relevant to the question whether or not the conclusion is true. Precisely what information is relevant to the truth of a particular conclusion may sometimes be difficult to determine, but it is clear that what we are looking for is relevant information. Our second criterion, therefore, is that each individual premise should be RELEVANT to the conclusion.

The logical strength requirement also gives rise to our third criterion, namely, that the premises must be adequate to support the conclusion. A premise may be both true and relevant to the conclusion, but it may nevertheless not be adequate to support the conclusion. Adequacy is usually (but not always, as we shall see later) a matter of degree. In most cases a true, relevant premise can provide support that ranges from very little to a great deal. Consider the following:

My neighbour, my wife, and all the people I work with, all of whom voted Tory in the last election, have decided to vote Liberal in the next election. Therefore, the Liberals will probably win the next election.

The premise of this argument is obviously relevant to the conclusion, and it does provide some, albeit minimal, support for the conclusion. It is, we might say, a straw in the wind. We would be foolish to bet on the outcome of the election on the basis of this evidence. By itself, therefore, this premise is not adequate. If, however, we keep asking friends and neighbours, or better yet undertake a proper public opinion survey, we may accumulate more information that shows that large numbers of voters are switching from Tory to Liberal. If this extra information is included as additional premises, then the support provided for the conclusion is much more adequate. The third criterion, therefore, is that the premises, considered collectively, must provide ADEQUATE support for the conclusion.

Thus there are three different criteria that a sound argument must meet:

(1) The premises must be acceptable.
(2) The premises must be relevant.
(3) The premises must be adequate.

Notice how in moving from (1) to (2) to (3) the criteria become more complex. Acceptability concerns the assessment of each premise considered on its own. The other two criteria ask us to assess the inference from the premise(s) to the conclusion of an argument. Relevance concerns the relationship between each individual premise, considered on its own, and the rest of the argument. And adequacy concerns the relationship between all the premises considered collectively and the conclusion. We are not entitled to pass final judgement on any argument until we have assessed it against each of these criteria. If it meets all three criteria, we should conclude that it is a sound argument. If it fails to meet any one criterion, we should regard it as a weak or defective argument.

5.3 Seven Rules for Assessing Arguments

At this point it will be useful to present a set of rules that should be followed whenever an argument is being assessed. The brief comments included here are intended only to highlight points that are made elsewhere.

RULE 1. IDENTIFY THE MAIN CONCLUSION

You may have noticed that none of the three criteria listed above asks us to assess the conclusion of an argument directly. When assessing an argument on the basis of these three criteria, we assess the conclusion indirectly by considering the evidence offered in support of it—that is, the acceptability, relevance, and adequacy of the premises. Still, even though we don't assess the conclusion directly, we must begin our assessment by identifying the conclusion. This is especially important when assessing the argument for relevance and adequacy.

The way to identify the main conclusion should be familiar by now. (1) Look for the main point of the passage, by asking, *What is the author driving at?* (2) Look for inference indicators, such as *therefore, hence, so, consequently,* and so on. (3)

Pay attention to the context and background for clues as to what the argument is all about. (4) Bear in mind the principle of charity when interpreting an ambiguous conclusion or when supplying a missing conclusion. If the conclusion is difficult to elicit, it may be because we are not dealing with an argument at all. We have already come across several passages that look like arguments but should not be regarded as genuine arguments. Reports of arguments (see section 4.4.1) and forceful assertions can be especially troublesome. Remember that every argument presents a claim *and* a reason to support that claim.

RULE 2. IDENTIFY THE PREMISES

The next step is to identify the premises. If the conclusion has been correctly identified, the rest of the argument will include the premises. But it may also include some material that is not specifically part of the argument itself, such as illustrations and examples. It may also include alternative versions of what is really a single premise. The question we should ask here is, *What information or reasons does the author provide to support the conclusion?* As always, it is important to pay attention to the context and the principle of charity when identifying the premises and when supplying missing premises.

RULE 3. IDENTIFY THE STRUCTURE OF THE ARGUMENT

Once the conclusion and the premises have been identified the structure of the argument must be identified. If the argument has a simple structure (see section 4.6.1), we can pass straight on to the critical assessment. In all other cases care should be taken to ensure that the structure of the argument has been correctly identified, if necessary by drawing a tree diagram (see section 4.6).

RULE 4. CHECK THE ACCEPTABILITY OF THE PREMISES

In Chapter 6 we will consider how truth-claims should be approached. Two warnings should be mentioned here. First, if the argument is intended to be a counterfactual argument (see section 1.3), it is irrelevant to ask whether the premises are true, since the author is not claiming that they are true. Second, we need to note that a false premise does not always deprive the conclusion of all support. If an argument has two independent premises, as in a V argument, the fact that one of them is false has no bearing on whether the other premise is true, and if the other premise is true, then the conclusion may still have some support.

RULE 5. CHECK THE RELEVANCE OF THE PREMISES

In Chapter 7 we will examine some common ways in which premises can seem relevant when in fact they are not. It should be stressed that the premises must be considered in context, for a premise that is irrelevant when considered by itself may have its relevance established by other premises in the argument.

RULE 6. CHECK THE ADEQUACY OF THE PREMISES

In Chapter 8 we will examine the common ways in which premises can fail to provide adequate support for the conclusion. When assessing adequacy it is important to notice the degree of support which the argument claims is provided by the premises.

RULE 7. LOOK FOR COUNTER-ARGUMENTS

Finally, we should look for counter-arguments. Are there any reasons we can think of that would support a conclusion that is inconsistent with the conclusion of the argument being assessed? Strictly speaking, this goes beyond the assessment of a given argument, but if there is a sound counter-argument we know that the given argument must be deficient. Otherwise, we would have two sound arguments with inconsistent conclusions, which is impossible. We will discuss the role of counter-arguments in Chapter 13.

6. Assessing Truth-Claims

6.1 Theories of Truth

Pontius Pilate, before sentencing Christ to death, asked, *what is truth?* but, being a practical man, did not stay around to debate the question. In its most general sense, the question is deeply troubling, for no one has yet been able to provide an entirely satisfactory answer. Philosophers have made numerous attempts to develop theories of truth, but all are open to plausible objections. However, our interest in truth, like Pilate's, is more practical than theoretical, so we need not delay too long over purely theoretical issues. Nevertheless, we should note the three main theories of truth, for they provide a useful background to our discussion of how truth-claims are to be assessed.

6.1.1 THE CORRESPONDENCE THEORY

What makes a statement or belief true? (We can speak interchangeably here of beliefs or statements.) The most obvious answer is that a statement or belief is true when it corresponds to the facts. The statement *My birthday is October 22* is true if, and only if, it is a fact that I was born on October 22. The fact that I was born on October 22 is a necessary and sufficient condition for the truth of the statement *My birthday is October 22*. Anyone who is not sure whether this statement is true need only check my birth certificate. It seems reasonable, therefore, to hold that truth consists of a correspondence between a statement and a fact; that when the correspondence holds, the statement is true; and when it does not hold, the statement is false. This is the COR-RESPONDENCE THEORY OF TRUTH.

There are a number of objections to this account of truth. The most obvious is that there are many statements that we believe to be true for which there seem to be no corresponding facts. But according to the correspondence theory, if there are no corresponding facts then we would have to conclude that these statements are false.

Consider the following statements: what facts would we check to determine whether they are true?

> *There is no greatest prime number.*
> *You should keep your promises.*
> *God created the universe.*
> *Bach was the greatest composer of the eighteenth century.*
> *If Hitler had died in 1918, World War II would not have occurred.*

Supporters of the correspondence theory have developed some ingenious strategies to overcome this objection. Some have held that there really are facts that correspond to these statements. They claim that there are mathematical facts, moral facts, etc. But these are not ordinary facts since they are not accessible to us in the way that facts about my birthday are, so the introduction of these special kinds of facts solves nothing. (There are, however, many philosophers who accept the existence of evaluative facts, but we need not pause over this interesting theoretical controversy.) Others have argued that some or all of these statements are not really true or false at all. They hold that when we say that you ought to keep your promises, we are expressing an attitude and that it is a mistake to regard our statement as making a truth-claim.

Despite this difficulty, the correspondence theory is an adequate account of one kind of truth. Sometimes the truth of a statement or belief does consist of a correspondence between the statement and certain facts. Whenever a statement makes a factual assertion, then, as long as there are facts that could be checked to determine whether they are as the statement claims they are, we can use the correspondence between the statement and the facts as our criterion of truth. But when a statement makes a non-factual assertion, or asserts a fact that is non-checkable, we cannot use correspondence as a criterion of truth.

The notion of checkable facts is important and needs some elucidation. We can only check facts, either directly or indirectly, by making observations. This is another way of saying that the fact must be empirical. An EMPIRICAL FACT is a fact that is observable in principle, that is, it could be observed if we could get ourselves into the right place at the right time. The notion of an empirical fact allows us to define an EMPIRICAL STATEMENT as a statement that asserts an empirical fact (or set of empirical facts). The correspondence theory of truth, therefore, provides an appropriate criterion of truth for all empirical statements. And since the world around us consists, by and large, of empirical facts, the correspondence theory is an appropriate criterion for our knowledge of the external, observable world.

6.1.2 THE COHERENCE THEORY

But the critics have a second objection to the correspondence theory. Besides claiming that it is inadequate as a criterion for non-empirical statements, they also object that it is inadequate even for empirical statements. They point out that the theory presents us with two distinct and separate worlds, the world of facts and the world of statements and beliefs. Its claim that truth consists of a correspondence between empirical facts and statements or beliefs requires that the world of facts must be *brute* facts, or facts that are independent of our beliefs about them. Otherwise, we could not compare the facts with our beliefs about them in order to see whether they correspond. But, the critics ask, how can we know anything at all about the world of facts, since as soon as we turn to the facts the only thing we can obtain is yet another belief about the facts? We can never, it seems, have any knowledge of such brute facts, for we can never get beyond our *beliefs* about them. Brute facts presumably exist but we can never know them directly. The very act of recognizing or knowing that something is a fact necessarily involves an element of selection and interpretation. Facts, as many philosophers of science claim, are never brute but are always constituted by a presupposed theory of what exists and what we should focus on when making observations. The empirical facts upon which correspondence theorists rely, therefore, presuppose that some theory or interpretation is already true, which means that the correspondence theory not only fails to provide a criterion of truth but presupposes some other criterion of truth.

This objection has led the critics to propose the COHERENCE THEORY OF TRUTH, according to which truth is defined by reference to the reasons we have for believing something to be true. When we consider whether any particular belief is true, we appeal to reasons, but these reasons are themselves beliefs. The only things available to us as justifications for believing something to be true are other beliefs. A particular belief, therefore, may be regarded as true when it is part of a coherent set of mutually supported beliefs. To show that any belief is true we appeal to our other beliefs: if it can be supported by some of them and is not inconsistent with the rest, we are entitled to regard it as true. But if it is inconsistent with one or more of our other beliefs, then one of the inconsistent beliefs has to be rejected, since we cannot simultaneously hold two inconsistent beliefs. In short, according to the coherence theory of truth, a belief or statement is true if, and only if, it coheres with a system of beliefs or statements.

Where do the beliefs that make up this system come from? They come from our experience. Some beliefs impress themselves upon us very strongly (for example, that you are now reading a book) while others seem less secure (for example, that you spent New Year's Eve, 1994, with your cousin). But the question whether any of these beliefs is true is not to be answered by looking at their source; this is the error made by correspondence theorists. Rather it is to be answered by appeal to other beliefs. Ultimately, the only test of truth lies in the appeal to the coherence of our beliefs.

The issue between correspondence and coherence theorists is quite theoretical and abstract, and we will not attempt to resolve it here. Since our interest is essentially practical, however, we should note that the coherence theory is strongest precisely where the correspondence theory is weakest—when dealing with non-empirical statements. Consider again the examples of non-empirical statements given in section 6.1.1. It seems obvious to some philosophers that we can only deal with the question of their truth or falsity in the way the coherence theory suggests. The coherence theory, therefore seems to be an appropriate criterion of truth only for non-empirical sentences.

6.1.3 THE PRAGMATIC THEORY

Some philosophers reject both these theories on the ground that they ignore the problem-solving function of human beliefs. They argue that all human activity, including thinking and using language, arises from our need to solve problems. This is true at the level of the human species: humans would never have learned to notice colours if, for example, colours were not helpful in deciding when fruit is ripe enough to eat. It is also true at the individual level: we learn the multiplication table because it is useful in figuring out how much wallpaper to buy to paper a room. Since thought and language are essentially problem-solving tools, they argue, truth should be thought of as a property of beliefs or statements that can actually solve problems. A true statement or belief is one that is useful in solving a problem.

Not all the problems we face are practical problems, but the pragmatic theory is not limited to practical problems. Any real problem can give rise to a true solution. To understand what a real problem is, we have to ask the following sorts of questions. Why do we want to know whether World War II would not have occurred had Hitler died in 1918? What difference would it make if this claim were true rather than false? What would we do differently if we knew it were true? Such questions force us to reflect upon what the solution is needed for. For pragmatic theorists a problem is only a real problem if we have to solve it in order to go on to do something else. Otherwise it is only a pseudo-problem, one that makes no difference to anything. Thus, for the PRAGMATIC THEORY OF TRUTH a statement or belief is true if, and only if, it leads to the successful solution of a real problem.

One basic objection raised against the pragmatic theory is that many beliefs that we are quite certain of cannot be regarded as solutions to problems. Mathematicians are quite certain that there is no greatest prime number because they are certain that they have a valid proof, although they would be hard pressed to say what the real problem is to which their belief is a solution. We can be reasonably sure that Caesar crossed the Rubicon in 44 BCE, even though this is unlikely to help in the solution of any real problem. At a more mundane level, it can be proven that when people hiccough, air travels through their windpipes at speeds of up to 140 kilometres per hour, but for what conceivable problem could this be a solution?

A rather different objection arises when we look at other types of problems. What problem is the belief in God's existence intended to solve? Suppose we say that the problem is how to find solace in a vast universe that seems to have no purpose? If, as is usually the case, belief in God does provide this kind of comfort, then we would have to conclude that a belief in God is true. But this puts the cart before the horse. Doesn't the belief in God have to exist *before* it can provide solace? Would the argument that belief in God provides spiritual solace to believers prove to an atheist that God actually exists? Surely not.

Critics of the pragmatic theory argue that while there is a connection between truth and problem solving, it cannot be as close as the pragmatic theory claims. It is true that when we act on the basis of true beliefs, our actions are much more likely to be successful than when we act on the basis of false beliefs. But it is a mistake to conclude that every belief that leads to a successful action must therefore be true. Consider the following situation:

> *I believe (a) that there is only enough gas in my car to drive 300 kilometres, and (b) that it is 250 kilometres from Guelph to Parry Sound. On this basis I conclude that I can drive to Parry Sound without refuelling.*

Clearly if both (a) and (b) are true, I will be able to drive to Parry Sound without refuelling. But (a) or (b), or both, may be false, and yet I may still get to Parry Sound without refuelling. Suppose that (a) is false because there is really enough gas in my car to drive 400 kilometres; in this case if (b) is true, I will still be able to drive to Parry Sound without refuelling. Or suppose that (b) is false because it is really 285 kilometres to Parry Sound; in this case if (a) is true, I will still get to Parry Sound without refuelling. Or suppose both (a) and (b) are false, because I really have only enough gas to drive 250 kilometres, and because it is really only 225 kilometres to Parry Sound; in this case I will still get to Parry Sound without refuelling. So false beliefs do not necessarily lead to unsuccessful actions.

It is also a mistake to hold that every belief that leads to unsuccessful actions must therefore be false. Many medical researchers have dedicated years to searching for the causes of cancer, although as yet none has been entirely successful. They all believe that cancer does have causes, that is, that it is not a purely spontaneous or uncaused phenomenon. This belief is one of the factors that has led them to conduct their unsuccessful research. Does this mean that their belief is false? Surely not.

The weakness of the pragmatic theory can also be seen when we consider what we have to do in order to tell whether a problem has actually been solved. To know whether we have solved a problem, we have to appeal either to empirical facts (as the correspondence theory tells us to do) or to reasons (as the coherence theory tells us to do). The empirical facts tell me whether or not I drove to Parry Sound without refuelling, and reasons tell me whether I have really solved a mathematical equation. So, far from being a theory of truth, the pragmatic theory actually presupposes the two other theories of truth.

6.2 Types of Truth-Claims

Every statement can be regarded as making a claim to be true or, in other words, as making a truth-claim. The process of determining whether or not a truth-claim is true is called verification. If we can show that a truth-claim is true, it has been VERIFIED. If we can show that it is false, it has been FALSIFIED. (Sometimes, of course, we can do neither, so the truth of the claim remains UNDETERMINED.) The method of verification we use depends upon the type of truth-claim being made. There are two main types of truth-claims, the empirical and the non-empirical. The first step in verifying any truth-claim should always be to decide which of these two types of claim we are dealing with. Since a non-empirical truth-claim is simply a truth-claim that does *not* make an empirical claim, it is best to begin by asking simply, *Is this an empirical claim?* If it is not, we will know that it is non-empirical.

6.2.1 EMPIRICAL TRUTH-CLAIMS

In section 6.1.1 we defined an empirical fact as a fact that could be checked, i.e., a fact that is observable in principle. Thus, when we want to verify an empirical truth-claim, we must be prepared to do the appropriate checking. Consider the following:

> *My car won't start.*
> *Jim has shaved off his moustache.*
> *The library owns a first edition of Fielding's* Tom Jones.

These are empirical statements because we can attempt to verify them by checking the relevant facts. If you doubt my claim that my car won't start, you can check it by trying to start the car yourself; if you cannot start it, then you will agree with my claim, and if you can, then you will have proven that my claim was false. If you doubt the claim that Jim has shaved off his moustache, all you need to do is look at him and you will know whether it is true or false. And you can check whether the library owns a first edition of Fielding's *Tom Jones* by looking in the catalogue.

However, not all empirical claims can be verified as easily as these: some are more difficult to deal with. Statements about the past or about the future rest only indirectly on the empirical facts that support them. For example:

> *Caesar crossed the Rubicon in 44 BCE.*
> *Sebastian first ran a four-minute mile five years ago when he was still in high school.*
> *Audrey will win the gold medal in physics next year.*
> *It will rain tomorrow.*

It is obvious that the empirical facts that would directly verify or falsify these statements are not available to us. For statements about the past, we have to rely on records and memories. For statements about the future, we have to use empirical evidence about the past and present that makes the predicted event likely to occur. Of course, we could wait and see whether the predicted event actually occurs, in which case we would have direct empirical support.

Our examples so far have been of PARTICULAR EMPIRICAL STATEMENTS, that is, statements about particular empirical facts. Sometimes, however, we have to deal with statements about *classes* of objects or events. These are called GENERAL EMPIRICAL STATEMENTS and have to be approached somewhat differently because they usually make a claim that goes beyond the available empirical evidence. There are two types of general empirical statements. The first are STATISTICAL EMPIRICAL STATEMENTS, which make claims about some, or a certain proportion of, a class of objects or events. For example:

A majority of Canadians support the use of capital punishment.
Ninety per cent of snapping turtles do not survive the first three months of life.

These claims would be impossible to check if we had to do a survey of the entire population of Canada and every snapping turtle in the world. However, there is a procedure—called inductive generalization—that can provide us with an empirical basis for statistical statements. It allows us to use a representative sample of a class as an empirical basis for making statements about the entire class. Public opinion polls, for example, work on this basis. We will examine this procedure in detail in section 10.2.

The second type of general empirical statement consists of UNIVERSAL EMPIRICAL STATEMENTS, or statements about *every* member of some class. These are even more difficult to check. Consider the following:

All swans are white.

This is a statement about all swans, and, like statistical empirical statements, it too makes a claim that goes far beyond any available empirical evidence. But there is an important difference between statistical and universal empirical statements that allows us to approach universal statements differently: universal empirical statements can be refuted by a single exception. If we can find one swan that is not white, the universal statement must be false. In other words, even though we cannot verify the statement, we can *falsify* it on the basis of empirical evidence. This suggests a procedure for dealing with universal empirical statements that gives them a secure empirical basis. If we make a systematic attempt to find exceptions to some universal empirical statement and nevertheless fail to find any, we are entitled to assert that it is true. But since this procedure does not rest upon direct empirical evidence, we must always regard universal empirical statements as tentative. They are tentative because we will never be in a position to rule out the possibility of finding an exception. In principle, they can never be verified as conclusively as particular empirical claims in the present tense, but can only be imperfectly verified (though they can be conclusively falsified).

When gathering empirical evidence, we must be careful not to misinterpret it. Since empirical evidence rests upon observation, it can sometimes be misinterpreted in ways we are unaware of. An object that looks blue under artificial light may look green in natural light. Railway tracks really do look as if they come together in the distance. Sometimes we misinterpret our observations because we have not observed carefully enough. We think the bowl contains sugar because it looks like sugar, but had we tasted it, we would have realized it is salt. We will later look at certain ways in which empirical facts can be misinterpreted, but in general there are no rules that will prevent us from misinterpreting empirical evidence except for the injunction to be careful.

All the various types of empirical statements rest, one way or another, on empirical facts. To decide whether a statement is an empirical statement, we must ask whether there could be empirical evidence that would verify or falsify it. If there could be such empirical evidence, then it is an empirical statement, and all that remains is for us to do our best to obtain this empirical evidence. On the other hand, a statement that could never be verified or falsified by empirical evidence must be non-empirical.

6.2.2 NON-EMPIRICAL TRUTH-CLAIMS

We now turn to non-empirical statements. Non-empirical statements are identified by the fact that empirical evidence would not be sufficient to verify or falsify them. Consider:

The government should provide free day-care programs.

What empirical facts could possibly show that this statement is true or false? It is an empirical fact that many people believe that the government should provide free day-care programs, but this clearly doesn't show that the statement is true. Nor does the fact that many people believe that the government should not provide free day-care programs show that the statement is false. It might be an empirical fact that the government promised it would provide free day-care programs, but by itself this doesn't show that the statement is true; to do so it would have to be assumed that governments should keep their promises, and *this* is not an empirical fact. It is impossible to specify any empirical evidence that would be sufficient to show the statement to be true or false, so we must conclude that it is a non-empirical statement.

How then are we to assess whether non-empirical statements are true or false? According to the coherence theory of truth we have to look not to the empirical facts but to other beliefs we have that are secure enough to serve as justifying reasons. What these justifying reasons will be depends upon the nature of the non-empirical statement we want to verify. If we want to verify the mathematical statement that the square of the hypotenuse of a right-angle triangle is equal to the sum of the squares of the other two sides, we have to work out the mathematical proof. It is not sufficient to draw several right-angled triangles and then measure their sides: mathematics teachers won't let us get away with this manoeuvre since it uses empirical evidence where a proof is required. If we wish to verify a moral statement like the one in the preceding paragraph, we must appeal to some general moral principle that is secure enough to justify it. We might, for example, appeal to the principle that governments ought to respond to the wishes of the majority of the voters, and this, along with the empirical claim that a majority of voters wants free day-care programs, would be sufficient to justify the moral claim. In short, to the extent that non-empirical statements can be assessed, they are verified or falsified by appealing to other non-empirical statements that can serve as justifying reasons.

There are several different types of non-empirical statements. Analytic and contradictory statements (see section 3.4) are clearly non-empirical: once we know what they mean, we can determine their truth or falsity without reference to any empirical facts. Ethical statements, like the example above, are non-empirical. So too are aesthetic statements. For example:

J.S. Bach is the greatest composer of the eighteenth century.

Any empirical evidence about Bach's music and the music of his contemporaries is not going to be sufficient to show whether this claim is true or false.

Most religious statements are non-empirical as well. For example:

God is eternal and unchanging.

It is clear that there could not be any empirical evidence that we can appeal to that would be sufficient to determine whether this claim is true or false. It is, most theologians believe, something that must be accepted on faith, although some would regard it as analytic. For all such statements, determining whether they are true or false depends not on empirical evidence but on the strength of the justifying reasons we can provide.

Not every statement in an ethical, aesthetic, and religious work is non-empirical, for sometimes these works make claims that can be supported by empirical evidence. For example:

People who are treated unjustly feel entitled to compensation or retaliation.
Of all Dickens's novels, Pickwick Papers *relies most extensively on the use of caricatures.*
Jesus Christ was crucified by Roman soldiers.

Each of these statements is empirical, because empirical facts are sufficient to determine their truth or falsity. Sometimes, however, it is difficult to tell whether statements are empirical or non-empirical. For example:

In democratic countries, citizens have a duty to vote.
All music must have a recognizable rhythm.
God created the world.

These are difficult statements to deal with precisely because it is difficult to know how to determine whether they are true or false. If we regard them as empirical, we would need to look for the appropriate empirical evidence; if we regard them as non-empirical, we need to look for non-empirical justifying reasons. Each of these statements can plausibly be interpreted in both ways, so whether we should regard them as empirical or non-empirical will depend upon what we think is the most reasonable interpretation of them. Ultimately, it is up to anyone who makes such claims to interpret them in one way or the other. It is, after all, the speaker who should be the final arbiter of what he or she means.

Finally, we should mention an important class of non-empirical statements consisting of what might be called foundational principles. These are principles that lie at the basis of all knowledge claims, including empirical claims. Consider what is sometimes called the Law of Causality:

Every event must have a cause.

Unlike most scientific laws, the Law of Causality is not an empirical law. It is a presupposition that underlies all of science and all common sense as well. How we are to show that the Law of Causality is true is a difficult philosophical question about which there are different and conflicting theories.

Many foundational principles are not as secure as the Law of Causality. We saw in section 6.1 that there are at least three plausible theories of truth. These theories express alternative foundational principles about the nature of truth, all of which are non-empirical in nature. Most foundational principles are like this: there is agreement that some foundational principle is needed but disagreement on precisely what it is. Some foundational principles are subject to even deeper disagreement. The statement that God exists is a foundational principle for those who believe in God but is a principle that atheists reject altogether. Foundational principles also underlie moral reasoning, and we will examine some of these in Chapter 12.

6.3 Acceptability

In section 5.2.1 we noted that it is not always appropriate to demand that truth-claims be *proven*. Conclusive proofs are often hard to come by, and if we were not entitled to make assertions unless we could prove them, we would have a great deal less to say. Fortunately, we do not need to insist on a proof for every truth-claim we make. The first question we need to ask about a truth-claim is not *Can it be proven?* but *Are we justified in accepting it?* Sometimes, indeed, we do need a proof in order to be justified in accepting a truth-claim, but usually proofs are not needed. In fact, there are varying standards of acceptability, depending upon the nature of the statement and the context in which it is made.

The most stringent standard of acceptability is that of a strict proof. There are in fact two types of strict proofs, depending upon whether the statement is empirical or non-empirical. In section 6.2 we saw how empirical statements rest on empirical evidence in various ways. An empirical proof is one in which the empirical evidence is subjected to scrutiny designed to eliminate as far as possible any error. The evidence is, as it were, cross-examined. Is the evidence available to any normal observer? Does it avoid questionable interpretations? Have alternative explanations been refuted? Only when these questions have been answered satisfactorily are we entitled to regard empirical evidence as constituting a proof.

Non-empirical statements, we saw, rest on justifying reasons rather than on empirical evidence. A non-empirical proof, therefore, is an argument in which the premises are shown to be true and whose conclusion follows necessarily from them. Of course, showing that the premises of the proof are true requires another proof of the same sort, which in turn requires yet another proof. If we are to avoid an infinite regress we must ultimately reach premises that we are entitled to assert in the absence of proof. In other words, the premises from which a non-empirical proof is derived must ultimately be statements whose truth we can be quite certain of without proof. There are profound philosophical difficulties about the notion of statements whose truth is certain but not provable, which need not detain us here. It is sufficient for our purposes that there are premises that seem certain to us even though we cannot prove them. The best examples of non-empirical proofs are found in mathematics, for in mathematics we typically begin from premises that are known to be true and deduce conclusions that follow necessarily from them.

Strict proofs, of either the empirical or non-empirical sort, are only rarely called for. In most contexts it is irrelevant and a waste of time to demand, or to attempt to provide, a strict proof for every truth-claim. In other words, it is often reasonable to demand or provide less stringent support for our claims. When is it appropriate to look for strict proofs, and when is it not? The answer depends upon the context in which the claim is made. Suppose someone claims that a low-cholesterol diet reduces the chances of a heart attack. What can we demand of the speaker in order to show that the claim is acceptable? If it is made in the context of a discussion among people who are only interested in a healthy diet for themselves and their families, it would be sufficient to defend the claim by referring to what doctors and nutritionists commonly say or are reported as saying in magazine articles. But if the claim is made by a professor who is giving a university course on nutrition, we should demand better evidence. If the professor defends the claim by saying,

> Well, a lot of nutritionists say that a low-cholesterol diet reduces the chance of heart attack, and besides there was an article in a recent issue of Reader's Digest that says so,

we would suspect the competence of the professor. The claim ought to be defended by citing research that has been generally accepted by qualified nutritionists. Finally, if the claim is made by the researcher who conducted the research, we should not allow that researcher simply to refer to his or her own published articles on the subject but should expect a defence of the research itself.

Deciding what kind of support is required by the context is largely a matter of common sense. Unfortunately, most of us have a tendency to accept or reject claims too readily because we fail to pay attention to the context. We should use our common sense to answer the question, *What is the appropriate defence for this claim in this context?* but should be cautious about using our common sense to answer the question *Is this claim true?* In the latter case we have a tendency to make one of two errors. If we want to believe something, we tend to ignore the context if it requires a stronger defence than we can easily provide. On the other hand, if we want to reject something, we tend to ignore the context and demand a strict proof where such a demand is not warranted.

In some contexts there are statements that are a matter of common knowledge and for which it is quite unnecessary to require a defence. Consider the following:

Canada has 10 provinces.
Christmas day is December 25.
Snow melts when the temperature is above freezing.
Shakespeare wrote Hamlet.

In most contexts such statements will be common knowledge among all those involved in a discussion, and any demand that they be defended will be inappropriate. When used as premises in arguments, they will be acceptable, even though we might find it difficult to defend them. If we are challenged to defend them, we should first attempt to discover the reason for the challenge, for this will tell us what kind of defence is needed. It may be sufficient merely to check an encyclopedia, if, for example, the challenger is obviously ignorant of the common view. But it is possible that the challenger may require a more thorough defence. There are people who believe that many of the plays usually attributed to Shakespeare were in fact written by Francis Bacon; if this is the reason for the challenge, we should be prepared to admit that we may be wrong and that a great deal of careful analysis and argument would be needed to settle the issue. The idea of *common knowledge* is a relative term that depends upon the shared assumptions of a community or group. If some item of our common knowledge is challenged, we should be prepared either to defend it or to concede that there is a possibility that we are mistaken.

Let us consider some examples of statements where the kind of defence required depends upon the context and purpose of the argument:

> *Christ died on the cross for our sins.*

If said by a preacher in a sermon or by a theology student in a course on New Testament theology, this statement would be accepted because it has a biblical source. But if said in an ethics or philosophy course, it could not adequately be defended by appeal to the Bible.

> *The Liberal party lost the 1911 general election because it ran on a platform of free trade with the United States.*

If said by a student in a history essay, this claim would be acceptable if it could be supported by the textbook for the course. If said by a historian, it should be supported by historical documents and analysis of the evidence.

> *Smith is guilty of first-degree murder.*

If said by a member of the jury while attempting to reach a verdict, this should be supported by a very careful assessment of the evidence presented in court. If said by someone after the trial, it should be supported by newspaper accounts of the verdict.

To decide whether or not a statement is acceptable, then, we should proceed as follows:

(1) If the statement is common knowledge, we should regard it as acceptable, unless the context requires a higher standard of proof.

(2) If the statement is not common knowledge, we should ask for, or be prepared to offer, the evidence upon which it is based, and accept it only if the

evidence meets the appropriate standard, for example, personal experience, appeal to a recognized authority, or strict proof.

It is important to remember, however, that whenever we rely upon anything less than a strict proof, there is a possibility that a truth-claim may turn out to be false. All the weaker standards of acceptability presuppose that a strict proof could be found if we were to take the trouble to look for it or to work one out for ourselves, and this is a presupposition that may turn out to be false. History is littered with discarded "truths" that were once believed to be true in the absence of a strict proof. We should not forget this lesson.

6.4 Self-Test No. 11

Which of the following are empirical claims?

1. The Conservatives won the last New Brunswick election.

2. My children are hoping for a white Christmas this year.

3. St. Paul's Cathedral in London is one of the great architectural achievements of Western civilization.

4. Human beings will not survive the destruction of the ozone layer.

5. The sum of the interior angles of a triangle is 180 degrees.

6. If the Toronto Maple Leafs win the Stanley Cup this year, I'll eat my hat.

7. If the Canadian government ever succeeds in eliminating the federal debt, there will be a substantial reduction in taxes.

8. Paula won the prize last year for the best student in the school.

9. It is a sad reflection upon our society that suicide rates are highest around Christmas.

10. The illegal killing of elephants in Africa has been significantly reduced by the international ban on the sale of ivory.

11. Three out of four people make up 75 per cent of the population.

12. According to the American Academy of Motion Picture Arts and Sciences, *Titanic* was the best picture of 1997.

13. We do know with certainty that Osama bin Laden is either in Afghanistan, or some other country, or dead.

6.5 Questions for Discussion

The following statements require some analysis and interpretation in order to determine whether they are empirical claims. Several contain both empirical and non-empirical claims that must be carefully distinguished.

1. Christians believe that the Bible is the word of God.

2. The human race was not created by God, but evolved from lower forms of life.

3. Everyone has a conscience, even those who deny it.

4. You should apologize to Miss Rothwell as soon as possible.

5. Every society has the values that are most appropriate for that society.

6. I know that President Gorbachev was very unpopular in the former Soviet Union, but you really have to admire him for bringing about the end of communism in what was one of the largest countries in the world.

7. I absolutely adore Robertson Davies' novels.

8. Science explains why things happen.

9. People who believe in God generally lead happier lives than atheists.

10. The fact that suicide rates are highest around Christmas is a sad reflection upon the failure of our society to deal with the breakdown of the family structure.

11. The game would have ended in a 0–0 draw, if Sidney Crosby had not scored an instant before the final buzzer sounded.

6.6 Assessing the Acceptability of Premises

Clearly, an argument with one or more unacceptable premises suffers from a major defect. Since the function of premises in an argument is to provide support for the conclusion, if the premises are unacceptable, then the argument provides no support for its conclusion. Such an argument fails to meet the first of our three criteria for a sound argument. Whenever we have reason to think that a premise lacks appropriate support, we can charge the argument with failing to meet the first criterion. To back up the charge, however, we must be able to state our reasons for claiming that it lacks the appropriate support.

In section 6.3 we examined what we need to do to determine whether a statement is acceptable. When a statement functions as a premise in an argument we should approach the question of its acceptability in the same manner. Sometimes we know that a premise is false and can easily refute it. But often we are sceptical of the truth of an opponent's premise without being able to refute it. For example:

> P1. Potential murderers would be less likely to commit murder if they knew they would be executed if they were caught.
> P2. We should do whatever will reduce the number of murders in Canada.
> C. Therefore, we should reinstate the death penalty.

In this example, P1 cannot be defended on the ground that it is common knowledge. Anyone who has followed the debate on capital punishment will be aware that many people who have examined the statistical evidence believe that it shows that P1 is false. Even if we are not familiar with this evidence ourselves, we should at least ask the speaker to produce the evidence he or she believes supports P1. In this case the evidence will be empirical and will consist of facts about the frequency of murders in countries where murderers are normally executed as compared to the frequency of murders in countries where murderers are not executed. If the evidence produced does not seem to be solid and accurate, we should charge the argument with violating our first criterion. Any good reason for thinking that a premise is unacceptable entitles us to raise this objection.

So the application of the first criterion for a sound argument is simply a matter of asking whether each of the premises is acceptable, and we do this using the approach outlined in section 6.3. We should always begin by deciding which of the various standards of acceptability we should use, and this, as we saw, should be decided on the basis of the context. In fact, the argument itself provides important information about the context that is usually helpful in deciding which standard of acceptability we should use.

6.7 Some Particular Fallacies

We now turn to four particular fallacies that describe special kinds of unacceptable premises. The first two—*begging the question* and *inconsistency*—are important because they identify arguments where it is unnecessary even to ask whether its premises are acceptable. The other two—*equivocation* and *false dichotomy*—are easy to commit and often difficult to spot if we are not on our guard and deserve special mention for this reason.

6.7.1 BEGGING THE QUESTION

An argument BEGS THE QUESTION when its premises presuppose, directly or indirectly, the truth of its conclusion. An argument of this sort obviously fails to support its conclusion, since any reason we might have for doubting the conclusion will obviously also lead us to doubt any premises that presuppose it. The function of the premises of an argument is to support its conclusion, and if we have to accept the truth of the conclusion in order to accept the premises, then obviously the premises have failed to do their job. The argument actually presupposes what it is supposed to prove. Begging the question is sometimes referred to by its Latin name: *petitio principii*. Many people nowadays use the phrase *beg the question* to mean *raise the question*. This was originally a mistake, but by now has achieved such wide currency as to be found acceptable by many authorities. But careful language users (and logicians) stick to the original meaning of the phrase.

Begging the question typically arises when we want to defend some claim, yet have difficulty in finding reasons that will persuade others of its truth. For example:

> *We can be certain that [C] Dr. Drake is a good physician, because [P1] he's on staff at the General Hospital and [P2] all the medical personnel at that hospital are good at their jobs.*

The conclusion of this argument may be true, but the evidence offered by the argument does not support it because P2 presupposes that Dr. Drake is good at his job. Only someone who already accepts the conclusion would be able to accept that premise. We are especially prone to beg the question when we want to defend a conviction that we hold strongly but have trouble finding reasons. For example:

> *Morality is very important, because without it people would not behave according to moral principles.*

We are even more likely to beg the question when we are challenged by a sceptical opponent to defend an important claim. For example:

> NORTH: *I believe I was justified in lying to Congress because I was doing so in order to protect the national interest.*
> SOUTH: *How can you defend such a position?*
> NORTH: *Because a good citizen should always protect the national interest even if they have to tell lies to do so.*

Notice that North's second statement (the premise) is roughly equivalent to the first statement (the conclusion). Anyone who is unwilling to accept North's conclusion will obviously be equally unwilling to accept North's premise. Perhaps telling lies to protect the national interest is justified, but the argument fails to show this because it begs the question.

A somewhat more complex way of begging the question is when we use premises that are clearly different from the conclusion, and thus do not beg the question directly, but that are themselves defended by other premises that presuppose the truth of the original conclusion. For example:

EAST: *I deserve a larger salary than you because as sales manager my job is more important to the company.*
WEST: *I dispute that. As production supervisor my job is just as important as yours.*
EAST: *No it isn't. My job is more important because I get paid more than you.*

East is arguing in a circle: *A therefore B, and B therefore A*. Notice that neither of East's two arguments begs the question when considered in isolation from the other. It is only when they are taken together that they beg the question.

6.7.2 INCONSISTENCY

The fallacy of INCONSISTENCY arises when an argument contains, implicitly or explicitly, a contradiction, usually between two premises. In section 3.4 we defined a contradictory statement as one that is false by definition. The kind of contradiction we are now referring to is that where two statements, neither of which is contradictory on its own, create a contradiction when they are asserted together. For example, consider the following statements:

Mary is older than Gord.
Gord is older than Mary.

Neither statement by itself is a contradiction, but asserting them together amounts to saying,

Mary is older than Gord and Gord is older than Mary.

Since this is a contradiction, we know that it must be false without having to check the facts. We may not know which of the contradiction's components is false, but we know that one of them must be. Clearly, any argument that includes a contradiction must fail to provide support for its conclusion.

Arguing from a blatant inconsistency is not common, doubtless because even the most irrational person can see that an argument with contradictory premises is not going to succeed. We sometimes get carried away and contradict ourselves when under pressure, but usually the contradiction is implicit. Some parents will recognize the following:

SON: *Dad, I'm going over to the park for my football practice.*

> FATHER: *Son, you missed school today and were excused from raking leaves for being sick.*
> SON: *Oh, I can play football. I feel better now.*
> FATHER: *Well, then you must rake the leaves and catch up on your missed school work first.*
> SON: *But, dad, you know I can't do anything strenuous when I'm sick.*

The son argues (a) that he feels well enough for football practice, and (b) that he is not feeling well enough to do chores or school work. Assuming that football is more strenuous than leaf raking and homework, (a) and (b) are inconsistent. It's easy to imagine the son making the last remark as a joke, and in fact inconsistency is often used in humour. Consider this old joke about a couple on an all-inclusive, vacation cruise:

> WIFE: *The food they serve on this ship is so awful it's inedible.*
> HUSBAND: *I agree entirely. And the portions are too small.*

Recognizing the husband's inconsistency is essential for catching the humour here: on one hand, the husband agrees that the food is inedible, but on the other hand, he wants to eat more of it. It's humorous because it's fallacious.

In serious contexts, however, the fallacy of inconsistency usually arises when the contradiction is implicit rather than explicit. In these cases we need to make the contradiction explicit by showing how it arises. For example:

> *There are three reasons why the free trade agreement with the US is bad for Canada. First, open competition has created a significant increase in unemployment and will eventually produce a drastic reduction in the GNP as more and more branch plants are closed by their American owners and Canadian industries are driven into bankruptcy. Second, we are under continual pressure to dismantle social programs such as medicare and family allowances, which the Americans regard as "unfair" subsidies to industry. Third, all the new wealth that is being created in Canada is concentrated in the hands of a prosperous middle class while the workers become poorer.*

Now, it certainly seems that the first and third reasons are inconsistent with each other. The first predicts *a drastic reduction in the GNP* while the third admits that *new wealth is being created.* Are these two claims really inconsistent? The principle of charity would require us to give the speaker a chance to explain, or explain away, the apparent inconsistency, but in the absence of a convincing explanation, we can charge the argument with committing the fallacy of inconsistency because it relies on inconsistent premises.

A more common type of inconsistency in argument is between what someone says in the course of an argument and other relevant things they have said on other occasions. For example:

JOCK: *The city cannot afford a performing arts centre. Taxes are already too high and cause hardship for many ordinary people.*

ART: *Wait a minute. Last year you made a presentation to City Council in support of a proposal to build another hockey arena, and that would have cost even more than a performing arts centre. Fortunately, the Council turned down that proposal.*

Art's charge is that Jock has presented two arguments dealing with the same subject (i.e., city taxes) that contain inconsistent premises. In the argument above, Jock has used the premise that taxes are too high, while in his earlier argument he used the premise (or perhaps presupposed as a missing premise) that taxes are not too high. But this by itself does not entitle Art to charge Jock with the fallacy of inconsistency. Because the inconsistency arises between two arguments presented at different times, Art must allow for the possibility that Jock has changed his mind. Jock might respond to the charge by saying that since last year he has reconsidered his position and now thinks that his earlier argument was unsound because it used a premise he now believes is false. If Jock takes this line, then Art's charge of inconsistency will fail. Of course, Jock may be only pretending to have changed his mind in order to avoid having to respond to Art's charge. In this case Jock will have avoided the charge of inconsistency at the price of being a hypocrite.

There is another type of hypocrisy, however, that can give rise to the charge of inconsistency. This is where the inconsistency is between what someone says and what he or she does, that is, between words and actions. For example:

MARY: *I'm just appalled at my sister-in-law. She had an affair and then when my brother found out, she expected him to forgive her. That sort of thing is unforgivable, and I think he should leave her. It would be good riddance to bad rubbish.*

FRANCINE: *Cool it, Mary. I know about the little extramarital fling you had a couple of years ago, and when your husband found out, you were grateful when he forgave you.*

Francine's accusation of hypocrisy is probably justified, assuming she has her facts right. Mary's premise is that an extramarital affair should not be forgiven by a spouse. But, as Francine points out, Mary not only had an affair herself but wanted her husband to forgive her. Clearly, Mary's premise is inconsistent with her earlier actions, and her conclusion—that her brother should not forgive, and should leave, her sister-in-law—lacks real support. Francine should, however, give Mary a chance to explain her apparent hypocrisy. Perhaps her affair took place during a period when her husband was also having an affair, and this might allow her to argue that the two situations are not parallel. But in the absence of some such explanation, Francine is justified in refusing to accept Mary's premise and charging her with the fallacy of inconsistency.

6.7.3 EQUIVOCATION

In Chapter 3 we examined various ways in which language can be ambiguous, and we indicated the importance of ensuring that the meaning of what we say is clear and unambiguous. We now consider some ways in which ambiguities can destroy or weaken an argument. The fallacy of EQUIVOCATION arises when a premise has two interpretations, one acceptable and one unacceptable, and when it is the unacceptable interpretation that is required by the conclusion.

Here is a silly example that clearly illustrates the nature of this mistake:

Noisy children are a real headache.
An aspirin will make a headache go away.
Therefore, an aspirin will make noisy children go away.

There is a sense in which noisy children are a headache, but it is only a metaphorical sense. When taken literally, the claim is false. The conclusion of this argument, however, follows only if the first premise is literally true. The argument, therefore, commits the fallacy of equivocation.

Usually, the equivocation arises in more subtle ways. For example:

There's a lot of talk these days about how we shouldn't discriminate. Well, I don't agree at all. Everybody discriminates all the time. It is unavoidable. We discriminate when selecting a wine or buying a car or choosing new wallpaper. We discriminate when deciding which friends to invite to a party or which candidate to vote for. We discriminate when we hire someone, or admit someone to a college. We always make such decisions on the basis of the qualities we admire: i.e., we discriminate. So there is nothing wrong with discrimination.

The equivocation here is with the term *discrimination*. In the premises the speaker uses the term to mean *making decisions on the basis of relevant qualities*. This is an accepted sense of the term, which is reflected in sentences like *He is very discriminating in his choice of clothes*. But the conclusion uses the term to mean *making decisions on the basis of irrelevant qualities such as race, religion, or gender*. This is the sense of the term that is obviously used by those who believe we should not discriminate. The sense in which the premises are true is not the sense required by the conclusion, so the argument commits the fallacy of equivocation.

Any of the types of ambiguity we discussed in Chapter 3 can give rise to the fallacy of equivocation. Sometimes it may rest on a failure to recognize linguistic ambiguities, for example, the ambiguity between the collective and distributive use of a term. Or it may arise through the failure to distinguish between the analytic and synthetic interpretations of a statement, between the descriptive and evaluative meanings of a term, or between necessary and sufficient conditions.

Here are two more examples of arguments that commit the fallacy of equivocation:

Professor Jones says that no one will get an A in his course unless they attend every seminar.
Well, I've attended every seminar so I'm expecting an A.

According to Judge Wapner's ruling, the Country Club cannot build an indoor swimming pool unless the membership agrees. Well, I am a member, and I most certainly do not agree. Therefore, the Club cannot build its new pool.

6.7.4 FALSE DICHOTOMY

We often have to deal with alternatives. Sometimes there are only two alternatives: either we are pregnant or we are not. But frequently, when we are offered two alternatives, there are really more than two: we may be neither rich nor poor, neither young nor old, neither hairy nor bald. In addition, some alternatives do not exclude each other. When we are offered a choice of cake or pie for dessert, we may, if we are lucky, be able to choose both. With any range of alternatives we can ask whether they are exhaustive and whether they are exclusive. Alternatives are EXHAUSTIVE when they cover all the possibilities. *Being pregnant* and *not being pregnant* are exhaustive alternatives, for there is no other possibility. *Being young* and *being old* are not exhaustive alternatives, for there is a third possibility: *being middle-aged*. Alternatives are EXCLUSIVE when the choice of one rules out the other(s). For example, the designations *a.m.* and *p.m.* are exclusive, at least when applied to a time on a particular place on earth. *Being a faculty member* and *being a student* are not exclusive, since some faculty are also students.

Thus, every set of alternatives will be either exhaustive or non-exhaustive *and* either exclusive or non-exclusive. The famous choice between liberty or death (*Give me liberty or give me death*) is exclusive but not exhaustive. It is exclusive because one cannot choose both liberty and death, but it is not exhaustive because one could choose neither liberty nor death but slavery. The American bumper sticker *America: Love It Or Leave It* presents a choice that is neither exhaustive nor exclusive. It is not exhaustive because it is possible to neither love it nor leave it: for example, to be indifferent to it but stay. It is not exclusive because it is possible to love it and to leave it.

The fallacy of FALSE DICHOTOMY arises when the premise of an argument presents us with a choice between two alternatives and assumes that they are exhaustive or exclusive or both when in fact they are not. Most commonly it arises when the alternatives are presented as if they were exhaustive when in fact they are not. For example:

DAVID: *Let me get this straight, Paul. You mean that you have been going out with your girlfriend for almost a year, and she never told you she has a three-year-old daughter by a previous marriage?*
PAUL: *That's right. And I only found out by accident last week.*
DAVID: *Well, whatever you do, Paul, don't marry her. She is a liar.*

David is assuming that telling the truth and telling lies are exhaustive alternatives, when in fact not telling the truth is not the same as telling a lie. We can fail to tell the truth by not saying anything, which is what Paul's girlfriend did, and this is quite different from telling a lie. Here are three more examples of the fallacy of false dichotomy:

I'm against giving aid to countries in which people are starving. We will never be able to eradicate starvation completely, so it is a waste of time even trying.

Good students will study and learn if there are no examinations, and bad students won't study and will learn nothing even when there are examinations. So exams are useless.

These days students have to choose whether they want to get good grades or whether they want to have fun. Well, Tamsen has decided she wants to have fun at college, so I guess she's not going to get good grades.

6.8 Self-Test No. 12

Identify the weaknesses in the following arguments, after making sure you have correctly identified the conclusion.

1. If we want economic prosperity for Canada, we should be looking for wars to get involved in. Every nation that has fought a major war in this century emerged from the war economically stronger than it was before. It seems to be the one sure path to economic prosperity.

2. In our democratic system, government is supposed to be based on the consent of the governed. Well, I am one of the governed, and I certainly do not consent to the GST (General Sales Tax on goods and services). So the government has no right to force me and others who think the way I do to pay this iniquitous tax.

3. The outboard motor I bought last year turned out to be a real lemon. As soon as the warranty expired everything started going wrong; it has cost me over $600 in repairs so far this year. The trouble is there's nothing I can do about it. I thought about suing the manufacturer, but the lawyer's fee would cost more than I could ever hope to win.

4. History shows that only in democracies does the human spirit flourish. And the reason is clear: undemocratic societies deny to most of their members any opportunity to take part in the political life of the community, and without such participation the human spirit withers and dies.

5. Members of the jury, there are two compelling reasons why you should find my client not guilty. First, the prosecution has failed to prove beyond a reasonable doubt that he was anywhere near the warehouse on the night the theft occurred. And second, even if he was there, I have presented evidence to show that he was acting under threats from his companions. In either case he should be found not guilty.

6. Most people are much more interested in local issues—such as property taxes, garbage collection, their children's education, and zoning by-laws—than they are in provincial and national political issues. This is shown by the fact that a much higher percentage of the electorate votes in municipal elections than in provincial or federal elections.

7. It never ceases to amaze me that so many scientists deny that the miracles reported in the Bible actually took place. After all, science itself has presented us with many miracles, such as lasers, antibiotics, computers, and space flight. Since scientists accept that these modern miracles actually exist, they should accept that biblical miracles also actually occurred.

8. The choice confronting us is clear. Do we want a defence policy that relies upon the threat of nuclear annihilation to deter aggression, or do we want a non-aligned foreign policy that is aimed at reducing international tensions? It is obvious that we should reject the first alternative since it embodies a dangerous and outmoded cold war mentality, and that we should therefore adopt a non-aligned foreign policy.

9. Last year I took a great course in history of science that was developed and team-taught by Professors Smith, Jones, and Brown. They were excellent teachers; in fact they received an award for teaching excellence for the course. So I am going to register next term for a new course being offered by Professor Smith. I am sure it will be a great course, too.

10. There are 13 chapters in this book, and I am now almost finished Chapter 6. Therefore, I am almost halfway through the book.

6.9 Questions for Discussion

Each of the following arguments involves a weakness, although it may take careful analysis to identify the precise nature of the weakness.

1. There is no such thing as an unselfish act. If you examine any so-called unselfish act, such as donating money to charity, you will always find that there is a selfish motive. There has to be, for nobody can do anything unless they

think it will give them some kind of satisfaction. Seeking self-satisfaction is the only reason why anybody does anything. So every act is selfish.

2. Individuals are born, struggle through childhood, grow to maturity, and after a few years decline and finally die. So we should expect all societies, which are mere aggregations of individuals, to do the same.

3. I have attended several operas, and I always come away with the same reaction, which is that opera is a vastly over-rated art form. The plots could never be described as great literature, and some are as bad as any TV melodrama. Even when performed superbly, the music itself is always a mixture of good and mediocre, usually more mediocre than good. The costumes and the staging are often well done, but the whole experience is always destroyed for me by the atrocious acting. Why can singers never learn to act? The fact that opera lovers always seem to be unaware of these drawbacks is a great mystery to me.

4. The great experiment in communism that began in Russia in 1917 with such high hopes finally came to an inglorious end in 1991, and all that is left is to diagnose the fatal flaw that destroyed the noble dream. The view one hears most frequently is that it was the failure of the communist system to provide its citizens with material goods that brought it down. But this view ignores the role of the denial of freedom that has characterized the Soviet Union since its inception. If the history of the Soviet Union proves anything, it is that the human spirit needs freedom not merely to flourish but to survive. People will tolerate the denial of their freedom for a time in order to achieve security, but eventually the demand for freedom will burst forth, destroying everything that stands in its way. The death of communism can only be explained by its denial of freedom, not by its admitted failure to give its citizens material prosperity.

5. In his book *Utilitarianism*, John Stuart Mill defends the view that the ultimate test of right and wrong is the greatest-happiness principle. The principle states that we should always seek to promote the general happiness, which he defines as the greatest happiness of the greatest number of people. To show that the principle is true, Mill argues as follows: Each person's happiness is a good to that person. Therefore, the general happiness is a good to the aggregate of all persons.

7.   Assessing Relevance

7.1 The Criterion of Relevance

Our second criterion for a sound argument is that the premises must be relevant to the conclusion. An argument whose premises are irrelevant to its conclusion obviously suffers from a major weakness. But what precisely is relevance? What are we looking for in an argument when we ask whether its premises are relevant? What we need from our premises, if they are to be relevant to the truth of the conclusion, is that they should make it more likely that the conclusion will be true. We cannot expect that the truth of a premise will always guarantee the truth of the conclusion, but we can demand that it make the conclusion more likely to be true than it would be if the premise were false. In brief, a premise is relevant when it helps to make it reasonable to accept the conclusion.

The idea of relevance is easier to grasp if we compare some examples of arguments with relevant premises and arguments with irrelevant premises:

> *You should vote for Johnson because she is honest and is well informed about the issues.*
> *You should vote for Johnson because her mother used to be my kindergarten teacher.*

The first of these arguments supplies two reasons for voting for Johnson, both of which are clearly relevant. Anyone who thinks they are irrelevant would have to hold that it is a matter of indifference whether a politician is honest or well informed about the issues and would see no reason to vote against a politician who was dishonest or poorly informed about the issues. Such a view is unacceptable to most of us because we are convinced that being honest and well informed are desirable qualities in a politician. If pressed, we could defend this view by pointing to the disastrous social and political consequences of having dishonest or poorly informed politicians. The second of the above arguments supplies an irrelevant reason for voting for Johnson. It is difficult to imagine why anyone would seriously think that the fact that the candidate's mother was a kindergarten teacher is a good reason to vote for that candidate. If pressed to justify our view that this is an irrelevant premise, we could argue that there is no evidence that the children of kindergarten teachers make better politicians than anyone else.

Thus, for any premise we can always ask whether it has any relevance to the acceptability of the conclusion. Usually it is quite clear whether a premise is relevant, but where it is not clear, we can address the question directly by trying to find an argument that will determine the question one way or the other. This is not always a straightforward matter. Consider the following:

You should vote for Johnson because she is the only female candidate.

Is the fact that Johnson is a woman a relevant reason to vote for her? This is a debatable question. Many people believe that there should be more women elected to public office, and they defend this view by arguing that women bring a different and better perspective to politics, that women are more likely than men to address women's issues seriously, that women are still handicapped in politics by their gender, and so on. On the other hand, many people reject this view on the ground that we should vote only for candidates whose policies we agree with, and that not all women candidates support the policies we may agree with. It is not obvious whether a candidate's gender is relevant; to decide whether it is, we have to grapple with the issue on its own terms.

There is one complicating feature of questions of relevance we must note. Sometimes the question whether a premise is relevant depends upon the standard of acceptability that is appropriate in the context. In section 6.3 we discussed the different standards of acceptability that we can use when determining whether statements are acceptable. These varying standards also have a bearing on whether premises are relevant. If we want to show that a high-cholesterol diet increases the chances of a heart attack, the context will determine which premises are relevant and which are not. Appealing to an article in *Reader's Digest* will be relevant in a casual conversation with friends about diet, but irrelevant in a discussion by nutritionists about recent research. Again, measuring the interior angles of a triangle with a protractor to show that they add up to 180 degrees may be relevant in some contexts but irrelevant when a mathematical proof is called for. Generally, when the standard of acceptability is very demanding, premises that may be relevant with a lower standard of acceptability will become irrelevant. Whenever we raise the question of relevance about a premise, we should always take account of the standard of acceptability that is appropriate in the context.

7.2 Recognizing Irrelevant Premises

The traditional term used to describe arguments with irrelevant premises is *non sequitur*, which means, literally, *it does not follow*. It is an unfortunate human tendency to believe that much more follows from premises than really does. We are too willing to appeal to premises that may be irrelevant on the off chance that they might convince others or even ourselves. Fortunately, it is usually easy to decide whether a premise is relevant if we can remember to ask ourselves whether the premise, if accepted for the sake of the argument, makes the conclusion more likely to be true. Simply raising the question often suggests a plausible argument that shows whether the premise is relevant. The kind of argument we need is not usually a lengthy one, but it should be clear and specific. For example:

> I washed my car this morning. So we can be certain that it's going to rain later today.

We can show the irrelevance of the premise of this argument by noting that there is no reason to believe that washing a car has any role to play in the weather. If someone were to say this while laughing and rolling their eyes, the principle of charity would oblige us to interpret this claim as a joke. But if it is asserted seriously, the conclusion simply does not follow. Many superstitions exhibit *non sequitur*s of this sort.

Here are two more arguments with irrelevant premises:

> I am opposed to the proposed anti-smoking by-law and will vote against it at the Council meeting. Such a by-law is inappropriate in a city in which the Imperial Tobacco Company is one of the largest employers.

> The movie of Anna Karenina *was pretty boring; it is really nothing more than a soap opera set in Imperial Russia. I'd always thought it was supposed to be a great novel. I guess I was wrong.*

The irrelevance of the premise of the first argument can be shown by arguing that the fact that the Imperial Tobacco Company is one of the city's largest employers has no bearing on whether the citizens want or are entitled to an anti-smoking by-law. But, presumably, the reason for an anti-smoking by-law is based on the threat of smoking to public health. There is no direct reason to think that the status of Imperial Tobacco as a local employer has any bearing on this threat. In the second case, a comparison of even a few great novels with films that have been based on them is sufficient to show that the quality of the film usually has very little to do with the quality of the novel. Unless we have some special reason to believe that the film version of *Anna Karenina* is a faithful re-creation of the Tolstoy's novel, we should not judge of the book on the basis of the film.

There is no limit to the kinds of irrelevant premises people can appeal to except for the limits of their imagination. Certain types of irrelevant appeals, however, occur so frequently that they have been given particular labels. These labels are useful because they remind us of the common kinds of irrelevancies we should be on the lookout for and because they help us to explain why the premises are irrelevant. The APPEAL TO PITY that we mentioned in section 5.1 is one such. Here is another example of an appeal to pity:

> The judge was very unfair. He shouldn't have found Evelyn guilty. She is a single parent with three small children and an ex-husband who refuses to make

his support payments, and I'm sure she would not have started shoplifting if she weren't really hard-pressed for money.

Evelyn certainly deserves our pity (or sympathy), but this has no bearing on whether or not she is guilty of shoplifting. If there is strong evidence that she shoplifted, then the judge has no option but to find her guilty. There are situations, however, where the appeal to pity is relevant. If the conclusion of the above argument were

The judge shouldn't have given Evelyn a jail sentence

then the appeal to pity would be relevant, since we could argue that single parents with small children should not be jailed for non-violent criminal offences.

Another type of irrelevant appeal is the APPEAL TO FORCE. It arises when the premise of an argument threatens the use of force (either physical force or other kinds of pressure, such as economic pressure or emotional blackmail) as a reason for accepting the conclusion. Obviously, an appeal to force normally provides no reason for accepting the truth of a claim, although it might well provide a good reason for pretending to accept it. For example:

Listen, I'm telling you that my son did not cheat on his exam: if you don't agree, we'll step outside and settle the matter man to man.

Clearly, the son's innocence cannot be established by beating up his teacher, although the son might nevertheless be innocent. And even if the teacher agrees with the father out of fear, the son has obviously not been shown to be innocent.

An appeal to force may be relevant when it is used in an attempt to get someone to do something, rather than to accept a truth-claim. However, in order to decide whether we are justified in using threats of force to get people to do something, we must establish a moral or political principle to serve as an additional premise. The criminal law, for example, works on the basis of the principle that society is entitled to use the threat of punishment to secure obedience to the law. If we accept this principle, then it is relevant to argue that people should not commit murder because otherwise they will be punished.

Another type of irrelevant appeal worth mentioning is the APPEAL TO POPULARITY. It arises when an argument uses the popularity of a belief as a reason for holding that the belief is true, when its popularity is irrelevant to its truth or falsity. Obviously, the mere fact that a belief is popular is usually no guarantee that it is true. History provides many examples of discarded beliefs that were once widely held to be true. Typically, the popularity of a belief is not a good reason for accepting it. For example:

Well, obviously capitalism is the most efficient economic system ever devised by humankind. Everybody knows that.
Phrenology is unscientific nonsense. Nobody believes it any longer.

Clearly, the popularity of capitalism does nothing to show that it is the most efficient economic system, nor does the unpopularity of phrenology do anything to show that it is false. It is also easy to recognize the cases where the appeal to popularity is relevant, that is, cases where the conclusion makes a claim that depends upon the popularity (rather than the truth) of some belief. If we are trying to predict who will win an election, or the future sales of a product, or the size of an audience for a concert, we will obviously need to use the appeal to popularity.

There are, however, harder cases where the relevance of the appeal to popularity is unclear. For example:

> *According to public opinion polls, more than 60 per cent of Canadians are in favour of the death penalty for first-degree murder. This is supposed to be a democratic country, so the government ought to reinstate capital punishment.*

Is this a sound argument? It does not attempt to show that capital punishment is justified in itself, but only claims that it ought to be reinstated because the majority support it. It thus relies upon a missing premise: the political principle that government policy ought to reflect the will of the majority. It is on the acceptability of this principle that the strength of the argument depends. If it is acceptable, then the argument is strong. If it is not acceptable, then the argument is weak, for it appeals to an irrelevant premise.

7.3 Appeals to Authority (1)

Often in discussion we make numerous claims that we do not attempt to defend. When we are challenged to do so, a common response is to cite an authority, in other words, we present an argument of the form:

> *So-and-so says X.*
> *Therefore, X is true (or probably true).*

The authorities we appeal to in order to defend a claim are many and varied: the prime minister, the family doctor, Uncle Fred, the weatherman, mom, the encyclopedia, a physics professor, the media, Wayne Gretzky. In each case, the argument is in effect claiming that the mere fact that so-and-so says something is a good reason for us to accept it as true.

It is obvious that sometimes such appeals are quite irrelevant and give rise to very weak arguments. When Uncle Fred tells me that the Tiger-Cats are the best team in the CFL, it is unreasonable for me to agree with his view merely because he holds it. He is an enthusiastic fan, but he knows very little about football. What he says is irrelevant to the issue of whether or not the Tiger-Cats are the best team in the CFL. But not all appeals to authority are as obviously weak as the appeal to Uncle Fred. Consider the following examples:

Albert Einstein, even after all his research into the nature of the universe, still believed in God. He once wrote, "I do not believe that the universe was the result of blind chance." If belief in God made sense to Einstein, then it makes sense to me.

I've decided not to take any more philosophy electives. Some philosophy is kind of interesting, but the problem is that it consists merely of opinions and not knowledge. At least that's what my psychology professor says.

These arguments may seem plausible, but they appeal to irrelevant authorities. It is (or should be) evident that the fact that a famous physicist believed in God is not a good reason for believing in God. And the fact that a psychology professor thinks that philosophy consists merely of opinion and not knowledge is not a good reason for accepting his or her claim.

However, not all appeals to authority are irrelevant. In fact, our lives would be intolerable if we were never to rely upon authorities. The reason we consult lawyers, doctors, architects, and engineers, is that we have to rely upon their advice on matters about which we lack knowledge. In general, an appeal to authority is relevant whenever the following two conditions are met: (1) we lack information or experience that is needed to make a reasonable decision, and it is difficult or impossible on the matter in question to obtain it directly for ourselves; and (2) the authority appealed to is entitled to authoritative status. The first condition recognizes that if we could get the needed information and experience directly and without appealing to some authority, we ought to do so. For example, we should not rely upon someone else's view that a book is offensive if we could easily read it and decide for ourselves. Similarly, we shouldn't accept the view that euthanasia is right merely because some person we admire for their general good judgement holds that it is. The appeal to authority, even when it is legitimate, should always be regarded as second best; if we are in a position to learn about the matter and decide for ourselves, we should do so. Only in situations where we lack the expertise needed to make some decision or judgement are we entitled to turn to an authority, such as a doctor, lawyer or engineer. But when we do so, we must bear in mind the second condition and make sure we are relying upon the judgement of someone who really is entitled to be treated as authoritative on the matter in question. There should be good reasons to believe that what the authority says really is likely to be true. How much reliance we should place on authorities will be discussed in section 8.2.

7.4 Some Particular Fallacies

The particular fallacies described in this section all involve an irrelevant appeal of some sort. They deserve a more extended discussion because they are so common and because recognizing them requires sensitivity to their complexities. They figure prominently in arguments about virtually every controversial issue and account for much of the frustration we typically experience when we are drawn into such debates.

Understanding them will not only help us to avoid them but also show us how to respond when our opponents use them against us.

7.4.1 AD HOMINEM

The AD HOMINEM FALLACY is committed when the premise of an argument provides information about the author of some statement in an attempt to show that this statement is false, when this information is irrelevant to the truth or falsity of the statement. Loosely speaking, the ad hominem fallacy involves a personal attack upon someone in an attempt to discredit what that person says, when such an attack is irrelevant to the issue. The traditional name for this fallacy is *argumentum ad hominem*, which literally means *argument against the man*. Some contemporary logicians call this fallacy *abusing the person*, or *attack on the person*, but the Latin name is still widely used in ordinary speech, and we shall follow this usage here.

Let us look at some examples of arguments that commit the ad hominem fallacy:

> *According to the supporters of capital punishment, the death penalty is an effective deterrent against murder. This is nonsense. These people are not interested in deterrence at all. They want vengeance pure and simple. They suffer from a kind of blood-lust; they are the people who flock to see* Dirty Harry *movies. They get turned on by the thought of shooting up the bad guys.*

What makes this an ad hominem is that the facts (or alleged facts) cited about the personal qualities of supporters of capital punishment are completely irrelevant to the question of whether or not the death penalty is an effective deterrent against murder.

The ad hominem is usually easy to detect as long as we can remember to separate our views about the personal qualities of people whose opinions we do not share from our views about their opinions. We may not like to admit it, but nasty people sometimes say what is true and sometimes argue impeccably. The ease with which so many people commit the ad hominem fallacy doubtless derives from the fact that it is psychologically satisfying to attack nasty people. This also explains why an ad hominem can be so successful in public debates and discussion: audiences enjoy seeing nasty people under attack and often feel that such attacks actually refute their opinions and arguments. It is important, therefore, not to allow ourselves to be taken in by such attacks when they constitute an ad hominem, especially in situations where we feel very strongly that someone's opinion is not only false but deeply immoral as well. These are the types of situations where we may commit an ad hominem without realizing it. We should strive to develop the intellectual self-discipline to separate our views about our opponents from our views about the truth or falsity of what they say.

Not every attack upon a person's personal qualities, however, constitutes a fallacy. It is only when such attacks are irrelevant to the point at issue that the fallacy arises. Sometimes the personal qualities of someone are precisely what is at issue. When we are looking for a baby-sitter, or considering asking someone out on a date, our decisions should be based upon a judgement about personal qualities. In such cases the personal qualities of the person are not used as a basis for rejecting what the person says, and for this reason no ad hominem fallacy is committed.

There are two types of arguments that seem to, but do not actually, commit the ad hominem fallacy. First, in some situations it is appropriate to argue that a person's opinions should not be relied upon because he or she is untrustworthy. When we are trying to assess the reliability of someone's testimony about an event, it is relevant to point to facts about the person's character. If you tell me that you have no idea how my bicycle came to be in your garage, the fact that you were convicted for bicycle theft last year is relevant to the question of whether I should accept your claim of innocence. This does not, of course, prove that you stole my bicycle, but it is relevant to the question of whether or not it is reasonable to believe you. Or, if I tell you that you will get better grades in school if you buy a particular encyclopedia, the fact that I get a 10 per cent commission is relevant to the question of whether you should accept my claim.

Second, sometimes it is appropriate to argue that a person's opinions should not be taken into account because of a conflict of interest. When a body such as a city council or school board makes decisions that might affect the financial interests of its members, it is an accepted principle that any member whose financial interests might be affected should not participate in such decisions. Here we do not dispute what a person says, but rather whether that person's views ought to be taken into account in the decision-making process. An argument that someone ought to abstain from voting on an issue because of a conflict of interest does not commit the ad hominem fallacy.

7.4.2 TU QUOQUE

The TU QUOQUE FALLACY is a special case of the ad hominem. Like the ad hominem, it typically arises in an argumentative context when someone attempts to refute or rebut something said by another person. The tu quoque fallacy is committed when the conclusion of an argument claims that an accusation is unwarranted and supports it by claiming that the accuser is also open to a similar accusation. This fallacy is sometimes called the *Two Wrongs* fallacy, but we shall use the traditional Latin name (pronounced tew-kwoh-kway), which means *you too.*

It is clear that a tu quoque response to an accusation can never refute the accusation. Consider the following:

> WILMA: *You cheated on your income tax. Don't you realize that's wrong?*
> WALTER: *Hey, wait a minute. You cheated on your income tax last year. Or have you forgotten about that?*

Walter may be correct in his counter-accusation, but that does not show that Wilma's accusation is false. Wilma's guilt can in no way reduce or eliminate Walter's guilt.

It is easy to understand why tu quoque arguments are so popular. After all, what better way to avoid an accusation than to hurl the same accusation back at our accusers. Many important public issues suffer from an abundance of tu quoques. For example:

I don't see why our company should be singled out by the city just because of some leakage problems at our chemical storage facility. The city should pay more attention to the more serious pollution that is occurring at its landfill site.

The opposition is in no position to attack the government for increasing the deficit. When they formed the government a few years ago, they created a massive deficit that we are still coping with.

Tu quoque arguments are probably popular because they are deceptively similar to a type of argument that is sound. For example, when the issue is not whether an accusation is true, but whether someone has the right to make that accusation, it may be legitimate to use a tu quoque response. Recall our example from section 6.7.2:

MARY: *I'm just appalled at my sister-in-law. She had an affair, and then when my brother found out, she expected him to forgive her. That sort of thing is unforgivable, and I think he should leave her. It would be good riddance to bad rubbish.*
FRANCINE: *Cool it, Mary. I know about the little extra-marital fling you had a couple of years ago, and when your husband found out, you were grateful when he forgave you.*

Here the issue is not whether Mary's sister-in-law has had an extra-marital affair, but whether she should be forgiven for it. Since Francine is really charging Mary with hypocrisy, Francine herself does not commit a fallacy. In such cases an underlying moral principle is being invoked. We shall discuss how these arguments work in more detail in section 12.3.

7.4.3 STRAW MAN

This, too, is a very common fallacy. It usually arises in debates over controversial issues when one side is attempting to avoid or deflect criticisms presented by the other side. The STRAW MAN FALLACY is committed when someone attacks a position that appears similar to, but is actually different from, an opponent's position, and concludes that the opponent's real position has thereby been refuted. The opponent being attacked, however, is not the real opponent but an unreal opponent, a *straw man* who has been constructed by the attacker solely for the purpose of destruction. To recognize this fallacy we must, of course, know what the opponent's real position is in order to see that it is different from the position being attacked. The question we need to ask when a position is under attack is, *Is the position being attacked really held by those under attack, or is it a false interpretation of their position?*

Examples of the straw man fallacy abound. When the issue is controversial, the straw man fallacy is often committed by both sides. Consider the following arguments:

What I object to most about those people who oppose capital punishment is that they believe that the lives of convicted murderers are more important than the lives of the policemen and prison guards who protect us.

Those who want the death penalty restored have not really thought their position through. They hold that every murderer would have been deterred from committing murder had the death penalty been in force, and this is absurd. Otherwise, countries with the death penalty would have no murders, which is obviously false.

With regard to the first argument, there is no evidence that anyone who is against the death penalty has ever believed that the lives of murderers are more important than anyone else's lives. With regard to the second argument, there is no evidence that anyone who supports the death penalty has ever seriously argued that the death penalty would deter all potential murderers. In both cases, the accusers have attacked an unreal position and have thus committed the straw man fallacy.

Clearly, the principle of charity is being ignored in these cases. We have no difficulty recognizing when our opponents have committed a straw man fallacy by attacking a travesty of our position. We know that they have violated the principle of charity. It is more difficult for us, however, to avoid stooping to the same level as our opponents. We need to remind ourselves that committing the straw man fallacy accomplishes nothing other than perhaps making us feel better for the moment. Our opponents are certainly not persuaded by such arguments; neither should anyone else be persuaded, since the position our opponents really hold has not been attacked at all and survives unscathed. Even worse, people who are not yet committed to either side of the issue may well conclude that our position must be very weak indeed if our straw man attack is the best that can be said against the other side.

Here are some other examples of straw man arguments:

If the New Democratic Party ever forms the government in Canada they would nationalize the whole economy. After all, they have repeatedly made it clear that they are opposed to business and to the profit motive.

The government's immigration policy allows anyone who claims to be a refugee to enter Canada. This is an indefensible policy. What we want are laws that will make it easy for legitimate refugees to enter Canada, while at the same time requiring all non-refugees to apply to immigrate like anyone else.

The demands made by the Aboriginal peoples are totally unacceptable. They claim that the whole country was stolen from them without their consent and are demanding compensation for their loss. This is crazy. There isn't enough money in the world, let alone in Canada, to pay compensation for the whole country.

7.5 Self-Test No. 13

Explain the weaknesses, if any, in the following arguments.

1. I wouldn't take his word for anything, if I were you. His father has been convicted for fraud, and you know what they say: Like father, like son.

2. *Survivor* is the best show on television. It must be the best because it gets higher ratings than any other show.

3. Many mathematicians used to believe that formal logic could provide a foundation for the whole of mathematics. But they were wrong. Their view was decisively refuted by Kurt Gödel in his famous paper published in 1931.

4. How can anyone seriously believe in evolution? I certainly don't. How can you take seriously a theory that claims that humans are just monkeys with less hair and that our ancestors were apes?

5. I'm fed up with the feminist movement. I used to think they had some valid concerns, but they are just another special-interest group who are upset because they aren't getting all the good jobs. They talk a lot about justice but it all comes down to selfishness.

6. Throughout recorded history, the family unit has always had a single head, usually the father, but sometimes the mother or a grandparent. But in recent years this tradition has been challenged by those who think that the mother and father can be equal partners. Do these people really think that their limited perspective is better than the wisdom of history? The idea is preposterous.

7. I hate flying, and I don't see why everyone thinks I'm just being silly. Look at Janine. She hates flying as much as I do.

8. My son wants to be an opera singer, but he'll have to do it without any support from me. I've tried to persuade him to go into something useful, like business or law, but he insists on being a singer. He seems to think that everybody should be free to do whatever they want in life. Well, where would we be if everybody did whatever they wanted? That's what I said to him when he told me he wanted to study music at university. And his only response was to walk out of the room.

9. For years francophone (French-speaking) Quebeckers had to put up with an economy that was dominated by anglophones (English speakers). Often they could not even get a job, and usually could never get a promotion, unless they spoke good English. The shoe is now on the other foot. Now, because of the measures adopted by the Quebec government, anglophones are finding that

they are barred from many jobs unless they can speak good French. In my view, this is entirely justified. Let the anglophones suffer for a change.

10. (BACKGROUND: A schoolteacher resigned his position, charging that the principal persistently treated him in an unfair and arbitrary manner. A school board official gave the following response.)
We conducted a thorough investigation to determine whether or not there is any validity to the charge, and we have concluded that there is not. The teacher in question seems to have embarked upon a campaign to undermine the authority of the principal. It is not clear whether his reasons for doing so were ideological or personal, but in either case he seems to have been a troublemaker.

11. (BACKGROUND: A cabinet minister in the House of Commons responding to complaints that a new government program is more expensive than it was supposed to be because of inefficiencies.)
Naturally, I would expect this member of the opposition to complain about these things. She objected to the program when it was first proposed, argued against it both in the House and in the media, and voted against it when it was passed in the legislature. She just won't accept that this is a valuable program.

12. The Prime Minister promised that infrastructure development would reduce unemployment, stimulate the economy, and improve the standard of living for the poor. This is a ridiculous, simple-minded policy, for it doesn't address the need to develop international trade, reduce taxes, or reduce the national debt.

7.6 Questions for Discussion

Each of the following arguments relies upon a premise that might be regarded as irrelevant. Identify the offending premise and suggest an argument that shows it is irrelevant.

1. There are no absolute values, i.e., no values that are valid for all times and all places. To see this you only have to look at the wide variety of values that have been held by other societies and at earlier times in our history. Pick any value you like: there will be some society somewhere that has rejected it. You simply cannot find a value that has been valid at all times and all places.

2. Although there are no strict proofs that God exists, it is still rational to believe that He does exist. Suppose God does exist: in this case heaven and hell exist and God will send unbelievers to hell for eternity, while believers stand a good chance of going to heaven. Obviously it is rational to do whatever is necessary to avoid hell and to get to heaven, so it is rational to believe in God if He actually exists. On the other hand, suppose God doesn't exist: in this case there is no heaven or hell, so even if we believe He exists, we run no risk of

being punished for having a false belief. It is rational, therefore, to believe in God even if He does not exist. So it is rational to believe God exists, whether He exists or not.

3. The Israeli government should accept the right of Palestinians to a national homeland, because otherwise the Palestinians will continue their campaign of terrorism indefinitely. Israel will never have peace until it recognizes this right.

4. Recently, a number of manufacturers have begun marketing so-called green products, i.e., products that are supposed to be environmentally friendly. The supermarket shelves are now full of them, everything from detergent to peanut butter. These companies seem to think that these products will show their concern for the environment. This is absurd. They have developed these products not because they care about the environment but because they think they can make more money. Sadly, they probably will make more money because the public wants to help preserve the environment and thinks that buying green products will make a difference. But don't be fooled into thinking that these manufacturers care about the environment. It is profit, pure and simple, that motivates them.

5. There are a few people who believe that prostitution is morally acceptable, but in fact it is immoral behaviour. It is contrary to the accepted standards of our community as reflected in public opinion and in the legal system. The vast majority of Canadians strongly believe that prostitution is immoral and therefore quite properly reject any proposal to legalize prostitution.

6. Why does the public get so upset when people refuse to render assistance to someone in need? That incident last month where a woman was beaten in a park by her boyfriend while several hundred people looked on and did nothing produced a great outpouring of righteous indignation. But I can't for the life of me see why everyone gets so upset at the bystanders. According to the law, these people did nothing illegal, since the law imposes no duty on ordinary citizens to go to the aid of someone who is in distress. That's what the law says, so I don't see that the bystanders did anything wrong at all.

8.   Assessing Adequacy

8.1 The Criterion of Adequacy

Our third criterion of a sound argument is that its premises should be adequate to support its conclusion. We need this criterion because even if an argument satisfies the first two criteria (i.e., each premise is acceptable and relevant to the conclusion), the set of premises may nevertheless be inadequate to support the conclusion. Clearly, an argument with premises that are inadequate to support its conclusion suffers from a major weakness. Relying on premises that are inadequate to support a conclusion is sometimes called jumping to conclusions, or reaching a hasty conclusion.

We saw in section 5.2.1 that adequacy is a matter of degree. In this respect the criterion of adequacy differs from the first two criteria. If the premises of an argument are *unacceptable*, then they give us no reason to think that its conclusion is true. Again, if the premises are *irrelevant*, then they give us no reason to think that the conclusion is true. But if the premises are inadequate, they may still provide some support for the conclusion, although this support may be too weak or inadequate to make the conclusion acceptable. The fact that premises may be partly but not entirely adequate to support a conclusion is often reflected in the tentative way we assert the conclusion. For example:

> *Look at those dark clouds on the horizon. We might be in for some rain, so maybe we should head back to the car.*

Notice the tentative nature of the inference. By using the words might and maybe, the speaker is acknowledging that the evidence is not conclusive. Suppose, however, the argument had been:

> *Look at those dark clouds on the horizon. It's going to rain, and if we don't head back to the car right away, we're going to get soaked.*

Here, the inference is not tentative at all. The speaker is arguing that the dark clouds mean that it will rain, and since, as we all know, the presence of dark clouds on the horizon does not always mean that it will rain, the argument violates the criterion of adequacy.

When assessing the adequacy of the premises of any argument, therefore, we always need to look for the degree of strength that the argument claims to have. If it claims to *establish* or *prove* its conclusion, it is more likely that it may violate the criterion of adequacy. If its conclusion is presented tentatively, it is less likely to violate the criterion. It is important to interpret an argument with this question in mind before asking whether it violates the criterion of adequacy. Frequently, it is unclear what degree of strength a speaker is claiming for an argument, and we have to rely upon the contextual clues and the principle of charity when interpreting the argument.

However, we also need to make a judgement regarding the degree of support the premises actually provide for the conclusion, as opposed to the degree of support that is claimed by the speaker. This degree of support can range from none to a great deal and may fall anywhere in between. When an argument violates the criterion of adequacy, it may be because the premises provide no support for the conclusion, or it may be because the premises provide some, although not enough, support to justify accepting the conclusion. Thus, many arguments that violate the criterion of adequacy can easily be amended to meet the criterion by changing the wording of the conclusion to reflect the degree of support actually provided by the premises. This is what we did in the above example. To determine the degree of support provided by a set of premises, we need to examine the full context and use whatever relevant background knowledge we possess in order to make the best judgement we can.

Once we have decided, however, that an argument violates the criterion of adequacy, we must be prepared to say why the premises are inadequate to support the conclusion. The reasons we offer will depend upon the content of the argument. In the above example, we pointed out that a few dark clouds on the horizon do not always mean that it is going to rain. In other cases we will explain the inadequacy of the premises by pointing out other relevant factors. For example:

> *Steve always got A's in high school, so we expect him to get high marks in university.*

> *All Margot's classmates think that Mr. Braithwaite is a great teacher, so I'm sure she does too.*

The fact that Steve always got A's in high school provides some support for concluding that he will get high marks in university, but, as many of us know to our sorrow, it is no guarantee. And that Margot's classmates think Mr. Braithwaite is a great teacher is no guarantee that she agrees with them. We would have to know more about both Margot and Mr. Braithwaite to know how much support this argument provides for its conclusion.

When assessing the adequacy of an argument, it is sometimes important to take account of what the consequences would be if the conclusion turns out to be false or unacceptable. If we are considering major surgery, the consequences could be very serious if the operation fails; in a matter as important as this, we should normally demand a very high standard of adequacy, and it would therefore be reasonable to seek a second medical opinion. But when an auto mechanic recommends that we use higher octane gasoline, the relative unimportance of the consequences, if it turns out to be bad advice, means that it would normally be inappropriate to demand a second opinion.

Jumping to conclusions, and thus violating the criterion of adequacy, is the product of a very widespread human tendency. We have a small amount of relevant evidence and cannot resist claiming that we have a good argument, or even a proof. We all know of cases like the following:

> *Classical music is terrible; I sang in the school choir for a year, and we had to do some really boring classical music.*

> *Sure, I believe in astrology. The day I broke my leg my horoscope said I should avoid risky situations, but I went skiing anyway. After that, I started taking it seriously.*

Additionally, there are practical reasons why we might act on a conclusion that is not adequately supported by the evidence at hand; in such cases, we might be aware that the available evidence is weak, but the consequences of acting or not acting are such that we accept the inference. For example, if someone tells you they once read that eating potatoes with green patches under the skin can cause cancer, then you might accept the conclusion even though this is very weak evidence. It is easy to avoid eating these potatoes, and the consequences of not accepting the conclusion, if it is true, are very serious. We can say in this case that the cost of a false negative is low, and the danger of a true positive is high; therefore, the conclusion is accepted for practical reasons. Also, anyone who comes to the hospital complaining of chest pains is treated as if they are having a heart attack, even though chest pains alone are weak evidence of a heart attack. There is no real harm in being cautious with every complaint of chest pain, but there may be a serious, preventable harm if an actual chest pain is left untreated while they wait for more conclusive evidence of a heart attack. Again, the cost of a false negative is low, and the danger of a true positive is sufficiently high that the conclusion is accepted for practical reasons.

There seems to be no limit to the different ways in which we can violate the criterion of adequacy, but it is possible to identify two generic criteria of adequacy. The first and most stringent generic criterion is called deductive validity, which is explained in Chapter 9. The second generic criterion, inductive strength is explained in Chapter 10. For the rest of this chapter, however, we will concentrate on a few familiar types of argument where determining the adequacy of the premises raises special difficulties.

8.2 Appeals to Authority (2)

In section 7.3 we saw that appeals to authority are relevant in circumstances where we lack information or experience that is needed for some decision and which we are unable to obtain for ourselves directly. But not all appeals to authority are equally strong. The adequacy of any appeal to authority depends upon a number of factors, all of which must be taken into account. There are five criteria we should use when determining the adequacy of any appeal to authority.

1. THE AUTHORITY MUST BE IDENTIFIED. The reason for insisting that an authority must be identified is obvious: if we don't know who the authority is, we cannot determine whether he or she is reliable. Using an *anonymous* authority undermines the very purpose of citing an authority at all. An expert's acknowledged good judgement in previous situations gives us reason to be confident in their judgement in the situation at hand. We must beware of unnamed authorities because we have no way to know the track record that justifies the appeal in the first place.

2. THE AUTHORITY MUST BE GENERALLY RECOGNIZED BY THE EXPERTS IN THE FIELD. The characteristics someone must have to be an authority depend upon the particular field in question. In some fields there are licensing requirements that are intended to ensure an appropriate level of expertise, as in medicine, dentistry, and many other professions. In fields where there are no licensing requirements, there are often generally accepted standards of expertise, such as a PhD or a diploma in auto mechanics. Meeting licensing requirements or accepted standards, however, does not by itself guarantee that what an expert says is true. There are "qualified" crackpots in every field. The best general test is whether the expert is generally recognized as an expert by other experts in the field. Beware of authorities who lack the support of their fellow-experts.

3. THE PARTICULAR MATTER IN SUPPORT OF WHICH AN AUTHORITY IS CITED MUST LIE WITHIN HIS OR HER FIELD OF EXPERTISE. No one is an expert on everything, and the authority that experts can legitimately claim is limited to their field of expertise. Bank presidents are presumably experts on banking, but when they make pronouncements on what is a fair tax system they probably lack the relevant kind of expertise. Beware of authorities who make claims beyond their area of expertise.

4. THE FIELD MUST BE ONE IN WHICH THERE IS GENUINE KNOWLEDGE. In certain fields individuals may have a great deal of experience, but this experience does not produce genuine knowledge. By genuine knowledge we mean a systematically ordered body of facts and principles that are objective in nature. In this sense, an experienced novelist may not have any knowledge of how to write a good novel and may be an abysmal teacher. In some fields there is no expertise: experience may produce familiarity but no genuine knowledge and hence no expertise. Experience is sometimes not merely the best but the only teacher. Beware of authorities who pretend to have expertise in a field in which there is no genuine knowledge.

5. **THERE SHOULD BE A CONSENSUS AMONG THE EXPERTS IN THE FIELD REGARDING THE PARTICULAR MATTER IN SUPPORT OF WHICH THE AUTHORITY IS CITED.** In virtually every field of knowledge there are some controversial issues. This is true in mathematics, law, medicine, economics, accountancy, and molecular biology, as well as in plumbing, wine-making, and coaching athletes. Such controversies mean that on that particular issue there is no knowledge, even though the field in general may have a secure knowledge base. Always be cautious when authorities disagree among themselves.

When deciding whether an appeal to an authority is adequate, we should always apply these criteria as best we can. In practice, it is sometimes difficult to gather the information that would show they have all been satisfied, but at the very least we should always look for evidence that one or more criteria is not met. To the extent that the criteria are not satisfied by some authority, we should reduce our reliance upon that authority, especially when there is something important at stake. We can be forgiven if we accept the authority of our grandmother that chewing a garlic bud will stave off a cold, but it would be foolish in the extreme to accept our horoscope as an authority on whether to undergo surgery.

8.3 Appeals to Ignorance

Sometimes people defend a claim by appealing to the fact that there is no evidence that it is false. By itself this is a completely inadequate reason, for it assumes that in some mysterious way the absence of evidence that something is false supports the claim that it is true. For example:

> *I believe in astrology and always read my horoscope in the paper every day. I can't actually prove that it is true, but nobody can disprove it.*

In fact, the absence of evidence against something is by itself never a good reason for believing it. Otherwise, we would have a good reason to believe all sorts of silly things. For example:

> *The world will come to an end at exactly 12:00 noon EST on a Saturday.*

> *There are seven invisible leprechauns living in my garden.*

> *Bill Clinton was never the president of the United States. The real Bill Clinton died in his sleep in 1991, but his body was taken over by creatures from outer space.*

None of these statements can be disproved, even though there is no evidence that they are true.

In certain contexts, however, the absence of contrary evidence can be a good supporting reason for a conclusion. If we have some evidence that supports a claim, then the absence of contrary evidence does add some additional support. This additional support is even stronger if we have actually looked for contrary evidence and failed to find any. This is what medical doctors sometimes do when faced with a condition that is difficult to diagnose. The symptoms suggest the patient has a certain disease; a test is performed that could prove that the patient does not have that disease, but the test result is negative. The absence of this piece of contrary evidence is then used as additional support for the initial diagnosis. The legitimacy of the appeal to the absence of contrary evidence in such cases, however, usually requires that there be some direct supporting evidence. And even then, the additional support it provides is usually only of secondary importance. Thus, the tree diagram for an argument with an appeal to the absence of contrary evidence as a premise would have to be a T-argument structure, since it only provides support when joined to other premises. Even in cases where such an appeal is relevant, however, its adequacy as a supporting premise should be assessed by appeal to the criterion of adequacy in the usual way.

8.4 The Slippery Slope Fallacy

We often want to assess a proposal to take some action or adopt a new policy. One important and legitimate way of doing so is to examine the consequences that would result if the action were taken or the policy adopted. If the action or policy is likely to lead to undesirable consequences, then we have a good reason to reject it, and if it is likely to lead to desirable consequences, then we have a good reason to support it. This method of assessment involves making predictions about the future, and it is important to realize that such predictions are always somewhat tentative. Even when there is a wealth of empirical support for predictions we know how easily they can be wrong: think of weather forecasts and stock market predictions. There is one important aspect of predictions that needs to be noted. When we chain predictions together in the following way:

A will probably lead to B; B will probably lead to C; C will probably lead to D; D will probably lead to E, and E will probably lead to F;

we are not entitled to conclude that A will probably lead to F. This is because when we multiply probabilities, the resulting probability is always reduced. There may be a 50 per cent chance that the next person to walk around the corner will be a woman, and a 50 per cent chance that the woman will be married, but that means that there is only a 25 per cent chance that the next person to walk around the corner will be a married woman. So if each of the probabilities between A and F is 80 per cent, the probability that A will lead to F is only 33 per cent. Clearly, to conclude that A will probably lead to F would be a mistake. Such arguments commit the SLIPPERY SLOPE FALLACY. The premises of a slippery slope argument present a chain of predictions each of which may be very strong, but the chain as a whole is weak. The conclusion of such an argument is not adequately supported.

Usually, however, when we make a chain of predictions we cannot, or do not bother to, assign numerical probabilities to each step in the chain. But it is clear that even a chain of "pretty likely" predictions will become weaker as it becomes longer. And if, as often happens, one step in the chain violates the criterion of acceptability, then the prediction of the final outcome will be very weak indeed. For example:

If abortion on demand were to become legal, there would be a great increase in abortions. And once abortion became commonplace, there would be a weakening of respect for human life in general. Once the respect for human life was weakened, we would see an increase in euthanasia of all kinds: the elderly, the mentally handicapped, and the physically disabled. Before long we would be getting rid of anyone who is unproductive. In short, it would threaten our civilization. Therefore, we should oppose any move to broaden the grounds for legal abortions.

This is a clear example of a slippery slope fallacy. Which step is the weakest in the chain is debatable, for none of them is very strong. But the second step—that if abortions become commonplace, there would be a weakening of respect for human life in general—seems especially weak. It might be true that there would be a weakening of respect for human life in general, but there is very little evidence to support this claim.

This example shows another common characteristic of slippery slope arguments: they often omit some of the steps in the chain. It is possible that if society began to get rid of anyone who is unproductive, our civilization would be threatened, but clearly there must be a number of intermediate steps, which the argument omits. There are missing premises that would have to be supplied in order to undertake a complete assessment of the argument.

Sometimes slippery slope arguments omit all the intermediate steps in the chain. For example:

You should never drink during the day. Once you start doing that, you will end up as a skid-row bum.

The only charitable interpretation of this argument is to regard it as having a series of missing premises that would provide the intermediate steps in the chain. Of course, it is difficult to assess a series of missing premises of this sort. All we can do is use our own knowledge to decide whether the chain would be a strong one if it were spelled out in detail. (And there are some cases in which the slope genuinely is slippery. Alcoholics who stop drinking are aware that one drink really can lead to disaster, because they find it so difficult to stop after the first one.)

Slippery slope arguments are superficially similar to another kind of argument that is not open to the same kind of objection. Sometimes we explore the consequences of a policy by predicting the different consequences that would arise if we were to adopt the policy. Here our reasoning is as follows:

A (the policy) will probably lead to B; A will probably lead to C; A will probably lead to D; A will probably lead to E, and A will probably lead to F.

If these consequences are bad we will reject the policy, and if they are good we will accept the policy. But we need to note that each of these predicted consequences is independent of the others, and thus they do not constitute a *chain* of predictions. Chained predictions can be diagrammed as follows:

A ⟶ B ⟶ C ⟶ D ⟶ E ⟶ F

We are now considering a series of independent predictions that are diagrammed as follows:

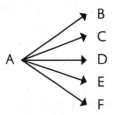

It is important to understand the crucial difference between the two types of reasoning. In slippery slope arguments, our interest is in the last item in the chain, and it, as we have seen, is vulnerable to the weakness that results from the cumulative effect of each step being only probable. But when we work out a series of independent predictions, our interest is in all the predictions taken together. Any weaknesses in our predictions are therefore not cumulative. In slippery slope arguments, a single false prediction breaks the chain, whereas a single false prediction in a series of independent predictions leaves the others intact. An argument whose conclusion rests on a series of independent predictions thus is not a slippery slope argument.

Sometimes an argument that commits the slippery slope fallacy will not at first appear to be a slippery slope argument because the author uses another metaphor. In particular, arguments that invoke a *domino effect* or arguments claiming that one action is the *thin edge of the wedge* have the same logical structure of slippery slope arguments. Because they have this structure, they commit the slippery slope fallacy. Here are two more slippery slope arguments. Note that the first is part of a reductio ad absurdum argument:

Revenue Canada's recent decision that many of the perks employers give their employees are taxable benefits is a silly and dangerous precedent. It is one thing to tax food and lodging when it is routinely provided by employers. But now they are going after things like free parking. Next will be the pencils and paper clips we all take home from work. Then it will be office Christmas parties: there will be auditors hovering, clipboards in hand, keeping track of how many free drinks and peanuts we have consumed. And when they realize that for many of us the greatest perk is being able to daydream on the job, they will even begin to tax our dreams.

Everyone accepts the general principle that lying is immoral. Many people also believe that some exceptions to the rule are permitted. This, of course, raises the question of what these exceptions should be. People always start with the easy ones: we should be prepared to lie, they say, if it is the only way of preventing the death of an innocent person, and they point to examples such as lying to the Gestapo to protect Jews. But then, they argue, since lying in these cases is justified, surely it is justified to tell lies to protect your country in wartime; for example, when captured by the enemy. And then, of course, lying would be justified to protect your country in peacetime, and so also must lying to protect your government. It is then but a very short step to lying to protect your reputation if you happen to be a government official. Once you allow that any lie is capable of being justified, you are inexorably led to telling lies whenever you feel like it.

8.5 Causal Fallacies

We now come to a group of fallacies that often arise when reasoning about causes. But first we need to say something about the concept of causation. The idea of a cause is an extremely elusive concept, and a great deal of philosophical and scientific energy has been devoted to giving an adequate account of it. Scientists often avoid the term altogether and refer instead to correlations between variables. It is clear, however, that these correlations are intended to reveal causal factors (see section 11.1). These causal factors can best be expressed as statements of necessary and sufficient causal conditions in the way described in section 3.8.

It is misleading to speak of an event as having a single cause, for there are always a large number of causal conditions involved in any event. When we ask, *What caused the explosion at the mill?* we are not usually looking for a complete causal explanation of the explosion. We don't want to know about the various necessary conditions (the presence of oxygen, the presence of a combustible gas, etc.). We are usually looking for the one condition that, along with these necessary conditions, is sufficient to cause the explosion. In explaining the causal fallacies, we shall simplify the causal picture by assuming that events have only a single cause. It is possible to explain these fallacies without this simplifying assumption, but the explanations would be extremely cumbersome. The nature of the fallacies is the same in either case.

8.5.1 POST HOC

If A causes B then A must occur before B occurs, since the cause must always precede the effect. If watering and fertilizing a house plant causes it to bloom, then we have to water and fertilize it before we can expect it to bloom. But the fact that a cause must always precede its effect does not mean that everything that precedes some event must be its cause. It is a necessary, but not a sufficient, condition of a cause that it must precede its effect. If we forget this distinction, we can be led to commit the fallacy of POST HOC. The name comes from the Latin phrase *post hoc ergo propter hoc*, which means *after this therefore because of this*. The fallacy of post hoc is committed when it is argued that something that occurs before some event must be its cause. For example:

> The stove in your apartment was working perfectly until you moved in, but the next day the oven stopped working. It must be something you're doing that has caused the problem.

This inference is obviously fallacious. It is possible that the landlord's conclusion is correct, but the argument provides very little support for it.

Here are some more examples of post hoc fallacies:

> In the 1960s the trend towards married women working outside the home began to emerge. Within a few years we began to see a significant increase in the divorce rate, which has now reached alarming proportions. Obviously, if we value the family as an institution, we should try to prevent married women from working outside the home.

> I tried some Russian caviar at Mattie's cocktail party last Saturday and was so sick when I got home that I got almost no sleep that night. There must have been something wrong with the caviar or else I'm allergic to the stuff.

> In Aesop's fable, the rooster reasoned as follows: Every morning without fail, the sun rises just a few minutes after I start crowing. I must be the greatest creature in the world since I cause the sun to rise every day.

8.5.2 CONFUSING CAUSE AND EFFECT

If A causes B, then whenever A is present (under the appropriate circumstances) we will find B as well. If inflation causes unemployment, then wherever we find inflation we should also find unemployment. This fact can sometimes make it difficult to know which is the cause and which is the effect. The fallacy of CONFUSING CAUSE AND EFFECT is committed when an effect is identified as a cause and the cause is identified as the effect. For example:

> According to a recent Statscan report, married couples with no children have approximately 20 per cent more disposable income than married couples with children. This shows that it is affluence which causes declining birth rates.

The conclusion of this argument is not as well supported by the premise as the conclusion that having children leads people to have less disposable income. It is, of course, *possible* that affluence causes declining birth rates, but not very likely.

Here are some more examples of arguments that commit (or seem to commit) the fallacy of confusing cause and effect:

As the population of dark spotted moths grew larger throughout the Industrial Revolution in nineteenth-century England, smog and air pollution in the country grew worse. Therefore, the increasing number of dark spotted moths was the source of the smog and air pollution.

Did you notice at the party last night that, as soon as Kevin and Paula arrived, she told him not to drink too much, and then Kevin proceeded to get really drunk? That always seems to happen when they are at a party together: she always complains about his drinking, and he always gets drunk. If only she would shut up about it, he probably wouldn't get drunk at all.

Most people are afraid of hospitals. They have friends and relatives who have gone into hospital for routine surgery or for some tests and then either died or came down with some chronic debilitating illness. In fact, when you come to think of it, almost everyone who dies seems to die in a hospital. Hospitals really are dangerous places.

8.5.3 COMMON CAUSE

One reason why A and B may always occur together is that one of them causes the other (either A causes B or B causes A). But there may be another explanation: it may be that A and B are each caused by some third event, C. In these cases, if we ignore C, we can easily misinterpret the causal relationship. The fallacy of COMMON CAUSE is committed when it is claimed that there is a causal relation between A and B when in fact both A and B are caused by a third factor, C. For example:

During the trial of a 17-year-old Toronto youth accused of raping and then murdering a 26-year-old suburban housewife, the prosecution presented evidence that the youth had a large collection of pornography hidden in the attic of his home. He had over 500 magazines of what is normally classified as hard-core pornography, and 37 pornographic video-cassettes. Before passing sentence, the judge made the following observation: "If anyone still needs persuading that pornography causes violence against women, this case provides conclusive proof."

The relationship between pornography and violence is a complex one, and we cannot say that the judge's conclusion is false. But the judge's evidence is quite weak. The evidence cited is probably better interpreted as showing that the youth's fascination with pornography and his crime were both caused by some underlying psychological factor.

Here are some more arguments that commit (or seem to commit) the fallacy of common cause:

Recent studies have shown that people who are commonly regarded as being successful have much larger vocabularies than average. This is no accident. Having an extensive vocabulary is an important factor in producing success.

The solution to the problem of poverty in Canada is obvious. People who live below the poverty line normally have very little education: more than half have less than a grade eight education. Therefore, the way to overcome poverty is to provide incentives and encouragement for poor people to go back to school to complete their education.

The best way to clear up the sinus congestion that usually accompanies a sore throat is to get rid of the sore throat by taking some of those medicated throat lozenges you can get at the drug store. After all, it's the sore throat that causes the congestion: haven't you noticed that you always get a sore throat just before your head gets stuffed up?

8.6 Self-Test No. 14

Explain any weaknesses in the following arguments:

1. They say there is no proof that living near nuclear power plants causes birth defects. Well, my sister-in-law, who lives only two kilometres from the Pickering nuclear power plant, had a miscarriage last year, and they can't prove that it wasn't caused by the power plant.

2. A recent study showed that students who cram immediately before examinations usually get lower grades than those who do not. Well, I certainly won't make that mistake this term. I'm not even going to open a book during the exam period.

3. Our major objection to the free trade deal with the United States is not with the short- and medium-term consequences, since it is likely that, on balance, Canada will benefit economically. Our concern is with the long term. Gradually, our governments will lose the ability to interfere in the market place in ways designed to benefit the people of Canada, unless the US government approves. Each time the government capitulates to US pressure, it will be another nail in the coffin of Canadian independence, and the final outcome will be the complete loss of Canadian sovereignty.

4. I was in good health until they started that darn fluoridation program. Within a few weeks I started getting an upset stomach every day or two, and within three months I was having really bad stomach cramps. I went to the doctor, who discovered that I had a duodenal ulcer. The doctor treated me, of course, but I knew what I needed to do—start drinking bottled water, which I

do now. That was two years ago, and I've been fine ever since. But it just goes to show how dangerous fluoridation is.

5. The high-school drop-out rate in Ontario has declined by more than 50 per cent since 1950. During the same period, there has been an increase of about 40 per cent in the rate of juvenile delinquency. I can't believe this is a mere coincidence. Clearly, we should have higher academic standards in school to force the weaker students out and into the real world where they will develop a sense of responsibility.

6. Pope Benedict XVI is one of the most learned pontiffs ever, and he has spent years studying and thinking about what is best for the Roman Catholic church. If he believes that it would be wrong to admit women into the priesthood, then we should accept his judgement.

7. (Comments by a city politician on a proposal that the city should fund a drop-in centre for unemployed workers.)
I would be prepared to support the proposal if I thought there was a need for it. But I really don't see that there is a need. I get phone calls from taxpayers about all sorts of things, but I cannot recall ever getting a phone call from anyone suggesting we need such a centre.

8. All the public opinion polls for the last year have shown that the government has a lower approval rating than either of the two opposition parties. So the Premier obviously knows the government is not going to be re-elected and will postpone calling the election until the last possible moment.

9. Last weekend there was a large demonstration in front of the US Consulate by people protesting against US involvement in the middle east. There were so many people that they spilled out all over the northbound lanes of University Avenue, and the police had to re-route traffic. Like many other innocent people, I was seriously inconvenienced by the inconsiderate behaviour of the demonstrators. The incident has convinced me that the time has come to ban all demonstrations on public property.

10. If some of the poorest developing nations are released from their debts, then other poor, developing countries will also want their debts forgiven, too. And if all the national debts of these poor countries are forgiven, then they won't feel obliged to pay back loans in the future. After a while wealthy countries won't see the point of paying off their own debts, and all the lending institutions will be bled dry. So we can't release very poor countries from their debts without crippling the global economy.

11. Our family physician says that marijuana should not be decriminalized for medical use because it has no real value for treating any physical condition.

According to him, people who want to decriminalize it just want to get high, not help people with medical problems. With 30 years of medical training and practice behind him, that's enough for me. We shouldn't trust these people who are lobbying to decriminalize marijuana.

12. "This bill and the foregoing remarks of the majority remind me of an old Arabian proverb: 'If the camel once gets his nose in the tent, his body will soon follow.' If adopted, the legislation will mark the inception of aid, supervision, and ultimately control of education in this country by the federal authorities." (US Senator Barry Goldwater)

8.7 Questions for Discussion

Discuss the strengths and weaknesses of the following arguments:

1. Almost all military experts hold that we must have standing armies because of the continuing threat of war. The reality is quite different: the continuing threat of war is caused by the existence of standing armies.

2. There has been a great deal of criticism recently of the quality of high-school education in Alberta. People seem to think the quality is declining. But the statistics don't bear this out; in fact they show that quality is increasing. The average grades of high-school graduates have increased by at least 10 per cent since 1977.

3. People who believe they have a duty to help those who are less fortunate than themselves almost always get pleasure from their unselfish actions. This just proves that it is the expectation of pleasure which causes people to act morally or to adopt their moral beliefs.

4. Athletes who earn multi-million-dollar salaries deserve them. Those who are so critical of these "astronomical" salaries conveniently overlook two reasons that make such salaries entirely justified. First, these athletes are supremely talented. They are able to perform better than almost everyone else, including most other athletes. Second, they have only a few short years to make their fortune, since in most cases they will have retired from professional sport by their mid-thirties. To compare their salaries with what most people earn you would have to spread athletes' million-dollar salaries out over 40 years to make the comparison fair.

5. Ken is the leading scorer on the university hockey team this year. He is averaging one goal per game this year whereas last year he scored only three goals in the entire season. He claims that what made the difference is that he found God last summer; before each game he prays to God to give him the strength

and concentration to score at least one goal. Well, maybe he's right, and we should try to get the rest of the team to get religion. If it works for Ken, who is to say it won't work for the other players.

6. The [federal] Liberal government plans to endorse same-sex marriage based on a lower-court ruling in Ontario. Once it does, the well-defined definition of traditional marriage in Canada will be forever altered. The following letter responds to the debate:

> If we allow people to marry without regard to their sex, who is to say that we can't discriminate on the basis of number? It is a small step then to legal-izing polygamy.
> Once we open up marriage beyond the boundary of one man and one woman only, there will be no difference based on the Charter of Rights and Freedoms between gay marriage and polygamous marriage (Letter to the edi-tor, *Globe and Mail*, June 19, 2003).

9.   Deductive Reasoning

In this and the next chapter we consider two types of reasoning, each of which has distinctive features and that therefore requires special treatment. Both of these types still rely upon the three criteria of a sound argument for assessment, but the application of the criteria requires a detailed understanding of how these arguments work.

9.1 The Nature of Deductive Reasoning

In section 1.2, we defined logical strength as the property of an argument whose premises, if true, support its conclusion. We also pointed out that logical strength is a matter of degree, and we distinguished deductive and inductive arguments on that basis: deductive arguments are those whose premises guarantee the truth of the conclusion, and inductive arguments are those whose premises make it reasonable to accept the conclusion but do not absolutely guarantee its truth. To understand the nature of deductive reasoning, it is essential to understand the fundamental difference between the two types of reasoning.

Most of the logically strong arguments we have considered so far in this book have been inductive arguments, i.e., arguments that do not provide absolute guarantees. This is not necessarily a weakness, for in many cases the most we can expect of an argument is a degree of strength that falls somewhat short of constituting an absolute guarantee. Consider the following inductive argument:

The Gordon Street bridge is regularly inspected by qualified engineers.
Vehicles have been driving over it for years.
Therefore, it will be safe to drive over it tomorrow.

This is a logically strong argument, but it does not provide an absolute guarantee that it will be safe to drive over the bridge tomorrow. There is a remote possibility that it will collapse at the very moment I cross it. If the premises are true, then the conclusion will very likely, or probably, or almost certainly, be true; but the truth of the premises cannot absolutely rule out the possibility that the conclusion will be false. In other words, the conclusion might turn out to be false even though the premises are true.

But deductive arguments are not like this. The conclusion of a logically strong deductive argument cannot possibly be false if its premises are true. Consider the following argument:

> *If you are under the age of 18, then you are legally a minor.*
> *If you are legally a minor, then you cannot be sued.*
> *Therefore, if you are under the age of 18, then you cannot be sued.*

Unlike the argument about the Gordon Street bridge, it is impossible for the conclusion of this argument to be false unless at least one of the premises is also false. If its premises are true, the truth of the conclusion is guaranteed.

Logically strong deductive arguments are able to guarantee, or conclusively establish, their conclusions because the logical strength of deductive arguments does not depend upon their specific content, but on their form or structure. Consider another example of a deductive argument:

> *If Sadie lost her purse, then she lost her student ID card.*
> *If she lost her student ID card, then she won't be allowed to write her exams.*
> *Therefore, if Sadie lost her purse, then she won't be allowed to write her exams.*

This argument has the same logical form or structure as the previous example. This form can be expressed as follows:

> If p then q.
> If q then r.
> Therefore, if p then r.

What is significant about these arguments is not merely that they have the same form but that their logical strength is derived from their form. If we ask why the premises provide strong support for the conclusion, we can ignore the particular content of the arguments because the facts about being under 18 or losing ID cards have no bearing on the logical strength of the argument. It is the form of the argument (i.e., the form or structure of the premises and conclusion and the formal relationships among them) that makes these arguments strong. They are strong arguments *because* of their form. This means that *every* argument with this form will be a logically strong argument. It is their form that determines their strength.

9.2 Truth-Functional Statements

Deductive reasoning relies upon what are called TRUTH-FUNCTIONAL STATEMENTS: every deductive argument includes at least one truth-functional statement. In order to understand deductive reasoning, therefore, it is necessary to understand what a truth-functional statement is. All statements can be divided into two classes: simple and complex. A SIMPLE STATEMENT is one that does not contain any other statement as a part, and a COMPLEX STATEMENT is one that contains another statement as a component part. Here are some simple statements:

Virginia got a job with the Bank of Montreal in 1973.

I lost the keys.

Mark has had a great deal of experience dealing with emotionally disturbed children.

Shirley loves him.

Here are some complex statements with the component statements underlined:

<u>Virginia got a job with the Bank of Montreal in 1973,</u> and <u>she became a vice-president after 22 years.</u>

Either <u>I lost the keys,</u> or <u>they have been stolen.</u>

It is false that <u>Mark has had a great deal of experience dealing with emotionally disturbed children.</u>

Tom believes that <u>Shirley loves him.</u>

Truth-functional statements are a sub-class of complex statements that are distinguished by the way their truth is determined. Ordinarily, when we want to determine whether a statement is true, we look directly for facts or reasons to tell us whether what the statement says is true. With truth-functional statements, however, the procedure is a little different. We have to proceed indirectly, for the truth of truth-functional statements is determined not by directly seeing whether what *it* says is true but by seeing whether *its components* are true. The truth of truth-functional statements is thus a function of the truth values of its component statements.

Consider the first example given above. It is a truth-function because in order to determine whether it is true, we must separately determine the truth or falsity of its two component statements. If they are both true, then the complex statement will also be true. But if either component is false—either because Virginia did not get a job with the Bank of Montreal in 1973, or because she did not become a vice-president after 22 years—then the statement as a whole will be false. The second example is also a truth-function. Unlike the first example, however, it asserts an *either/or* relationship between its two components. In order for the statement as a whole to be true, only one of the component statements needs to be true. The third example is also a truth-function. It is true only when its component statement is false.

The fourth example, however, is not a truth-function even though it is a complex statement, because its truth is not a function of the truth value of its component statement. Tom might believe that Shirley loves him even when she does not, in which case the statement *Tom believes that Shirley loves him* will be true even though the statement *Shirley loves him* is false. Or, Tom might not believe that Shirley loves him even when she does, in which case the statement as a whole will be false even though the component statement is true.

Each of these truth-functional statements includes what is called a LOGICAL OPERATOR: *and, either/or*, and *it is false that*. The presence of the logical operator is crucial, since it tells us precisely how the truth of the statement as a whole is determined by the truth values of its component statements. The logical operators define the different kinds of truth-functional statements. There are four kinds of truth-functions that are important for understanding deductive reasoning. We shall follow the standard convention in logic and use the letters p, q, r, and so forth, to stand for the component statements, which may be either simple or complex statements.

1. NEGATION: The statement *p is false* is a negation. (Sometimes, negations are written as *not-p*.) A negation is true when its component statement is false, and false when its component statement is true. Thus, the statement *p is false* is true when *p* is false, and false when *p* is true. For example:

   It is false that falcons mate while flying.

This statement is true if the statement *falcons mate while flying* is false. If falcons do mate while flying, then the statement is false.

2. CONJUNCTION: The statement *p and q* is a conjunction. It is true only when *p* is true and *q* is true; it is false when *p* is false, or when *q* is false, or when both *p* and *q* are false. For example:

   Ted and Alice have been married for six years, and they have no children.

This statement is true only if both its component statements, or CONJUNCTS, are true. If either conjunct is false, then the conjunction as a whole is false. If Ted and Alice have been married for only five years, then the statement is false even though it may be true that they have no children. If they have a child, then the statement is false, even though it may be true that they have been married for six years.

3. DISJUNCTION: The statement *p or q* is a disjunction. It is true when *p* is true, or when *q* is true, or when *p and q* are both true; it is false when both *p and q* are false. For example:

Either Mac did it or Bud did it.

This statement is true if either or both of its component statements, or DISJUNCTS, is true. If both disjuncts are false, then the disjunction as a whole is false. If Mac did it, then the statement is true. If Bud did it, then the statement is true. If they both did it, then the statement is true. If neither of them did it, however, the statement is false.

It is important to note that in a disjunctive truth-function the two disjuncts are exhaustive but not exclusive. (Recall the discussion of false dichotomy in section 6.7.4.) This means that the disjuncts cannot both be false, since they are exhaustive, but both may be true, because they are not exclusive. In other words, a sentence such as

Stephen will drive his car or Karen will drive her car

will be true if Stephen drives his car and Karen does not, or if Karen drives her car and Stephen does not, or if both drive their cars; it's only false when neither one drives their own car. This is not how most of us understand disjunctions, however. Ordinarily, we think it is false if both disjuncts are true. But logicians use *or* in a way that suits truth-functional logic but is counter-intuitive to most people. The technical reasons behind this special interpretation of *or* need not detain us, but we need to be aware that this is how truth-functional disjunctions operate.

4. IMPLICATION: The statement *if p then q* is an implication. The two component sentences in an implication have different names since, unlike conjuncts and disjuncts, each plays a different role: the first is called the ANTECEDENT, and the second is called the CONSEQUENT. An implication such as *if p then q* is false only when p is true and q is false; in all other cases (i.e., when p is false, or when q is true), it is true. For example:

If Moe studies hard, then he will get an A average.

This statement is true if both the antecedent and the consequent are true, that is, if Moe studies hard and also gets an A average. And it is clearly false if the antecedent is true while the consequent is false: if Moe studies hard and does not get an A average. But what about the other two possibilities? If both the antecedent and consequent are false—if Moe doesn't study hard and fails to get an A average—logicians regard the original implication as still being true. And if the antecedent is false while the consequent is true—if Moe doesn't study hard and yet does get an A average—logicians also regard the original implication as true. These last two cases are somewhat counter-intuitive. What we want to say is that the original implication *could* still be true in these cases, but not that it *is* true. Logicians admit the oddity but defend it by pointing out that it results from treating implication as a truth-function, and that the power of deductive reasoning is greatly enhanced when implication is given a truth-functional interpretation.

Truth-functional statements are expressed in a variety of ways in English, but it is usually easy to recognize that they are truth-functions. Here are some alternative ways of expressing negations:

It is not true that organized crime is controlled exclusively by the Mafia.

John did not win the Alexander Prize for Physics.

His claim that he was at a concert when the break-in occurred isn't true.

It is easy to see how these statements can be rewritten in the standard *p is false* form.

Here are some truth-functional conjunctions that do not use the word *and* but rely on an equivalent word or phrase:

Sarah always worries about getting poor grades, even though she has never had a grade of less than B+.

The rent on my apartment has increased by 40 per cent in the last ten years, but my income has only increased by 35 per cent during the same period.

Our conference lost more money this year despite the fact that twice as many people attended as last year.

All these statements express truth-functional conjunctions, since each asserts that both its component statements are true.

Here are some disjunctions that are expressed in variant terms:

You should either fix his lawnmower or buy him a new one.

He must have been extremely upset to have trashed his bicycle like that, or maybe he was just drunk.

There are just two possibilities: raising taxes or reducing expenditures.

Each of these statements is clearly equivalent to a disjunction expressed in the standard *p or q* form.

Implications may be expressed in a wide variety of different sentences. For example:

Since your lease has expired, the landlord is free to raise the rent up to the limit set by the Rent Review Board.

Being a teenager these days means that you have to face a tremendous amount of peer pressure.

Anyone who takes horoscopes seriously must be very gullible.

The theory of evolution implies that God did not create human beings in the way described in the Bible.

Whenever the pressure reaches 300 psi, the release valve automatically opens and reduces the pressure to a safe level.

Being wealthy entails having obligations to those who are less fortunate.

If we rewrite these statements in the appropriate *if p then q* form, we can see that their meaning remains the same:

If your lease has expired, then the landlord is free to raise the rent up to the limit set by the Rent Review Board.

If you are a teenager these days, then you have to face a tremendous amount of peer pressure.

If someone takes horoscopes seriously, then that person must be very gullible.

If the theory of evolution is true, then God did not create human beings in the way described in the Bible.

If the pressure reaches 300 psi, then the release valve automatically opens and reduces the pressure to a safe level.

If you are wealthy, then you have obligations to those who are less fortunate.

9.3 Formal Validity and Soundness

The concept of logical strength is central in our approach to the assessment of arguments, since, as we saw in section 5.2.1, it provides the basis for the second and third criteria of a sound argument—acceptability, relevance and adequacy. When applied to deductive arguments, however, the concept of logical strength has narrower meaning than it does when applied to non-deductive arguments. Logical strength is the property of an argument whose premises, if true, provide support for its conclusion. But the support claimed by a deductive argument amounts to a guarantee of the truth of its conclusion. The term *formal validity* is used to describe this special kind of logical strength; a FORMALLY VALID argument is defined as an argument such that, if its premises are true, then its conclusion must also be true. The phrase *must be* in this definition is to be interpreted strictly. Since it expresses the idea of a guarantee, it does not mean *is very probably*, but *is necessarily*.

The concept of validity or formal validity has a corollary that it is useful to note. It follows from the definition of formal validity that a valid argument cannot have true premises and a false conclusion, and this means that if we know that the conclusion of a valid argument is false, then we know that at least one of the premises must be false. Otherwise, the argument would violate the definition of a valid argument.

Notice that the definition of validity does not claim that the premises of a valid argument *are* true, but only that *if* the premises are true then the conclusion must also be true. Conversely, an argument can be valid even if its premises are false, since validity is entirely a structural feature. Saying that an argument is valid thus does not mean that it satisfies the first criterion of a sound argument—that is, that it must have acceptable premises. On the other hand, all valid arguments satisfy the second and third criteria—that is, relevance and adequacy. This is the great strength of deductive reasoning: once we know that a deductive argument is valid, we know that it completely satisfies both the second and third criteria, and we know this simply because the form or structure of the argument constitutes a valid argument form. A valid argument form thus guarantees both that the premises of the argument are relevant to the conclusion and that they are adequate to prove the truth of the conclusion. Let us now identify some of these valid argument forms.

9.4 Valid Argument Forms

A valid argument form is any set of statements such that every argument with that form is a valid argument. In other words, if an argument has a valid argument form, then if its premises are true, its conclusion must also be true. To show that an argument is valid, therefore, we need only to show that it has a valid argument form. There are a great many valid argument forms, but we shall consider only four basic forms from truth-functional logic. They are basic in the sense that they frequently occur in everyday use, and that all other valid argument forms can be derived from these four forms.

1. AFFIRMING THE ANTECEDENT
   If p then q
   p
   Therefore, q

2. DENYING THE CONSEQUENT
   If p then q
   Not-q
   Therefore, not-p

3. CHAIN ARGUMENT
   If p then q
   If q then r
   Therefore, if p then r

4. DISJUNCTIVE SYLLOGISM

Either p or q
Not-p
Therefore, q

Whenever we find an argument whose form is identical to one of these valid argument forms, we know that it must be a valid argument. We identify the form of a deductive argument by reconstructing it. But when reconstructing deductive arguments, we proceed a little differently from the way described in Chapter 4. Consider the following argument:

> *If the police knew that Jones had a motive for the crime, then he would be a suspect. But he is not a suspect, so they obviously don't know that he hated the victim.*

To reconstruct this argument we first need to identify the truth-functional statements and their logical operators. This would give us:

> *<u>If</u> the police knew that Jones had a motive for the crime, <u>then</u> Jones would be a suspect.*
> *Jones is not a suspect.*
> *<u>Therefore</u>, the police do not know that Jones had a motive.*

(We'll explain why we changed the way the conclusion is formulated in a moment.)

But now, instead of numbering the premises and drawing a standard tree diagram, we symbolize the statements to bring out their truth-functional relationships:

If p then q.
Not-q.
Therefore, not-p.

Now, we simply compare this form with the valid argument forms. If it matches one of them, then it is a valid deductive argument. Our example has the form of denying the consequent, so we know that it is a valid argument. Note that the tree diagram for each of these valid argument forms is always a T-argument structure, since clearly it is only if both premises are true that they provide support for the conclusion.

When reconstructing deductive arguments, there are two things we need to watch for. First, we must be careful to ensure that the meaning of the component statements is the same each time it appears in the argument. If a statement is used ambiguously in an argument, the argument will not be valid. In the above argument, for example, we have changed the wording of the conclusion from *They obviously don't know that he hated the victim* to *The police do not know that Jones had a motive*. In the context of the argument, it is clear that these two statements have the same meaning, since hating the victim means that Jones had a motive.

Second, we must be consistent in symbolizing negative statements. A statement such as:

Jones is not a suspect

can be symbolized either as *not-p* or as *p*. If the argument has the form of affirming the antecedent or of a chain argument, it is better to symbolize a negative statement simply as *p*. But in arguments whose form is denying the consequent or disjunctive syllogism, the negative statements play a special role, and if a negative statement appears in the first premise it should always be symbolized simply as *p*. For example:

If he has an alibi, then he is not a suspect.
But he is a suspect.
Therefore, he does not have an alibi.

The first premise should be symbolized as *if p then q*. And this means we must symbolize the second premise as *not-q* since it is the negation of the consequent of the first premise. Since the conclusion must be symbolized as *not-p*, it is now easy to see that the argument has the form of denying the consequent.

As long as we have correctly identified the form of an argument as valid, then, to repeat the point made earlier, we will know that, if its premises are true, its conclusion must also be true. Of course, when a valid argument has false premises, the guarantee is voided: the conclusion may be true or it may be false, for we have lost our guarantee.

These valid argument forms underlie many arguments we encounter in a variety of contexts. Often they are combined together in the same argument, and sometimes they produce quite complex logical structures. Consider the following argument:

If we want a healthy economy, then we must have a balanced budget, and if we are to have a balanced budget, then government funding for social programs will have to be cut back drastically. But if government funding for social programs is cut, then the private sector will have to do more to support education, health care, and private welfare organizations. So, if we are to have a healthy economy, then the private sector must provide much more support for social programs. The question is whether the private sector is willing to provide this support. There is little doubt that the private sector wants, indeed demands, that a healthy economy should be our top priority. Therefore, I am confident that the private sector is willing to do much more to support social programs.

When we reconstruct this argument we have the following:

(1) If we want a healthy economy, then we must have a balanced budget. (if p then q)
(2) If we are to have a balanced budget, then government funding for social programs will have to be cut back drastically. (if q then r)

(3) If government funding for social programs is cut, then the private sector will have to do more to support education, health care, and private welfare organizations. (if r then s)

(4) Therefore, if we are to have a healthy economy, then the private sector must provide much more support for social programs. (if p then s)

(5) There is little doubt that the private sector wants, indeed demands, that a healthy economy should be our top priority. (p)

(6) Therefore, I am confident that the private sector is willing to do much more to support social programs. (s)

Is this a valid argument? If the premises are true, must the conclusion be true as well? Even though some of the premises may be false or unacceptable (for example, 2 and 5), this is a valid argument. To show that it is valid, however, requires us to show that it uses only valid argument forms. To do this, we first write down the forms of the statements that constitute the argument:

(1) If p then q
(2) If q then r
(3) If r then s
(4) If p then s
(5) p
(6) s

To show the validity of this argument we reason as follows:

(a) 1 and 2 are the premises of a chain argument whose conclusion is if p then r.
(b) This conclusion (i.e., if p then r) and 3 are the premises of another chain argument whose conclusion is 4. (This means that 4 is validly derived from 1, 2, and 3.)
(c) 4 and 5 are the premises of an argument affirming the antecedent whose conclusion is 6.
(d) Therefore, 6 has been validly derived from the given premises.

In other words, if 1, 2, 3, and 5 are true (these are the premises whose truth we are being asked to accept) then we can derive 4 and 6. Therefore, the argument is a valid one. If we believe that the premises are true, then we must accept the conclusion. On the other hand, if we believe that the conclusion is false, we will have to reject one of the premises.

9.5 Formal Invalidity

Just as there are certain arguments whose strength depends solely upon their form, there are certain arguments whose weakness depends solely upon their form. Such arguments are called formally invalid. A formally invalid argument is one that lacks formal validity; if its premises are true, its conclusion may nevertheless turn out to be false. Formal invalidity is not always a crushing verdict on an argument, for many strong arguments (including most strong inductive arguments) lack formal validity. Arguments can be strong even when they are formally invalid, for all strong inductive arguments lack formal validity. The strength of such arguments depends upon their particular content; the premises do provide support for the conclusion, but the support does not derive from the logical form of the argument.

However, there are two types of fallacies involving formal invalidity that are worth considering. Both occur frequently in real life, and sometimes it is difficult to recognize them because of their similarity to the valid argument forms of affirming the antecedent and denying the consequent.

1. FALLACY OF DENYING THE ANTECEDENT
If p then q
Not-p
Therefore, not-q

For example:

> If the police knew that Jones had a motive for the crime, then he would be a suspect. But the police do not know that Jones had a motive. Therefore, he is not a suspect.

The form of this argument shows that it commits the fallacy of denying the antecedent. We can see why this is a fallacious argument by noting that there are other reasons for regarding someone as a suspect besides knowing that the person had a motive. For example, those who had the opportunity to commit a crime are usually treated as suspects. So the fact that the police do not know that Jones had a motive does not rule out the possibility that he may still be a suspect. Thus, the truth of the premises of this argument would be consistent with the falsity of the conclusion, which of course means that the argument must be invalid.

2. FALLACY OF AFFIRMING THE CONSEQUENT
If p then q
q
Therefore, p

For example:

> If the police knew that Jones had a motive for the crime, then he would be a suspect. And he is a suspect. Therefore, the police must know that he has a motive for the crime.

The form of this argument shows that it commits the fallacy of affirming the consequent. We can see why this is a fallacious argument by noting that there are other reasons the police might have for regarding Jones as a suspect. They may, for example, have an eyewitness who claims to have seen Jones at the scene of the crime. In this case, the fact that Jones is a suspect might not rest on the police claim that he has a motive but on the testimony of the eyewitness. Thus, the truth of the premises of this argument would be consistent with the falsity of the conclusion, which means that the argument must be invalid.

9.6 Self-Test No. 15

Reconstruct the following deductive arguments and determine whether they are formally valid, and, if they are not, whether they are formally invalid.

1. Look, if you buy a new coat, you won't be able to buy your text books for next term. And if you don't have the textbooks, your grades will suffer. So if you get a new coat, your grades are going to suffer.

2. I'm sure it wasn't Ellen who violated the confidentiality of the committee by revealing what took place at the meeting. If she had done that, then she would have harmed herself more than anyone else. And you know what Ellen is like: she would never do anything that was not in her self-interest.

3. I have an appointment to see my doctor this afternoon. He called yesterday to tell me that after consulting several specialists he has decided that surgery would be useless, but he wants to see me today. In general, as I understand it, there are only two treatments for my condition that are likely to do any good: either surgery or a long program of physiotherapy. So I suppose he wants to see me to set up a physiotherapy program.

4. The coach is worried that the football team will lose if it rains during the game next Saturday: he thinks the team doesn't play very well when the field is muddy. But the weather forecast is for sunny weather for the whole weekend. That's good news; it means we will win the game on Saturday.

5. If the Conservatives had won more than 50 per cent of the votes in the 1989 election then they certainly would have gained a mandate from the voters to implement the free trade agreement with the United States. But although the Conservatives won more seats than either of the other parties, they received less than 40 per cent of the popular vote. So they certainly did not have a mandate to implement the free trade agreement.

6. Chris has decided to run for president of the students' council. That's a pity because he is bound to lose. If Chris is going to win the election, he will have to be known to a lot of students. But hardly anyone knows Chris.

7. I told you Chris would lose the election. If he had been known to a lot of students, then he would have won. But hardly anyone knew who he was.

8. Left-wing radicals talk a great deal about their right to freedom of speech when they are under attack, but are strangely silent when it is the freedom of speech of conservatives that is under attack. If they were really committed to freedom of speech, then they would defend freedom of speech whenever and wherever it comes under attack. Their silence when conservative intellectuals like Philippe Rushton are under attack shows that they are not really committed to freedom of speech at all.

9. If this is really question 5, then I must be losing my mind. But this is not question 5, so (thank heavens) I'm not losing my mind.

10. If I have not lost my mind, then this must be question 810. This is question 810. Therefore, I have not lost my mind.

9.7 Questions for Discussion

The following deductive arguments may combine two or more argument forms, and may have missing premises. Supply the missing parts you think are intended, and test for validity.

1. Ken says that he does not have a logical mind: he complains that whenever he hears the word *validity*, he goes into a state of intellectual shock. Well, he is just being perverse. Anyone who can pass university-level courses must be able to think rationally, and anyone who can think rationally must have the capacity to reason logically. And Ken is obviously successful in passing his courses. So, he must have the capacity to reason logically.

2. JAY: There is a rumour going around that Fred is going to resign. This creates a really interesting situation. You see, if Fred resigns, then Grace will be promoted to Fred's position. And if Grace gets promoted, then Howard is going to be so upset that he will certainly quit. So, if Fred resigns then Howard will quit.
ALF: But I happen to know that Fred is definitely not going to resign. Therefore, Howard will not quit.

3. If he tells his teacher he cheated, he will be punished by the principal. But if he doesn't tell his teacher he cheated, he will be punished by his parents. Either way he is going to be punished.

4. Despite the fact that the social sciences must, if they are to sustain their status as sciences, claim to be able to make accurate predictions of human behav-

iour, it is not surprising that the social sciences have such an abysmal record when it comes to making actual predictions. To predict anything, including human behaviour, one must rely upon a deterministic theory about the causes of whatever behaviour one is trying to predict, whether it is the movements of the planets, a rise in the inflation rate, or an increase in violent crime rates. Therefore, since the social sciences are committed to the claim that they can predict human behaviour, they must rely upon a deterministic theory of human behaviour. But these deterministic theories are false, as can be seen by the following argument. If some human behaviour is genuinely free, then it is false that all human behaviour is subject to deterministic laws. But we all know from our personal experience that some of our behaviour is free: every time we deliberate about something, we are directly conscious that what we decide is not determined by anything, but is a decision freely arrived at. Otherwise, we would not waste our time thinking about the matter, and would just let deterministic fate decide for us. So, since we know that some human behaviour is free, we know that deterministic theories must be false. This, of course, means that the social sciences cannot really predict human behaviour, and their failure to do so should no longer surprise us.

5. In Dostoevsky's novel, *The Brothers Karamazov*, Alyosha tries to persuade his brothers that if God did not exist, then everything would be permitted. He means by this that if there is no God, then anything we do would be morally acceptable. Alyosha's brother Dmitri happily accepts Alyosha's claim, apparently because he reasons that since there is no God, then everything really is permitted. The other brother, Ivan, is deeply troubled by Alyosha's claim. He believes that not everything is permitted, since he is convinced that the slaughter of innocent children is inherently wrong. But he is unwilling to accept Alyosha's claim because then he would have to accept that God exists. He refuses to believe in God because he believes that if God exists, He would not tolerate the slaughter of innocent children.

10. Inductive Reasoning

10.1 The Nature of Inductive Reasoning

Inductive arguments are distinguished from deductive arguments by the fact that they lack the ability to guarantee their conclusions. (The ability to guarantee their conclusions, as we saw in Chapter 9, is a defining characteristic of valid deductive arguments.) It will help us to understand the nature of inductive reasoning if we explain this difference in more detail. The ability of valid deductive arguments to guarantee their conclusions derives from the fact that deductive reasoning merely draws out, or makes explicit, information that is already contained in the premises. Consider any formally valid argument, and it can be seen that the premises always implicitly contain the information that is stated in the conclusion. Often this is quite obvious, but sometimes it is not. When it is not obvious, however, seeing that the argument is formally valid is the same thing as seeing that the conclusion is implicit in the premises. But if the conclusion is implicitly contained in the premises, then to assert the premises *is* to assert the conclusion. Clearly, then, if the premises are true, then the conclusion must also be true. Stating that the conclusion is true is only making explicit what has already been stated in asserting that the premises are true.

But this characteristic reveals the major weakness in deductive reasoning, namely, that its usefulness is limited to exploring the implications of what we already know or assume to be true. Wherever there is an organized body of knowledge or truth-claims—as in science, law, theology, history, mathematics, indeed any academic discipline—deductive reasoning can generate knowledge that seems to be new, but this knowledge is actually implicit in our current knowledge. Genuinely new knowledge, however, cannot be derived from deductive reasoning alone. When we want to generate genuinely new knowledge, we must rely upon inductive reasoning. Almost every increase in scientific knowledge and most new common-sense knowledge is genuinely new and was not implicit in our previous knowledge. The knowledge of the causes of cancer or of how the stock market will behave if the price of oil drops suddenly cannot be discovered merely by drawing out the logical implications of our current knowledge. Our current knowledge is indeed necessary as a basis for such discoveries, but it is not sufficient. Genuinely new knowledge can only arise through the use of inductive forms of reasoning. Inductive reasoning is thus much more powerful than deductive reasoning. It can overcome ignorance in a way that deductive reasoning cannot.

But the power of inductive reasoning comes at a price. The absolute guarantee that valid deductive reasoning can provide for its conclusions is beyond the capacity of inductive reasoning: the conclusion of an inductive argument can never be more than probably true. This is because inductive reasoning *extrapolates* on what we know, using our current knowledge to arrive at conclusions that go beyond what is strictly, deductively implied by the available evidence. The probability that a conclusion reached through inductive reasoning is true may be very high and may even approach certainty. But certainty can never, in principle, be achieved. There is only one way of achieving certainty through reasoning, and that is by using a deductive argument. If we want to reach new knowledge that goes beyond what is implicit in our premises, we have to settle for something less than certainty.

The strength of inductive arguments depends not on their form but on their content. Only deductive arguments derive their logical strength from their form alone. This means that we cannot produce a catalogue of logically strong inductive argument forms as we could for valid deductive arguments. There are certain important inductive argument forms, but these forms by themselves tell us nothing about the logical strength of the arguments. To determine the strength of an inductive argument, we must always examine its content. For example, as we saw in section 8.2, in order to determine whether appeals to authority are legitimate, we have to examine the particular authority being appealed to and the particular claim involved. Indeed, most of the weaknesses described in Chapters 6, 7, and 8 rest upon an analysis of content.

There are, however, four types of inductive arguments that are widely used and that are strong arguments when certain conditions are met. It is useful to examine briefly these inductive argument forms, in order to learn what these conditions are and what weaknesses to look for. If any of these weaknesses is present, then the probability that the conclusion will be true is reduced. Each inductive argument form is prone to its own type of weaknesses, so it is important to be able to recognize the form of an inductive argument before assessing it. The four inductive argument forms we will examine all play a significant role in both the natural and social sciences, but they are also frequently and legitimately used outside the domain of science.

10.2 Inductive Generalization

The inductive generalizations we will look at have the following form:

Z per cent of observed F's are G.
It is probable, therefore, that Z per cent of all F's are G.

For example, suppose we want to know what percentage of students at a particular university believe in God. Clearly, it would be extremely difficult to ask every student at the university whether they believe in God. It is much easier to select a *sample* of students and determine their religious beliefs and then to generalize the results to the whole student body. SAMPLING involves observing a portion of a population in order to draw a conclusion about the entire population. This is a useful method for making justifiable claims about what trends can be found in a population without observing each and every member. Moreover, if the population size is large, it may be the only way to make such claims. Whenever we use a sample of some population as the evidence from which we draw a conclusion about the whole population, our reasoning will be in the form of an inductive generalization. Thus, our example would be written out as follows:

> *Sixty per cent of students at the University of X who were questioned believe in God.*
> *It is probable, therefore, that approximately 60 per cent of all students at the University of X believe in God.*

There are two possible weaknesses in inductive generalizations, both of which pertain to the nature of the sample. The first and most important is that the sample may not be representative of the population it is drawn from. If it is an *unrepresentative* or *biased* sample, the argument is significantly weakened. So when assessing any inductive generalization we should always ask:

(1) IS THE SAMPLE REPRESENTATIVE?

In other words, is the sample of observed F's referred to in the premise representative of the entire class of F's referred to in the conclusion? Suppose we had questioned only science students. Would this weaken the argument? Unless we are sure that studying science (rather than economics or philosophy) has no bearing upon one's religious beliefs, we would have to conclude that the argument is weak, since the sample is unrepresentative or biased in a way that might affect the conclusion. In a similar way the sample would be biased if our sample included only graduate students, or only first-year students, or only students who were in the pub on Friday night. Ideally, the sample should reflect the same percentage distribution as the entire student body at the University of X as regards degree program, major, year, grade average, age, sex, place of birth, type of religious upbringing, drinking habits, and marital status, to name a few variables. The more closely the sample is representative of the entire student body, the stronger the argument.

The second weakness that can arise with inductive generalizations is that the sample may be too small, and thus there is a second question we should ask:

(2) IS THE SAMPLE LARGE ENOUGH?

Even if a sample is adequately representative, it may nevertheless be so small that an inductive generalization from it is weak. We might, for example, be fortunate and discover a sample of 20 students who are more or less representative of students at the

University of X in general, but the argument clearly would be stronger with a sample of 40 students who were equally representative. In general, the larger the sample the stronger the argument. However, as the size of the sample is increased, the increase in strength becomes smaller with each additional increase in the size of the sample. For example, an increase from 20 to 40 students produces a much greater increase in strength than an increase from 220 to 240. In practice, therefore, we can often work with relatively small samples, especially if the population is homogeneous and we are careful to ensure that our sample is representative.

When an inductive generalization is weak for either of these two reasons it violates the criterion of adequacy. The premises of the above argument are presumably acceptable and are clearly relevant, but if the sample is unrepresentative or too small then the premises will be inadequate to support the conclusion.

10.3 Statistical Syllogism

All statistical syllogisms have the following form:

> Z per cent of all F's are G.
> x is an F.
> It is probable to the degree 0.Z, therefore, that x is G.

In this schema, *x* refers to a single individual. The phrase *It is probable to the degree 0.Z* ... is the way statisticians normally express degrees of probability. It means the same as *There is a Z per cent chance that* ....

Statistical syllogisms always start from a generalization and use it as the basis for determining the likelihood that it will apply to a particular individual case. So we have seen two forms of induction: generalizations, which move from the particular to the general, and statistical syllogisms that move from the general to the particular. For example, if we want to predict how likely it is that a particular student at the University of X believes in God, we would start with the conclusion of our previous inductive generalization and develop the following statistical syllogism:

> *Sixty per cent of students at the University of X believe in God.*
> *Fred is a student at the University of X.*
> *It is probable to the degree .6, therefore, that Fred believes in God.*

To determine whether a statistical syllogism is weak, it is necessary to look beyond the premises for any other information that might be relevant. The question we need to ask is:

> *Is there additional relevant information available concerning x that has not been included in the premises?*

For example, if we know that Fred is a regular churchgoer, then it is likely that the chance that he believes in God is much higher than 60 per cent. Or if we know that Fred refuses to go to church even for family funerals or his friends' weddings, then it is likely that the chance that he believes in God is much less than 60 per cent. Or if we know that Fred is a history major *and* that only 40 per cent of history majors believe in God, then it is likely that the conclusion of our argument will be false. Whenever we use or assess a statistical syllogism, it is important to ensure that no relevant information has been overlooked.

When a statistical syllogism leaves out relevant information, we can usually charge it with violating the criterion of adequacy, since the missing information significantly weakens the argument. In some cases, however, leaving out relevant information will lead to the charge of violating the criterion of relevance. For example, if it is known that Fred has explicitly stated that he is a committed atheist, the appeal to the generalization about University of X students becomes quite irrelevant.

10.4 Induction By Confirmation

Induction can be used to provide support for a hypothesis. A hypothesis is a principle or statement that, if true, would explain the event(s) or situation(s) to which it applies; for example, that Third World poverty is caused by international monetary policies, or that excessive exposure to sunlight causes skin cancer. To test the truth of a hypothesis we follow a two-stage procedure. First, we deduce from the hypothesis a number of *observation statements*. An observation statement is an empirical prediction, that states that under certain conditions a certain fact will be observed. By deducing observation statements from our hypothesis, we are claiming that, if our hypothesis is true, then we would expect to find that these empirical predictions are true. We then proceed to the second stage and make observations to determine whether or not our empirical predictions turn out to be true. If our actual observations agree with the predicted observations, they inductively support the hypothesis from which the predictions were deduced. They provide *confirming instances* for the hypothesis.

The form of such arguments is:

If h then o.
o.
It is probable, therefore, that h.

In this schema, *h* stands for a hypothesis and *o* stands for an observation statement that is logically deducible from *h*. When, as is usual, we have several observation statements, the form would be:

If h then o1, o2, o3, and o4.
o1.
o2.
o3.

o4.
It is probable, therefore, that h.

Induction by confirmation is widely used in the sciences, especially in the physical and natural sciences. For example:

> If the theory of general relativity is true, then it follows that light rays passing near the sun will be bent.
> During the solar eclipse of 1919 it was observed that light rays passing near the sun were deflected.
> It is probable, therefore, that the general theory of relativity is true.

Induction by Confirmation is also used in other contexts. It is often used for solving such mundane problems as discovering why a car won't start. It is used by doctors when diagnosing diseases. It is also used in criminal trials, where the evidence presented by the prosecution is intended to provide inductive support for the prosecutor's hypothesis that the accused is guilty. Consider these two examples:

> If my car has failed to start because the battery is dead, then I should find that the radio and lights don't work.
> The radio and lights don't come on properly.
> It is probable, therefore, that the battery is dead.

> If the bookkeeper intended to embezzle money, she would have kept a second copy of the company's financial records and a secret bank account to store large sums of money.
> We have found a second copy of the company's financial records and a bank account in the bookkeeper's name with over $300,000 in it.
> It is probable, therefore, that she was embezzling money from the company.

There are two possible weaknesses in inductive arguments by confirmation, and hence there are two questions that need to be asked. The first is:

(1) Is the number of confirming instances relatively high?

One swallow does not a summer make, and one confirming instance of a hypothesis usually does very little to show that the hypothesis is true. It is therefore important to gather a large number of confirming instances before asserting that the hypothesis is probably true. How large this number should be depends upon several factors: the range of different kinds of confirming instances, the scope of the hypothesis (i.e., does it apply to a large or small range of phenomena?), and whether the hypothesis is consistent with other well-established hypotheses. In general, the larger the number of confirming instances the stronger the argument and the more likely it is that the hypothesis is true. This means that if the number of confirming instances for some hypothesis is relatively small, the argument could be charged with violating the criterion of adequacy.

The second question that needs to be asked is:

(2) Are there any disconfirming instances?

A disconfirming instance arises when an observation statement that is predicted by the hypothesis is found to be false. Unlike the first weakness, which is a matter of degree, the presence of any disconfirming instances does not merely weaken the hypothesis, it refutes it altogether. Any hypothesis will be refuted by a single disconfirming instance. There is an asymmetry between confirming and disconfirming instances in the way that they affect the hypothesis. Each confirming instance adds a little strength to the hypothesis, whereas a single disconfirming instance conclusively refutes the hypothesis.

This asymmetry is important. To understand the reasons for it, we need to recall two of the argument forms discussed in Chapter 9, the valid argument form of denying the consequent and the formal fallacy of affirming the consequent. Since observation statements are logically deduced from the hypothesis, we have to treat *if h then o* as a truth-functional statement. A disconfirming instance, therefore, presents us with a formal argument of the form:

If h then o.
Not-o.
Therefore, not-h.

This is a valid argument because it has the form of denying the consequent. Any disconfirming instance, therefore, entails that the hypothesis is false. On the other hand, a confirming instance presents us with a formal argument of the form:

If h then o.
o.
Therefore, h.

This, however, has the form of Affirming the Consequent and thus is fallacious. Clearly, we cannot rely upon a single confirming instance to prove that a hypothesis is true. It is a mistake, however, to regard Induction by Confirmation as relying upon an invalid argument. Induction by Confirmation is genuinely inductive in nature, as is indicated by the fact that its conclusion is claimed only to be *probably* true. Each confirming instance does add support to the hypothesis by making it more probable that the hypothesis is true, unless, of course, we have one or more disconfirming instances, in which case we must conclude that the hypothesis is false.

In practice, however, scientists do not usually give up a hypothesis merely because of a single disconfirming instance. If the hypothesis is one that seems very promising and fruitful, it is reasonable to look for some other explanation for a disconfirming instance. Perhaps one of the test tubes was dirty, or there were impurities in the acid, or a piece of equipment malfunctioned, or a laboratory assistant was distracted when taking measurements, or any of a hundred other possibilities. If some such explanation seems likely, then it is reasonable not to reject the hypothesis. But if a plausible explanation is unavailable, the hypothesis should be rejected, since the argument in support of it actually refutes it. Scientists usually refer to disconfirming instances as *negative results*. Although it is disappointing to obtain negative results from one's research, it is important to report that fact to other scientists so that they will know that a particular hypothesis has been refuted.

Another way of saving a hypothesis for which there is a disconfirming instance is to revise the hypothesis. Often only a minor revision is needed to save a hypothesis. For example, a hypothesis put forward to explain how a particular disease is transmitted may be saved by adding the qualifications ... *at temperatures between 0 and 100 degrees Celsius*. Strictly speaking, the *original* hypothesis has not been saved: the revised hypothesis is a different one, even though the difference is slight. Much scientific research consists of this kind of refinement in an attempt to discover hypotheses that can withstand testing, that is, for which there are a large number of confirming instances and no disconfirming instances.

Induction by Confirmation should not be regarded as a description of the temporal order of steps in which scientific research is conducted, but as an analysis of one kind of scientific reasoning. If it is regarded as a simple description of how scientists do research it is somewhat misleading. The method suggests that we must have a hypothesis *before* we can make the observations to test it. In fact, many scientists reverse this order. They gather data that they believe might be helpful in explaining some phenomenon, and then attempt to find the hypothesis that best explains the data. There is nothing wrong with proceeding in this way, although it needs to be noted that no scientist would ever set out to gather data without having at least a vague idea of the kind of hypothesis that will explain the data being gathered. But data by itself is scientifically meaningless; it explains nothing. Data becomes meaningful only when it is used to support or reject a hypothesis, and science can only explain phenomena when it can produce a hypothesis that is supported by the data. Thus, induction by confirmation, regarded as a method of reasoning, is still necessary to transform data into a scientific explanation.

Two more points must be made before we complete the account of induction by confirmation:

(1) While Induction by Confirmation is a common form of reasoning within the sciences, it is common in other contexts, too. In fact, it is one of the most common forms of reasoning we use everyday. Here are some examples of Induction by Confirmation in non-scientific contexts:

Stephanie's family moved when she was six, and before her first day at a new school her parents told her that being pleasant and outgoing with strangers is a great way to meet people and make new friends. Her family moved seven more times by the time she finished high school, and she always made an effort to be pleasant and outgoing with her new classmates. In every new school she developed friends quickly, so there must be something correct about her parents' advice.

The defendant insists that he didn't intend to shoot his wife. But the only conclusion that fits the facts is that he did intend to kill her. If he intended to do it, then he would have purchased the gun ahead of time, which he did. He would have taken her to a secluded place, which he did. He would have arranged an alibi, which he did. He would have had a motive, which he does. All the evidence you have heard supports the conclusion that he intended to kill his wife, and you should therefore find him guilty of first-degree murder.

For several years Alfred had been bothered by insomnia. He had a hunch that it was caused by drinking coffee during the evening, so he began keeping a record of when he drank coffee in the evening and whether or not he suffered insomnia that night. After a month he analyzed his records and discovered that on 17 of the 18 nights when he suffered insomnia he had drunk coffee after 8 p.m. and on 11 of the 12 nights when he did not suffer insomnia he had drunk no coffee at all. He concluded that it was the coffee that caused his insomnia.

(2) Not only can we find Induction by Confirmation outside scientific contexts, but we also find other forms of reasoning within scientific contexts. So it is not *the* method of scientific reasoning, it is *one* method. In fact, entire books have been written about the repertoire of argument forms that have been used in science. We won't be able to conduct a full survey of all these forms, but in Chapter 11, besides returning to Induction by Confirmation, we will look at some common and important ones.

10.5 Analogical Reasoning

Reasoning by analogy is probably the most creative form of reasoning. Whenever we encounter something we do not understand, it is a natural reaction to try to understand it by reference to something that is familiar to us. When we see a man behaving erratically in a way that reminds us of Aunt Ethel, we conclude that he too is suffering from Alzheimer's disease. When an election gives the winning party a minority of seats, political commentators immediately look at past minority governments in order to understand the possibilities of the new situation. Sometimes scientists seeking an explanation for a new phenomenon begin by comparing it with other phenomena which have already been subsumed under familiar laws or principles. In all such cases the reasoning presupposes an analogy between two things (objects, classes of objects, situations, relationships), one of which is familiar and one unfamiliar.

Some analogies are better than others, and some are downright misleading. The quality of an analogy depends upon the purpose of drawing it. If the purpose is merely to clarify a difficult concept, any analogy will be a good one if it succeeds in clarifying the concept. For example:

According to quantum mechanics, particles move in accordance with wave-like principles. They are not physical waves, however, but probability waves. They are not like the waves on a lake but are more like a crime wave.

The crime-wave analogy is helpful in grasping the concept of a probability wave, and for this purpose it is a good analogy. In general, any analogy that helps us to understand something is a good one.

Another purpose of analogical reasoning is to suggest possible explanations. Charles Darwin got the idea for the principle of natural selection, which is central to the theory of evolution, by reading a book on economics by Thomas Malthus. Some scientists have used the digital computer as a source of possible explanations for how the human mind works. In these cases, the analogy is used not to prove anything but merely to suggest a hypothesis that would have to be defended independently of the analogy.

Our concern, however, is with analogies that are used in arguments, that is, where the analogy is being used to provide support for a conclusion. Here we need to be careful in choosing our analogies, for a weak analogy will fail to provide the support our conclusion needs. Analogies by themselves are never sufficient to prove anything, and if an argument claims to prove its conclusion, any premise that introduces an analogy would be irrelevant. However, a strong analogy can provide an adequate reason for conclusions which are claimed to be only probably true. For example:

Last year I put some fertilizer on my strawberries in the fall and got about 20 per cent more strawberries. You should do the same with your strawberries, since you've got the same kind of soil. You'll probably get more strawberries too.

Clearly, this conclusion is not derived with the certainty of a deductively sound argument, but the analogy between your soil and mine is strong enough to make it reasonable for us to accept it, at least tentatively. A weak analogy, on the other hand, is one that is used as a premise in an argument but fails to provide adequate support for the conclusion. For example:

Driving a car is basically just like riding a bicycle: it's all a matter of physical coordination and keeping an eye on where you are going. Well, I taught myself how to ride a bicycle, so I reckon I can teach myself how to drive a car.

Clearly there are some similarities between riding a bicycle and driving a car, but the analogy is not strong enough to provide much support for the conclusion of this argument.

The usefulness of analogical arguments derives from the similarities between different things. If there are enough important similarities between the two things being compared in an analogy, we can draw conclusions about things we do not know based on evidence from comparable things that we know better. In the first example in the previous paragraph, for instance, similarities between the soil in the two gardens help predict how fertilizer will encourage the growth of strawberries in one garden based on how it affected another garden. We should say that the analogy compares two *cases*. The SUBJECT CASE is that about which we are trying to draw a conclusion in an analogical argument. The ANALOGUE CASE is that with which we are more familiar and which is used to draw the conclusion in an analogical argument. In this example, the speaker's garden is the analogue case and the garden of the person the speaker is addressing is the subject case. The speaker's garden is used as an analogue because the soil in that garden and the plants being grown in it are comparable to the soil and plants in the garden of the person being addressed. Since there is no direct evidence of the effect of fertilizer on the production of strawberries in the subject case, the analogy is used to provide indirect evidence, which is reasonable to use because of the similarities.

The easiest way to identify the subject case and the analogue case in any analogical argument is to find the conclusion. The conclusion will always be about the subject case. The conclusion will also indicate what the *target feature* of the analogy is. The TARGET FEATURE is that feature of the subject case about which the conclusion is being drawn. This is the focus of the comparison between the two cases. For example, the conclusion above is *You'll probably get more strawberries too*. The conclusion is not about every feature of the garden, but rather only about the production of strawberries in the garden. Similarly, the conclusion of the second passage is not about every aspect of driving a car, but only about the prospect of the speaker teaching himself how to do it.

There are two kinds of analogical argument, each with its own form. The first analogical argument is based on a comparison of the *properties* of the subject case and those of the analogue case, and the second is based on a comparison between *relations* that obtain in the subject case and those of the analogue case. The difference between a property and a relation is important and straightforward, although it is abstract and may require some practice to get used to. But because analogies by properties and analogies by relations are different in important respects, it will be helpful to make this clear before we look at the two analogical argument forms. A PROPERTY is a feature that is attributable to a thing considered on its own and as a single entity, whereas a RELATION is a feature that is attributable to the relationship between two or more things. So, for example, *red*, *juicy*, and *sweet* may be properties of an apple, whereas *inside*, *next to*, and *in front of* may describe the relation between the same apple and a bowl. Similarly, *exciting*, *realistic*, and *647 pages long* may be properties that are attributable to a novel, whereas the same novel may be related to other things in ways such as "*shorter than* War and Peace," "*written before* the author won the Nobel prize," or "*not as good as* the movie based on it."

One special set of examples must be noted before we turn to the forms of analogical arguments based on properties and those based on relations. Sometimes we might describe a single thing by noting the *relations* between its *parts*. For example, we might say that "a clock's minute hand *moves faster than* its hour hand," or "Chapter 2 of this book is *longer than* Chapter 5." Even though *a clock* or *this book* are single entities, the italicized phrase expresses a relation because the sentences are about the relations between parts of a clock or this book. These may look like exceptions to the distinction between properties and relations specified above, but they really are not, because the parts (the minute and hour hands of the clock, Chapter 2 and Chapter 5 of this book) are themselves treated as different things.

An ANALOGICAL ARGUMENT BY PROPERTIES has the form:

> x has A, B, C.
> y has A, B.
> It is probable, therefore, that y has C.

In this schema, x refers to the analogue case, y refers to the subject case, and A, B, and C refer to properties. The first premise describes the analogue case (x) as having properties A, B, and C, and the second premise describes the subject case (y) as having properties A and B. The target feature is C, which is one of the properties of the analogue case. On the basis of the analogy between x and y, there are probable grounds to infer that y also has property C. Here are some examples of analogical arguments by properties:

> *Canada Geese are water birds that nest in Canada in the early spring and migrate south to a warmer climate for the winter months. Ducks are also water birds that nest in Canada in the early spring. Therefore, ducks probably migrate south for the winter, too.*

> *The Montreal Symphony Orchestra's last recording was of a Beethoven piano concerto, led by their current conductor, featuring Marc-André Hamelin as the soloist and on the CBC recording label. I loved it. The orchestra's next Beethoven recording will have the same conductor and the same pianist and is also recorded on the same label. I'm confident that I'll enjoy it as well.*

> *Running a university is like a running a business: just as a business cannot function in the face of massive debts, so a university cannot function with a debt load; just as a business must make itself appealing to prospective customers, so a university must make itself appealing to prospective students; just as a business must meet the practical needs of its paying customers, so must a university meet the practical needs of its tuition-paying students. Therefore, each university must cover its own costs, just as each business should cover its own costs.*

An ANALOGICAL ARGUMENT BY RELATIONS has the following form:

> x is to y as a is to b.
> x is R to y.
> It is probable, therefore, that a is R to b.

In this schema, x and y are related in the analogue case, and a and b are related in the subject case. The target feature is specified as R, which is said to describe the relation between x and y in the analogue case. On the basis of the analogy, there are probable grounds to infer that R describes the relation in the subject case. Here are some more examples of analogical arguments by relations:

Just as Pavlov's dog salivated whenever it heard a bell ring, so can my kids get excited whenever they hear the theme song to Hockey Night in Canada. Pavlov's dog started salivating because it associated the sound of the bell with food. I suppose my kids associate the theme song with the fun of watching a hockey game.

Politicians are like doctors for the country. Like doctors, they are there to cure the ills of an economy. When you go to a doctor, you acknowledge that she knows more about good health than you do, and you happily follow her advice. There is no point in electing politicians if you aren't going to give them a free rein to act once they are in power. Criticising politicians is defeating them and yourself, and it's just as silly as going to the doctor and then refusing to act on her advice.

The proposal to give clean needles to prison inmates to stop the spread of the AIDS virus from the use of dirty needles is ridiculous. It is like giving bank robbers normal bullets to stop them from using dum-dum bullets, which are much more damaging to the victim.

To determine the strength of an analogy, we examine the similarities and dissimilarities between the two cases. A strong analogy is one in which there is a large number of relevant similarities and a small number of relevant dissimilarities between the cases. A weak analogy is one in which there is a small number of relevant similarities and a large number of relevant dissimilarities between the cases. It is important that the similarities and dissimilarities are relevant. The fact that riding a bicycle and driving a car are done in a sitting position is not a relevant similarity. The fact that I learned to ride a bicycle in June whereas I am proposing to teach myself to drive a car in September is not a relevant dissimilarity. On the other hand, the fact that both require good physical coordination is a relevant similarity. And the fact that cars are faster and more powerful than bicycles is a relevant dissimilarity. The relevance of a similarity or dissimilarity depends upon the target feature of the analogy and the conclusion being inferred. For each of the above similarities and dissimilarities, we would have to be prepared to say why we think it is or is not relevant, and to do this we would have to rely upon what we know about riding bicycles and driving cars, as well as what we know about learning to drive a car. Determining the strength of an analogy involves weighing the relevant similarities against the relevant dissimilarities. We have to make a judgement, in the light of the similarities and dissimilarities, as to whether the analogy is strong enough to support the conclusion. There are no hard and fast rules here: all we can do is to look for relevant similarities and dissimilarities and make our judgement on that basis.

10.6 Self-Test No. 16

For the following passages, (1) indicate the type of inductive argument being used and (2) identify within each passage the parts that correspond to parts of the schematic forms provided in this chapter. Then (3) assess the strength of the argument by identifying, describing any weaknesses.

1. In order to discover whether people were satisfied with the recreational facilities provided by the City, a questionnaire was included with the tax bills that were mailed out last spring. The results showed that almost 80 per cent were satisfied with the current recreational facilities.

2. Giving fathers a period of paid leave when their wives give birth would not be prohibitively expensive. In Sweden, where such a policy has been in effect for more than a decade, only 12 per cent of Swedish men take the leave.

3. The Ontario Minister of Tourism responded yesterday to recent charges by some resort operators that Ontario provides inadequate facilities for tourists. He claimed that the tourists themselves—about 80 per cent of them—stated that they were satisfied with the facilities provided for tourists and cited a study conducted by the Ministry last summer, in which questionnaires were distributed to every car with non-Ontario licence plates leaving Ontario and entering the United States. Approximately 18,000 questionnaires were returned. The results showed that 23 per cent were very satisfied and 56 per cent were satisfied with the facilities provided for tourists.

4. The Career Placement office predicts that 90 per cent of this year's graduates will find a job within three months of graduation. This is good news indeed for my roommate. He will be relieved to know that even though he will have only a general BA with a D average he still has a 90 per cent chance of getting a job.

5. Almost everyone would throw a life preserver to a drowning person; indeed, someone who could easily do so but refused would be regarded by everyone as a sick or immoral person. The same thing applies to nations when a famine occurs in a Third World country. We should be prepared to throw them a life preserver in the form of emergency aid. Yet, we continually hear complaints from those who are opposed to such aid. Surely we are entitled to regard them as sick or immoral people.

6. Recently the Philosophy Department surveyed all students registered in its introductory courses. One of the questions asked students whether they expected that a university education would improve their communication skills, and 88 per cent answered yes to this question. So it seems that 88 per cent of

students at the university think that a university education will improve communication skills.

7. Many people support gun control legislation because they think it will reduce the number of murders. They are making a serious mistake, however. Have they forgotten the failure of prohibition to reduce the amount of drunkenness?

8. I recently read about a survey which showed that 90 per cent of Americans knew less about the Canadian political system than the average Canadian ten-year-old. Well, there's an American student in my Canadian politics course, and I don't know how he hopes to pass the course when he's that ignorant to begin with.

9. Those of us who grew up in rural and small-town Ontario in the 1940s and 1950s never met or heard of any local communists or even communist sympathizers. If any existed, and according to the press there were a few around, we all believed they must be spies and could be found only in Toronto, Ottawa, or Montreal. But now we are told that during this period one of the largest and most powerful trade unions in northern Ontario was controlled by communist sympathizers. Well, I for one simply don't believe it. I lived through that period, and I should know.

10. Last year both Frances and Rhonda spent six hours a day training with Jim Birkin and followed his special diet, and both made Canada's national swim team. This year I'm training just as hard with the same coach and following the same diet. So I bet I'll make the team.

11. The Student Union conducted a telephone poll of students to see how much support there was for a fee increase to help pay for new athletic facilities. Every twentieth name in the student directory was telephoned last weekend. The results showed that only 44 per cent supported the proposal.

12. Perhaps we cannot know for certain that many animals feel pain, but there are three reasons for holding that they do. First, they exhibit behaviour that in humans is invariably associated with feeling pain. Second, they have a central nervous system that is similar to humans'. And third, the ability to feel pain would have the same kind of evolutionary advantage for many animals that it does for humans.

10.7 Questions for Discussion

Answer the questions accompanying the following passages in light of the appropriate criteria for the kind of argument in each passage.

1. A few years ago, Ann Landers asked the women readers of her newspaper column to send her a card stating which they would prefer: "to be held close and treated tenderly," or to have sex. Of the 90,000 people who replied, 72 per cent said they would prefer the former. She concluded that most women preferred being held close and treated tenderly to having sex. How strong is this inductive generalization?

2. Fifty per cent of those who voted in the 2000 federal election voted for a Liberal candidate, presumably because they wanted a Liberal government. Many people concluded from this that 50 per cent of all Canadians wanted a Liberal government. Is this a reasonable conclusion?

3. It is sometimes suggested that racism is caused by two types of bad inductive reasoning. First, it is argued that racial stereotypes are caused by weak inductive generalizations: racial stereotypes arise because people tend to notice individuals who stand out from the crowd, and then they use this sample as the basis for their generalizations about race as a whole. But such a sample is necessarily unrepresentative since it is based only on those few individuals who stand out, that is, who are different. Second, it is argued that individual members of other races are discriminated against because of weak statistical syllogisms: all evidence that an individual does not fit the generalization is ignored. Is this a plausible explanation for racism?

4. It is clearly unreasonable to argue as follows: *I have known three Irishmen in my life, and all were drunkards with violent tempers; therefore, all Irishmen are drunkards with violent tempers.* Why then is it not equally unreasonable to argue as follows: *I have read three Harlequin Romance novels, and all had uninteresting characters and predictable plots; therefore, all Harlequin Romance novels have uninteresting characters and predictable plots?*

5. The following passage comes from a seventeenth-century author whose information about other planets in the solar system was much more limited than ours. Even so, what problems might one of his contemporaries have spotted in the argument? *We may observe a very great similitude between this earth which we inhabit, and other planets, Saturn, Jupiter, Mars, Venus, and Mercury. They all revolve round the sun, as the earth does, although at different distances and in different periods. They borrow all their light from the sun, as the earth does. Several of them are known to revolve around their axis like the earth and, by that means, must have a like succession of day and night. Some of them have moons that serve to give them light in the absence of the sun, as our moon does to us. They are all, in their motions, subject to the same law of gravitation, as the earth is. From all this similitude, it is not unreasonable to think that those planets may, like our earth, be the habitation of various orders of living creatures. There is some probability in this conclusion from analogy.*

6. When medical treatment is unsuccessful and the patient dies or is permanently incapacitated, many people feel that the doctor must be guilty of negligence, and the patient or the family often launches a suit for medical malpractice. Is this reasonable, given that the reasoning that lies behind all treatment decisions must be inductive in nature?

7. Are there any inconsistent assumptions in the following argument that are exposed by schematizing it? *I am conscious of a series of facts connected by an uniform sequence, of which the beginning is modifications of my body, the middle is feelings, and the end is outward demeanour. In the case of other human beings I have the evidence of my senses for the first and last links of the series, but not for the intermediate link. I find, however, that the sequence between the first and last is as regular and constant in those other cases as it is in mine. In my own case I know that the first link produces the last through the intermediate link and could not produce it without. Experience, therefore, obliges me to conclude that there must be an intermediate link; which must either be the same in others as in myself, or a different one;... by supposing the link to be of the same nature... I conform to the legitimate rules of experimental enquiry* (J.S. Mill, *An Examination of Sir William Hamilton's Philosophy*, 1867, pp. 237–38).

part four
APPLICATIONS

11.   Scientific Reasoning

In this section of the text we turn to applications of the fundamental concepts covered in earlier chapters. In particular, the next three chapters examine some of the methods and forms of reasoning found in scientific contexts (Chapter 11), the forms of reasoning used for deliberating over moral issues (Chapter 12), and effective ways of responding to arguments by other people (Chapter 13). Each of these contexts requires us to argue with a fairly well-defined purpose in mind, and these purposes may be described in broad terms. One important purpose of scientific reasoning is to expand our knowledge of the world by answering questions about *why* things happen as they do. The purpose of moral reasoning is to formulate reasonable moral judgements about what is right, wrong, good, bad, fair, and unfair. And the purpose of arguing back is to engage the arguments of other people in a rational and critical manner. Each of these purposes presents special difficulties that must be dealt with in order to argue effectively in these contexts.

An essential task of science is to explain how and why things happen. From physical sciences (such as mechanics, chemistry, or biology) to social sciences (such as economics, sociology, and psychology), every branch of science has this task. For this reason, a great deal of effort is invested in formulating, testing, and refining the explanatory concepts that are at the heart of each scientific discipline. Accordingly, part of this chapter is devoted to some of the inductive procedures that help generate explanatory causal statements (section 11.2). Another part examines some problems connected to the application of explanatory hypotheses, in particular, deciding which ones to accept and apply when more than one is available (section 11.4). Finally, we finish the chapter with a case that will illustrate how the various methods, argument forms, and concepts that we have covered can be used in combination with each other (section 11.5). But, first, let us consider what makes a scientific concept genuinely explanatory.

11.1 Causation/Correlation

To appreciate some important wide-spread features of scientific reasoning, let us return to a concept that first came up in connection with argument adequacy, causation. In Chapter 8 the elusiveness of causation was noted in passing before we turned to the fallacies of *post hoc, confusing cause and effect*, and *common cause*. Now we must consider causation in a little more detail, because it is a central concept in many different kinds of scientific reasoning. Since Aristotle's time, philosophers and scientists have attempted to understand many types of phenomena in a scientific way by discovering their causes. In these cases, we explain particular events and general patterns by identifying the causal factors involved.

To begin, we must note that there are a couple of ways in which two or more events may be related. First, there is a causal relation that is important for a scientific understanding. Second, there is the temporal relation of events, i.e., their order in time. We can *observe* the order of two events in time and note whether one occurred before, after, or simultaneously with another. In other words, a statement about the temporal relation of events is empirical. But when we claim that one event *caused* another one, the connection between the two is much stronger than anything we observe directly about their order in time. When someone says that moderate levels of rainfall in June *caused* a bumper crop of corn the following August, that claim goes beyond what is strictly observable about the temporal order of these events. Similarly, to say that an explosion was *caused* by a gas leak in the presence of an open flame goes beyond the strict observation that both the gas leak and open flame occurred simultaneously. As both these cases illustrate, while the temporal relation is observable, the causal relation is not. This is because a *complete* causal account specifies the NECESSARY and SUFFICIENT CONDITIONS for something to occur, and both of these conditions involve *counterfactual statements* (see section 1.3). Counterfactual statements are about what would have happened had the purported necessary and sufficient conditions not been satisfied. These possibilities are not directly observed; one purpose for experimental research, then, is to test whether these implicit claims about necessary and sufficient conditions can be satisfied empirically.

For these reasons, the concept of causation must be carefully distinguished from the concept of correlation. Two events that regularly occur at the same time or in the same sequence may be both correlated and related as cause and effect *or* they may be correlated without being in a direct causal relationship. A CORRELATION is observed when different events occur at the same time or occur regularly in the same sequence. With CAUSATION, one event (the cause) is responsible for, or brings about, another event (the effect). We can see the need for this distinction by considering one of the causal fallacies outlined earlier, *common cause* (see section 8.5.3). Someone might notice that a sore throat is always accompanied by sinus congestion (a correlation). On the basis of this observed correlation the sick person might fallaciously believe that the sore throat *causes* the sinus congestion. But really the sore throat and the sinus congestion are both caused by a third factor, namely, a cold virus. So while the sore throat and congestion have a common cause, neither causes the other. In this case, there is a correlation but no causal relationship between the sore throat and the congestion. At the same time, there is both a correlation and a causal relationship between the cold virus (the cause) and the congestion (an effect) and between the virus and the sore throat. If the sick person takes the time to think about these relations, they may be able to correct their own fallacious reasoning. Suppose this person takes a decongestant that relieves the sinus congestion but does nothing for the sore throat. This "experiment" would reveal the falsity in the original counterfactual, *If the sinuses were not congested, then the throat would not be sore.* This person is now in a much better position to understand both the sore throat and sinus congestion as effects of some other cause.

Causal claims attempt to identify what is responsible for, or what brings about, a state of affairs. They answer questions that take the form *Why ...?* For example, we might ask

> *Why does the price of gold go up when the stock market is down?*
> *Why do the tides alternate as they do?*
> *Why did the plane miss the runway during landing?*
> *Why did wheat production in Manitoba drop dramatically during the 1930s?*

Each of these questions can be reworded as a question about what causal factor is responsible for the event in question:

> *What is responsible for the rising price of gold when the stock market is down?*
> *What is responsible for the alternation of tides?*
> *What was responsible for the plane missing the runway during landing?*
> *What was responsible for the drop in wheat production in Manitoba in the 1930s?*

Under either formulation, each question treats the phenomenon being asked about as an effect. Also, each one is answered when the cause is specified:

> *Investors seeking a secure commodity during periods of market uncertainty* cause the price of gold to rise.
> *The mutual gravitational attraction of the moon and the earth* causes the tides.
> *Fog and pilot error* caused the plane to miss the runway.
> *Drought, soil erosion, and swarms of crop-eating insects* caused a reduction in wheat production.

In each example, the answer is a circumstance (or set of circumstances) that is both correlated with the phenomenon being asked about and is responsible for it. Because the correlated circumstances usually occur prior to the event in question, they are called *antecedent circumstances.*

Mere correlations identify antecedent circumstances without answering *Why ...?* questions, such as those found in the previous paragraph. Suppose the price of gold happens to go up every time polka dot ties become fashionable. In this case, we have a strong correlation between two phenomena. However, there are no good grounds to causally and directly connect trends in tie fashion and trends in the gold market. Even if the correlation has been strong in the past, we shouldn't expect it to be repeated in the future. On its own, this correlation does not answer the *Why ...?* question about the price of gold, and we have no reason to believe it has been anything more than a curious coincidence. To answer a *Why ...?* question, it isn't enough to notice what circumstances precede the phenomenon in question. We must have some reason to believe that the correlated antecedent circumstances played a role in bringing about the event.

Of course, noticing a correlation between one event and another can help us to identify the cause of some phenomenon, even if a correlation is not sufficient to establish a causal relation. Where there is *no* correlation, we will find no causal relation between two events. For example, because the phases of Venus are not correlated with patterns associated with tides, we discount these phases as a cause of the tides. But because the position of the moon with respect to the earth is correlated with the tides, we have some reason to suspect that the moon might be involved in the cause we are looking for. If a correlation holds in a wide range of instances and over an extended period of time, then we should suspect that an underlying causal relationship is at work here. Better still, if all the correlated incidents can be organized systematically, then we can use our observations to *infer* a causal relationship. The methods of reasoning described in the next section are designed to help determine whether certain correlations provide strong grounds for making causal claims.

11.2 Mill's Methods

John Stuart Mill, the nineteenth-century philosopher, formulated several ways of collecting and organizing observations so that they could be used to infer causal relationships. These inferences will always be inductive, because they require us to extrapolate from premises about observable events to conclusions about the underlying causal relationship between these events. So the conclusions we draw on the basis of these methods can never be guaranteed in the way deductive conclusions are. What Mill has provided is a set of procedures for systematically and methodically extrapolating from the observable temporal order of things to the causal order which is not directly observable. By being methodical in the ways he recommends, we can increase the probability that our conclusions about the causal order are correct.

Mill outlines five methods: (1) the Method of Agreement, (2) the Method of Difference, (3) the Joint Method of Agreement and Difference, (4) the Method of Concomitant Variations, and (5) the Method of Residue.

11.2.1 METHOD OF AGREEMENT

When we observe several instances of the same phenomenon, we expect that all of them are the result of the same cause. And if we also observe the same antecedent circumstances in all these instances, then we have reason to believe that this may be the cause we are seeking. The METHOD OF AGREEMENT helps us identify significant correlations between the phenomenon and antecedent circumstances, which then provide probable grounds to infer a causal relationship.

Suppose there is a dinner party attended by 10 people, and that six of the diners subsequently develop food poisoning. Naturally, we expect one of the food items served at the dinner party to be the cause. We can determine which item on the menu was responsible for the food poisoning by charting which items were eaten by each person, then check to see if anything was eaten by the six people who became ill and not by any of the other guests. In this case, food poisoning is the phenomenon, all the items on the menu are the antecedent circumstances, and the 10 guests provide evidence of the cause. The chart might look like this (only "yes" answers are indicated in the appropriate spaces, "no" answers are left blank):

INSTANCES	SALMON MOUSSE	LIVER PATÉ	GARDEN SALAD	ASPARA-GUS	CAKE	PHENOMENON (FOOD POISONING)
Terry	yes	yes	yes	yes	yes	YES
Peter		yes	yes	yes	yes	
Rowan			yes	yes	yes	
Gillian	yes			yes	yes	YES
Polly		yes		yes	yes	
Eric	yes	yes		yes	yes	YES
Prunella		yes	yes		yes	
John	yes	yes		yes	yes	YES
Graham	yes		yes		yes	YES
Michael	yes		yes	yes	yes	YES

First, compare the two columns on the right. All those who developed food poisoning ate cake. But four people ate cake without getting food poisoning, which makes it unlikely that the cake is the cause. Next, compare the list of people with food poisoning and the list of people who ate asparagus. Not only are there instances of people who ate asparagus without getting sick, but one person who got sick (Graham) didn't eat that item. Again, we have reasons to eliminate this antecedent circumstance as the cause. For both the cake and the asparagus, there is no correlation between the list of people who ate it and the list of people who became ill. There is also no correlation between food poisoning and four other items on the menu. In fact, there is only one item that correlates with the people who developed food poisoning. All those who ate the salmon mousse became ill; furthermore, none of those who didn't eat salmon mousse became ill. This is a SIGNIFICANT CORRELATION because it is the only antecedent circumstance that correlates with the phenomenon. Therefore, there are good probable grounds to infer that the cause of the food poisoning was the salmon mousse.

The argument form associated with the Method of Agreement is as follows:

P occurs in 1 in circumstances x, y, z
P occurs in 2 in circumstances x, z
P occurs in 3 in circumstances x, y
Therefore, it is probable that x is the cause of P.

In this schema, *P* is the phenomenon for which we are attempting to determine the cause. *1, 2,* and *3* refer to the instances of the phenomenon, and *x, y,* and *z* are the antecedent conditions. It says that when we look at all the observed instances and find only one antecedent circumstance that correlates with the phenomenon, then it is probable that the correlated circumstance is the cause.

Two qualifications about this argument form must be noted, however. First, the form isn't restricted to exactly three antecedent conditions or three instances of the phenomenon; it can be expanded to include more than three antecedent conditions or more than instances. More importantly, if more than one antecedent circumstance corresponds with all instances of the phenomenon, as both cake and salmon mousse do in the food poisoning example, then the immediate conclusion to be drawn is *Therefore, it is probable that either x or y is the cause of P.* If only one of these antecedent circumstances correlates with the phenomenon, as the salmon mousse does, we should add the premise *But only x is correlated with P,* then draw the conclusion as it is stated above. In fact, this is what we did when we ruled out cake as a possible cause of food poisoning.

As with other kinds of reasoning we have examined, it is important to be aware of the limitations of the Method of Agreement. In order to assess an argument based on the Method of Agreement we must check to see whether it exhibits any of the weaknesses to which arguments of this sort are vulnerable. First, it is possible that there will be agreement between the list of instances in which the phenomenon is observed and *two or more* antecedent circumstances. In these cases, we do not have a *significant* correlation; that is, we cannot narrow the list of potential causal factors down to one uniquely best candidate. It is also possible that two or more antecedent circumstances are *jointly necessary and sufficient* causes of the phenomenon. In these cases, we need to investigate further to identify a significant correlation before we can draw an inference. Second, it is possible that some *unobserved* factor may be playing a role in the instances being considered. An observed correlation provides only indirect evidence about the causal factor that is responsible for the phenomenon in question. Inevitably with this method, the antecedent circumstances that we select to observe will be determined by what we already think are potential causes. But it is possible that the real cause is something we simply do not expect and are not looking for. Third, even though we have a significant correlation in the dinner party example, we have not identified the causal factor *precisely*—i.e., we have not identified what is sometimes called the causal *agent.* We would want to know what kind of food poisoning was caused in this case (botulism, salmonella, staphylococcus, etc.), which ingredient in the salmon mousse harboured it, and how it got there. Answers to these questions will help explain why poisoning occurred in this particular dish (because ordinarily salmon mousse doesn't have this effect).

11.2.2 METHOD OF DIFFERENCE

When all the antecedent circumstances in two instances are the same except one and a specific phenomenon is observed in one instance but not the other, then we have reason to believe that there is something significant about the single difference in the circumstances. The METHOD OF DIFFERENCE helps us identify the causal factor in one observed instance of a phenomenon by comparing it with a *nearly similar* instance in which the phenomenon is not observed. If we compare Terry and Peter at the dinner party, there is a significant difference between the two. Terry sampled from every dish being served, whereas Peter ate everything except the salmon mousse. So the *only* difference between what Terry ate and what Peter ate is the salmon mousse. The fact that Terry subsequently developed food poisoning and that Peter did not provides reason to believe that the mousse, the only item in Terry's meal that Peter did not also eat, was the cause of his food poisoning. Therefore, it is probable that the salmon mousse caused Terry's food poisoning.

The argument form associated with the method of difference is as follows:

P is observed in 1 in circumstances a, b, c, ...z
P is not observed in 2 in circumstances b, c, ...z
Therefore, it is probable that a is the cause of P

In this schema, *1* and *2* refer to the two comparable things being observed. Again, *P* is the phenomenon for which we are seeking the cause, and the list of antecedent circumstances is *a ... z*. The argument says that because all antecedent circumstances for 1 and 2 are the same except *a*, we may infer that *a* is the cause of P in 1.

There is a variation of the argument form associated with the Method of Difference that we must also consider. Often when the Method of Difference is used in experimental contexts, it is not particular cases that are compared; rather, *groups* of cases are compared. In these cases, a researcher begins with a uniform population, then introduces a change into some members of the population while leaving the other members unchanged. Any subsequent difference between the two groups is inferred to be due to the change introduced to the one group. The change being introduced is called the EXPERIMENTAL VARIABLE, and the subsequent change to be observed is the OBSERVED VARIABLE OF INTEREST. The two groups are called the *subject group* and the *control group*. The SUBJECT GROUP is the part of the population in which the *experimental variable* is being manipulated. The CONTROL GROUP is that part of the population in which the *experimental variable* remains unchanged. If there is a subsequent difference in the *observed variable of interest* between the two groups, then it is probable that the *experimental variable* played a causal role in producing that difference.

Suppose a biologist is able to grow a thriving population of a microorganism species in a laboratory Petri dish. Suppose also that a divider is inserted into the centre of the dish so that the two sides are now completely sealed off from each other, with the population on each side of the dish being the same size. We now have two comparable groups. One group can serve as the control by having all circumstances remaining constant. The other group can serve as the subject group, in which one antecedent condition is manipulated as the experimental variable. Consider what might happen to these groups when salt is added to the subject group. In this case, salt is the experimental variable, and population size within each group is the observed variable of interest. If the population sizes become noticeably different, then we may infer that the salt *caused* this difference. That is, we may infer that the presence of salt is responsible if the value of the observed variable of interest in the subject group is different from that of the control group. Moreover, we may make an inference of this kind as long as there is *any* significant difference between the two populations. If the size of the subject group diminishes, while that of the control group grows or remains constant, we may infer that salt caused the population reduction. Alternatively, if the population of the subject group is observed to grow while the population of the control group remains the same or diminishes, we may infer that salt caused the population growth. Finally, if no difference is observed after salt is introduced to the subject group, then we may infer that salt has no causal role to play in the life of this species.

The form of argument associated with the Method of Difference when used to compare groups in this way is much like the argument form described above in connection with particular cases.

P is observed in the subject group in circumstances a, b, c, ...z
P is not observed in the control group in circumstances b, c, ...z
Therefore, it is probable that a is the cause of P.

As with other inductive forms of reasoning, the strength of these arguments is never purely a matter of form. Both premises could be true, yet the conclusion could be false. For the argument to be strong, the subject and control groups need to be designed in the right way. They must be comparable with each other, which is difficult to achieve when the population from which the groups are drawn is not as homogenous as the microorganism population described above. If, for example, the population consists of human beings, then some members will be older than others, some taller than others, some healthier, some heavier, some male, some female, etc. How do we get comparable subject and control groups when the group members are so diverse? To begin, rather than aim to make every member of the two groups identical, we can aim to make the distribution of traits the same in both groups. We can assign to each group comparable numbers of tall people, healthy people, males, females, etc. This can be done in one of two ways: (1) the proportion of group members with a certain trait can be *matched* to the proportion of members in the other group with the same trait; or (2) the selection process can be *randomized*. MATCHING means ensuring that the percentage of females in the subject group is the same as the percentage of females in the control group, and so on for other traits. RANDOMIZING means assigning members to the subject and control groups without any regard for specific traits;

if this is done arbitrarily, both groups should roughly equally reflect the distribution of traits within the overall population.

In order to assess an argument based on the Method of Difference, we must check to see whether it exhibits either of two weaknesses. First, we must consider whether there are any unobserved factors that may be playing a causal role in the occurrence of the phenomenon. As in the case of arguments based on the Method of Agreement, the antecedent circumstances that we notice will depend on what we think is relevant before we make our observations. But it is always possible that there might be other, unobserved differences that are causally more important than the ones we notice. Suppose, for example, that by mistake the salt added to the subject group in the Petri dish was iodized table salt rather than pure sodium chloride. Perhaps the observed change in the subject group was due to the iodine rather than the salt? Secondly, even if we have not missed anything relevant, we might not have isolated the specific causal factor involved, i.e., the causal agent. As we noted in connection with the Method of Agreement, there must be something in the salmon mousse that is the more precise cause of the food poisoning (botulism, salmonella, staphylococcus, etc.). These potential weaknesses, like the potential weaknesses with the Method of Agreement, are not reasons to distrust the method; rather, these are the reasons why we must take the conclusions of arguments based on these methods as being only probably true and not deductively certain.

11.2.3 JOINT METHOD OF AGREEMENT AND DIFFERENCE

It is possible to use the Methods of Agreement and Difference together in one extended line of argument. In fact, with the JOINT METHOD OF AGREEMENT AND DIFFERENCE the two methods can yield mutually confirming conclusions. We can see how they complement each other in the dinner party example. The entire argument can be developed in two stages. First, we can consider all the people who got sick, using the Method of Agreement to uncover the correlation between the instances of diners who ate salmon mousse and the instances of those who developed food poisoning. If we look at only the people who got sick, however, *two* antecedent circumstances seem to correlate with the phenomenon. At this point, the method of difference can be used to determine if either of these potential correlations constitutes an actual correlation or a significant correlation. Terry and Peter are then compared using the Method of Difference.

A schematic account of how the two methods can be used together in the food poisoning example looks like this:

STAGE I: METHOD OF AGREEMENT

Food poisoning [P] is observed in Terry [1] subsequent to eating salmon mousse [a], paté [b], garden salad [c], asparagus [d], and cake [e].

Food poisoning [P] is observed in Gillian [2] subsequent to eating salmon mousse [a], asparagus [d], and cake [e].

Food poisoning [P] *is observed in Eric* [3] *subsequent to eating salmon mousse* [a], *paté* [b], *asparagus* [d], *and cake* [e].

Food poisoning [P] *is observed in John* [4] *subsequent to eating salmon mousse* [a], *paté* [b], *asparagus* [d], *and cake* [e].

Food poisoning [P] *is observed in Graham* [5] *subsequent to eating salmon mousse* [a], *garden salad* [c], *and cake* [e].

Food poisoning [P] *is observed in Michael* [6] *subsequent to eating salmon mousse* [a], *garden salad* [c], *asparagus* [d], *and cake* [e].

Therefore, it is probable that either the salmon mousse [a] *or the cake* [g] *is the cause of the food poisoning* [P].

STAGE 2: METHOD OF DIFFERENCE (NOTE THAT [2] AT THIS STAGE IS NOW PETER, NOT GILLIAN):

Food poisoning [P] *is observed in Terry* [1] *subsequent to eating salmon mousse* [a], *paté* [b], *garden salad* [c], *asparagus* [d], *and cake* [e].

Food poisoning [P] *is not observed in Peter* [2] *subsequent to eating paté* [b], *garden salad* [c], *asparagus* [d], *and cake* [e].

Therefore, by the Method of Difference it is probable that salmon mousse [a] *is the cause of food poisoning* [P].

Therefore, by the Joint Method of Agreement and Difference it is probable that salmon mousse [a] *is the sole cause of food poisoning* [P].

Because both arguments identify salmon mousse as the cause, after accounting for the data in different ways, the probability that we have concluded correctly in this case is greatly increased.

Now consider an example that uses the second version of the Method of Difference. In developmental genetics, experimental research can be conducted on genes by removing or altering a gene or part of a gene that is thought to be responsible for the development of a particular feature of an organism. If members of the subject group have genetic material "knocked out" and they subsequently develop in a way that is different from what is normal, then the missing genetic material is inferred to be responsible for normal development. In this research, the experimental variable is the genetic material, which is not changed in the control group but removed from members of the subject group. Suppose a particular gene sequence is knocked out in a subject group of mice and that all these mice subsequently grow abnormally short, dense bones. If the bones in mice of a control group grow normally, then the conclusion may be drawn that the missing genetic material is a *necessary* causal factor in the development and elongation of bones. Like the earlier example, the argument associated with this experiment can be analyzed as developing in two stages.

STAGE 1: METHOD OF DIFFERENCE

Abnormally short, dense bones [P] are observed in the subject group of mice when they are deficient only in specific genetic material [antecedent circumstances b, c,... z].

Abnormally short, dense bones [P] are not observed in the control group of mice who have the specific genetic material [antecedent circumstances a b, c, ... z].

Therefore, by the Method of Difference it is probable that the genetic material [a] is the cause of bone growth.

STAGE 2: METHOD OF AGREEMENT

Short, dense bones [P] are observed in mouse 1, which had gene X manipulated [a], was weaned at 3 weeks [b], fed a diet of sunflower seeds [c], and received regular exercise [d].

Short, dense bones [P] are observed in mouse 2, which had gene X manipulated [a], was weaned at 4 weeks [e], fed a diet of sunflower seeds [c], and received regular exercise [d].

Short, dense bones [P] are observed in mouse 3, which had gene X manipulated [a], was weaned at 3 weeks [b], fed a diet of corn [f], and received no exercise [g].

Short, dense bones [P] are observed in mouse 4, which had gene X manipulated [a], was weaned at 5 weeks [h], fed a diet of corn [f], and received regular exercise [d].

Short, dense bones [P] are observed in mouse 5, which had gene X manipulated [a], was weaned at 3 weeks [b], fed a diet of peanuts [i], and received no exercise [g].

Short, dense bones [P] are observed in mouse 6, which had gene X manipulated [a], was weaned at 5 weeks [h], fed a diet of peanuts [i], and received regular exercise [d].

Short, dense bones [P] are observed in mouse 7, which had gene X manipulated [a], was weaned at 4 weeks [e], fed a diet of millet [j], and received regular exercise [d].

Therefore, by the Method of Agreement it is probable that the manipulation of gene X [a] is responsible for the short, dense bones [P] in this group of mice.

Again, we see in this example how the two methods can be used jointly to arrive at a conclusion. Not only can they be used jointly in this way, but the same set of observations can be used in both stages. In Stage 1 the subject group is considered in relation to the control group. Then in Stage 2 the members of THE SUBJECT group are considered in relation to each other. These arguments are assessed by checking each stage for the same weaknesses that are associated with the method used in that stage.

11.2.4 METHOD OF CONCOMITANT VARIATIONS

When we observe that variations in two phenomena coincide with each other, we have reason to believe that they are causally related. The METHOD OF CONCOMITANT VARIATIONS helps identify correlations between two distinct phenomena. This method is useful for diagnosing the source of changes over time or across different populations. It is especially useful when the variations may be described in terms of a proportion. For example, as the temperature increases in a closed container of liquid, the internal pressure increases, while as the temperature decreases, the internal pressure decreases. Also, as we move to higher altitudes, the air pressure decreases, while as we move to lower altitudes, it increases. And finally, we might discover that the average number of cavities in children in various populations varies inversely with the amount of fluoride in the water supply. In the first case, the observed variations are *proportional*, which means that as one value increases, the other increases in a fixed proportion. In the second case, the observed variations are *inversely proportional*, which means that as one value increases, the other decreases. The third case is inversely proportional, too. Not all uses of this method are so easily described as mathematical proportions, however. Mill's own example of this method concerns the relationship between the ocean tides and the moon. In this case, there is a correlation between the position of the moon relative to the earth and the locations of high and low tides on the earth. On the basis of this observed correlation (along with other things we know about gravity), we infer that tides are caused by the moon.

There are two argument forms associated with the Method of Concomitant Variations. The form for proportional relations is as follows:

P1 occurs with P2 in 1
P1+ occurs with P2+ in 2
P1- occurs with P2- in 3
Therefore, it is probable that changes in P2 cause proportional changes in P1.

In this schema, 1, 2, and 3 refer to the instances. P1 is the phenomenon for which we are seeking the cause, and P2 is the associated phenomenon that correlates with P1. It says that when the value of P1 increases, so does the value of P2 increase, and that when the value of P1 decreases, so does the value of P2 decrease. This form of the argument describes what happens when the method uncovers a proportional correlation. When the method uncovers an inversely proportional correlation, the form of argument associated with it is slightly different:

P1 occurs with P2 in 1
P1- occurs with P2+ in 2
P1+ occurs with P2- in 3

Therefore, it is probable that changes in P2 cause inversely proportional changes in P1.

In this schema, the argument says that when the value of P1 increases, the value of P2 decreases, and when the value of P1 decreases, the value of P2 increases. From this it is inferred that the second phenomenon is inversely related to the first.

   With this method, especially, a conclusion about the precise causal relationship between the two phenomena is difficult to establish. For while the Method of Concomitant Variations can identify a pattern of simultaneous or successive changes in the phenomena, this establishes only a correlation. We must go beyond the information in the premises to infer what is responsible for this correlation. For example, on the basis of available data about the tides and position of the moon alone, we cannot discount two other possibilities. It may be that the tides are responsible for the position of the moon, or it may be that a third factor is the cause of both. The first alternative simply reverses the causal order of the conclusion stated above. The second alternative says that Mill's sample argument about the tides commits the fallacy of common cause. We eliminate these possibilities, however, not because they are logically less secure than the original conclusion. Rather, because of what we believe about universal gravitation, we *interpret* tidal activity as the causal effect of the moon when we notice a correlation. Again, we are reminded that Mill's methods are inductive and that, however systematically they organize the data, they do not generate deductively certain conclusions. In order to function, this kind of reasoning requires a context within a larger body of knowledge about how the world operates. In this case, universal gravitation happens to be part of this body of knowledge.

11.2.5 METHOD OF RESIDUE

When we have a complex phenomenon the cause of which is partly explained by one or more antecedent circumstances, then we have reason to believe that any unexplained aspect of the phenomenon is caused by the remaining antecedent circumstances. The METHOD OF RESIDUE helps to identify the final causal factor in cases when the list of causal factors is nearly complete. For example, if we want to determine the mass of a certain quantity of liquid, we can weigh an empty container first, then weigh the container again with the quantity of liquid in it. Suppose the mass of the empty container is 1 kilogram, and that the mass of the container filled with liquid is 10 kilograms. By subtracting the mass of the container from the total mass of the container and liquid, we can determine that the mass of the liquid alone is 9 kilograms. More complex examples are possible. Suppose we want to determine what percentage of cases of hepatitis C have been transmitted sexually, and we have evidence to believe that there are three routes of transmission. If we know that 60 per cent of cases are caused by intravenous drug use, and that 15 per cent are caused by blood transfusions, then it is probable that the remaining cases (25 per cent) are transmitted sexually.

The form of the argument associated with the Method of Residue is as follows:

P consists of parts P_1, P_2, and P_3
P occurs in circumstances a, b, and c
a causes P_1
b causes P_2
Therefore, it is probable that c causes P_3.

In this schema, P is a complex phenomenon with parts P_1, P_2, and P_3, while a, b, and c are the antecedent circumstances. It says that the phenomenon consists of three parts, with all but one part being caused by all but one of the antecedent circumstances. From this we can infer that the remaining part is probably caused by the remaining antecedent circumstance.

As with the Method of Difference and the Method of Concomitant Variations, the Method of Residue has a variant with a slightly different form. The second version of the method is used to identify an interfering factor when we are dealing with a well-understood cause-and-effect relationship. Suppose a medication is ordinarily effective for reducing high blood pressure. If it is observed to be ineffective when taken at the same time as another medication, then the second medication is an interfering causal factor. The form of the argument associated with this version of the Method of Residue is as follows:

Ordinarily, a causes P
P does not occur in circumstances a and b
Therefore, it is probable that b interferes in the causal relation between a and P.

In this schema, P is the phenomenon and a and b are antecedent circumstances. The argument says that while a usually causes P, it does not do so in the presence of b. On the basis of this, it is inferred that b probably interferes in the causal connection between a and P.

To assess arguments based on the Method of Residue, we must first determine whether the background causal relationship asserted in the first premise is sufficiently well understood to support the conclusion. While the other methods described by Mill infer a causal relation from a correlation, the method of residue infers something about *part* of a causal relation from an account of the *whole* causal relation. Of course, this concern about the first premise is not a *logical* problem, since it amounts to a concern about premise acceptability. Still, because this legitimate concern can never be eliminated, the inference to the conclusion using this method is only probable, it's not deductively certain. Secondly, not only does it remain possible that we do not understand the causal process as well as the first premise alleges, but it is also possible that the part of the phenomenon to be accounted for is entirely due to unobserved circumstances or to an unobserved circumstance *and* the residual observed circumstance. Perhaps the remaining 25 per cent of cases of hepatitis C infections are due to sexual transmission *and* some other source that has not been noticed before.

11.3 Self-Test No. 17

For each of the following passages, identify which of Mill's methods is being used and describe the argument in the passage using the schematic form associated with that method.

1. Epidemiologists traced the illness [Severe Acute Respiratory Syndrome] back to a professor from China who was staying at Hong Kong's Metropole Hotel. Five other people who have come down with SARS stayed at the same hotel, with some of them staying on the same floor as the professor. (CBC News Online; March 20, 2003)

2. The mortality rate of SARS in the general population is not as high as news reports might suggest, and usually it can be treated successfully. The most recent estimates peg the general mortality rate at 10-15 per cent. However, this is deceptive, for the mortality rate is not the same for all groups. For those who are otherwise healthy and under 25 years of age, it is slightly less than 1 per cent. But for the elderly and for those who are already suffering from respiratory conditions, the rate rises to almost 50 per cent. So it is probable that SARS is much more difficult to treat successfully when the patient is elderly or suffering from a prior respiratory condition.

3. In case the central bank wants to slow down the economy it may ... increase ... lending rates. The increase in the lending rates would ultimately lead to a decrease in the money flow in the system. The decrease in the money flow in the system would lead to the slowing of ... demand. Slow down of ... demand would help to bring down inflation.
   In case the central bank and the government wants to put the economy in a growth trajectory then ... interest rates is one of the important tools it uses. A lowering of ... interest rates will lead to the increase of money in the system. Increase of money in the system will lead to an increase in the disposable income of the people and in turn increase the demand. Thus the decrease ... in the interest rates imparts buoyancy to the economy. (http://www.indiainfoline.com/nevi/ecin11.html)

4. All domesticated dog breeds become quite adept at responding to human gestures such as pointing. By contrast, neither their genetically close relatives, wolves, nor intellectually superior primates, such as chimpanzees, respond as well as dogs to the same cues. Therefore, it is likely that something happened in the evolutionary heritage of dogs (i.e., a combination of breeding and social-

ization) since they split off from wolves and that factor is responsible for this ability.

5. Former US Olympic hockey coach Herb Brooks probably fell asleep at the wheel before his fatal car crash last month, according to a report released yesterday [by] the [Minnesota] state police. The report confirmed that Brooks wasn't drinking, speeding, talking on his cellphone, or having a health problem before the crash. Police said weather and road conditions were ruled out [as the cause]. (*The Globe and Mail*, S4, September 17, 2003)

6. Twins ... have a [significantly] lower suicide rate, reports the *British Medical Journal*. Danish researchers ... identified 21,653 same-sex twins born between 1870 and 1930 and established the date and cause of their deaths from 1943 to 1993. They compared the number of suicides with the general population. The lower rate for twins supports the view that strong family ties reduce the risk for suicidal behaviour....

The strongest risk factor for suicide is mental illness, and other studies have found mental illnesses to be slightly more common among twins than single-tons. "This should lead to a higher proportion of twins committing suicide compared with the general population, but our findings show exactly the oppo-site, further underscoring the importance of strong family ties," they conclude. (*Toronto Star*, D3, August 22, 2003)

7. Stressed children are more likely to go for high-fat foods and snacks than their placid peers, regardless of whether they respond to anxiety by eating more or less than usual. A study of 4,320 British schoolchildren, appearing in the journal *Health Psychology*, found a strong relationship between stress and fatty foods. Those 11-year-olds who were the most stressed ate nearly twice as much fatty foods as their less anxious classmates. They also were the biggest snack-ers. At the same time, they "were also less likely to consume the recommended five or more fruits and vegetables a day and eat a daily breakfast," said Jane Wardle, director of the Cancer Research UK Health Behaviour unit. (*Globe and Mail*, A22, September 3, 2003)

8. In a famous experiment conducted 27 years ago by the Stanford University psychologist Philip Zimbardo, a car was parked on a street in Palo Alto, where it sat untouched for a week. At the same time, Zimbardo had an identical car parked in a roughly comparable neighborhood in the Bronx, only in this case the license plates were removed and the hood was propped open. Within a day, it was stripped. Then, in a final twist, Zimbardo smashed one of the Palo Alto car's windows with a sledgehammer. Within a few hours, that car, too, was destroyed. Zimbardo's point was that disorder invites even more disorder—that a small deviation from the norm can set into motion a cascade of vandalism and criminality. (*The New Yorker*, June 3, 1996)

11.4 Argument to the Best Explanation

In section 10.4 we examined how Induction by Hypothesis can be used to explain a set of observations. At the same time, observations can be used to test the truth of a hypothesis. When an observation statement that has been deduced from a hypothesis turns out to be true, we have inductively *confirmed* the hypothesis. When the observation statement is not true, we have *disconfirmed* the hypothesis. As we saw in Chapter 10, inductive *confirmation* falls short of deductive certainty, and a *disconfirmed* hypothesis can be saved or revised in a number of ways. So while we are concerned with the *truth* of a hypothesis, we do not have a direct and conclusive test to establish whether it is true or false. Moreover, a good hypothesis is not only true, it is also *explanatorily adequate*. EXPLANATORY ADEQUACY means that the hypothesis explains *all* instances of the phenomena, and that it does so with as much *precision* as possible. The first component of explanatory adequacy concerns the *scope* of the hypothesis; that is, it tells us how many instances of the phenomenon the hypothesis explains and specifies what restrictions apply. Naturally, the wider the scope the better the hypothesis. The best hypotheses have a universal scope; in other words, they cover *all* instances. The second component concerns the *accuracy* of the hypothesis; that is, it tells us how much detail the hypothesis is able to provide as an explanation of any particular observation. Naturally, the more detailed a hypothesis is the better, for it explains each instance *precisely*. For a hypothesis to be completely explanatorily adequate, there should be no unexplained instances of the phenomenon (in which case, we say its scope is *universal* or *unrestricted*), and the observation statements should be deducible from the hypothesis with as much precision as we are able to achieve in making the observations themselves.

Of course, if every observation is explained by a single hypothesis, then we have good grounds to accept the hypothesis. But there are two common situations in which the evidence is not so decisive. (1) Sometimes two or more rival hypotheses may each purport to explain *some* observations without either one explaining all of them; that is, both hypotheses are *restricted* in scope. If the hypotheses are inconsistent with each other, then at least one of them is not true. How do we decide which one to accept? (2) Sometimes two or more hypotheses purport to explain *all* the observations; that is, both hypotheses are *unrestricted*. Again, if they are inconsistent with each other, then at least one of them is not true. How do we choose which of these to accept?

The most decisive strategy for resolving an impasse of either kind is to devise a *crucial experiment*. A CRUCIAL EXPERIMENT is designed to generate an observation that is predicted to occur by one of the rival hypotheses and predicted not to occur by the other(s). In this way, one rival is confirmed and the other(s) disconfirmed. However, a disconfirmed hypothesis may be qualified, some of its key concepts may be redefined, its scope may be limited, or another part of the theory that generated it may be revised (see section 10.4). For these reasons, it is difficult to eliminate any of the rival hypotheses once and for all. There are, after all, people who still maintain that the world is flat and not spherical. Still, this doesn't mean that all hypotheses are equally acceptable or that there are never reasons to favour one hypothesis over others. Usually, we must assess hypotheses by asking which, on balance, is better than its rivals. The components of *explanatory adequacy* provide standards for making such comparative assessments. We can determine which of the rivals has the widest *scope*, and we can determine which is more *accurate*.

In section 11.4.1 we will consider what rational grounds are available to decide which hypothesis to prefer when two *restricted* hypotheses compete for our acceptance. Then in section 11.4.2 we will consider what rational grounds are available to decide which to prefer when two *unrestricted* hypotheses compete to explain the observations. These are not purely theoretical disputes, for they go right to the heart of what a science is supposed to do. Sciences are supposed to provide explanations for observed phenomena, and we want to use the best explanatory hypothesis available when we formulate an explanation. So it is important that we find a way to settle these disputes in a rationally defensible manner.

11.4.1 CHOOSING BETWEEN RIVAL RESTRICTED HYPOTHESES

Rarely, if ever, is there only one hypothesis that purports to explain something. When we have more than one hypothesis, we might say that the different hypotheses *compete* with each other for our acceptance. In these cases, we need to choose between RIVAL HYPOTHESES. Suppose Louis notices that the last piece of chocolate birthday cake that he has been saving in the fridge is gone and that the plate it was on is sitting in the sink, licked clean. If the only people who have been in the house since he put away the cake are his two brothers, Leo and Paul, then Louis might formulate two rival hypotheses. These are as follows:

> H1: *Leo ate the last piece of cake.*
> H2: *Paul ate the last piece of cake.*

Suppose also that Paul cannot stand the taste of chocolate or cake, and that chocolate cake is Leo's favourite dessert. Bearing this in mind, Louis will be able to recall many occasions when Leo devoured chocolate cake enthusiastically, and countless times when Paul declined cake (and other chocolate treats). All these memories of Leo eating cake can be counted as confirming observations for H1, and the memories of Paul declining can be counted as disconfirming observations of H2. In this case, the choice between H1 and H2 is pretty easy. H1 is far more likely to be true than H2. It isn't always as easy to choose between rival hypotheses as it was for Louis. But, in general, the logical situation is not fundamentally different from this. Let us develop a more sophisticated example to illustrate how this is so.

In the seventeenth century, physicists were divided over a controversy about the nature of light. Isaac Newton maintained that observations about the movement of light were best explained by thinking of it as an emission of particles. Christian Huygens, on the other hand, maintained that observations were best explained by thinking of its motion as a travelling wave. A summary of this controversy, which lasted until the early years of the twentieth century, illustrates the problem that arises when restricted hypotheses compete with each other (i.e., when some observations are explained by each hypothesis, but neither hypothesis explains all of them).

Both camps appealed to observations that seemed to confirm one hypothesis but not the other. According to Newton and other particle theorists, the hypothesis that light moves as a particle is confirmed by the observations that light travels in a straight line and that it reflects off mirrors in the same way a ball bounces off a wall. And according to Huygens and other wave theorists, the hypothesis that light moves as a wave is confirmed by observations that two beams of light can pass through each other without either one being disturbed and that light passing through a double-slitted screen diffracts in a pattern that resembles waves on a lake passing through two openings in a barrier. At the same time, however, the scope of both hypotheses is limited. The particle hypothesis cannot explain diffraction, and the wave hypothesis cannot explain why light does not move around corners.

The two hypotheses and their respective confirming observations can be described using the argument form for Induction by Hypothesis as follows:

HI: LIGHT AS A PARTICLE

If light is a particle [h1], *then a beam of light will travel in a straight line* [o1], *and a beam of light striking a mirrored surface will reflect off the surface at the same angle as the angle of incidence* [o2].

A beam of light does travel in a straight line [o1].

A beam of light striking a mirrored surface does reflect at the same angle as the angle of incidence [o2].

It is probable, therefore, that the hypothesis that light is a particle is true [h1].

H2: LIGHT AS A WAVE

If light is a wave [h2], *then two beams of light will cross paths without disturbing each other* [o3], *and a beam of light passing through a double-slitted screen will diffract* [o4].

Two beams of light do cross paths without disturbing each other [o3].

A beam of light passing through a double-slitted screen does diffract [o4].

It is probable, therefore, that the hypothesis that light is a wave is true [h2].

If one of these hypotheses had been more accurate than the other, then that might have tipped the scales in favour of the more accurate hypothesis. But in this case, it was not possible to settle the dispute in this way. Consequently, because neither hypothesis explained all the observations, the challenge for physicists was to find a formulation of one hypothesis that would expand its scope to cover the observations previously associated with the other hypothesis. The hypothesis with the greater scope will then have more explanatory power, which tips the scales in its favour.

Essentially, the wave hypothesis gained wider acceptance over the course of the eighteenth and nineteenth centuries because it was able to explain o1 and o2, while the particle hypothesis could not accommodate o3 and o4. However, waves require a medium, just as water is the medium of waves on a lake, and an *auxiliary hypothesis* about the nature of this medium was accepted along with the wave hypothesis. An AUXILIARY HYPOTHESIS is a second hypothesis that is logically required by the hypothesis under investigation. In this case, the *auxiliary hypothesis* postulated that all space (even a vacuum through which light can travel) is permeated with aether, a transparent, intangible, massless substance that acts as a stationary medium for the propagation of light waves. It was this *auxiliary hypothesis* that eventually raised concerns about the wave hypothesis. In 1895 two American scientists, Albert Michelson and Edward Morley, performed an experiment that disconfirmed the existence of aether. Huygens's formulation of the wave hypothesis could not be sustained without the *auxiliary hypothesis* about aether (although, as it turns out, the real change concerned the assumption that waves require a medium in which to travel). Because the particle hypothesis still could not accommodate o3 and o4, it became necessary for physicists to look for a new hypothesis about the nature of light. Accordingly, the new hypothesis had to accommodate all the observations about the phenomena associated with light (which by this time was believed to be only the visible part of the range of the electromagnetic spectrum) and to overcome the duality of the wave particle controversy. The new hypothesis, that light is a quantum of electromagnetic energy, became a central part of quantum theory.

For our purposes, there is no need to dwell on the technical, theoretical details of this controversy and the transition from the classical seventeenth-century hypotheses about light to the contemporary, quantum mechanical hypothesis. Our interest in this controversy lies in tracing out the rational principles involved in the process of searching for the best explanation. Both the original hypotheses were confirmed by some observations, and each one was restricted in its scope. The wave hypothesis gained wider acceptance as the best explanation because it came to cover a greater and greater range of observations. (In fact, the double-slit phenomenon [o4] was not observed by Thomas Young until the early part of the nineteenth century.) As the scope of the wave hypothesis expanded, it became more explanatorily powerful; that is, it became a better explanation. But the Michelson-Morley experiment disconfirmed a necessary *auxiliary hypothesis*, and it became difficult to accept the wave hypothesis that presupposed it. In view of the discovery that aether does not exist, it was no longer plausible to see the wave hypothesis as explanatory at all. This last development (along with several others that have been left out of this summary) encouraged physicists to reconsider the assumed wave/particle dichotomy and formulate a new hypothesis that synthesized the two.

Most importantly, this case illustrates how a dispute between two rival *restricted* hypotheses can be conducted as a rational debate and how its resolution can be described in rational terms. We must assess the rival hypotheses using the components of *explanatory adequacy*. We can do this by asking two questions: (1) is one hypothesis more accurate or precise than others? If not, then (2) does one hypothesis cover more observations than others? And, of course, if one hypothesis is both more accurate and covers more observations, it is that much better.

11.4.2 CHOOSING BETWEEN RIVAL UNRESTRICTED HYPOTHESES

Since the middle of the nineteenth century, evolutionists and creationists have debated over how to explain the existence of fossils and certain other geological phenomena. On one side, evolutionists claim that fossils are the petrified remnants of plants and animals that died millions of years ago. A central hypothesis of evolutionary theory is that the earth is millions, indeed billions, of years old and that this explains the observed fossil record. On the other side, a popular hypothesis among creation theorists is that the earth is only approximately 6,000 years old, and fossils are explained as taking their present form in the original moment of creation. A summary of this controversy illustrates the problem that arises when two rival hypotheses compete to explain *all* the same observations. Because this debate is still ongoing, and because it would divert us from our purpose to enter the fray as participants, we won't attempt to trace it through to a resolution (as we did in section 11.4.1). Instead, we'll use the debate to explore one further dimension of scientific reasoning.

In the wave/particle debate the two camps were initially divided not only by their respective hypotheses, but also by the observations that each side deemed to be relevant for testing the hypotheses. In the evolution/creation debate the disagreement may be even more fundamental, for both sides appear to accept the same observations as relevant. The fundamental difference can be shown by considering the following descriptions of the two lines of reasoning using the form of Induction by Confirmation.

EVOLUTION

> *If the earth is millions of years old* [h1], *then the part of lithosphere (i.e., the rocky crust of the earth) will be stratified* [o1], *and there will be fossils within these layers* [o2].

> *Parts of the lithosphere are stratified* [o1].

> *Fossils are found in the layers* [o2].

> *Therefore, it is probable that the earth is millions of years old* [h1].

CREATION

> *If the earth was created 6,000 years ago* [h2], *then part of the lithosphere will be stratified* [o1], *and there will be fossils within these layers* [o2].

> *Parts of the lithosphere are stratified* [o1].

> *Fossils are found in the layers* [o2].

Therefore, it is probable that the earth was created 6,000 years ago [h2].

How could two incompatible hypotheses both be confirmed by the same observations in this way? This is one of the most difficult and controversial theoretical questions associated with scientific reasoning. Fortunately, it's not necessary for us to solve this problem here. For our purposes, it will be enough to outline what lies behind the division between the two hypotheses and to indicate how the debate over a controversy of this sort can be conducted.

Because o1 and o2 are worded as neutral descriptions of facts, it looks as if evolutionists and creationists are both making arbitrary deductions in the first premise of each argument. But, as we pointed out above, *explanatory adequacy* requires that the observations deduced from a hypothesis be both true for all observation statements and *precise*. It is in attempting to meet the second part of the standard of explanatory adequacy, precision or accuracy, that the deep difference between these two hypotheses emerge. Neither evolutionists nor creationists should be content with the bland, undetailed description of the facts as o1 and o2 describe them. For example, consider how each would elaborate on o2 to improve its precision. Each camp will define *fossil* differently. An evolutionist might define it as *the petrified remains or traces of any organism that lived in the distant geological past*, whereas a creationist might define it as *mineral patterns that have the appearance of plants or animals*. Moreover, an evolutionist will maintain that petrification of organic material takes place under certain conditions in a process that requires millions of years to complete, whereas a creationist will maintain that the mineral patterns that distinguish fossils were produced by God in the act of creation. Now we begin to see how the observation statements can be explained so differently by the two hypotheses: what evolutionists and creationists disagree over is the *interpretation* of the observed phenomena. *This* is the deep problem that divides evolutionists and creationists so sharply.

In section 10.4 we saw that hypotheses can be disconfirmed, but also that a disconfirmed hypothesis can be saved in a number of ways—for example, by restricting its scope. Then in section 11.4.1 we saw that when two incompatible restricted hypotheses compete for acceptance, the balance of confirming and disconfirming instances can tip the scales in favour of one over the other. This was how the original particle hypothesis was eventually ruled out as an explanation of light by the late nineteenth century. We also saw in section 11.4.1 that a hypothesis can come to be rejected if a necessary auxiliary hypothesis is unacceptable. This is how the original wave hypothesis also lost favour among physicists. In all these cases, hypotheses were tested by determining whether the observation statements that could be deduced from them were true. Now we see that in order for two scientists to come to the same assessment of a hypothesis, each must *interpret* the observed phenomena in the same way. Differences of interpretation will become evident in the way observational details are described with *precision*. Moreover, the precise way these details are described depends on the entire *theory* within which the hypothesis is set. A THEORY is a systematically integrated set of general principles, methods of investigation, and concepts whose function is to explain a wide array of phenomena. Theories generate hypotheses about specific phenomena, but, significantly, they also provide the filter or lens through which we interpret the observations that test hypotheses. (This is quite different from the popular, unscientific conception of a theory as an untested hypothesis or a guess, by the way; in science, a theory is much more systematic and regulative than these popular notions suggest.) The interpretive role performed by a theory in formulating a precise observation statement is the ultimate source of some profound controversies in science, such as over the age of the earth. For the most part, the rivalry between the wave hypothesis and the particle hypothesis was a rivalry between two players in the same game, so to speak; both hypotheses attempted to explain the nature of light within the larger theoretical framework of a *mechanistic* theory of the universe. The mechanistic theory attempts to explain all phenomena as material elements that interact in a mathematically determined fashion. Because both waves and particles can be described in these terms quite well, both were attractive models for the nature of light. But in the debate over the age of the earth, the two rival hypotheses may not be playing the same game, which is illustrated by the disagreement over how to formulate observation statements precisely; rather, what may be ultimately at stake here concerns which game rules to apply. If two games are very similar (e.g., ice hockey with bodychecking and ice hockey without bodychecking), then it may not be difficult to debate over which rules apply. If two games are similar in some ways but quite different in others (e.g., ice hockey without bodychecking and ringette), then this debate is more difficult. And if two games are very different (e.g., ice hockey with bodychecking and golf), then the debate is going to be much more difficult, if not impossible.

When theories differ so much that it's impossible to test any of their respective hypotheses with the same observation statements, then we must consider the possibility that the theories are *incommensurable*. INCOMMENSURABILITY literally means *not capable of being measured by a common standard*, and it refers to the relationship between two things that are so different that it's not possible to make an objective comparative judgement about them. (In essence, this is what the cliché about the impossibility of comparing apples and oranges means.) Theories are incommensurable when there is no available standard that is independent of both theories and by which we can test to determine which theory is better. It may well be that evolutionism and creationism are indeed incommensurable. This itself is a matter of much debate. But within the scientific community, evolution has been the preferred theory, and along with it, the hypothesis that the earth is millions (indeed billions) of years old has been the preferred hypothesis about the age of the earth. How has this happened?

Evolutionism has simply offered more opportunities to pursue research into the questions that give science its distinctive purpose, that is, the *Why ...?* questions about the way natural processes work. No decisive refutation of creationism has been involved in this preference. And because theories can be saved from refutation in all the same ways that hypotheses can be saved from disconfirmation, no such refutation should be expected. Still, this doesn't mean that the preference for one theory over the other, such as the preference for evolution over creationism, is arbitrary. For in this case, the research program offered by creationism seems always to lead to the same answer. For creationism, all the *Why ...?* questions are ultimately resolved in terms of God's intentions, which are often said to be beyond human comprehension. It's not that there aren't interesting and thoughtful ways to provide answers to such questions with creation theory. But, however interesting and thoughtful they may be, they have not been interesting to scientists because the justification for them rests as much, if not more, on biblical exegesis than on empirical investigation. Creationism does not suggest observation statements that are testable by empirical scientific research. In contrast, evolutionism suggests many avenues of empirical research. For example, if one genus of animal is hypothesized to have evolved from another genus (e.g., birds may have evolved from reptiles), then we should find no evidence of the later evolving genus below a certain point in the layers of rock and we should find some evidence of the earlier evolving genus below that point. It is primarily because evolutionism has generated so many detailed hypotheses of this sort that it has been accepted by most scientists.

Here again, we see that the standard of *explanatory adequacy* provides guidance in the scientific choice between two hypotheses, even when the hypotheses are unrestricted and may be incommensurable. In these cases an assessment can be made using the standard of accuracy: the hypothesis that generates more *precise* observation statements to confirm it is more explanatorily powerful.

11.5 Case for Discussion: Semmelweis's Discovery of Antisepsis

The process of discovery recounted below may be described using several of the concepts and argument forms covered in this chapter, along with a few from earlier chapters. There are several discrete stages in the overall line of reasoning that begin with the first observation of the phenomenon and end with a conclusion about the cause of that phenomenon. Using the information from this account (1) identify the hypotheses being tested and (2) identify the separate stages in the overall line of argument. Also, (3) identify what kind of argument form is used at that stage, and (4) describe the argument using the appropriate form for each stage.

Ignaz Semmelweis (1818–65) was a professor of medicine in the Doctor's Ward of the Vienna General Hospital from 1844 to1848. The hospital was dedicated exclusively to the obstetrical care of poor women. For many years before Semmelweis arrived and for many of his first months there, the hospital had an unusually high mortality rate among the patients who came there to deliver their babies. In particular, there were frequent outbreaks of a life-threatening illness known as puerperal fever, which is better known as childbed fever.

We now know that childbed fever is a bacterial infection of the female genital tract which is contracted during childbirth. In the nineteenth century, however, the source and transmission of infectious disease was very poorly understood. It was not until 1857 that Louis Pasteur discovered germ theory, which explained both the specific cause of infectious diseases as being microorganisms and how these diseases are spread in a community. Without Pasteur's theory, it was much more difficult to understand childbed fever. (Even then, it was not until the 1870s that Pasteur himself identified the microorganism responsible.) Furthermore, in the 1840s there was no treatment for the condition, and very few women who contracted it survived.

The hospital had two divisions, the Doctor's Ward where Semmelweis and other professors delivered babies and taught obstetrics students, and the Midwives' Ward where midwives and their students delivered babies; the two divisions were in separate but adjacent wings. Besides providing obstetrical training on live births, physicians in the Doctor's Ward performed autopsies as part of the course of instruction for their students. For many years the Doctor's Ward had a maternal mortality rate of approximately 10 per cent, which means that of the 3,000 or so births in any year 300 women died. During epidemic periods the maternal mortality rate rose as high as 20–50 per cent. In the Midwives' Ward, however, the rate of death due to childbed fever was much lower. In 1844 it was 2.3 per cent, in 1845 it was 2.0 per cent, and in 1846 it was 2.7 per cent.

When Semmelweis raised concerns about the rate of childbed fever in the Doctor's Ward and asked his supervisor how it could be so high, he was told that the fever was inevitable with patients at this hospital, who were among the poorest in Vienna (expectant women from higher economic classes were generally attended to by a private physician in their own homes). He was told that the women treated in the Vienna General Hospital were from an "inferior" class of society, which made them susceptible to *miasma* (which means *pollution*), or atmospheric forces that harboured childbed fever in the air. Semmelweis found this explanation unsatisfactory for two reasons: (1) women who gave birth on the way to the hospital were far less likely to die from childbed fever than those who actually made it there in time to give birth (this rate was nearly 0 per cent). Why would the atmospheric conditions in the neighbourhood outside the doors of the hospital be different from those inside the hospital? (2) Since every woman admitted to the hospital came from the same socioeconomic class and the two wards were adjacent, *all* the women at the hospital should have been equally affected by the *miasma*. But the infection rate in the Midwives' Ward was much lower than in the Doctor's Ward, despite the fact that both divisions were equally exposed to the "atmospheric conditions" that were said to be responsible. Why was there a significantly different rate of infection between the two divisions?

Someone suggested that overcrowding in the Doctor's Ward might be the problem. But the Midwives' Ward was more crowded than the Doctor's Ward, so this couldn't explain the difference. (In fact, many women contrived to be admitted to the Midwives' Ward, because the rate of maternal mortality in the Doctor's Ward was notoriously high.) Another suggestion was that foreign medical students in his division (of which there were many) were too rough with women during examination. But, Semmelweis noted, delivery was far more traumatic than anything that might be done during examination; besides, there was no evidence that foreign students were rougher than other students or the physicians themselves. Semmelweis also noted that there seemed to be no differences in the patients of the two divisions with respect to the diet or general care. Finally, Semmelweis noticed that there was a higher incidence of childbed fever in the Doctor's Ward among women who had long labours than those whose labours were brief.

Looking for what may account for the differences between the two divisions, Semmelweis noticed that priests coming to perform last rites in the Doctor's Ward entered at one end of the hall, then proceeded down the entire hallway, past all the beds of new mothers to the room to which infected patients were removed after being diagnosed. By contrast, a priest entering the Midwives' Ward to perform last rites could get to the dying patient without passing any other patients. Perhaps the psychological stress of having the priest pass by otherwise healthy women in the Doctor's Ward to perform this task was provoking periodic epidemics? Semmelweis arranged for the priests to enter by a secondary staircase hoping that this would reduce the infection rate. No reduction in the rate of infection was observed. Other, similar changes were introduced to the protocols of the Doctor's Ward, all equally ineffective.

Early in 1847 one of Semmelweis's colleagues, Jakob Kolletschka, died after receiving a puncture wound from a scalpel while performing an autopsy. While examining the pathology report on Kolletschka's death, Semmelweis noticed that his colleague exhibited the same symptoms as childbed fever. Semmelweis thought that "cadaveric matter" had entered Kolletschka's blood through the scalpel wound and caused his illness. Kolletschka's death led Semmelweis to believe that the women under his care had died from a similar kind of poisoning, not from something in the air. Semmelweis, his colleagues, and their students had been inadvertent carriers of the infectious "cadaveric material." They often came to deliver babies directly from performing autopsies, and routinely they examined patients after only superficially washing their hands. In contrast, the midwives never performed autopsies; therefore, they were not infecting their patients with "cadaveric matter."

Semmelweis ordered physicians and students to wash their hands in a chlorinated lime solution as a chemical means to disinfect their hands after performing autopsies. The results were immediate and dramatic. The maternal mortality rate had been 13.1 per cent in July 1846, and 18.05 per cent in August 1846. In May 1847, just before Semmelweis's antiseptic hand-washing practice was introduced, it was still as high as 12.24 per cent. But in the first month after the practice was instituted, June 1847, it dropped to 2.38 per cent. The rate dropped in July 1847 to 1.2 per cent, and in March and April 1848 there were no deaths due to childbed fever in the division. By 1848 the annual mortality rate due to childbed fever in the Doctor's Ward fell to 1.27 per cent (correspondingly, it fell to 1.3 per cent in the Midwives' Ward).

For many months after the practice was introduced in the Doctor's Ward, the infection rate of childbed fever remained close to this low level. Then, after a period of stability, a wave of infections temporarily spread through the division. One day during rounds, physicians first treated a pregnant woman who had an ulcerated cervical tumour, then they proceeded to examine several other women immediately afterwards. Since physicians had already disinfected their hands before treating the first patient, they didn't disinfect them again afterwards. Eleven of the 12 women treated after this woman died of childbed fever. In light of this incident, Semmelweis revised his initial claim about the source of infection. Now he maintained that it was caused by "cadaveric matter or putrid organic matter." We now know that the more precise description of the cause is microscopic bacteria, but Semmelweis's imprecise description was enough for practical purposes. As long as physicians and students in the division washed their hands with the chlorinated lime solution before examining any patient, the rate of infection remained low.

Independently of Semmelweis's work, Oliver Wendell Holmes (1809–94, poet and father of the famous jurist, Oliver Wendell Holmes, Jr.) came to the same conclusions about both the contagiousness of childbed fever and how to prevent it. And shortly after Semmelweis's death, Joseph Lister (1827–1912) designed a similar antiseptic system for clinical practice based on Louis Pasteur's germ theory. Semmelweis is now acknowledged to have been at the leading edge of this revolution in hospital practice.

12.   Moral Reasoning

Moral reasoning—reasoning that leads to judgements about right and wrong, good and bad, fair and unfair—presents special difficulties. Much of what we have dealt with so far in this book is of only limited use when dealing with moral arguments. The primary difficulty is that the criteria we actually use to assess moral judgements are themselves moral in nature, at least in part. In fact, at first glance it seems that when we criticize the moral judgements of others, we are doing nothing more than setting our moral standards in opposition to theirs. You think a progressive income tax is unfair and I think it is fair, and it seems that when we have finished berating each other for being hard-hearted or soft-headed, there is nothing else we can say to one another. Certainly, it often seems that there is nothing *rational* that two people can say to each other when they have a moral disagreement. Some people conclude from this that moral judgements are essentially like judgements of taste: I like the taste of parsnips, you can't stand it. As they say, there's no accounting for tastes, and if moral judgements are merely matters of taste, then there is no room for rational debate and discussion, and our critical thinking skills will be of no use to us. Is this a reasonable view?

12.1 Moral Judgements and Judgements of Taste

Moral judgements and judgements of taste are obviously similar in some respects. But the suggestion that they are essentially the same rests on a weak analogy, for there are major differences between them. First, their subject matters are quite different. Moral judgements are always about how people *ought* to be treated, either how we should treat others or how others should treat us. Judgements of taste, on the other hand, are always about the kinds of experiences we *like* or *dislike*. Some of these experiences may involve other people, such as playing hockey or having a party, but when judgements of taste involve others, they do not involve judgements about how we ought to treat them. Judgements of taste, in other words, are nothing more than descriptions or expressions of our feelings and imply nothing about how we ought to treat one another.

Second, almost everyone believes that moral judgements are capable of being justified, whereas almost no one believes that judgements of taste can be justified. People may think you are pretty peculiar because you like parsnips, but it would never occur to anyone to suggest that you should be called upon to justify your liking for parsnips. If you were, what could you say? Only that, odd as it may seem, you really do like parsnips. You might add that you like them because of the way your mother used to cook them when you were a child; this does not, of course, justify your taste, it only explains it. In the end, all you can do is to reiterate that you just do like parsnips. Judgements of taste, in other words, are immune to demands for justification. With moral judgements, on the other hand, we always accept, and usually respond to, the demand for justification. I think a progressive income tax can be justified on the grounds that it redistributes wealth to those whose need is greatest and also contributes to economic growth by increasing demand for goods and services. This justification may not persuade you to change your views, but it is clearly an attempt to provide a justification, that is, to provide reasons in support of my view.

Third, moral judgements, unlike judgements of taste, are always generalizable. What this means is that whenever we make a particular moral judgement (i.e., a judgement about what is right or wrong for me or someone else to do in a particular set of circumstances), we are committed to making a similar moral judgement about what would be right or wrong for others to do in similar situations. For example:

> DIANE: *I don't see anything wrong with not paying Carl the $20 I owe him.*
> JEAN: *How can you say such a thing! How would you feel if someone refused to pay you money that they owed you?*

Jean's question presupposes that Diane's moral judgement can be generalized. Jean is in effect saying:

> *If it is morally acceptable for you not to repay Carl, then it must also be morally acceptable for someone who owes you money not to repay you.*

This is a way of making the point that there is a moral principle involved in Diane's judgement and that the principle is one that could be applied against Diane in certain (perhaps hypothetical) situations. With judgements of taste, on the other hand, there is no analogous move. If I like Mozart, you might think that I should also like Haydn, but if I don't, you cannot turn around and challenge my judgement that I like Mozart. I just do like Mozart and don't like Haydn, and that is all there is to the matter.

These three differences show that the analogy between moral judgements and judgements of taste is very weak. The second difference—that moral judgements call for some sort of justification—is crucially important because the only way to justify a moral judgement is by developing an argument, and arguments are, of course, always open to critical assessment. But what is a strong moral argument? What kinds of premises can we use to defend our moral conclusions? In other words, what premises can we appeal to that will be acceptable, relevant, and adequate?

12.2 Moral Justification

Before looking at the criteria for assessing moral arguments, we need to consider briefly the views of the radical sceptic. Radical sceptics hold that there are no criteria for moral justification at all and that the belief that there are such criteria is an illusion that is explainable only by reference to some deep psychological need or to our social and cultural history. (Those who claim that moral judgements are essentially matters of taste are usually radical sceptics.) Radical sceptics present us with a fundamental challenge, for they are in effect challenging us to prove our basic moral principles. The best refutation of this challenge would, of course, be a proof of some fundamental principle of morality, such as the principle that we should always seek to produce as much happiness as possible. If such a proof could be discovered, radical sceptics would have to give up their scepticism. However, philosophers have failed to find such a proof despite more than 2,000 years of searching. Each "proof" has, on reflection, turned out to be flawed in some way (usually because it begs the question) and thus is not sufficient to refute the radical sceptic. But the fact that we cannot refute radical scepticism does not force us to accept it. For just as no one has been able to prove that radical scepticism is false, so radical sceptics have been unable to prove that it is true. The fact that philosophers have failed to find an acceptable proof of any objective moral principle does not prove that there cannot be such a principle. Nor does it prove that it is unreasonable to believe in such principles. In fact, the force of the radical sceptic's challenge relies upon the assumption that it is unreasonable to believe in any objective moral principle unless it can be proven rationally. But this assumption is certainly not an obvious truth, and is open to serious objection. There are many fundamental principles of mathematics and science, for example, that cannot be proven to be true, but it would be quite unreasonable to reject them just for this reason.

We thus find ourselves in a dilemma. The radical sceptic cannot prove that objective moral criteria do not exist, and those who believe in such criteria cannot prove that they do exist. The most reasonable response to this dilemma is to ignore it. If proofs are unattainable, then we are free to choose between accepting and rejecting objective moral criteria.

Moral sceptics, while denying that basic moral principles are objective facts, capable of rational proof, almost always agree with those who believe in objective moral truths that morality is a deeply important part of life, and that it can be reasoned about. But the question arises for their position: if there are no objective moral truths, then isn't all morality just a matter of trivial individual subjective feeling, like taste in ice cream? Philosophical moral sceptics have tried to answer this question in various ways. What just about everyone agrees on is that morality should be taken seriously, and reasoned about.

There are two different sorts of reasoning that philosophers think we appropriately use when thinking about morality. Both are found in typical moral thought throughout history, and in all cultures. Each approach is systematized by a type of moral theory. Theories of the first type (called DEONTOLOGICAL theories) hold that the rightness or wrongness of an action is to be determined by appeal to an objective moral principle according to which actions of that type are right or wrong. The following are some principles that typically function in this way:

Thou shalt not commit adultery.
Never punish an innocent person.
Always tell the truth.
Everyone has the right to freedom of expression.

Theories of the second type (called TELEOLOGICAL or CONSEQUENTIALIST theories) hold that the rightness or wrongness of an action is to be determined by appeal to the goodness and badness of the consequences of all the actions open to the agent: the right action is the one which will have the best overall consequences.

Whenever we attempt to justify something we have done or intend to do, our justification inevitably rests upon one or other of these approaches. Either we appeal to some moral principle according to which our action is right, or we appeal to the consequences of our action and claim that they are better than the consequences of anything else we could have done, or we make both appeals together. For example, someone may justify a decision not to cheat on their income tax by appeal to the principle that one should tell the truth, or by appeal to the harmful consequences of cheating, or by both appeals at the same time. Every justification for an action will be of one or other of these types. (It should be noted that justifications are different from excuses, such as that we made a mistake, lost our temper, or were acting under duress. When we plead an excuse, we are in effect denying that we are really responsible for the action and hence do not need to provide any justification.) Once we accept the responsibility for an action and attempt to justify it, we inevitably appeal either to some specific moral principle or to the consequences of the action.

For our purposes we do not need to examine the details of particular theories. To do so would involve us in a number of issues that are of importance for a full understanding of ethics but that shed very little light upon moral reasoning. What we need is an understanding of how each type of approach gives rise to a method of moral justification, how each type can be assessed, and how the two types can come into conflict with one another.

12.3 Appeals to Principles of Right and Wrong

The initial step in justifying a particular moral judgement on the basis of an appeal to a principle of right and wrong is to articulate the principle involved. If we can find an appropriate moral principle, then we will have justified the particular moral judgement. This move is familiar to everyone. In the following examples the word *because* introduces the moral principles that are being appealed to.

He should not have killed his severely retarded daughter, because it is wrong to take an innocent life.
It was wrong for the police to use coercion to try to get Martin to confess, because the police ought to obey the law.
Ben Johnson should not have used steroids because cheating is wrong.

This is also how Jean argued in the example used in section 12.1:

Diane should repay Carl the $20 she owes him, because one ought to repay one's debts.

If Diane accepts this principle, she will be forced to accept the particular judgement. The principle thus justifies the judgement in the sense that anyone who accepts the principle must accept the particular judgement.

But conversely, if Diane rejects the principle, she will have no reason to accept the particular judgement on which it is based. Does this mean that the justification has failed? Not necessarily. Obviously it has failed to persuade Diane, but this may be Diane's fault rather than the principle's. How, then, are we to defend the moral principles we invoke to justify our actions and judgements? What can Jean say to Diane to persuade her to accept the principle? The most powerful argument that can be used to defend particular moral principles derives from the feature of particular moral judgements we noted in section 12.1, namely, that they can be generalized. This feature reflects what is called the *generalization* principle:

A right action is one that is entailed by a principle that is acceptable when applied generally, and a wrong action is one that is entailed by a principle that is unacceptable when applied generally.

When this principle is used to defend a particular moral principle, such as *one ought to repay one's debts*, the resulting argument is called a GENERALIZATION ARGUMENT. There is nothing mysterious about the generalization argument; it is very widely used by almost everyone and was used earlier by Jean:

DIANE: *I don't see anything wrong with not paying Carl the $20 I owe him.*
JEAN: *How can you say such a thing! How would you feel if someone refused to pay you money that they owed you?*

Whenever the question *How would you feel if everyone did that?* is used, the generalization argument is being invoked. The generalization argument is often expressed as the Golden Rule: *Do unto others as you would have them do unto you.* A more explicit rendering is: It is always wrong to treat others in a way that you would object to if others treated you that way, and it is always right to treat others in the way that you demand others treat you.

How is the generalization argument assessed? What are its strengths and weaknesses? To answer these questions we have to examine how such arguments work in more detail. When Jean invokes the generalization argument in the above passage, she is in effect saying that Diane should agree that refusing to repay Carl is wrong because she, Diane, would not agree that others would be justified in using that principle as a reason for refusing to repay a debt to her. Jean is claiming that Diane's refusal to repay Carl must be based upon the principle that it is morally acceptable to refuse to repay one's debts. Since Diane has already implicitly accepted this principle, she can legitimately be challenged to defend it, not just in the particular application where she wants not to repay a debt, but in general. A general defence of the principle requires her to accept the application that others may make of the principle even when it is applied against her. How would she feel if someone refused to pay her money that they owed her?

This argument puts Diane in a bind. On the one hand, if she rejects the principle when others apply it against her, then she cannot apply it against others. On the other hand, if she wants to apply it against others, then she must allow others to apply it against her. If she tries to eat her cake and have it too, by accepting the principle when she wants to apply it against others and rejecting it when others apply it against her, she is a hypocrite. (It is in circumstances of this sort that the *tu quoque* argument [see section 7.4.2] can be used legitimately.) To avoid hypocrisy, Diane must choose between the two alternatives: either give up the principle and repay her debt to Carl, or accept the principle and allow others to renege on their debts to her.

The generalization argument does, however, leave room for a counter-argument that, if successful, would allow Diane to escape the dilemma Jean has tried to put her in. Diane might refuse to accept the principle Jean claims is implicit in her judgement. She might, for example, reply to Jean as follows:

> *Look, I'm not basing my judgement on the principle that it is always morally acceptable for people to refuse to repay their debts. I accept the principle in general, but there is an exception to it: that it is morally acceptable to postpone repaying a debt if repaying it would cause personal hardship. Repaying Carl now would mean giving him my next week's grocery money. It is a pity, but he is going to have to wait for a few weeks.*

Diane's reply shows that she does not accept Jean's generalization of her particular judgement. Diane is claiming that the principle underlying her judgement is different from the principle Jean has attributed to her. Note that Diane is not denying that she must appeal to some principle to defend her judgement; her claim is that Jean has appealed to the wrong principle.

If Jean still wants to challenge Diane's judgement, she has to focus on this new principle. She can argue that Diane faces a new dilemma: if she applies this principle against Carl, she must allow other people to apply the principle against her, and if she is unwilling to allow others to apply it against her, she cannot apply it against Carl. Unlike the first dilemma Jean posed, the second one is such that Diane could reasonably accept it when others apply it against her. She might respond as follows:

But I am willing to allow others to apply the principle against me. When I lend money to someone, I do so on the basis that they should repay me only when they can afford to do so. If someone is never able to repay me, I would regard it as a kind of donation to a worthy cause.

By acknowledging that she is prepared to allow others to use her moral principle against her, Diane has provided a plausible justification for her initial judgement.

What are Jean's options at this point? She has two. First, she can challenge the sincerity of Diane's claim that she thinks it would be morally right for others to refuse to repay a debt to her if they could not afford to do so. Does Diane really believe this, or is she merely saying that she does? Jean might be able to point to another situation in which Diane had demanded repayment of a debt from someone who could not afford to repay her. Diane would then either have to admit she had been wrong to demand repayment (in which case she might be open to another charge of insincerity) or concede that she is now being hypocritical. The charge of insincerity is often difficult to sustain, for we have no direct access to the feelings and motives of others. Jean may suspect that Diane is being insincere but be unable to find much good evidence to support her suspicions. Even Diane may have to admit that she cannot be sure whether she would be so ready to forgive someone who refused to repay a debt to her: perhaps she is deceiving herself about the kind of person she is. However, the fact that generalization arguments leave us open to possible charges of insincerity shows the importance of ensuring that we should not make such claims unless we really mean what we say.

Second, Jean may challenge Diane's version of the principle she is implicitly appealing to. For example:

But you cannot use that principle unless you make sure that the person from whom money is borrowed realizes that the debt will be repaid only when the borrower can afford to do so. Did Carl know that he wouldn't get his money back until you felt you could afford it?

If Carl knew that the debt would be repaid only when Diane could afford it, then Diane can accept this new version of the principle, since it justifies her initial judgement and she can accept it when others apply it against her. On the other hand, if Carl did not know, then Diane faces the old dilemma: either she must accept that it is morally acceptable for others to mislead her when they are borrowing money from her, or she must concede that she is not morally justified in refusing to repay Carl.

The above example has been developed at considerable length because it illustrates the steps that may be involved in attempts to justify a particular moral judgement on the basis of the generalization argument. These steps can be summarized as follows:

(1) We appeal to some general moral principle according to which our particular moral judgement is correct.

(2) We defend the general moral principle by showing that we accept that it would be morally right for others to follow it, even when it is applied against ourselves.

(3) The claims made in step (2) must be sincere; if challenged, we must be able to make a believable case for our sincerity.

(4) If we are unsuccessful in steps (2) or (3), we must go back to step (1) and look for another general moral principle that will allow us to carry out steps (2) and (3) successfully.

These steps show not only what we must do to develop an adequate generalization argument, but also the kind of challenges we may have to respond to and how we can challenge a generalization argument put forward by another person. These challenges are, first, that the general moral principle invoked may not be acceptable because the person invoking it does not accept that others are morally entitled to use the principle against him or her (step 2), and second, that the person's claim to accept the principle may be insincere (step 3).

12.4 Self-Test No. 18

Suggest two different moral principles that, if accepted, would justify each of the following particular moral judgements:

1. I refuse to vote for Robinson because he was convicted two years ago for tax evasion.

2. I think what she did was wrong. I believe she should take her children and move back in with her husband as soon as possible, if he'll still take her back.

3. I have no sympathy for him. He should have informed the police as soon as he realized they were selling illegal drugs, and if he had to go to court to give evidence at the trial, then that's just too bad.

4. How can you even think of handing in an essay that someone else has written?

5. All those people who turn up in Canada claiming refugee status, like the boat people a few years ago, should be sent back to where they came from.

12.5 Questions for Discussion

Each of the following arguments appeals to a moral principle to justify a particular moral judgement. What kinds of questions should be asked to determine whether the reasoning is acceptable? If the reasoning is unacceptable, is there another principle that could justify the action or policy?

1. The school board should ban the use of corporal punishment by teachers. Only parents have the right to inflict physical punishment on their children.

2. We would all agree to condemn someone who inflicted pain on a child simply to obtain pleasure. Everyone agrees that inflicting pain for pleasure is inherently evil, and our condemnation is especially strong when the pain is inflicted on those who have done nothing to deserve it. Those who eat meat can only do so at the cost of great pain and suffering being inflicted on farm animals, both in the way they are raised and in the way they are slaughtered. So there can be no justification for eating meat.

3. It was wrong for Warren to break his promise to Marilyn that she could use his car to drive to her sister's wedding. The fact that he wanted to use his car to visit his mother who was having an operation is no excuse. Promises ought to be kept.

4. The government was right to prosecute the protestors who were involved in the confrontation at the G8 conference, since they clearly broke the law. A state is always entitled to punish those who break its laws.

5. Mrs. Robinson was entirely justified in not informing the police that her husband was involved in illegal arms sales to Iraq, even though she knew he was involved. When loyalty to one's family clashes with loyalty to the laws of one's country, one ought to prefer one's family.

12.6 Appeals to Consequences

Appeals to consequences are much easier to describe. They involve three steps.

First, we must identify the alternative actions open to us in the situation we face. Sometimes there may be only two alternatives, for example, to photocopy a library book illegally, or not to do so. Frequently, however, there are more than two alternatives, for example, to drink a lot, to drink a little, to drink nothing, or not to go to the party at all. There must always be at least two alternatives open to us. Moral decisions are made only when we face a choice: if there is no room for choice, then no moral decision needs to be made. But when we are identifying the alternative actions open to us, it is important to ensure that we consider all the options. Failure to do so leaves us open to the charge of committing the fallacy of false dichotomy (see section 6.7.4).

Second, for each alternative we identify the consequences that, so far as we can tell, will result if we performed that action. The consequences for each alternative are then assessed to determine how much good and how much bad each will produce. For example, if we were considering visiting a sick friend in hospital, we would consider the good that would be produced (such as reducing the friend's boredom and preserving the friendship) as well as the bad effects (such as the money spent driving to and from the hospital and the time lost from other activities). It is important that all the consequences be assessed in this way. We should not exclude the long-term or indirect consequences, and we should not exclude the effects on any other person. We must consider the good and bad consequences for anyone, anywhere, at any time.

To make such assessments it is necessary to use some criterion of goodness (and badness). There are several possibilities: some philosophers have suggested pleasure (and pain), others have preferred benefit (and harm). Traditionally, a common approach has been to use happiness (and unhappiness) as the criterion. There are difficulties with each of these, but we shall here use happiness since it comes closest to expressing the idea that most people seem to have in mind when they use this method of moral reasoning. The idea of happiness is a little vague, and is notoriously difficult to define adequately. But most people are able to use the concept without being puzzled, and as long as we can put up with a little vagueness, it works reasonably well as a criterion.

The third step is to compare the net amount of good produced by each alternative and choose the alternative that produces the greatest net amount of good. The net amount of good is the total amount of good reduced by the total amount of bad. For example, if an action would produce an equal amount of good and bad, the net amount of good produced would be zero. There is, obviously, a difficulty in the idea of subtracting the amount of bad from the amount of good. It suggests that we could actually measure amounts of goodness and badness. This is clearly an absurd suggestion (although not so absurd that no one has ever seriously proposed it). Fortunately, however, we do not have to measure quantities of goodness and badness in order for this approach to be feasible. If we take happiness as our criterion, we can usually make reasonable judgements about the net amount of happiness that an action will produce. Such judgements do not normally need to be precise; we need only as much precision as is necessary to enable us to make reasonable comparative judgements between the net amounts of happiness produced by the alternatives we are considering. For example, it is not difficult to show that getting drunk the night before a final examination will produce less net happiness than not getting drunk.

These three steps provide us with a method of justifying particular actions. They embody what is usually called the PRINCIPLE OF UTILITY or the GREATEST HAPPINESS PRINCIPLE, according to which we ought always to choose, from among the actions open to us, the action that will produce the greatest happiness of the greatest number of people affected by it. (*Utility* means "fitness for a practical purpose," and the practical purpose that guides utilitarianism is a commitment to generate as much happiness as possible; hence, the names for the principle of utility and the greatest happiness principle.) The fact that the appeal to consequences rests upon a principle such as this does not mean, however, that it is really an appeal to a principle of right and wrong like those considered in section 12.3. The principle of utility functions quite differently from principles of right and wrong. When we appeal to a principle of right and wrong to justify an action, it is the fact that the action is covered by the principle that justifies it. It is the nature of the act itself that brings it within the principle and makes it right. When we appeal to the principle of utility, on the other hand, the nature of the act itself is quite irrelevant; what counts are the consequences of the act. The fact that generalization arguments provide justifications for particular *judgements* whereas utilitarian arguments provide justifications for particular *actions* reflects this basic difference between the two approaches.

To illustrate how a utilitarian argument works, let us return to Diane and Jean. Had Jean wanted to challenge Diane on the basis of the principle of utility she would have proceeded quite differently. Instead of looking for a general moral principle that might apply to Diane's action, she would have examined the consequences of the actions open to Diane. If we assume that there are only two alternatives—repaying Carl the $20 she owes him, and refusing to do so—Jean would compare the consequences of the two alternatives in the following manner:

ALTERNATIVE 1: REFUSING TO REPAY CARL.

Good Consequences:

» Diane gets to keep the $20 to spend on food.
» Diane avoids the embarrassment of having to sponge a few meals from her other friends.
» Diane's friends do not have to put up with her sponging a few meals.

Bad Consequences:

» Carl has $20 less to spend on the things he wants.
» Carl feels a sense of grievance against Diane.
» Diane may lose Carl as a friend.
» Diane may get a reputation for being untrustworthy.
» Diane may find it much more difficult to borrow money the next time she needs to do so.

ALTERNATIVE 2: REPAYING CARL.

Good Consequences:

» Carl gets $20 to spend on the things he wants.
» Diane preserves her friendship with Carl.
» Diane will gain or preserve her reputation as a trustworthy person.
» Diane will avoid having an argument with Jean.

Bad Consequences:

» Diane will have to sponge some meals from her friends.
» Diane may harbour a grudge against Jean for having pressured her into repaying Carl.

This is merely a sketch of the kinds of consequences that will have to be examined. There could be many more. If, for example, Carl plans to donate the $20 to Oxfam, then Jean will need to take account of the good that this would produce. And making reasonable estimates of how much happiness or unhappiness each of the consequences would produce will depend upon the particular facts of the situation, such as whether Carl is likely to complain to others about Diane's refusal to repay her debt.

Appeals to consequences can be criticized in two ways. The first way is quite straightforward. We may be able to argue that certain consequences have been overlooked. For example, someone who appeals to consequences in order to justify longer jail sentences for criminals may be challenged if the effects on the family of the criminal or the costs of building new prisons have been ignored. Such a criticism may not be sufficient to undermine the conclusion, but at the very least it will force a reconsideration of the calculation of the greatest net amount of good. Since the method of appealing to consequences requires us to take *all* the consequences into account, if we invoke this appeal but overlook some of the consequences, we can legitimately be challenged to rethink our conclusion. The second way in which appeals to consequences may be criticized is by challenging the assessment of the goodness or badness of a particular consequence. For example, a particular act may have the effect of making a person or group feel somewhat insecure, but it is not clear whether this should be regarded as a bad effect, and if so how bad it is. There are no easy answers to questions of this sort. They require careful thought as well as discussion with others whose feelings about the matter may be different from our own. In the end, our judgements should always be regarded as somewhat tentative.

12.7 Self-Test No. 19

Briefly outline some of the good and bad consequences of each of the following proposed actions or policies. Include only consequences that are good or bad solely on the basis of the happiness and unhappiness they produce. A consequence that is good or bad because it violates some moral principle should be excluded since it would not be part of a utilitarian's calculation.

1. Submitting an essay written by someone else.

2. Failing to declare $500 of income on one's income tax.

3. Providing a false alibi for a friend to prevent him from being charged with leaving the scene of an accident.

4. Legalizing the sale of marijuana.

5. Selling non-nuclear arms to right-wing rebel groups in Central America.

12.8 Questions for Discussion

Can a case be made for the following policies or actions solely on the basis that they produce the best consequences?

1. Legalizing the manufacture and sale of alcoholic products without any government regulation or control.

2. Making it illegal for doctors to charge their patients a fee in addition to the fee the doctor receives from Medicare.

3. Banning all magazine, radio, and television advertising of alcoholic beverages.

4. Using laboratory animals in research that is aimed at finding a cure for AIDS.

5. US President George W. Bush's decision to launch an attack upon Iraq in 2003.

12.9 Rational Agreement

There can be no guarantee that the use of these two types of argument will produce actual agreement on moral issues. Each type of argument is rational on its own terms, but each allows for different moral conclusions to be drawn about the same situation by two different people. The problem with generalization arguments is that they cannot rule out the possibility that two different people, each of whom argues rationally, will come up with somewhat different general principles. The problem with utilitarian arguments is that they provide no rational way of resolving disputes over precisely how much happiness or unhappiness will be produced in particular cases. What is surprising, perhaps, is that within each approach there is usually substantial agreement in practice. Only rarely will two people reach opposite conclusions about whether promises ought to be kept on the basis of the generalization argument. And in most cases utilitarians will reach agreement on what is the best action.

One of the major causes of moral disagreement is the fact that we can appeal to both types of arguments. Virtually everyone recognizes that both embody an important form of moral reasoning; both carry moral weight. The problem is that, although they often support the same conclusions, sometimes they support opposing conclusions. The generalization argument may lead to the conclusion that an action is wrong, while the utilitarian argument may lead to the conclusion that the action is right. Many of the tough moral dilemmas we face are like this. And many controversial moral issues facing society (e.g., abortion, capital punishment, pornography) arise because the generalization argument tends to support one position while the utilitarian argument tends to support another.

Moral philosophers have long attempted to resolve the fundamental dispute between the two approaches, but this dispute, like the dispute with the radical sceptic, has failed to produce any generally accepted proof that one approach is superior to the other. In the absence of a conclusive proof, it is probably best simply to recognize that both approaches are necessary and that when they clash, we have to make the best judgement we can and hope we will not regret it later. We must recognize that human life is inherently problematic and that what is most important is not reaching provable moral conclusions but taking moral questions seriously and facing them as sensitively and honestly as we can. This may well be the most reasonable conclusion to reach: that the way we deal with moral issues is even more important than the moral decisions we make. This does not mean that the decisions themselves don't matter. It does mean that we should strive to develop maturity in our moral thinking. Moral maturity is important because moral decisions require more than rationality and because we should not allow others to make our moral decisions for us.

12.10 Moral Maturity

We conclude this chapter with a brief description of moral maturity. The material in this section has been adapted from the pamphlet *Ethical Discussion in the Classroom*, written by the Ethics Research Group, Department of Philosophy, University of Guelph. Be warned, however, that it is not, or not entirely, an empirical description, nor is it simply a description of the way rational criteria apply to moral decision-making. It is both of these, but it also incorporates an ethical ideal that may be open to challenge on moral grounds.

Moral maturity is best characterized by describing the qualities that we would expect a morally mature individual to exemplify. These are not necessary conditions, however, for an individual who is deficient in one or two respects could still be morally mature, although less so than someone who embodies them all. It should also be noted that it is an ideal: it is unlikely that anyone could live up to it all the time with regard to every moral decision. But it is a quality that is worth striving to achieve in our lives and is widely recognized as such in many cultures.

The first three characteristics of moral maturity are implicit in what has been said earlier in this chapter, and need only be noted here.

1. *Independence of judgement*. We make or accept moral judgements only for reasons that we believe can withstand critical scrutiny and never simply because we accept someone else's authority.

2. *Justification by appeal to principles*. We recognize that we must always be prepared to appeal to some general justificatory principle (either the greatest happiness principle or some specific moral principle) when called upon to justify our judgements.

3. *Generalization of moral judgements*. We recognize that what we think is right (or wrong) for one person to do in certain circumstances must be right (or wrong) for any other person to do in relevantly similar circumstances.

There are several other features of moral maturity we have not yet touched upon:

4. *Consistency*. The moral judgements we make should as far as possible be consistent. There are three ways in which consistency is important. First, our actions should be consistent with our judgements. If we believe it is wrong to cheat on our taxes, then it is immature to go ahead and cheat anyway. Second, there should be

consistency between our judgements on different issues. If we believe that it is wrong for baseball players to assault one another during a game, but also believe that it is morally acceptable for hockey players to assault one another, we would attempt to remove the inconsistency either by changing one of our judgements or by showing that the circumstances of the two sports are significantly different in a way that justifies treating them differently. Third, there should be consistency between the different principles we invoke. If we believe that euthanasia is morally acceptable but that capital punishment is not, we would recognize the apparent inconsistency between the deliberate taking of human life in the one case and the refusal to do so in the other and would deal with this inconsistency either by changing one of our principles or showing that there is a morally significant difference between the two cases.

5. *Awareness of complexity*. Moral principles (such as *Love your neighbour as yourself, Respect all life, Keep your word, Be just*) typically need to be interpreted and balanced against one another when they are applied to specific concrete situations. How, precisely, are we to respect life? Who, exactly, is our neighbour? And how are respect for life and our neighbours to be balanced against one another when we are in a situation where it is difficult or impossible to do both? A morally mature individual recognizes these elements of complexity and does not pretend that an issue is simpler than it really is.

6. *Getting the facts straight*. A mature ethical judgement is adopted only after all the relevant facts have been taken into account. Since most of the moral issues we face pertain to complex situations, we should refuse to make moral judgements about them until we have gathered all the relevant facts. This is especially true of issues that arise because of developments in modern technology, such as the use of animals in medical research, surrogate motherhood, invasions of privacy by computers and electronic devices, technological aid to developing countries, and a host of similar issues. The very complexity of such moral issues means that we usually have to rely upon the advice of experts in these matters. But our reliance upon experts should be restricted to the factual domain. The moral decisions themselves should, of course, remain our own.

7. *Recognition of our fallibility*. The complexity of many moral issues and the difficulty of knowing that we have taken into account and properly understood the facts makes it hard to be sure that we have made the correct moral judgement on any specific issue, even when we have done our best. Moral maturity implies that we recognize that there is always an element of personal judgement in our moral beliefs. No matter how confident we feel about a moral judgement we should always be open to the possibility that future reflection may lead us to revise it.

8. *Tolerance*. Moral decisions are never made in a vacuum. We are affected by the moral decisions of those around us, as they are by ours. If we want our judgements and our reasons for them to be respected by others, then we must respect the judgements and moral reasoning of others. We should therefore be tolerant of those with whom we disagree. Because of our fallibility, not only are we never in a position to claim that we must be right and those who disagree with us must be wrong, but we are always in the position of being able to learn from others, even those with whom

we disagree, at least in cases where they exhibit the kind of moral maturity we strive to achieve for ourselves.

These characteristics represent an ideal that is often not fully realized in practice. When we face moral issues that are important to us personally, or that have generated public debate, we find all too often that emotions, bigotry, and prejudice tend to get in the way of reasonable and mature discussion. When ethical discussion falls too far short of the ideal, it is extremely unlikely that it will lead either to moral insight or to a genuine resolution of the dispute. This is especially true when dealing with clashes between the utilitarian appeal to consequences and the appeal to moral principles.

12.11 Questions for Discussion

Identify the type of moral reasoning and any weaknesses involved in the following arguments.

1. I have no objection to erotic materials, but I think hard-core pornography should be banned because it legitimizes and encourages violence against women. There are many males in our society whose attitudes to women are deeply influenced by hard-core pornography. It encourages them to think that many women really want to be raped and that inflicting violence and cruelty on women is both morally and socially acceptable.

Hard-core pornography is often defended by an appeal to the right to freedom of expression. But surely no one believes that freedom of expression has no limits. In fact, there are a number of limitations on freedom of expression that everyone accepts: there are the laws against libel and slander, for example, as well as the duty to keep certain information confidential. All I am advocating is that hard-core pornography be added to the list of types of things that cannot be defended by appeal to freedom of expression.

2. I am opposed to all forms of censorship, including censorship of hard-core pornography. The right to freedom of expression is fundamental in our society, and it is important that it be defended whenever it is threatened. Once we start restricting freedom of expression because of some real or alleged harm, we have started down the road to totalitarianism, where the government decides what we should be allowed to think. This is a question of fundamental human rights. If we don't like the way some people exercise their rights, we simply have to put up with it. I wouldn't have it any other way.

Perhaps some pornography has harmful consequences—personally, I find some of it quite disgusting—but even if it is sometimes harmful, there is good reason to think that pornography also has beneficial consequences. It allows males to satisfy their sexual fantasies harmlessly in their imaginations. Otherwise they would have to inflict their fantasies upon women. Pornography therefore provides a harmless outlet for men with sick sexual fantasies. Perhaps we need more rather than less pornography to deter those males who now inflict violent and degrading treatment on women.

3. I believe that the law should be changed to permit euthanasia in certain cases. Specifically, I believe that terminally ill individuals who are mentally competent should be free to consent to having their life ended by a medical doctor. There are three reasons why I think this would be a good thing. First, it would make it possible for individuals who are suffering the ravages of some terminal disease to end their suffering in a manner of their own choosing. Second, it would allow these individuals to have the satisfaction of being able to choose to die at a time that they feel is appropriate for them. Third, by reducing the demand for medical services, it would allow medical resources that are now devoted to the terminally ill to be used for other kinds of treatments and services that are not now available under Medicare.

4. The legalization of euthanasia is immoral even in strictly limited circumstances. The problem is that, once you start euthanizing people, there is no morally significant stopping point. The current proposal is to permit euthanasia only for a terminally ill patient who, while competent, has given his or her prior consent. But now some people are calling for the legalization of euthanasia for those who are severely retarded if their family consents. But having started down this road, why stop here? What about elderly patients who are a burden to their families and who seem not to be enjoying life? What about children who suffer from severe physical handicaps? What about children or adults who are likely to be a permanent burden to society? There is only one moral reason for not employing euthanasia in these and similar cases, namely, that we place an intrinsic value on all human life. But if this is so, then we have a compelling reason for not allowing euthanasia at all. In short, if there is a reason to stop euthanizing people at some point, then there is an equally strong reason not to start euthanizing people in the first place.

13. Arguing Back

In debates and other argumentative contexts we are not usually content to remain passive and merely note the weaknesses in our opponents' arguments. Usually we want to argue back. We may want to help our opponents to see the truth (as we understand it). Or, if we do not know what the truth of the matter is, we may want to pursue the argument in hopes of increasing our understanding and perhaps getting closer to the truth. Or, we may simply want to persuade our opponents of the error of their ways because we don't want them to get away with weak arguments. Whatever the reason, we all want to be able to respond effectively to the arguments of our opponents. In this chapter we examine the main strategies of arguing back against an opponent or an opponent's position.

13.1 Explaining the Weakness

In Chapters 5 to 8 we examined the criteria a sound argument must satisfy and the kinds of weaknesses arguments may be subject to. In Chapters 9 to 12 we examined certain specific types of arguments and their weaknesses. These chapters provide us with the basic ammunition for arguing back. When we detect a weakness in our opponents' arguments we can point it out, and hope that they see what is weak in their argument. Unfortunately, not everyone we are likely to debate with has studied critical thinking. If we accuse them of relying upon an unacceptable empirical premise or committing the post hoc fallacy, they may not know what we are talking about. If we are trying to convince an opponent who is not familiar with logical terminology, it is usually necessary to explain, and not merely name, the weakness.

A full explanation involves two stages. First, we need to explain the nature of the weakness being charged. It is usually best to begin by explaining the relevant criterion for a sound argument. If a fallacy is being charged, it is best to name it only after the relevant criterion has been explained. The purpose of this part of the explanation is to ensure that our opponents understand what we are accusing them of. We should always ensure that our opponents understand the nature of a charge before we try to persuade them that the charge is correct. If an opponent disputes a charge, we should immediately attempt to determine whether he or she fails to understand the charge or understands it but believes we cannot back it up.

The second stage of a full explanation is backing up our charge. This involves reconstructing the argument, supplying missing premises, identifying the logical structure, and so on, in the way described in previous chapters. If done properly, our explanation should convince our opponents that their argument does indeed contain a weakness. An opponent who is unwilling to respond to a full explanation of a weakness in his or her argument is probably not interested in serious discussion, and we should (politely, of course) change the topic of conversation.

We should note here that sometimes it is difficult to decide whether a particular weakness results from violating the criterion of relevance or the criterion of adequacy. We have seen that sometimes an appeal to authority may be irrelevant (for example, when a strict proof is called for) and sometimes it may be relevant but inadequate. Appeals to ignorance are also sometimes difficult to classify. This can be a problem with other types of weak arguments as well. All we can do when faced with this problem is to make the best judgement we can as to which criterion will most clearly explain the weakness of the argument to our opponent.

13.2 Counter-examples

Fully explaining a weakness is a laborious method of arguing back. The method of counter-examples is a short-cut method that is easy to use and can sometimes be remarkably effective. Its use is limited, however, to arguments that rely upon a generalization in the premises that can be challenged as being unacceptable. The method consists simply of presenting an exception to the generalization that shows that the generalization should not be relied upon. For example:

> MIKE: *You should try the wine cooler I just bought. It's really good. It is a new product, just put on the market by the producers, so it's bound to be better than their old ones.*
> ELAINE: *Just like the new Coke, eh?*

Elaine attacks the missing premise of Mike's argument, that a new product is always better than existing products, by citing an example of a new product that was (or was commonly believed to be) inferior to the product it replaced.

Here is another example:

> JOHN: *I've decided to invest most of my savings in gold and gold-mine stocks. I read a book that came out a couple of months ago, written by a business professor at Harvard, and he strongly recommends gold as the best investment for the next few years.*

PETER: *A few years ago my cousin followed the advice in a book written by a business professor. She invested her life savings in an oil-exploration company and lost the bundle.*

Peter's counter-example responds to the missing premise in John's argument—that all business professors are good investment advisors. The counter-example shows that there are exceptions to this generalization. As long as John gets the point of the counter-example, this is a more effective method of challenging his appeal to authority than a detailed explanation of why his appeal has failed to meet the criteria for accepting an appeal to authority.

Unfortunately, the method of counter-examples usually allows our opponents an easy reply. Since most generalizations admit of some exceptions, an opponent can concede the counter-example but argue that, generally speaking, the generalization still holds. For example, Mike might argue that since most new products are better than existing ones, the new wine cooler is likely to be better than the old coolers. And John might claim that most business professors are likely to understand the investment market better than he does. If Mike and John respond in this way, we will either have to concede that our counter-examples have failed to show the weakness or undertake the slower process of explaining the weakness.

Here are some examples of the use of counter-examples with differing degrees of effectiveness:

FRED: *I don't see that there is anything really wrong with an occasional extra-marital fling. Everybody needs some variety in their lives. It's like food. I mean, if we had to eat the same thing for dinner every night, we'd soon come to hate it.*
ALICE: *Does that mean you want to trade in the children for a couple of new teenagers?*

SON: *But, Dad, everybody I know is going to the rock concert. You say it might be dangerous, but it's not. How can it be dangerous if everybody else's parents are letting them go?*
FATHER: *What about that rock concert last summer where there was a riot and three teenagers were killed? I'm sure their parents let them go because they thought it wouldn't be dangerous.*

BRUCE: *I don't see anything wrong with the school board firing teachers whose moral standards are different from those of the community. After all, the members of the school board are democratically elected in free elections and represent the will of the people.*
MARGARET: *That is exactly what they said in Nazi Germany. Don't forget that Hitler was democratically elected in a free election.*

13.3 Absurd Examples

A more effective way of displaying a fallacy is the method of absurd examples. It is similar to the method of counter-examples but can be used against a broader range of weaknesses, often with devastating effectiveness. It involves constructing an argument that is parallel to the weak argument, but which has true or plausible premises and an obviously false or absurd conclusion. For example:

> BOB: *As far as I'm concerned, people who are against teaching scientific creationism in the schools are communists. They are all atheists, after all, and all communists are atheists.*
> CAROL: *Don't be silly, Bob. That's like arguing that since all men have two eyes and all women have two eyes, all men are really women.*

Carol's reply shows the weakness in Bob's argument by challenging its structure. Both arguments have an identical structure:

> All As are Bs.
> All Cs are Bs.
> Therefore, all As are Cs.

Carol is in effect saying to Bob that if his argument is a good one, then so is hers; if he is going to believe that all opponents of scientific creation are communists, then he must also believe that all men are women. Since Bob is presumably unwilling to accept Carol's conclusion, he must either reject his own conclusion or develop another argument to support it.

To be effective, an absurd example must be closely similar to the original argument. The similarity must always involve an identical structure, but it often involves similarity of content as well. In general, the more closely an absurd example resembles the original argument, the more effective it will be in showing a weakness. The above example relies on an absurd example with the same logical structure as the fallacious argument. Here is an example that relies mainly upon similarity of content:

> WALTER: *I think the government should ban all pornographic publications. It really bothers me to think of all those people reading all that mindless stuff.*
> WILL: *Great argument, Walt. And I think the government should ban the Toronto Sun. It really bothers me to think of all those people reading all that mindless stuff.*

Will's absurd example is structurally identical to Walter's argument, but its success as an absurd example depends not so much on this similarity as on the similarity of content.

The practical effectiveness of an absurd example depends on more than similarity of structure and content. To be effective the absurd example should use premises that are obviously true and uncontroversial, so that our opponent cannot reject it on the ground that it relies on unacceptable premises. Sometimes, we can get away with hypothetical premises. Will, for example, may not be bothered at all by the thought of people reading the *Sun*, but pretends to be in order to make his point. Of course, Walter might miss the point and respond by arguing that Will is not really bothered by people reading the *Toronto Sun*, in which case Will's absurd example has failed in its purpose.

The main drawback to the absurd example method is that it is often difficult to invent a good absurd example on the spur of the moment. If we use a poor absurd example we give our opponents a plausible excuse to ignore the serious point we are trying to make, on the ground that we have missed the point of their argument. The greatest strength of the absurd example method, on the other hand, is that it places our opponents on the horns of a very awkward dilemma: either they must accept our absurd conclusion, or they must admit that their argument fails to support their conclusion.

Here are two more absurd example arguments:

SADIE: *One of the primary responsibilities of parents is to provide their children with a sound moral education. Religion provides a solid foundation for morality. Therefore, any parent who cares about their children's moral education should give their children a religious upbringing.*

TAMSEN: *Sorry, Sadie, your argument is no good. It is just like the following argument: It is a responsibility of architects to design safe and sound buildings. Granite provides a solid foundation for a safe building. Therefore, any architect who wants to design safe buildings should design buildings with granite foundations.*

AUDREY: *The main reason I think abortion is wrong is that you can't draw a sharp line between a fetus that is 39 weeks old (i.e., one ready to be born) and one at any earlier stage of its development. Obviously, it would be wrong to kill a baby while its mother is in labour. But if it's alright to kill it at some earlier stage, then there must be some point at which you can say, "Up to this point it was not a person, but at this point it becomes a person." But no one can do this. Fetal development is absolutely gradual from beginning to end. So if you can't justify killing a fetus at the end of its development, you can't justify killing it at the beginning.*

BETTY: *There is something wrong with your argument. You are arguing as follows: You cannot draw a sharp line between when something is hot and when it isn't. When you boil water, it starts out cold and gradually becomes hot. There is no point at which you can say, "Up to this point it is cold, but at this point it becomes hot." Bringing water to a boil is absolutely gradual from beginning to end. So if it is hot at the end of the process, then it must be hot at the beginning. So cold water is really hot.*

13.4 Counter-arguments

The final method of arguing back goes beyond the intent of the first three. They attempt to display the weakness of our opponent's argument not by attacking the conclusion directly, but by attacking the way the conclusion is defended. A counter-argument, on the other hand, attempts to show that our opponent's conclusion is false or problematic by constructing a different argument altogether to support a conclusion that is inconsistent with the original conclusion. For example:

> ROY: *The state must retain the right to apply the death penalty in extreme cases. I believe that any person who commits cold-blooded, premeditated murder is unfit to remain a member of any civilized community. By their act of denying another's right to life, they have renounced their own right to life, and the state is therefore entitled to put them to death.*
>
> DALE: *The trouble with your position is that it brings the state down to the level of the murderer. If the right to life is so important, then don't you think the state ought to show how important it is by refusing to execute anyone, no matter how heinous his or her crime? The real question is whether you want to live in a society where the government from time to time kills some of its citizens.*

Notice that Dale makes no attempt to challenge any of Roy's premises and does not even suggest that Roy's conclusion does not follow from his premises. In fact, she is actually in partial agreement with one of Roy's premises: that there is a right to life. But she ignores Roy's argument and attempts instead to show that the state ought not to inflict the death penalty by appealing to a different set of premises. Every genuine counter-argument has this feature: it ignores the premises of the original argument and presents an independent set of reasons in support of a contrary conclusion.

Every weak argument is therefore open to a counter-argument. In fact, counter-arguments can often be developed against arguments whose weakness we are unable to identify. If we are presented with an argument whose conclusion we are reluctant to accept, there are two possible explanations for our reluctance: (a) the argument is weak, or (b) we are being irrational about the matter. If the argument really is weak, then we ought to be able to describe the weakness in such a way as to persuade our opponent. But if, as sometimes happens, we cannot do so, we would have to concede that our refusal to accept it may be irrational. In these circumstances it can be very useful to attempt to develop a counter-argument. If we can develop a plausible one, then we have a good reason to believe that our opponent's argument is weak and that we are not being irrational.

In addition, a good counter-argument can often suggest what is weak about the original argument. In the above example, Dale's counter-argument does suggest a line of attack on Roy's argument. Roy appeals to the fact that murderers have denied the right to life of their victims as a reason for claiming that murderers have renounced their own right to life. Dale's argument relies on the premise that the right to life cannot be lost by anyone, which suggests a way of attacking this sub-argument: she could argue that it violates the criterion of adequacy. We do not as a rule hold that, if A violates some right of B's, the state should deny A the same right; that if I, for example, violate your freedom of religion, the state should force me to become a Baptist. Consequently, Roy's sub-argument needs more support in order to be acceptable.

To develop good counter-arguments we have to be familiar with the subject matter under discussion, and we have to care about the issue as well. Counter-arguments cannot be developed merely as a reaction against an argument that looks weak. There are no logical rules for producing a good counter-argument. We have to be sceptical about our opponent's conclusion, which means we should have reasons for our scepticism. It is only on the basis of the reasons that lead us to be sceptical that we can develop a good counter-argument.

Counter-arguments are often found in debates over controversial issues. In fact, in controversial contexts we can most easily see the chief drawback to the method of counter-argument. We are all aware that in debates over controversial matters both sides often seem to pay no attention to the arguments of the other side. Both sides seem content to repeat, over and over again, their arguments (along with their slogans and, usually, a great deal of invective and frequent ad hominems), all the while ignoring the arguments of their opponents. To avoid such juvenile behaviour, we should use counter-arguments not as an excuse to stop thinking rationally about the issue but as a useful tool for carrying forward a rational enquiry. Not only can they suggest weaknesses in our opponents' arguments, but they can give us a better understanding of the issue. A serious attempt to develop a counter-argument against a given argument, and then to examine the two as dispassionately as we can, will give us a deeper understanding of any complex issue.

13.5 Self-Test No. 20

I. Suggest a counter-example that shows the weakness in each of the following generalizations:

1. Wealth always increases human happiness, since it removes one of the major barriers to achieving what we want out of life.

2. The function of law is to force people to do what they would otherwise choose not to do.

3. All humour is cruel: people never find anything funny unless it is at someone else's expense.

4. Women have still not been able to achieve real political power anywhere in the world.

5. Religion has always been a force for good in the world.

II. Suggest an absurd example that shows the weakness in each of the following arguments:

1. You might as well save your breath and go peddle your pamphlets somewhere else. I've been a Tory all my life. I was raised a Tory by my father, and if it was good enough for him, then it is good enough for me.

2. I don't think that taking things like pencils and paperclips from the company is really stealing because the company has never threatened to punish anyone for it.

3. If Jim had a steady job, then he'd be able to afford a new car; well, he has just bought a new car, so he must have a steady job now.

4. You shouldn't eat any of that stuff. It's deadly. They've proven that it kills laboratory animals when they give them a steady diet of it.

5. My wife always gets my breakfast for me. She's been doing it every morning for 14 years, so I'm positive she'll get my breakfast tomorrow.

13.6 Questions for Discussion

Suggest a plausible counter-argument against each of the following arguments.

1. The capitalist economic system is superior to any other system. Western civilization has advanced more since capitalism emerged in the late seventeenth century than in the previous 2,000 years, and these advances could not have occurred except for the tremendous explosion of productivity brought about by capitalism. It may not be perfect, but it is clearly superior to all its rivals.

2. Parliament committed a serious blunder in 1967 when it removed attempted suicide from the Criminal Code. Until then it had been a criminal offence for anyone to attempt to commit suicide. The value of the old law was not that it made it possible for the courts to punish those who were so disturbed or depressed that they wanted to end their lives. Its value was that it gave the police the right to apprehend someone who was threatening to take his or her own life. The way things are now, if the police find someone threatening suicide, they cannot interfere, for the person is doing nothing illegal. And since most people who threaten suicide are really pleading for help, we should have a law that permits the police to interfere first and ask questions later.

3. Teachers in primary and secondary schools should avoid introducing any controversial political or ethical issues into the classroom. Such discussions tend to be divisive and to create friction among students. They lead many par-

ents to feel that the school is subverting their authority as parents. And they allow teachers to abuse their authority and to impose their values upon their students.

4. Each year, *Maclean's* magazine publishes a ranking of Canadian universities. One of the criteria used is the grade average of students entering first year. This is an absurd criterion when used as a basis for determining the quality of a university. It is like determining the quality of a judge on the basis of the seriousness of the cases heard by him or her. The quality of a university should depend not on the quality of entering students, but on what happens to them after they arrive.

5. Most Western governments are willing to negotiate with terrorists to obtain the release of hostages or to achieve other goals. This is an ill-advised policy. What governments should do is to announce that their policy will always be to refuse to negotiate with terrorists under any circumstances and then to adhere rigorously to this policy. They should inform all their citizens that this is their new policy and that those who travel abroad should not expect the government to negotiate for their release should they be taken hostage by terrorists. Once terrorist groups realized that a government was serious about its refusal to negotiate under any circumstances, they would realize that their terrorist acts were useless or even counter-productive. They would be forced to cease their terrorist acts, and fewer people would suffer as a result.

6. Government spending on the arts is wasteful and should be abolished. If some particular artists or poets or singers are recognized as good by enough of the public, they will be able to make a decent living by selling their books or giving concerts, in which case they don't need government hand-outs. But if they can't make a decent living it must be because not enough people think they are good enough to buy their books or go to their concerts. In this case, there is no justification for subsidizing artists who are regarded by Canadians as second best. So all support programs for the arts should be eliminated.

14.

Irrational Techniques
of Persuasion

In this chapter we consider a variety of irrational devices that are commonly used as persuasive techniques. Several of these have already been touched on earlier but are repeated here in order to give a more complete picture of these techniques. Some logicians treat these devices as fallacies, on the ground that they are used in attempts to persuade us of something and thus at least pretend to supply a reason for us to accept it. However, if we treat them as fallacies, we would be obliged to reconstruct an argument from the passages in which they occur, which is often difficult and usually violates the principle of charity. It is usually better to treat them not as arguments at all, but merely as irrational techniques of persuasion. In fact, their success frequently depends upon their not being used in an explicit argument, since once the argument is spelled out, the weakness becomes glaringly obvious.

14.1 Loaded Terms

We saw in Section 3.6 that many words have both a descriptive and an evaluative meaning. A group of rebels may be called freedom fighters, or terrorists, or just plain rebels. All three terms have more or less the same descriptive meaning, but their evaluative meanings are quite different: *freedom fighter* has a positive evaluative meaning, *terrorist* has a negative evaluative meaning, while *rebel* has no (or a neutral) evaluative meaning. The first two of these—*freedom fighter* and *terrorist*—are frequently used as loaded terms. A LOADED TERM is any term with a clear descriptive meaning and a positive or negative evaluative meaning, which is used in an attempt to persuade us to accept the evaluation conveyed by the term. Thus, anyone who wants to create support for a group of rebels can do so by always referring to them as freedom fighters, just as anyone who wants to create opposition to them can do so by always referring to them as terrorists.

Loaded terms are most effective in a context where the audience is not already committed to accepting or rejecting the evaluation carried by the loaded term and where this question is not being discussed explicitly. In such situations people can more easily accept the loaded term because it sounds like it is a purely descriptive term. How many terrorists are there? How well-armed are the terrorists? Do the terrorists have support from outside the country in which they operate? These are all empirical questions that do not explicitly raise the ethical question of whether or not the rebels should be supported. But after a discussion of such factual questions through which we become accustomed to referring to the rebels as terrorists, when the ethical question is finally raised, we can easily find ourselves placed in a position where we *seem* to be committed to opposing the rebels. After all, terrorism *is* the kind of thing one ought to oppose, so the ethical question already seems to have been answered. In the same way, had we become accustomed to referring to the rebels as freedom fighters then, when the ethical question is finally raised, we *seem* to be committed to supporting the rebels. After all, freedom *is* the kind of thing one ought to support. In this way loaded terms can prevent us from making explicit value judgements, because the loaded term makes the judgement for us without our realizing it.

Advertisers are well aware of the fact that loaded terms can force value judgements upon the unwary. A company uses the slogan, *Seventy-five Years of Service to Canadians*; the fact that the company has been in business for 75 years means that it is not a fly-by-night outfit, but the phrase *Service to Canadians* suggests an affinity with service organizations such as the Red Cross. A blatant use of loaded terms sometimes occurs in naming certain products or even companies. A detergent is called *Joy* in an attempt to make us think we enjoy it. A car rental company is called *Budget* to suggest that it has low rates. But loaded terms are used in many contexts besides business. We are all aware of the impact of racist terms (e.g., *wop, kike, nigger, chink*) and of other derogatory terms (*pinko, fascist, nerd, shyster, egg-head, bleeding heart, yuppie, book-worm, jock*). Fortunately, most of these terms are so blatantly evaluative that they are unlikely to persuade anyone who is not already prone to accept the evaluation carried by them.

A loaded term must have both a clear evaluative meaning (positive or negative) and a fairly specific descriptive meaning. It is the *descriptive* adequacy of the use of the term that makes it possible to insinuate the evaluative meaning. Once we accept the descriptive adequacy of the term we are more likely to accept its evaluative meaning as well. It should be noted, however, that some evaluative terms, such as *good, evil, right,* and *wrong*, lack a descriptive meaning and therefore cannot function as loaded terms. They are pure evaluative terms (i.e., they have no specific descriptive meaning) and thus can be used in almost any context, since there is no descriptive meaning to determine their correct use.

14.2 Vague Terms

In Section 3.2.1 we distinguished vagueness from ambiguity on the basis that a vague sentence lacks a precise meaning, whereas an ambiguous sentence has two or more different but usually quite precise meanings. We noted that although vagueness is often acceptable, it should sometimes be criticized; in particular, it should be criticized in contexts where greater precision is needed. The fact that a vague sentence lacks a precise meaning makes it possible for vague language to be quite misleading. A vague sentence has a large number of possible meanings, and often some of these possible meanings will make the sentence true while others will make it false. As a result we usually recognize that a vague sentence is true on at least one possible interpretation (i.e., that it is partly, or in some sense, true), and if we are not careful we can be led to think that it is also true on other interpretations, when in fact it is false. For example:

> What I admired most about Ernest Hemingway was that he broke the mould.

The phrase *broke the mould* is exceedingly vague. There are several different meanings we might give to it. It might mean that Hemingway was unconventional in his personal life. In this sense the claim would be true. On the other hand, it might mean that he was a creative genius or that his prose style is entirely unique. But on these interpretations the claim may well be false.

Vague language can thus be used to persuade us to accept something that is either false or problematic. This technique is much used by advertisers, politicians, and others who want to persuade us to do something that we would be reluctant to do if we thought carefully about it. It is commonly used in slogans of all sorts. For example:

> Vote Jones—The People's Choice.

> Coke Is The Real Thing.

> Canadians want a leader who is human, who knows what it is to struggle, to have ups and downs, and who has compassion for the tribulations of ordinary people.

14.3 Loaded Questions

A question is not an argument and not even a statement, so it may be difficult to imagine how a question can be a technique of persuasion. Nevertheless, questions can sometimes suggest something in a way that may be persuasive. Sometimes the suggestion is explicitly contained in the question itself. For example:

> Have you stopped beating your wife?

The form of the question requires a yes or no answer, but both answers involve the admission that you used to beat your wife. If you answer *yes*, you are admitting that you used to beat your wife but no longer do so. If you answer *no*, you are admitting that you used to beat your wife and still do so. In either case you have admitted that you used to beat your wife. Such questions are called COMPLEX QUESTIONS because they contain an assumption that both possible answers will confirm. Complex questions thus are a way of making a claim without appearing to do so. The only way to respond to a complex question containing a false assumption is to refuse to answer it in the form in which it has been asked and to challenge the assumption directly. Here are some more complex questions:

Is your sister still as moody as she used to be?

Are you opposed to the practice of broadcasting pornographic programs on television during prime time?

Has the United States lost its reputation as guardian of the free world?

Did the government lose the election because they were incompetent or because they were arrogant?

There are other more subtle ways in which questions can make suggestions. The context in which questions are asked normally suggests that the questioner believes that there is no obvious answer to the question. As a result, if someone asks a question that has an obvious answer, the audience will tend to assume that the questioner has a plausible reason for believing that the obvious answer is true. Suppose a newspaper prints an article under the headline *Does The Premier Have A Secret Swiss Bank Account?* Even if the article makes no allegations but merely describes how the reporter, despite a thorough investigation, failed to turn up any hard evidence that the Premier does have a secret Swiss bank account, the unwary reader will suspect that the newspaper had some grounds for asking the question. Simply by asking the question the article suggests that the Premier is the sort of politician who would do that sort of thing, and the fact that no proof was found may only show that the reporter has not found it yet.

Any allegation can be turned into a question, and even if the answer is *no*, a suspicion that the allegation is true will remain. After all, if someone thought the question was worth asking, it is natural to assume there must have been some reason to think that the implied allegation might have been true, even if it turns out to be false. In some situations, the taint of suspicion will remain no matter how much evidence is produced to refute the implied allegation. Public figures are especially vulnerable to suspicions created through the adroit use of loaded questions, but the technique can be applied to anyone. For example:

Do you suppose he tries so hard to be macho because he is secretly afraid of impotence?

Was that essay really your own work, or did you crib it?

Is she just reacting emotionally to the situation, or has she actually sat down and thought it through?

Did you steal my Chemistry notes?

How long is it going to take before you learn to take some responsibility for your actions?

14.4 False Confidence

People are often willing to accept a claim if the speaker presents it with great confidence. The confidence can be conveyed both by the choice of words and by the manner in which they are expressed. If the speaker is genuinely confident of the truth of the claim, then presenting it with confidence is quite appropriate. But if a questionable claim is presented with confidence, the audience can be misled into thinking that it cannot seriously be questioned. For example:

> *I certainly don't want to suggest that all adopted children are miserable, but the fact is that a majority of adopted children do suffer from a serious problem of self-identity and that the problem is most serious during their teenage years.*

Is this claim true? It is certainly plausible, but in the absence of solid empirical evidence one could just as plausibly claim that it is false. But if it is asserted in a confident tone of voice, and in a way that suggests that everyone who knows anything about adoption would know that it is true, most people will be inclined not to challenge the speaker. They will believe that it is probably true.

False confidence is different from deliberately telling a lie. Of course, if a lie is to be convincing, the liar must tell it with confidence, so in a sense lying does require that the liar present false confidence. But we are here describing a different technique, one used by those who believe that what they are saying is true, but who want their audience to accept the claim without critical scrutiny. It is a way of suggesting, rather than saying, to the audience that there is no need to ask for the evidence. It suggests that anyone who did ask for evidence would only reveal their ignorance or naivety.

The effectiveness of false confidence in persuading an audience to accept a claim depends in large part upon the plausibility of the claim being made. No amount of false confidence would persuade most of us to accept a claim that flies in the face of common sense or is inconsistent with what we strongly believe to be true. For example:

> *Mongolian peasants use a method of predicting the sex of unborn children that is accurate more than 95 per cent of the time. On a night when there is a full moon, the father spits into a cup of the mother's urine and leaves it on the doorstep of their hut overnight. If the spit is still floating the next morning, the baby will be a boy.*

No matter how confidently such an assertion is made, most of us will refuse to believe the accuracy of this method of predicting the sex of unborn children. We have good reasons for believing that such a claim is inherently problematic and are unlikely to accept it without strong evidence. But if the claim is one we think could well be true, and especially if we think the speaker just might know something we don't, we can be taken in by the speaker's confidence.

It is not clear why so many people seem willing to accept any plausible claim if the speaker presents it confidently. It may be out of a sense of politeness: not to accept the claim is to suggest that the speaker is ignorant or dishonest. It may be that many people are afraid they may be called upon to present evidence and arguments to defend their scepticism, which they may be unwilling or unable to do. Or it may be a naive belief that most people never seek deliberately to mislead others. Whatever the reason, false confidence can frequently be very effective in persuading people to accept something without supporting reasons.

14.5 Selectivity

Many judgements rest upon a complex body of evidence. Inductive generalizations, as we saw in Section 10.2, rest upon a number of particular instances, and their strength depends upon these instances being a representative sample of the entire population; since populations are not usually homogeneous, we can be misled by an unrepresentative sample. This fact makes it possible for someone to create a misleading impression by bringing unrepresentative examples to our attention. Suppose, for example, we disapprove of the Canada Council's policy of giving grants to artists. Without presenting arguments against the policy, we can attempt to discredit it by looking for examples where the grants have been abused and mentioning them to anyone who will listen. We say nothing that is false, we make no claim that grants are always or usually abused, we present no arguments against the policy; we merely point out every abuse whenever we find one.

Presenting unrepresentative facts will mislead only when the audience is not aware of all the evidence. It may be that in 99 per cent of cases there is no abuse and that the policy is achieving its goal, but most people are unlikely to know this and will gain the impression that the grants are systematically abused. A rational response to such selectivity would be to ask for evidence that would show what percentage of grants are abused and how the abusers are dealt with, as well as to ask for evidence of the social and cultural benefits produced by the grants, for this is the kind of evidence we would need to pass judgement on the policy. But people who are deliberately selective in the facts they present usually want to avoid presenting such evidence, which is why they are usually careful to avoid even the appearance of presenting an argument. If they say, *Here is my evidence and here is my conclusion*, someone is sure to challenge the evidence, which will defeat the purpose of being selective.

The news media are frequently criticized for being selective in their approach to the news. Often the criticism is deserved, especially when the particular newspaper or television station has a strong political or ideological commitment. Stories that reflect favourably upon their cause are given prominence, and those that do not are ignored or relegated to the back pages.

Of course, if selectivity occurs in an argument, the argument would violate the criterion of adequacy. Most often it would involve both of the weaknesses discussed in Section 10.2.

14.6 Misleading Statistics

One of the more insidious types of selectivity involves the selective use of statistics. An extensive knowledge of statistics would be needed to be able to recognize the many different ways in which statistics can mislead, and we can here describe only a few of the more common types of misleading statistics.

It is often useful to know the average value of something. We may, for example, want to know the average grade for a course, the average grade of a student, the average wage paid by a company, the average rent for a one-bedroom apartment, or the average summer temperature in Australia. But averages can be quite misleading. Suppose we are told that the employees of a company earn an average of $1,000 per week. This is a quite respectable wage, and we would not have a great deal of sympathy if the employees complained of being seriously underpaid, since we would assume that most employees must be receiving around $1,000 per week. But this need not be so. Suppose the company has eleven employees who are paid as follows:

General manager:	$2,400
Sales manager:	$2,000
Production manager:	$2,000
Office manager:	$1,800
Bookkeeper 1:	$440
Bookkeeper 2:	$420
Shipper:	$410
Driver:	$390
Salesperson:	$390
Salesperson:	$390
Receptionist:	$360
TOTAL:	$11,000

The average weekly pay is $1,000, but everyone except the managers receives much less. In such a case most people will be misled by references to the average wage.

To avoid such misleading averages, statisticians make use of two related concepts that help to give a more accurate picture than a simple average. The MEDIAN is the middle point in the range: half the individual cases will be above it and half below it. In the above example, the median is $420. The MODE is the particular value that occurs most frequently. In the above example, the mode is $390. The median and the mode are quite different from the simple average, or MEAN, as it is called by statisticians.

A second way in which statistics can mislead is when they are used to describe quantitative changes, such as increases or decreases in prices, productivity, crime rates, and so on. The problem lies in an ambiguity in the way such changes are described. If a merchant buys an item for $6 and sells it for $10, what, in percentage terms, is the merchant's profit? Calculated as a percentage of the merchant's *buying* price, the profit is 66.6 per cent. But calculated as a percentage of the *selling* price, the profit is only 40 per cent. Both methods of calculating the merchant's profit are legitimate (even if one method is unconventional), but they are different and mean different things. If we are told that the mark-up used by a merchant is 50 per cent, we can be misled unless we know which method is being used. Similar problems can arise in a variety of other contexts. If a landlord says the rent on a $600 apartment has increased only 25 per cent in the last five years, does this mean the rent went from $480 to $600 (because the rent has increased by 25 per cent of the original rent of $480) or from $450 to $600 (because the rent has increased by 25 per cent of $600 from the original rent of $450)? If a friend brags about having increased his or her semester average 10 per cent last semester, did it jump from 60 per cent to 70 per cent or from 60 per cent to 66 per cent? In each case, in order not to be misled we should ask, *Percentage of what?*

A third way in which statistical information can be misleading is when it is presented as a graph. Once again, the actual statistical information is not false: the problem is that it can easily be misunderstood if we do not pay careful attention to how it is being presented. The two graphs shown below present identical information about the increase in the price of a commodity over a one-year period.

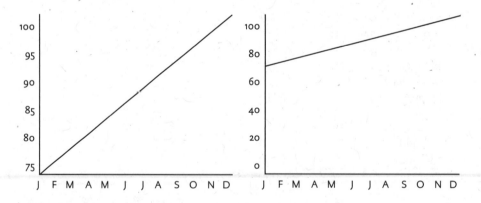

The graph on the left makes it appear that there has been a much more dramatic price increase than the graph on the right, even though both present *the same information*. The graph on the left suggests a greater increase because the bottom three-quarters of the graph has been cut off. The line looks different only because the vertical axis is drawn to a different scale. When interpreting any graph, we should always take the scale into account.

14.7 Humour

There is nothing wrong with using humour in a discussion. In fact, if a discussion starts to become boring, a little humour can be a very good thing. Every good public speaker knows the value of a good joke or a witty comment. For example:

> You've heard of the definition of a philosopher as a blind person in a dark room searching for a black cat that isn't there? Well, a theologian is the person who finds the cat.

> When I read what drama critics have to say about my work, I am reminded of Brendan Behan's comment that critics are like eunuchs in a harem: they know how it's done, they've seen it done every day, but they're unable to do it themselves.

There are, however, limits to the purposes for which humour can legitimately be used. In particular, it should not be used as a substitute for rational argument. In argumentative contexts, any use of humour functions *independently* of reasons in favour of the argument's conclusion. When we use humour to divert attention from a weakness in our argument or to have some fun at the expense of our opponents, no reasons have been provided to believe that our position is stronger than that of our opponent. If our argument was weak before we added some humour, it will be just as weak after.

The effectiveness of humour as a persuasive device depends, of course, upon the views and prejudices of the audience. If the audience is sympathetic to our opponent, our attempts at humour may backfire and make us look mean and petty. If our jokes are too cruel, they may create sympathy for our opponent. And if the audience feels that it is also a target, our humour may create hostility towards us.

But humour is not always used as a substitute for rational argument. It can be used to make a rational argument more effective. For example:

> Mr. Speaker, the Minister is still refusing to act on the unanimous recommendations of his own officials as well as several independent experts regarding the leakage at the PCB dump in my constituency. Everyone who has examined the situation agrees it constitutes a serious health hazard to the 20,0000 people living nearby. But when asked by a reporter yesterday what he was going to do about it, the Minister talked at great length about consulting all the interested parties. This is a totally inadequate response. As usual, the Minister's mouth is in high gear and his brain is in neutral.

In the face of unanimous recommendations regarding what to do about a serious health hazard, the Minister's response certainly seems totally inadequate. The humour helps to make this point in a more effective manner, even though it adds no logical or rational strength to the argument.

14.8 Red Herring

When responding to a criticism of some position we hold, it is often tempting to ignore the criticism and launch a counter-attack on our opponent by raising a different issue altogether. When we do this we have introduced a RED HERRING. (The label probably derives from fugitives trying to prevent dogs from tracking their scent by rubbing a stinky red herring across their path.) We are attempting to avoid a criticism by shifting the discussion to a new topic on which we can attack the critic. This device is regularly used by politicians when responding to attacks by opponents. For example:

> OPPOSITION MEMBER: *Will the Minister tell the House why nothing has been done to clean up the mercury poisoning in the Kenora area, 18 months after it was brought to his attention?*
> MINISTER: *The Honourable Member sounds like a broken record with his constant carping about health hazards. The fact is that my Ministry has been extremely successful in reducing, and in many cases eliminating, environmental pollution across this province. Our record is vastly better than the previous government's record.*

The Minister has clearly not responded to the question at all but has attempted to shift the discussion to the government's record of pollution control in general to avoid having to answer the question that was asked.

It is important to realize that there is nothing wrong with attempting to shift a discussion from one topic to another. Many discussions ramble naturally from topic to topic; as we get tired of one topic we move on to something else that is more interesting. Shifting topics is only illegitimate when the shift is introduced in an attempt to avoid a criticism.

Here is another example of a red herring:

> *Critics of the automobile industry frequently claim that our cars are not as safe as they could be. One critic has even suggested that we are criminally negligent because of our failure to produce safe cars. What these critics so conveniently forget is that cars do not cause accidents. Accidents are caused by bad drivers. We cooperate with governments in promoting safe driving and have taken numerous initiatives ourselves. We are not sure why our campaigns have been so ineffective. If we thought that spending more money on promoting safe driving would help, we would gladly do so, but no one knows what type of campaign would be most effective. This is where the critics could actually do some good, if they were to help us discover how to promote safe driving habits.*

14.9 Guilt By Association

One way of attacking an opponent or an opponent's position is by suggesting a similarity with another person or position that the audience regards in an unfavourable light. In a debate on the government's policy of attempting to create a sense of national unity, for example, someone might say:

> So what you are really advocating is a system like they had in Nazi Germany where the Propaganda Ministry attempted to foster a national ideology.

Such a comment is an attempt to create the same kind of hostility towards the government's policy that people feel towards Nazi Germany. It suggests that the policy is a totalitarian or fascist idea that ought to be rejected out of hand.

Guilt by association involves a faulty analogy. In fact, the analogy is usually so faulty that, if it were presented as a serious argument, its weaknesses would be immediately apparent and the purpose of drawing the analogy would be defeated. Here are some more examples of attempts to establish guilt by association:

> We should never forget that the politicians who gave us Medicare in Canada borrowed the idea from the communists, who first introduced socialized medical care in the 1920s.

> So, you are driving a BMW now. I guess you will soon be sending your children to private schools, like all the other yuppies.

14.10 Persuasive Redefinition

An especially effective device for changing attitudes is what is called PERSUASIVE REDEFINITION: the redefinition of a familiar term or phrase that has both a descriptive and an evaluative meaning in such a way as to change its descriptive meaning while keeping its evaluative meaning the same. Consider the term *poet*. The dictionary gives as one definition of a poet *a writer of verse*. This gives the term's descriptive meaning. The word can also be used with a strong positive evaluative meaning: to describe someone as a poet is normally to praise him or her. If we wanted to capitalize on this evaluative meaning, we might try a persuasive redefinition that involves dropping the requirement that a poet actually has to write verse: *A poet is a person with a deep and vivid imagination*. Given this definition, we could describe someone as a poet (and hence praiseworthy) who has never actually written a poem. If we are challenged, we could claim that we are not using the word in its ordinary or vulgar sense, according to which anybody who can scribble a rhyme would count as a poet, but rather in the true sense of the term. The essence of being a poet, we might say, is having a deep and vivid imagination. In other words, we attempt to justify shifting the descriptive meaning by claiming that our new definition is superior because it is truer. In fact, of course, such definitions are not usually superior at all but only different and, if judged as reportive definitions, wildly inaccurate.

To be effective, a persuasive redefinition must not change the descriptive meaning too much or else the audience will see the trick and not be fooled by it. If someone tried to redefine the term *intelligence* to mean the ability to use words of more than two syllables, no one would take the attempt seriously. But where the change preserves some of the original descriptive meaning, it may be harder to detect. A definition of intelligence as the ability to perform mental calculations quickly is closer to the original descriptive meaning and hence could be more successful as a persuasive redefinition. People who are good at doing mental calculations might well want to redefine intelligence in this way in order to attract the admiration that intelligence usually evokes.

Persuasive redefinitions are always stipulative, since the new descriptive meaning always differs from the original descriptive meaning to a certain extent. What distinguishes a persuasive definition from an ordinary stipulative definition is its purpose, for it always seeks to retain the original evaluative meaning. Most stipulative definitions are indifferent to the evaluative meaning of the term.

To illustrate the process of persuasive redefinition, let us consider an historical example. In the 1920s the term *fascist* came into use as a name for a political movement in Italy. It was strongly nationalistic and anti-communist and placed great emphasis on the role of a leader in expressing the spirit of the people and furthering the traditional values of the society. Similar movements in Germany and elsewhere also came to be referred to as fascist. Originally, the term lacked any clear evaluative meaning: people in many countries considered fascism as a serious political alternative, and many well-meaning people adopted a number of fascist views. The events of World War II, however, gave the term a strongly negative evaluative meaning. With the defeat of fascist regimes in Germany and Italy, one might have expected the term to fall into disuse. In fact, it has become an accepted part of our political vocabulary, probably because a number of influential political writers wanted to preserve it as a term of abuse. To do so, however, its original descriptive meaning had to be revised to take account of the fact that the original fascist movements no longer existed, and it now refers to any government with totalitarian or racist policies. The original descriptive meaning has largely, although not entirely, disappeared.

14.11 Self-Test No. 21

Identify the irrational techniques of persuasion used in the following passages.

1. So the city of Edmonton has launched an advertising campaign to attract tourists. It reminds me of the time when a Calgary newspaper had some kind of contest: first prize was a weekend in Edmonton, and second prize was a whole week in Edmonton.

2. We take great pride in our products. We've had over 80 years of experience making furniture and we've learned how to balance the highest standards of craftsmanship with a range of styles to suit the tastes of the modern consumer.

And our customers agree. When people walk into our showrooms the words we hear most frequently are, *Ah, that's what I've been looking for!*

Pardon us if we're smug. We are the best and can't see why we shouldn't brag about it.

3. Frankly, I don't think it matters whether pornography is harmful to women or not. We live in a pluralistic society in which there are many different voices, all of which are entitled to be heard. Silencing opinions and points of view that some group doesn't agree with goes against what this country stands for.

4. What is Adam like? Well, he's kind of hard to describe. He's basically just a neat guy: lots of personality, sort of laid back, the kind of person you would like.

5. If you are one of the minority of wage earners over 30 who doesn't have the protection an RRSP provides, you should be asking yourself, *Why do I keep putting it off?*

6. Remember, the next time you're in the market for a new lawn mower, try a Titan. They've got what it takes.

7. I'm fed up with those people who keep insisting that we shouldn't violate the rights of criminals. What I want to know is, what are they prepared to do for the victims of violent crimes?

8. He's not really a scientist. Sure, he has a PhD in chemistry and works in a research laboratory, but all he does is try to find cheaper ways of making soaps and cosmetics. Real scientists are dedicated to making discoveries, take pride in what they are doing, and care deeply about the progress of the whole discipline. He is nothing more than a glorified lab technician.

9. There sure is a lot of talk these days about the free trade deal, and it's probably going to get a lot worse before it gets better. I don't know about you, but I'm having a helluva time figuring out who's right and who's wrong. You've got the union leaders bleating about the loss of jobs, and the business types telling us we're all going to get rich. I mean, who are you to believe? One thing I want to know is, is there any reason to think that this time Mulroney isn't just serving the interests of his tycoon friends in corporate boardrooms?

10. Did you see that, Doris? That car went right through the stop sign without even slowing down. And it was a woman driver too, just like the one that rear-ended Ken last month.

14.12 Questions for Discussion

Some, although not all, of the following passages present real arguments. However, all rely in part on one or more irrational techniques of persuasion to attempt to put their point across.

1. Religious cults are extremely dangerous, and we must do everything possible to warn people against them. They always prey upon the young, who are at that vulnerable age when they still retain their idealism but are beginning to learn that the world is a less moral place than it should be. Once they have ensnared a victim they completely take over his or her life. Cult members become slaves: they do exactly what they are told and any questioning or criticism is severely discouraged. They are forbidden all contact with their families and former friends. Their dependency is so complete that it is virtually impossible to rescue them without the risk of doing serious psychological damage.

2. Communism always presented itself as a scientific theory of history and politics, but the reality was that it was essentially a religion. Like religion, its claim to an objective basis was more apparent than real and rested more upon faith than anything else. And it offered its adherents personal salvation: the assurance that they were right and that in the fullness of time they would be seen to have been right. It also offered an evil enemy that had to be opposed at every turn and whose ultimate overthrow would produce a new Jerusalem where at last the lion would lie down with the lamb.

3. For years many of us have regarded the NDP as an interesting and worthwhile third party. It has lots of ideas as to what the government should be doing, and some of those ideas are practical enough to deserve a hearing. And they're a decent bunch of chaps; they often take themselves too seriously, but basically they're honest and concerned people. But now that the polls suggest that they might actually win the next election, we have to ask whether the NDP has the competence—the ability to make tough economic decisions, for example—to govern a country as complex as Canada. How Canadians answer this question may well determine whether or not Canada will soon have its first socialist prime minister.

4. There can be no doubt whatever about the fundamental correctness of the government's fiscal and monetary policies, for we absolutely must get the deficit under control or else face economic disaster within ten years. There is, quite simply, no alternative to what the government is doing. Of course, the Opposi-

tion pretends that it has some magic wand that it can wave at the deficit and make it disappear. The reality, however, is that while the ship of state is in danger of sinking, the Opposition has only a sardine can to bail with. It would be funny if it were not so tragic.

5. During the twentieth century, mankind, at least in the industrialized world, has achieved a standard of living that would have astonished people only a century ago. The average person today has more money, more comfort, and better health than ever before. He has a better job, his children are better educated, he travels more widely and more often, he has a better home with more possessions, and can retire at age 55 to enjoy another 25 years of comfortable living.

15. Critiquing the Media

For most of us, the main source of information about the world beyond our immediate personal experience is the media. Most of the skills we need to assess this information have already been covered in earlier chapters, especially Chapter 6, which dealt with determining the acceptability of truth-claims, and Chapter 14, which outlined various irrational techniques of persuasion. However, there are some special problems associated with the media that require more detailed discussion. In this chapter we will discuss how to critique the media and will consider some of the problems that arise in doing so. In particular, we will examine how the media reports factual news stories and how to determine whether or not these reports are unbiased. In addition, we will examine the ways in which the media can influence how we interpret the information that comes to us from all sources as well as how the media can shape many of our deeply held values.

It is important to remember that the media plays a very important role in democratic societies, namely, that of watchdog on the actions of government. This role is so important that in many countries the media is given special legal protection against direct interference by the government. Indeed, in some countries this protection is entrenched in the constitution in order to make government interference virtually impossible. In Canada, for example, Section 2 of the *Charter of Rights and Freedoms* specifically protects "freedom of the press and other media of communications." In the United States, the first amendment to the constitution protects freedom of speech, which the courts have interpreted as including freedom of the media. This protection is important because the threat of exposure by a legally protected media is the best way to deter governments who may be tempted to lie to the people about their competence or to cover up their misdeeds or to manipulate public opinion. As we all know, even in the face of a protected media, governments still try to deceive us with some regularity. Of course, usually we know that these attempts have been made only because of exposure by or through the media. In addition, there is no reason to think that all such attempts have been detected and exposed by the media. However, it is clear that, without a legally protected media, we would be utterly helpless in the face of government manipulation.

But the very fact that the media enjoys special protection against interference carries with it the risk that the media may abuse its role. Of course, the media is subject to the laws of libel and may be sued for publishing false information which harms someone. But apart from this restriction, which applies to all of us, the media is free to publish whatever it chooses. Of course, if we value a free media we cannot advocate additional legal restrictions in order to ensure that the media performs its role in a responsible manner. If the media is free to report as it sees fit, then sometimes it will see fit to report irresponsibly. This is the price we have to pay for a free media. That is the nature of human freedom. However, while we have an obligation to respect and defend the freedom of the media, we also have an obligation both as citizens and as reasoning human beings to respond intelligently to it. There are two aspects to this obligation. First, we have an obligation to scrutinize the media in order to ensure that we understand its limitations and possible biases. If we don't do this, we risk being unknowingly misled and manipulated. Second, we have an obligation to criticize the media when it behaves irresponsibly. The underlying reason for protecting the freedom of the media is that the health of a democracy depends crucially upon the freedom of the media to criticize the government and to advocate policies that are at variance with those of the government. When the media behaves irresponsibly, it is weakening its role as a defender of democracy, and it is important to challenge the media whenever this happens.

It is important to understand the difference between criticizing the media and attacking the freedom of the media. Some people respond to criticism of the media by appealing to the principle of the freedom of the media. This response in effect claims that freedom of the media includes freedom from criticism. Such a response sadly misunderstands the nature of the freedom of the media. Freedom of the media requires only that the government not control the media. In a society where freedom of the media is respected, publishers and editors will be free to publish whatever they think is appropriate, and anyone who wants to start a newspaper or other news organization will be free to do so. In other words, freedom of the media means that control of what gets published should remain in the hands of private citizens. Criticizing the media does not challenge in any way the principle that the media should be free. Criticizing the media assumes only that editors and journalists sometimes do their job badly and that when they do they can legitimately be criticized for their failings. People who criticize the media are almost never calling for government intervention. On the contrary, they are calling for the particular editors concerned to do their job better voluntarily.

15.1 Determining Bias

The most obvious failing of the media is biased reporting. The two most important sources of bias in reporting were discussed in Chapter 14: loaded terms (Section 14.1) and selectivity (Section 14.5). Loaded terms are used most often and most blatantly in newspaper headlines, but can, of course, also occur in the text of stories. Consider the following pair of headlines:

(a) *PM Blames Staff for Fiasco*
(b) *Military Accepts Responsibility for Embarrassing PM*

The first headline conveys the idea that the Prime Minister has refused to accept responsibility for something that is his or her responsibility, which strongly suggests that the Prime Minister is a moral and political coward. The second headline makes no such suggestion and is consistent with the idea that the Prime Minister has behaved responsibly. Here are some other pairs of headlines in which loaded terms convey quite different views:

(a) *City Council "Cover-Up" of Hospital Fraud*
(b) *Councillor Alleges Cover-Up of Hospital Fraud*

(a) *Critics Disgusted by More Olympic Corruption*
(b) *Olympic Scandal Deepens: IOC Will Investigate New Charges*

(a) *More Food Aid Disappears: Canadians Conned by Corrupt Officials*
(b) *Food for Starving Gets Through: Delays Blamed on Rebels*

(a) *Butchered 7 Teenage Girls: Now Seeks Freedom*
(b) *Serial Killer's Parole Application Denied*

In each case it is easy to see that one of the two headlines relies upon loaded terms to convey a specific value judgement. The use of quotation marks in the first example ("Cover-Up") is interesting because it allows the newspaper to deny a bias by saying that the headline did not claim that there was a cover-up but merely quoted someone else's allegation of a cover-up. In fact, most readers will not notice the quotation marks and will take the alleged cover-up as a fact and assume that the newspaper endorses the negative judgement conveyed by the phrase.

Selectivity is a more complex source of biased reporting. Selectivity occurs in three ways. First, editors have to make decisions as to what to report and what to ignore. After all, there are thousands of incidents that occur every day that we would all agree are not worth reporting. No one could blame a television network for failing to report that someone spilled a cup of coffee at breakfast. Every television news broadcast and every issue of a newspaper or news magazine reflects the editors' judgements as to what should be reported and what should not. There is no way around this; some selection has to be made by someone. Second, selectivity occurs when decisions are made as to the prominence that is given to each story. For newspapers, the question is which story will be the main front-page headline and which stories will be mentioned on page 38. For television news programs, the question is which story comes first and which stories are left to the end. Once again, these decisions are unavoidable. Only two or perhaps three stories can receive front-page coverage, and only one story can come first in a television news broadcast. Third, editors have to make decisions as to the amount of coverage to be given to each story. Should it receive detailed treatment, perhaps with additional related stories on the same topic from different reporters, or does it warrant only short cursory coverage? These three types of selectivity make it possible for the media to present biased coverage of a certain event or certain types of events. They make it easy to play up or play down a particular story to make it seem more or less important to the audience. The story is covered and all the relevant facts may be mentioned, but the impact of the story can be significantly affected by the prominence given to it.

It is usually easy to identify and describe biased reporting that results from the use of loaded terms. Bias that arises from selectivity is a little more difficult to recognize. Often it only becomes apparent when a pattern of bias is detected. For example, a newspaper that routinely gives front-page prominence to stories about welfare fraud and relegates to the back pages a government report that shows that only 6 per cent of welfare claims are fraudulent can legitimately be suspected of attempting to create an anti-welfare sentiment. Similarly, a newspaper that always gives prominence to reports of high salaries of business executives and record profits of corporations may legitimately be suspected of attempting to foster anti-business sentiment. In both cases, however, the bias becomes apparent only through the identification of a pattern of coverage.

15.2 Is Objective Reporting Possible?

Identifying bias in reporting is usually a straightforward task requiring only the use of critical thinking skills. But how easy is it to remove bias from a story? At first sight this task seems equally straightforward. After all, since a bias is something present in a story that shouldn't be there, once we identify it, we should be able to remove it, thus leaving an unbiased story. Removing a bias is only difficult if we cannot identify it; once we recognize and identify a bias, removing it is no more difficult than removing a pair of spectacles with tinted lenses. Many people think of bias this way because it seems to follow directly from the method we use to identify bias in a story. We identify a bias in a story, they argue, by comparing the actual story with an "ideal," unbiased account. We compare the two and note the differences: the bias will consist of whatever is in the actual story that is not in the ideal story and/or whatever is in the ideal story that is not in the actual story. On this view, bias is simply a failure to achieve objectivity. It is assumed that we understand what objectivity is and can recognize it when we see it. The ability to understand objectivity is thus a precondition for recognizing bias.

But this view is frequently attacked on the ground that it is unrealistic and naive to think that we know what objectivity is. There is no "ideal" objective story, the critics argue, and objective reporting is therefore impossible. All reporting is necessarily subjective and reflects the values and biases of the reporters and editors. It may appear that some accounts are unbiased, but this is misleading, for an "unbiased" account is simply one whose biases coincide with our own. I may think my favourite newspaper is unbiased and yours is biased, but from your point of view my favourite newspaper is biased while yours is unbiased. In reality, the critics argue, we are both wrong, for objectivity is unattainable. It is not only unattainable in practice, but is also unattainable in principle. Objectivity is not some ideal goal we can strive for even though we know we can never achieve it, like a sprinter who strives to run 100 metres in under 9 seconds. Objectivity is an unintelligible goal, like trying to draw a round square. This attack raises an extremely important issue which must be addressed in any assessment of the media. If the critics are correct and objective reporting is impossible, it makes no sense to criticize the media for biased reporting. All we can do is seek to identify bias so we can screen it out if we don't agree with it or turn to a different media source for our information.

Initially the view that unbiased objective reporting is impossible looks plausible. We all know from our own experience how difficult it is to attain objectivity. No matter how hard we might try to describe some event in totally objective terms, we realize we can never produce anything other than our interpretation of it. Two people who are asked to produce detailed objective descriptions of the same event will never agree down to the last detail. They might produce closely similar accounts but this will be merely a coincidence that arises only because they happen to share the same biases. It seems that every conceivable description of a given event can never be anything other than someone's interpretation of it. And since the media is just as inescapably biased as individuals, it makes no sense to expect anything other than some particular interpretation when we watch the news on television or read a newspaper. It therefore makes no sense to criticize the media for bias. How can we criticize anyone for doing what is unavoidable? We might as well criticize water for running downhill.

But does this conclusion really follow? Does the fact that interpretation is inescapable make nonsense of the idea that we can aim at objectivity and impartiality? Does it really rule out the possibility of criticizing media bias? It certainly would if all interpretations are equally legitimate. But is this so? Are all interpretations of an event equally reasonable? If we are confronted by two conflicting interpretations of some event, can we only shrug and treat them as equally valid? Consider the following hypothetical example of conflicting news reports:

(a) *Ronald Smith, a science teacher at Oak Lane High School, lost his temper yesterday and threw a book at a student, 17-year-old David Jones, hitting him on the head. Jones has complained about Smith's behaviour to the school principal, Marion Lee, but Lee has so far refused to take any action against Smith. Jones was unavailable for comment, but his friends say he is planning to charge Smith with assault. When contacted by reporters, Smith refused to answer questions and referred reporters to Ms. Lee. Mr. L. Rostock, Director of Education for the county Board of Education, also refused to comment on the incident.*

(b) *Ronald Smith, a science teacher at Oak Lane High School, was attacked yesterday by one of his students. The student, 17-year-old David Jones, had refused to stop laughing and talking in class despite repeated requests from Smith. When Smith ordered Jones to leave the room, Jones threw his text book at Smith, who caught it and tossed it back to Jones. Jones then stormed out of the room and left the school. When contacted, the school principal, Marion Lee, said she had interviewed both Smith and Jones, and that Jones had already apologized to Smith. She said she now regards the matter as closed.*

These two accounts present quite different interpretations of the event. There are also certain factual discrepancies. Did Smith throw a book at Jones and hit his head? Or did Smith merely toss the book back to Jones after Jones had thrown it at Smith? Surely anyone who actually witnessed the event would be able to say which account is correct. After all, either the book actually hit Jones on the head, or it did not. Similarly, either Jones did in fact apologize to Smith, or he did not. Since it is the reporter's job to uncover the relevant facts, the discrepancies between the two stories show that one of the reporters has failed to do his or her job properly and has misreported the facts. But there is also a significant discrepancy in how the two accounts interpret the actions of the principal. The first account suggests that the principal is attempting to cover up the incident. The second account makes it appear that the principal acted appropriately. Which of these is the more reasonable interpretation? The information provided by the two accounts doesn't answer this question, but further investigation into the incident would likely make the answer clear. For example, would it be reasonable to interpret Smith's action of throwing or tossing the book to Jones as an assault? In some cases, observers might find it hard to say, but usually it will be obvious whether it really was a threatening action or not. These are all legitimate questions that arise out of the discrepancies between the two stories. Asking them is reasonable and natural. The answers to them will enable us to decide which story is closer to the truth or which is the more reasonable interpretation. People who think that there is no way to decide between the two accounts (because all reporting is biased) are forced to view such questions as illegitimate. But this is surely wrong. Further investigation will almost certainly favour one story, or the other, or perhaps a third version combining elements from both. People who hold that there is no way to decide which story is more reasonable are in effect refusing to carry out further investigation. They have closed their minds to the possibility of further reasonable inquiry.

Here is another pair of hypothetical news reports:

(a) *A clinic in Mexico has developed a new treatment for cancer that can cure most types of cancers, according to reports from doctors at the clinic. It is a treatment that combines one of the drugs commonly used in conventional chemotherapy treatments with several organic compounds developed at the clinic. Doctors at the clinic have stated that as many as 200 patients have been helped by the treatment in the last three months. The treatment has not been approved by the federal government for use in Canada despite repeated requests from individuals who want to use the new treatment. And no provincial Medicare plan is willing to pay for patients to travel to Mexico for treatment. Officials insist that patients must follow the conventional treatments, which consist of massive doses of chemotherapy and radiation, and refuse to consider any alternative treatments. When asked about this refusal, a spokesman for the clinic* said, "we expected a hostile reaction from the medical establishment and are not surprised by it."

(b) *Claims by doctors at a Mexican cancer clinic that they have discovered a cure for cancer are disputed by scientists who are familiar with the treatment. Dr. Robert Park, a cancer specialist from San Diego, California, said yesterday that the treatment is very similar to one that was tested two years ago in California that was shown to be of no clinical value. He also said that the clinic refuses to allow independent scientists to examine its patient records. As a result, he said, there is no way to assess the clinic's claim. "They won't show us the evidence," he said, "so how can we tell whether it is just a scam." Officials in the Health Protection Branch of the Ministry of Health in Ottawa say they would be happy to assess any evidence submitted in support of the clinic's claim, but no evidence has been submitted, and no one has asked the Branch to investigate the claim.*

Which of these two stories is likely to be closer to the truth? Once again, there are some factual discrepancies between them which could be resolved by anyone prepared to undertake further investigation. Has anyone actually requested health officials to approve the treatment? If so, the second story contains a falsehood. If not, the first story contains a falsehood. This is an empirical question, which means that the discrepancy can be resolved through factual investigation. But there are also differences of interpretation. The first story suggests that the government's refusal to fund the treatment is caused by the prejudice of the medical establishment, while the second story suggests that the refusal to fund treatment is the result of the lack of evidence to support the claim that it is effective. Which of these interpretations is more reasonable? Further investigation would be needed to know for sure, but it is likely that the second story is closer to the truth at least as regards the central issue of whether the new treatment actually does cure cancer: it assumes that the clinic's claim is unproven until the evidence has been assessed by independent experts, whereas the first presents the clinic's claim as acceptable without evidence.

These brief discussions show that, when dealing with conflicting accounts of an event, we are led to ask certain questions in order to decide which account is better. The fact that we ask these questions shows that we reject the suggestion that all interpretations are equal. We ask them because we believe that some interpretations are better (i.e., more reasonable, or more defensible, or closer to the truth) than others. And the questions we ask are of a type that should already be familiar to anyone with well-developed critical thinking skills. For example, we asked whether certain factual statements were true and whether other statements were relevant. As we saw in Section 5.3, these are both questions we need to ask when assessing arguments. This does not mean that news reports are actual arguments, but it does mean that we can use our critical thinking skills to assess them.

15.3 How to Assess News Reports

There are two primary purposes of news reports and the news media in general: (a) to describe some event to the reader and (b) to persuade the reader to accept an interpretation of the event. (These are two of the functions of language discussed in section 2.3.) We sometimes get so caught up in the factual descriptions that we forget about the second purpose of news reports. Journalists, however, are always aware of the need to present the factual description in a way that gives it a certain interpretation. For example, a story about a fire in a retirement home may highlight the narrow escapes of the residents and the heroism of the fire department, or it may focus on the failure of smoke alarms and inadequate safety inspections. Both stories may include the same factual descriptions of the incident, but the interpretations will be different. The presence of the interpretive element does not mean that reporters and editors deliberately present a biased story. In most cases they see what they are doing as presenting a responsible interpretation. If challenged to defend the content of a story, they will usually claim that the facts are true and that their interpretation is a reasonable one. When we assess news coverage by news organizations (print newspapers, online sources, magazines, radio and television stations) it is important to realize that there are these two different aspects—the factual and the interpretive—to consider. And because they are different, they require different types of assessment.

15.3.1 ASSESSING FACTUAL CLAIMS

The factual aspect of news reporting should be assessed in the manner described in Chapter 6. Descriptions in news reports consist of empirical truth-claims, and we have already discussed how to assess such claims in Sections 6.2 and 6.3. The factual truth of news reports is in practice relatively easy to assess because news reports are usually quite explicit in identifying the source of their factual claims. Reporters sometimes present their own eyewitness accounts, as when they describe a riot or flood that they have themselves witnessed. Sometimes they quote what witnesses have said about some event, as when they interview the victims of fraud. They may quote from official police reports. They may quote someone with relevant expertise. In each case the source of the information is identified so that the reporter can justify the claims made in the report. It is sometimes important to remind ourselves that, when a reporter quotes witnesses or experts, the reporter cannot guarantee the truth of what is said. Occasionally we may suspect that a reporter may not be telling the truth or may be deliberately attempting to create a misleading impression of the facts. However, most news organizations are careful to avoid publishing anything whose factual truth is in doubt. They believe, probably correctly, that if they are perceived as unreliable on factual matters their audience or readership will decline. This is why they are quick to publish corrections and apologies whenever they have made a mistake by publishing a false statement.

Normally we do not need to check the factual reliability of the news media with respect to particular news reports. But if we are concerned about the general reliability of a news organization, there are certain questions we should ask. Does it have a reputation for carefully checking its factual claims? Does it apologize whenever it makes a factual error? If there are conflicting reports of an event by different news organizations, is there internal evidence that would indicate which story is correct? When we have personal knowledge of an event being reported or background knowledge of a situation, does the report match our knowledge of the facts? Sometimes, however, a factual story may be so important to us that we will want to do some independent checking to determine whether it is correct. This may present us with a difficult practical challenge, for it may require us to interview witnesses for ourselves and to obtain documents and reports that may be difficult to find. But in principle we know from the discussion in Section 6.2.1 what we need to do to check out any empirical claim.

15.3.2 ASSESSING INTERPRETIVE FRAMEWORKS

Assessing interpretations presented in news stories is much more complex. The interpretive aspect of a news report needs to be understood in the context of the kind of interpretation that is present in the overall news coverage of a particular news organization. To understand the interpretation in a news story requires more than merely recognizing that a bias is present. For example, we need to know more than that the news organization dislikes the Prime Minister. We need to know what reasons they would give to explain or justify their hostility. This requires us to pay attention to the pattern of coverage and bias over a significant period of time. Is the hostility based on dislike of the Prime Minister's character and personal qualities? Or the government's policies? Or the inability to overcome government inefficiency? If we want to understand the interpretation being given to stories about the Prime Minister, we need to know what reasons lie behind the hostility. What these reasons will reveal is an interpretive framework that influences and is present in all the coverage. This framework will always include a political perspective, sometimes including a commitment to a particular political party, but it extends far beyond the political sphere. It may, for example, include a view of the role of the arts, the value of amateur sport, support for certain educational policies, and concern about the role of organized religion in society. There are often subtle interconnections within an interpretive framework. It may be, for example, that although the hostility directed towards the Prime Minister is most evident with respect to certain personal qualities, it is the government's policies that underlie the hostility. The news organization may believe that the best way to undermine public support for the government's policies is not by attacking them directly but by ridiculing the Prime Minister's personal qualities. And if we decide that the news organization is hostile to the government's policies, we need to understand which particular policies are disliked most strongly. Is it the government's support for NATO? Is it the refusal to introduce major tax cuts? Is it that the government is soft on crime, or hostile to minority rights, or that it treats certain regions of the country unfairly? Only when we can answer these questions will we really understand the interpretive framework that lies behind the interpretations given to particular stories.

Once we understand the interpretive framework in the coverage provided by a particular news organization, we are in a position to assess it. It may be that some of the

Prime Minister's personal qualities are less than admirable, but if we are aware that news stories that focus on these personal qualities are part of an attempt to undermine public support for certain government policies, we will no longer regard these stories as innocuous. We will want to object that the Prime Minister's accent or clothes or protruding ears have nothing to do with any significant political issue. It may be that the law deals too leniently with criminals, but we will want to know whether news reports that focus on crimes committed by repeat offenders really show a failure of government policy and precisely what that failure consists of. In short, we will want to use our own judgement to decide what we think is the most defensible social policy regarding the treatment of offenders and on this basis decide whether we agree with the interpretation presented by a particular news organization. This is the kind of thing we must do for every element of the news organization's interpretive framework. We must identify each policy stance that is part of the interpretive framework and then decide for ourselves whether we agree with it or not.

Of course, an interpretive framework may not include a position on every controversial social and political issue. Sometimes a news organization is neutral with respect to certain issues. For example, it may be neutral on the question of whether more government action is required to achieve significant reductions of greenhouse gas emissions. Such neutrality can sometimes be deceptive, however, for while a news organization may be neutral on whether government action is needed, it may have strong views on what the government should do if further action is needed. For example, it may insist that if further government action is needed, it should take the form only of tax incentives to manufacturers. The neutrality may extend to only one specific aspect of an issue.

It would be a mistake to think that an interpretive framework must be accepted or rejected as a whole. There will likely be some coherence among the various elements that make up an interpretive framework, but this does not mean we cannot be selective in our judgements about the framework. We may, for example, agree with a news organization on matters of foreign policy and disagree with it on domestic policy issues. Or we may agree with it on the need to strengthen the role of religion and religious institutions in our society and disagree with it on the need for welfare reform.

15.4 Another Warning

The reason we need to understand and assess interpretive frameworks should be obvious. We want to avoid having our social and political attitudes influenced without our realizing it. If we are not on our guard, we will find that our views about the treatment of offenders, the extent of welfare fraud, the role of trade unions, the amount of harm caused by strikes, and a host of other matters will have been shaped and determined by the media and not by thinking these matters through for ourselves. In general, people are unwilling (or say they are unwilling) to allow the news media to do their thinking for them, but it seems that many people are reluctant to make the effort to think for themselves. This is not surprising given the nature of the task. Not only must we address a host of political and social policy issues, but we have to develop an understanding of the interpretive frameworks of all the news organizations that supply us with information.

The task of deciding issues for ourselves is made even more daunting because we cannot address social policy issues without having a good understanding of the relevant facts. We should not even attempt to decide whether or not offenders are treated too leniently without knowing the relevant facts about prison conditions, crime rates, sentencing patterns, the requirements of the criminal code with respect to determining guilt, and a host of other related matters. These are the facts we need to make an intelligent judgement about sentencing policy. Unfortunately, the major source of this information is the media itself. And if the media interprets this information in a way that supports a certain type of sentencing policy, the very information we need to decide the issue for ourselves is compromised. There is no easy solution to this dilemma. We can try to avoid news organizations whose interpretive framework we disagree with, but this is not always possible. We can try to sift out the biases we disagree with, but this is very difficult to do unless we have another source for at least some of the factual data we need.

Assessing the media thus constitutes a major challenge for all of us. We are confronted not with a specific problem that we can solve once and for all and then put behind us, but by an ongoing need to respond intelligently to the media and to its role in our lives and in the lives of our fellow citizens. This is not an easy task. In the end, we must try to be vigilant in seeking to avoid being influenced in ways we are not aware of and that our considered judgement would not support. And for this, of course, our most effective tool will be the full and regular deployment of all our critical thinking skills.

There are no direct methods for testing biases of the sort used to test logical strength, relevance, etc. in earlier chapters. But there are two things we can do to assess the reliability of a news source and to assess a particular news report for biases. (1) To assess a news source, we can observe the patterns evident in its coverage over a period of time. Does this source routinely put the policies of one political party in a favourable light and that of a rival party in an unfavourable light, regardless of which party is in power? What issues and what kinds of stories seem to get the most coverage (e.g., reports about strikes and union agitation or reports about layoffs and corrupt business practices)? These kinds of questions can help detect selectivity biases and help identify the interpretive framework that informs the editorial policy of that source. If we rely on several other media sources for our news about the world, it is possible to assess any single source over time if we consult it with a healthy, critical regard. (2) To assess a particular news report for biases, we can compare that story more systematically with other reports of the same event in other media sources. The presence of obvious loaded terms can be detected when reading one story on its own, but comparative reading reveals more subtle use of loaded terms and descriptions. In effect, this kind of comparison yields an assessment of *all* the stories being consulted.

15.5 Questions for Discussion

The following two items are expressions of opinion on a controversial topic. How strong are the arguments? Are there counter-arguments that should be taken into account?

1. The so-called "tabloid" press—weekly newspapers that are sold mainly in supermarket check-out aisles—feature two types of stories. (1) Bizarre stories about space aliens, two-headed babies, UFOs, and Elvis sightings. They are always presented as true accounts and never acknowledge that there are good reasons to be sceptical about their claims. In many cases the claims are so outlandish that they could not possibly be true. (2) Reports of scandals involving Hollywood and pop music celebrities. These reports are often heavily criticized for violations of privacy and sleazy journalistic practices and have led to many lawsuits from angry celebrities. They are frequently shown to be blatantly false or wild exaggerations.

Some people regard the tabloids as simple entertainment that is designed to amuse, rather than as serious attempts to report news. They think the tabloids are good for a laugh and that it is a mistake to criticize them. According to one media watcher, the usual criticisms of tabloids miss the point; the only legitimate criticism of a tabloid is when it isn't funny. But this is surely far too glib. It is true that some people buy tabloids just for their humour value. What ought to concern us, however, is their effect on those readers who think that the tabloids are reporting news. Surely for these readers the effect of a steady diet of tabloids must be to blunt their critical faculties and to encourage them to accept outrageous claims at face value. Instead of improving their ability to understand the world around them, the tabloids make them more ignorant and more likely to listen to any demagogue who comes along. Not only are the tabloids an insult to human intelligence, they are a dangerous influence in our democratic society. No one is suggesting that they should be banned but surely we should try to create a society in which the average citizen would be too embarrassed to buy a tabloid.

2. Intellectuals and culture snobs are fond of criticizing the popular media for giving the public what it wants. Recently some egg-head intellectual in Toronto called it "pandering to the unenlightened tastes of the ignorant." He also described the popular media as "a symptom of the dumbing down of contemporary society." Now, I think I understand what these people don't like about the popular media. They don't like to see photographs of large-breasted blondes staring back at them from their morning paper while eating breakfast. And they don't like to see women—usually large-breasted blondes, I admit—on television talk shows shouting insults and trying to scratch each other's eyes out for stealing a man. And they don't like to see simplistic headlines—like one I saw recently that screamed "Coddled Killer Escapes"—that express a view about the criminal justice system they don't share. I understand all this. In fact I

don't like these things either. But my solution is to refuse to buy the newspapers or watch the television shows I don't like. I think this is the only reasonable way to respond to media you don't like.

But the intellectuals and culture snobs among us won't do this. They persist in reading newspapers and watching television shows they don't like—now, that's an interesting perversion, isn't it—so that they can tell us at great length how terrible the popular media is. And after they have finished their tut-tutting and moaning, they demand that editors and producers embrace the standards of taste and decency that all right-thinking people share. Now, there is a large gap in their logic here that they are seemingly unaware of. How do they get from "I don't like this" to "This should not be published"? That's a huge leap, and one that is totally unjustified. The fact of the matter is that a majority of their fellow citizens like the stuff that these critics dislike. Surely in a free society people should be free to read and watch whatever they want. If they want to see pictures of large-breasted blondes they should be able to do so. Besides, no one is forcing these critics to look at the pictures.

There is a bottom line in all this. Newspapers and television stations are subject to the constraints of the marketplace. If they cannot sell their product, they will go out of business, and their product will no longer be available for anyone. Giving the public what it wants is not only not reprehensible, it is actually a requirement of a free market society. It is healthy when newspapers and television shows compete for the public's attention. A society in which there is vigorous competition within the media is a society that is vibrant and alive. What the critics fail to recognize is that there is no realistic alternative to "pandering to the public's taste" through marketplace competition. The only way to remove the media from the competition of the marketplace would be to abolish private ownership. No sane person wants state ownership of the media. But that, I'm afraid, is the only thing that would make our media critics happy.

The following items are print and online news articles on a single event, the execution of Saddam Hussein. As you read these reports look for (a) the use of loaded terms, (b) patterns within each article that may indicate a selective use of the facts, (c) patterns of emphasis within each article that may indicate how we are expected to interpret the event, and (d) implicit assumptions about what the events mean.

3. From The Financial Times (online edition, accessed, December 30, 2006
http://www.ft.com/cms/s/7fdc0e86-97b8-11db-b2ac-0000779e2340,
_i_email=y.html
HEADLINE: Saddam Hussein executed in Baghdad
BY-LINE: Demetri Sevastopulo in Washington and Steve Negus, Iraq correspondent
PUBLISHED: December 29 2006 12:04
LAST UPDATED: December 30 2006 09:44

Saddam Hussein, the former Iraqi dictator, was put to death at dawn on Saturday, Baghdad time, just days after an Iraqi appeals court refused to commute his execution.

Before he was taken to the gallows in Baghdad, the former Iraqi president was reportedly handed a "red card" signalling his imminent death—a reminder of the red cards dealt to those he had condemned to death during his time in power.

Iraqi state television said Mr Hussein's execution was captured in still photographs and on video.

Muaffak al-Rubbaie, the Iraqi national security adviser who witnessed the event, told CNN that Mr Hussein, who declined to wear a hood for his execution, appeared "really, really broken" as he awaited his death and appeared to show no remorse.

Mr Rubbaie added he was "proud" of the way the Iraqi government conducted the execution, saying it conformed with international, Iraqi, and Islamic standards. He said Mr Hussein had been treated with respect before and after the event.

President George W. Bush welcomed his death, saying it came after a "fair trial—the kind of justice he denied the victims of his brutal regime."

"Saddam Hussein's execution comes at the end of a difficult year for the Iraqi people and for our troops," Mr Bush said in a statement. "Bringing Saddam Hussein to justice will not end the violence in Iraq, but it is an important milestone on Iraq's course to becoming a democracy that can govern, sustain, and defend itself, and be an ally in the war on terror."

US officials on Friday said they had been unaware of when Mr Hussein would be executed. But a White House spokeswoman later said Stephen Hadley, the White House national security adviser, had informed Mr Bush at 7:15pm Washington time that Mr Hussein was expected to be executed within hours. Mr Hadley received the news from Zalmai Khalilizad, the US ambassador to Iraq, who had been informed of the pending execution by Mr Maliki.

Margaret Beckett, the UK's foreign secretary, said in a statement she welcomed "the fact that Saddam Hussein has been tried by an Iraqi court for at least some of the appalling crimes he committed against the Iraqi people."

"He has now been held to account," Mrs Beckett said. "The British government does not support the use of the death penalty, in Iraq or anywhere else. We advocate an end to the death penalty worldwide, regardless of the individual or the crime. We have made our position very clear to the Iraqi authorities, but we respect their decision as that of a sovereign nation."

Mr Hussein, who was captured by US forces in December 2003, was sentenced to death last month for ordering the massacre of Iraqi Shia civilians more than two decades ago.

While the execution of the former Iraqi strongman was long expected, it will be an emotional jolt to many Iraqis to hear that the man who dominated their nation's public life with an iron fist for nearly three decades has finally been put to death.

"It is a moment of remembrance for the victims of Saddam Hussein," Feisal al-Istrabadi, deputy Iraqi ambassador to the United Nations, told CNN. "This is a man who history will record as responsible for the deaths of two million Iraqis."

Mr Hussein's two sons, Uday and Qusay, were killed by US forces in 2003.

US officials on Friday were careful to avoid any appearance that they had played any role in the decision to proceed with his hanging. But the US military was placed on heightened alert ahead of the execution in case his death resulted in more attacks on US troops, or a spike in the sectarian violence that has engulfed Baghdad.

Sunni Arabs may view his hanging as yet another aspect of Iraq's long national humiliation, even though many did not condone his regime's excesses. Some Iraqis fear that his execution will set back the chances of a political settlement between Iraq's Shia-led government and the country's Sunnis that could undercut support for the country's insurgency.

But the execution may bolster the government's standing among militant Shia groups, many of whom suspected that the former dictator might be able to strike a last-minute deal with the Americans to escape the gallows.

President George W. Bush justified the 2003 invasion of Iraq on the basis that Mr Hussein possessed weapons of mass destruction. After US forces failed to find those weapons, the Bush administration argued that the invasion had still been justified because it had removed the dictator from power.

The execution comes as the Bush administration prepares to unveil a new policy to help stop the violence that has claimed the lives of tens of thousands of Iraqis and almost 3,000 US troops.

Iraqis had braced themselves for the execution of their former ruler on Friday following mounting speculation that Mr Hussein would be sent to the gallows before the Muslim holiday of Eid al-Adha, which began on Saturday morning.

Nouri al-Maliki, Iraqi prime minister, on Friday said nothing could overturn the death sentence.

"Our respect for human rights requires us to execute him, and there will be no review or delay in carrying out the sentence," he said. Mr Hussein, 69, was sentenced to death by an Iraqi special tribunal on November 5 for his role in a campaign of reprisals ordered against the Shia village of Dujail, where he suffered a 1982 assassination attempt. The campaign led to scores being executed and many others subjected to torture and long-term detention.

His trial was marked by allegations of political interference and procedural errors, and some international organisations had called on the government not to go through with Mr Hussein's execution.

In Washington late on Friday night, a federal judge rejected a last-ditch petition by lawyers for Mr Hussein to block the US military from handing the former president over to Iraqi officials.

Democratic Senator Edward Kennedy said Mr Hussein had been "a brutal tyrant and murderous dictator." "Now it is time for the people of Iraq to work to reconcile their differences and to heal the wounds of the past. Only that process will end the violence that has prevented Iraq from moving forward," he said.

Pete Hoekstra, the outgoing Republican chairman of the House intelligence committee, said: "I do not support the death penalty, but Saddam Hussein's fate was determined by an Iraqi judicial system that was created by the free Iraqi people. His sentence was delivered swiftly and the pain was minimised—the same cannot be said for his many hundreds of thousands of victims."

4. FROM: The Sun (online edition), accessed January 1, 2007
http://www.thesun.co.uk/article/0,,2-2006600608,00.html
HEADLINE: Evil Saddam's last moments
BY-LINE: Simon Hughes

SADDAM Hussein went to Hell with the vicious curses of executioners ringing in his ears, including one who snarled: "God damn you."

Dramatic exchanges between the monster and his guards were revealed yesterday after grainy video footage of his final moments was posted on the internet.

The Iraqis were so delighted at the despot's demise that immediately after his death they danced a jig around his body as it dangled from the noose.

Joining in the outpouring of joy was the masked hangman, guards and even Iraqi officials.

But Saddam had been left in no doubt of the contempt in which he was held in his last few minutes alive. As he prepared to move onto the trap-door of the gallows, one of his guards turned to him and spat out: "God damn you." The doomed tyrant was heard replying: "God damn you."

But then another voice could be heard urging Saddam to "go to hell."

The exchanges are contained in a dramatic clip of the execution filmed on a mobile phone either by a guard or one of the onlookers at the execution in Kadhamiya—the former HQ of Saddam's military intelligence.

Fittingly, it was where Saddam had thousands of enemies tortured and hanged on the same gallows.

The unofficial recording, lasting almost two and a half minutes, showed scenes not broadcast in an official Iraqi government video of the execution. It was shot from a different angle, with manacled Saddam seen facing the camera, shuffling towards the trap-door.

The 69-year-old, who ruled Iraq for 24 merciless years, is surrounded by five masked guards. An audience of 15, including representatives of the Iraqi government, were there too.

In the exchange with his guards Saddam attempts to justify his war against Iran, which cost a million lives, and laughably proclaims victory against the United States.

One of the guards then shouts: "You have destroyed us. You have killed us. You have made us live in destitution." Saddam counters: "I have saved you from destitution and misery and destroyed your enemies, the Persians and Americans."

The outraged guard then snarls: "God damn you"—and the former leader returns the insult. A voice is also picked up saluting Muslim Shi'ite leader Moqtada al-Sadr, whose father is thought to have been murdered in 1999 by Saddam's thugs. "Moqtada, Moqtada, Moqtada," intoned the unseen figure.

Several seconds pass as Saddam, dressed in a woollen black knee-length overcoat, black trousers and white shirt, stands on the trap-door.

The noose with its giant knot is placed around his neck and lays on his left shoulder.

Saddam had already declined a hood. He claimed: "Death does not frighten me. We are going to Heaven and our enemies will rot in Hell."

As the hangman prepares to pull the lever to open the trap-door, Saddam chants the Muslim profession of faith. "God is Great and Mohammed is his prophet. Palestine is Arab."

His last words are: "I bear witness that Mohammed."

It is the beginning of the second verse of the invocation, but before Saddam can complete it the executioner sends him hurtling to his death.

Saddam is seen plunging through the trap-door. As he dropped his neck snapped with an audible crack.

According to one witness he died with his eyes open. In the video his corpse is then seen dangling at the end of the rope with his head at a grotesque angle. One onlooker proclaims: "The tyrant has fallen."

Another voice orders: "Let him swing for three minutes."

But his motionless body was left to dangle for TEN MINUTES before a doctor pronounced him dead. During that time the guards and executioner performed their dance.

Iraqi national security adviser Mowaffak al-Rubaie who was present, said: "It's a very ordinary action of a number of people—some officials, some ordinary people, even the executioner, because they have lost their loved ones, their fathers, brothers, sisters, this is a natural reaction." The corpse was later taken down, washed and wrapped in a white shroud.

Traces of blood were seen where the noose had cut into the neck. Saddam's remains were then placed in a coffin.

Saddam had been sentenced to death for the mass murder of 148 Shia Muslims in 1982. The violence in Iraq continued yesterday. Six US troops were killed in ambushes following the hanging. Two children died in a rocket attack on Baghdad.

5. FROM: The Sydney Morning Herald (online edition), accessed December 30, 2006
http://www.smh.com.au/articles/2006/12/30/1166895509954.
html?page=fullpage#contentSwap1

HEADLINE: Saddam executed in Iraq—Associated Press story

Clutching a Koran and refusing a hood, Saddam Hussein went to the gallows before sunrise in Baghdad today, executed by vengeful countrymen after a quarter of a century of remorseless brutality that killed countless thousands and led Iraq into disastrous wars against the United States and Iran.

In Baghdad's Shi'ite enclave of Sadr City, people danced in the streets while others fired guns in the air to celebrate the former dictator's death.

The government did not impose a round-the-clock curfew as it did last month when Saddam was convicted to thwart any surge in retaliatory violence.

It was a grim end for the 69-year-old leader. Despite his ouster, Washington, its allies and the new Iraqi leaders remain mired in a fight to quell a stubborn insurgency by Saddam loyalists and a vicious sectarian conflict.

Ali Hamza, a 30-year-old university professor, said he went outside to shoot his gun into the air after he heard the news.

"Now all the victims' families will be happy because Saddam got his just sentence," said Hamza, who lives in Diwaniyah, a Shi'ite town 130 kilometres south of Baghdad.

"We are looking for a new page of history despite the tragedy of the past," said Saif Ibrahim, a 26-year-old Baghdad resident.

But people in the Sunni-dominated city of Tikrit, once a power base of Saddam, lamented his death.

"The president, the leader Saddam Hussein is a martyr and God will put him along with other martyrs. Do not be sad nor complain because he has died the death of a holy warrior," said Sheik Yahya al-Attawi, a cleric at the Saddam Big Mosque.

As a security precaution, police blocked the entrances to Tikrit and said nobody was allowed to leave or enter the city for four days.

State-run Iraqiya television initially reported that Saddam's half-brother Barzan Ibrahim and Awad Hamed al-Bandar, the former chief justice of the Revolutionary Court, also were hanged. However, three officials later said only Saddam was executed.

"We wanted him to be executed on a special day," National Security Adviser Mouwafak al-Rubaie told Iraqiyah.

Sami al-Askari, the political adviser of Prime Minister Nouri al-Maliki, told The Associated Press that Saddam struggled when he was taken from his cell in an American military prison but was composed in his last moments.

He said Saddam was clad completely in black, with a jacket, trousers, hat and shoes, rather than prison garb.

Shortly before the execution, Saddam's hat was removed and Saddam was asked if he wanted to say something, al-Askari said.

"No I don't want to," al-Askari, who was present at the execution, quoted Saddam as saying. Saddam repeated a prayer after a Sunni Muslim cleric who was present.

"Saddam later was taken to the gallows and refused to have his head covered with a hood," al-Askari said. "Before the rope was put around his neck, Saddam shouted: 'God is great. The nation will be victorious and Palestine is Arab'."

Saddam was executed at a former military intelligence headquarters in Baghdad's Shi'ite neighbourhood of Kazimiyah, al-Askari said. The neighbourhood is home to the Iraqi capital's most important Shi'ite shrine, the Imam Kazim shrine.

Al-Askari said the government had not decided what to do with Saddam's body.

Photographs and video footage were taken, al-Rubaie said.

"He did not ask for anything. He was carrying a Koran and said: 'I want this Koran to be given to this person,' a man he called Bander," he said. Al-Rubaie said he did not know who Bander was.

"Saddam was treated with respect when he was alive and after his death," al-Rubaie said. "Saddam's execution was 100 per cent Iraqi and the American side did not interfere."

The TV station earlier was airing national songs after the first announcement and had a tag on the screen that read "Saddam's execution marks the end of a dark period of Iraq's history."

US President George W Bush said Saddam's execution marks the "end of a difficult year for the Iraqi people and for our troops" and cautioned that his death will not halt the violence in Iraq. The execution took place during the year's deadliest month for US troops in Iraq, with the toll reaching 108. Yet, Bush said in a statement issued from his ranch in Texas, "it is an important milestone on Iraq's course to becoming a democracy that can govern, sustain and defend itself, and be an ally in the war on terror."

The Iraqi prime minister's office released a statement that said Saddam's execution was a "strong lesson" to ruthless leaders who commit crimes against their own people.

"We strongly reject considering Saddam as a representative of any sect in Iraq because the tyrant only represented his evil soul," the statement said.

"The door is still open for those whose hands are not tainted with the blood of innocent people to take part in the political process and work on rebuilding Iraq."

The execution came 56 days after a court convicted Saddam and sentenced him to death for his role in the killings of 148 Shi'ite Muslims from a town where assassins tried to kill the dictator in 1982. Iraq's highest court rejected Saddam's appeal on Monday and ordered him executed within 30 days.

A US judge yesterday refused to stop Saddam's execution, rejecting a last-minute court challenge.

US troops cheered as news of Saddam's execution appeared on television at the mess hall at Forward Operating Base Loyalty in eastern Baghdad. But some soldiers expressed doubt that Saddam's death would be a significant turning point for Iraq.

"First it was weapons of mass destruction. Then when there were none, it was that we had to find Saddam. We did that, but then it was that we had to put him on trial," said one soldier, Thomas Sheck, 25, who is on his second tour in Iraq. "So now, what will be the next story they tell us to keep us over here?"

The execution was carried out around the start of Eid al-Adha, the Islamic world's largest holiday, which marks the end of the Muslim pilgrimage to Mecca, the hajj. Many Muslims celebrate by sacrificing domestic animals, usually sheep.

6. FROM: Guardian Unlimited UK, accessed December 30, 2006
http://www.guardian.co.uk/Iraq/Story/0,,1980290,00.html
HEADLINE: Saddam Hussein executed
BY-LINE: Staff and agencies, Guardian Unlimited

Saddam Hussein was executed at dawn today following his conviction by an Iraqi court for crimes against humanity.

The death sentence was carried out at a former military intelligence headquarters in a Shia district of Baghdad at 6am local time (3am GMT).

One of those who witnessed the hanging, Sami al-Askari, an adviser to the Iraqi prime minister, said Saddam struggled when he was taken from his cell in a US military prison but was composed in his last moments. He expressed no remorse.

The former dictator, dressed in black, refused a hood and said he wanted the Koran he carried to the gallows to be given to a friend. "Before the rope was put around his neck, Saddam shouted. 'God is great. The nation will be victorious and Palestine is Arab'," Mr Askari told the Associated Press.

Another witness, Mowaffak al-Rubaie, Iraq's national security advisor, said Saddam was "strangely submissive" in the execution chamber. "He was a broken man," he said. "He was afraid. You could see fear in his face."

In a prepared statement, George Bush cautioned that Saddam's execution would not stop the violence in Iraq but said it was "an important milestone on Iraq's course to becoming a democracy that can govern, sustain and defend itself, and be an ally in the war on terror."

The office of the Iraqi prime minister, Nuri al-Maliki, released a statement that said Saddam's execution was a "strong lesson" to ruthless leaders who commit crimes against their own people. The Iraqi state broadcaster, Iraqiya, later aired film of the lead-up to the execution but not the hanging itself.

Saddam's execution was followed by reports of a car bombing with as many as 30 dead in the Shia city of Kufa.

In Sadr City, a major Shia area in Baghdad, people danced in the streets while others fired guns in the air to celebrate. The government did not impose a round-the-clock curfew as it did last month when Saddam was convicted.

The execution, which became imminent after his appeal was this week rejected, brought to an end the life of one of the Middle East's most brutal dictators.

Launching the 1980–88 Iran-Iraq war, campaigns against the Kurds and putting down the southern Shia revolt that followed the 1991 Gulf war—triggered by his invasion of Kuwait—put the casualties attributable to his rule into the hundreds of thousands.

But the conviction that led to his hanging was for a relatively lower figure—the deaths of 148 men and boys from the Shia town of Dujail, where members of an opposition group had made a botched attempt to assassinate him in 1982.

In Iraq opinion was divided sharply along sectarian lines, with Sunni Muslims warning of "bloodbaths in the streets."

Even among Shia Muslims, terrorised for decades by Saddam, there was a sense of hopelessness. "They can kill him 10 times but it won't bring safety to the streets because there is no state of law," said one Shia taxi driver who gave his name as Shawkat.

In the Kurdish north, jubilation was tempered by the fear of deeper sectarian tensions and disappointment that Saddam would now not be able to stand trial for other charges including the gas attack on the town of Halabja that killed 5,000 people in 1988.

"It would have been much better for the execution to have taken place in Halabja, not in Baghdad," said Barham Khorsheed, a Kurd.

Many critics dismissed the conduct of the trial and Saddam Hussein's defence team had accused the Iraqi government of interfering in the proceedings. The latter complaint was backed by the US-based Human Rights Watch.

The process that ended with his execution began with the launch of the 2003 US-led war to disarm Iraq's claimed weapons of mass destruction.

Mr Bush committed the US to a policy of regime change and Saddam was ousted within weeks of the invasion. Just over eight months later, US forces captured him from his hiding place in a hole near his hometown of Tikrit.

Paul Bremer, the US civilian administrator in Iraq, told a press conference: "We got him." For the first time, he showed video footage of a dishevelled former dictator, with unkempt hair and beard, being inspected by military doctors.

His rise was through the Ba'ath party. The party, which had participated in previous coups against Iraqi governments, took complete power in 1968.

Saddam was deputy president and regime strongman, responsible for internal security. But used his position to build a powerbase allowing him to supplant Ahmed Hassan al-Bakr as president in 1979. On taking power he launched a massive purge of the party.

Iraq under Saddam was under the thuggish rule of the dictator and, frequently, his relatives and cronies from Tikrit.

Saddam Hussein's half-brother, Barzan al-Tikriti, and Iraq's former chief judge, Awad Hamed al-Bandar, were also sentenced to death at the close of the Dujail trial.

Iraqiya television initially reported the two were also hanged today but officials later said only Saddam was executed.

7. FROM: The Los Angeles Times, accessed December 30, 2006
http://www.latimes.com/news/nationworld/world/la-fg- execute30dec30,0,341
8595,full.story?coll=la-home-headlines
HEADLINE: Hussein executed—and Iraq braces
SUB-HEADING: The deposed tyrant declines to wear a hood and shows no remorse in the death chamber. Violent reprisals by Sunnis are expected
BY-LINE: Molly Hennessy-Fiske and Solomon Moore (Times staff writers Alexandra Zavis and Saif Hameed in Baghdad, Paul Richter in Washington and James Gerstenzang in Crawford, Texas, contributed to this report.)

BAGHDAD—A defiant Saddam Hussein was hanged at dawn today in a secret concrete death chamber here as the Muslim call to prayer echoed over the capital.

Hussein and 14 Iraqi government representatives were flown by helicopter to the site, according to Iraqi High Tribunal Judge Munir Haddad. Guards escorted Hussein into the room, where he denounced the West and Iran.

Hussein then climbed the high ladder to the gallows.

As his executioners placed a noose around his neck, Hussein blanched but betrayed no emotion, Haddad said.

Hussein refused to wear a hood.

The charged silence that settled over the execution chamber was broken by an exchange between Hussein and four guards, who were apparently followers of Muqtada Sadr, the militant Shiite cleric whose father was killed by Hussein.

"Muqtada Sadr!" they cried out.

Hussein scoffed in reply.

His last word was a sarcastic "Muqtada," Haddad said. "And then he was hanged."

No cleric was provided. But as Hussein's life ebbed away, Haddad said, some of those present uttered a Muslim prayer often used by Shiite congregations to express gratitude: "May Allah bless Muhammad and his descendants."

The deposed Iraqi president had been convicted of crimes against humanity Nov. 5 for the killings of 148 men and boys from the town of Dujayl after a 1982 assassination attempt—a comparative handful among the tens of thousands of Iraqi deaths for which he was responsible during his nearly four-decade rule.

His execution officially ends a bloody chapter in this nation's history but is not expected to quell the sectarian civil war and violent insurgency that have racked the country since his overthrow by an American-led invasion in 2003.

As news of the execution spread, some Iraqis here celebrated with the customary gunfire into the air, and television channels broadcast Hussein retrospectives complete with film of his many victims.

The hanging was photographed and videotaped, in part to provide proof in this rumor-driven society that the former dictator was truly dead, Iraqi TV also reported. But such documentation was not immediately made public.

The deposed Iraqi president's death warrant was signed Friday by the nation's two vice presidents, and execution witnesses gathered in Baghdad's heavily fortified Green Zone, according to an Iraqi official with knowledge of the proceedings. The hanging took place in an intelligence facility in northwest Baghdad.

US officials said Iraqi Prime Minister Nouri Maliki met with Cabinet officials and other politicians throughout Friday to plan the execution. Security was Iraqi leaders' main concern. Most officials expect Hussein's death to be followed by a rash of insurgent attacks as former Baathists retaliate against the Shiite-led government.

The government also sorted through execution procedural requirements Friday, including the timing of the execution and the assembly of the gallows.

US military officials handed Hussein over to Iraqi officials around 8 p.m. Friday Baghdad time, according to one of Hussein's defense attorneys.

Hussein's execution seemed to be much less than the historic turning point many people in Iraq and the United States once thought it would be.

With Iraq mired in violence, the former dictator's demise no longer appeared to signal the beginning of new order. Instead, it seemed another reminder of the country's divisions.

And though Iraq has seen some positive developments, such as national elections, many Americans remain unconvinced that things in Iraq have fundamentally changed for the better.

President Bush said in a written statement that Hussein had been executed after receiving a fair trial, "the kind of justice he denied the victims of his brutal regime."

"Fair trials were unimaginable under Saddam Hussein's tyrannical rule. It is a testament to the Iraqi people's resolve to move forward after decades of oppression that, despite his terrible crimes against his own people, Saddam Hussein received a fair trial," Bush said in the statement issued in Crawford, Texas, where the president is taking a winter vacation at his ranch.

The execution "will not end the violence in Iraq," he said, "but it is an important milestone" in Iraq's effort to become a self-sustaining democracy and US ally in fighting terrorism.

Deputy White House Press Secretary Scott Stanzel said Stephen J. Hadley, Bush's national security advisor, briefed the president about 6:15 p.m. CST about the imminent execution.

Stanzel said Hadley told the president that Maliki had informed Zalmay Khalilzad, the US ambassador to Iraq, that the execution would take place within several hours. He added that Bush went to bed before the execution, around 9 p.m. CST, and was not awakened after it was carried out.

Maliki legal advisor Mariam Rayis said Hussein's death warrant was signed by Vice Presidents Tariq Hashimi, a Sunni Arab, and Adel Abdul Mehdi, a Shiite. President Jalal Talabani, a Kurdish death penalty opponent, was out of Baghdad on Friday and delegated his capital authority to Mehdi, Rayis said.

The gallows was set up by midnight Baghdad time, Rayis said, and Hussein was led to the scaffold dressed in normal clothes.

Defense lawyer Najib Nuaimi said US military officials asked him Friday morning to send someone to pick up Hussein's personal effects, such as clothing, books—including a Koran—and a manuscript Hussein had been writing.

"He was writing his biography," Nuaimi said. "But I don't think he had a chance to complete it."

Among the witnesses at Hussein's hanging were a representative from the Interior Ministry, Iraqi High Tribunal Judge Munir Haddad, chief prosecutor Munqith Faroon, a physician, and a cleric who read from the Koran, Rayis said. Mowaffak Rubaie, Iraq's national security advisor, also attended.

Survivors from Dujayl did not attend, Rayis said.

Ali Hassan Mohammed Haidari, the first witness to take the stand against Hussein in the Dujayl case, wanted to see the execution but decided he didn't want to risk the dangerous drive to Baghdad, 60 miles away.

He said the execution made his family "very happy" but would not quell suffering. "You can imagine a mother who has lost seven children cannot avoid shedding tears even in the midst of this happy moment," he said.

Other Dujayl victims said their relief over Hussein's death was dampened by the fact that they had not witnessed their tormentor's final moments.

"I have been waiting for the last 40 years for such a moment," said Dujayl Mayor Mohammed Zubaidi, whose father and brother were killed in jail by Hussein's regime. "I was always hoping that this execution would take place inside the town of Dujayl because this is where the case happened."

Hussein's wife, who is in Qatar, and a daughter in Jordan could not attend the execution because they are both fugitives from Iraqi justice, Rayis said, and Hussein's lawyers were barred from attending.

Hussein defense attorney Bushra Khalil said that Raghad Ali, Hussein's eldest daughter, wanted her father to be buried in Yemen "until Iraq is free of the occupiers." Hussein's family is "depressed," Khalil said.

Khalil said Hussein had told her that he refused sedatives offered by Americans to calm his nerves and he had been resigned to his fate.

"We asked him if he would like us to communicate anything to the leaders of the Arab world," she continued. "He said no. His only request would be to Allah."

Khalil warned that Hussein's death would have violent consequences for Iraq.

Hussein's lawyers sought a temporary restraining order Friday at an appellate court in Washington, D.C., to force the US military to retain custody of Hussein. Hours before Hussein's death, the court refused to intervene.

Hussein's execution coincided with the end of the hajj, the seasonal Islamic pilgrimage to Mecca. Most Sunnis began Eid al-Adha, the Feast of Sacrifice, after morning prayers today; most Shiites will begin Sunday morning.

Nuaimi said that Maliki, a Shiite, had pushed for Hussein's execution during the holiday to "make a gift during Eid to his party."

Hussein "will be the sacrificial lamb for the Shiites, and the Iranians in particular," said Nuaimi, referring to many Muslims' practice of slaughtering lambs after pilgrimage for celebratory feasts.

US officials expressed concern that news of the execution's imminence, which began circulating Thursday, might have given insurgents time to plan attacks. US military officials said they had beefed up security in Baghdad in advance of the execution and to ward off possible retaliatory violence.

Iraqi and US officials said the government would probably extend Friday's curfew indefinitely.

Hussein's family wants to bury him in his hometown of Tikrit in northern Iraq but are afraid the government will cremate him and scatter the ashes, Nuaimi said.

Rayis said Hussein's body was to be wrapped in a white sheet and would be buried by Iraq's Directorate of Social Welfare if it not claimed by a family member.

His execution ended other legal proceedings against Hussein, including his genocide trial involving the Anfal military campaign. That operation left tens of thousands of Kurds dead by gunfire, bombings and poison gas.

8. FROM The Globe and Mail, December 30, 2006, A1 and A13
HEADLINE: Saddam Executed at Dawn
Sub-heading: Former Iraqi president is sent to the gallows during the morning call to prayer
BY-LINE: Claudia Parsons and Alasdair MacDonald (Reuters News Agency, with reports from AFP, AP)

Saddam Hussein was executed as the day dawned in Baghdad, a dramatic end for the leader who ruled Iraq by fear for three decades before a US-led invasion and his conviction for mass murder.

As the call to prayer echoed out across a dark and cold Iraqi capital just before 6 am on of the holiest days of the Muslim calender, a cleric and other officials witnessed Mr. Hussein, 69, mount the scaffold clutching a Koran and hang from the gallows, US-funded Al Hurra television channel reported.

One of the witnesses, Iraqi national-security advisor Mowaffaq al-Rubaie, said "Mr. Hussein had fear on his face" before his death.

Some of those present at the execution danced around the ex-dictator's body as Shia chants were shouted, another witness said.

"Criminal Saddam was hanged to death," Iraqiya television station said in an announcement to Iraqis. The station played patriotic music and showed images of national monuments and other landmarks.

Mariam al-Rayes, a legal expert and former member of the Shia bloc in parliament, told Iraqiya television the execution "was filmed, and god willing, it will be shown. There was one camera present and a doctor was also present there."

Ms. Al-Rayes, an ally of Prime Minister Nouri al-Maliki, did not attend the execution. She said Mr. al-Maliki did not attend but was represented by an aide.

Early reports said Mr. Hussein was executed along with his half-brother and intelligence chief, Barzan Ibrahim al-Tikriti, and former Revolutionary Court judge Awad Hamed al-Bandar, but that was later called into question. Both men were convicted with the former leader, and they are said to be due for execution soon.

Celebratory gunfire could be heard in the streets of Baghdad, and Iraqis in Dearborn, Mich., a Detroit suburb home to a large number of expatriates, waved Iraqi flags and cheered. Chants of "Now there's peace, Saddam is dead" in English and Arabic rang into the night.

US President George W. Bush hailed the death. "Bringing Saddam Hussein to justice will not end the violence in Iraq, but it is an important milestone on Iraq's course to becoming a democracy that can govern, sustain and defend itself, and be an ally in the war on terror."

Defiant to the end, Mr. Hussein insisted during his trial that he was still the president of Iraq. He said in a letter written after his conviction in November that he offered himself as a "sacrifice."

"If my soul goes down this path [of martyrdom] it will face God in serenity," he wrote in the letter.

Najeeb al-Nueimi, a member of Mr. Hussein's legal team in Doha, Qatar, had requested a final meeting with the deposed Iraqi leader. "His daughter in Amman was crying. She said, 'Take me with you,'" Mr. al-Nueimi said late last night. But he said their request was rejected.

His daughter Raghad, who is exiled in Jordan, has asked that his body be buried in Yemen, a source close to the family said early today. She said that this burial would be temporary, "until Iraq is liberated and it can be reburied in Iraq," the source said by telephone

The appeals court this week upheld a Nov. 5 conviction for crimes against humanity over the killings of 148 Shia men.

With millions in Iraq's now dominant Shia Muslim majority thirsting for revenge for Mr. Hussein's three decades of oppression, US officials had been concerned since his capture three years ago that he be treated with judicial propriety.

An execution at the start of Eid al-Adha is highly symbolic. The feast marks the sacrifice the Prophet Abraham was prepared to make when God ordered him to kill his son, and many Shiites could regard Mr. Hussein's death as a gift from God. Such symbolism could further anger Sunnis, resentful of new Shia power.

International human-rights groups criticized the year-long trial during which three defence lawyers were killed and a chief judge resigned after complaining of political interference.

Lawyers for the former Iraqi president had asked US District Court Judge Colleen Kollar-Kotelly for a stay late yesterday afternoon, but were turned down.

The request was a long-shot based on a creative legal argument. Lawyers argued that because Mr. Hussein also faces a civil lawsuit in Washington, he has rights as a civil defendant that would be violated if he is executed. He has not received notice of those rights and the consequences that the lawsuit would have on his estate, his lawyers said.

16.   Writing and Assessing Argumentative Essays

In this chapter we examine argumentative essays—sometimes called extended arguments—from two points of view: that of the author and that of the critic. Much of what is said here is a repetition or a common-sense extrapolation of material presented in earlier chapters, but it should prove helpful to draw this material together and expand upon it in order to indicate some of the special problems involved in dealing with argumentative essays.

The term *argumentative essay* refers to a written attempt to present a coherent discussion of a subject with a view to defending a specific thesis. The thesis of an argumentative essay is its main conclusion: it is usually a position or point of view, but may consist of a simple statement. The key phrase in the definition is *defending a specific thesis*. This is what makes an essay argumentative in nature, for any attempt to defend a conclusion requires premises. An argumentative essay can thus be regarded as an extended argument.

There are three elements in every essay: content, structure, and style. The content—the particular facts and ideas that form the subject matter—is different for each essay and is thus beyond the scope of our discussion. Questions about structure and style, on the other hand, tend to be the same for every argumentative essay regardless of content. We shall consider some of these questions first from the point of view of the author and then from the point of view of the critic. In the next chapter we will return to questions about structure from the point of view of an author.

First, however, we need to address an aspect of good writing that is often overlooked. The goal of all writing is communication with an audience. This means we must know what audience we are writing for, and write for *that* audience. We must take the audience into account when deciding what we want to say and how we are going to say it. What is their level of education? How much political (moral, scientific, religious) sophistication do they possess? How much background information are they likely to have? What are their values likely to be? Answers to these and similar questions are relevant to many of the decisions we must make when writing. Writing a paper on capital punishment for a graduate seminar in criminology clearly requires a different approach from writing a column on the same subject for the Calgary *Sun*. When writing anything, we should always pay attention to the intended audience. An argumentative essay, obviously, is intended for an audience that is capable of being persuaded by arguments.

16.1 Writing Argumentative Essays: Structure

The largest structural feature of an essay consists of its division into three parts: the introduction, the body, and the conclusion. Next is the logical structure of the main argument of the essay or what is sometimes called the *macro-structure*. Finally, there is the structural detail or micro-structure—the structures of the sub-arguments of the essay and their relationship to each other and to the main argument. We shall deal with each of these structural features in turn.

The INTRODUCTION is not merely a way of getting started; it has several specific purposes. These purposes are not so distinct from each other that they can be achieved in isolation, but each represents an important aspect of the introduction. (1) The introduction should always announce the subject matter, and should also mention any restrictions being placed on the topic. For example, if the topic is capital punishment but the essay considers only capital punishment in Canada, this fact should be stated. (2) It should establish a context for the discussion. The context may be the political aspect of the capital punishment debate in Canada or current criminological research. (3) It should relate the essay to the views of others. These may be the views of the public, or the published work of scholars, or the views of lawyers and judges, or all three. (4) It should indicate what the essay hopes to contribute to the discussion. For example, *This essay attempts to show that there is no statistical basis for regarding the death penalty as an effective deterrent.*

These purposes are important not only because they tell the reader what to expect, but also because they are necessary aids for the reader in interpreting the essay. We have already seen how important it is to be able to appeal to the context and background when interpreting an argument and supplying missing premises and assumptions. The same is true of argumentative essays. If we want our readers to abide by the principle of charity we need to give them as much help as we can.

In the BODY of the essay the thesis is developed, elaborated, and defended. The body always consists of two elements. (1) It presents reasons and arguments to support the thesis. These reasons and arguments are the kind of specific arguments we have already considered in detail. They should, of course, be sound arguments. (2) It attempts to rebut objections. This second element requires us to anticipate the kind of objections we are likely to meet from our intended audience. We need to know which of our audience's beliefs we are challenging, and why they hold them. Once we know, we should address these concerns directly, for otherwise we may leave the audience with an easy way of discounting our arguments and ignoring our conclusion. They may be able to say, *Well, I see what you are driving at, but you don't really understand why we think differently about the matter, and you've given us no reason to give up our beliefs.*

Supporting reasons and rebuttals are closely related, since in practice most of the arguments that can be used to support a position either are themselves, or easily give rise to, arguments that can be used to rebut the standard objections from those who hold a rival position. But it is always useful in an argumentative essay to state explicitly our reasons for regarding the rival positions as untenable. We may think the weaknesses are too obvious to mention, but usually our opponents don't think they are obvious at all.

The body is the largest part of any argumentative essay and should embody some principle of organization. There is no one "right" organization here, only possible organizational structures that make coherent sense. It is common to present the arguments in support of our thesis first and then deal with the objections, but we could start by analyzing and criticizing the rival positions and use this discussion as a basis for developing the arguments in support of our thesis. Similarly, when presenting our arguments, it makes sense to move from the easy and obvious ones to those that are more difficult and less obvious, or from the traditional ones to the more recent ones, or from the general to the specific. We shall work with one principle of organization in the example essay in this chapter, then turn to three alternatives in the next chapter.

The CONCLUSION of an argumentative essay should present a brief summary of the main arguments and rebuttals and show how they support the main conclusion of the essay. It should also include a clear statement or restatement of the conclusion and should note any significant restrictions or limitations that may apply. The primary purpose of the concluding section is to remind the reader of what we think our essay has (and has not) accomplished.

The MAIN ARGUMENT of an argumentative essay can best be understood by thinking of the essay as consisting of a single argument of the sort that could be presented in a few sentences. The thesis of the essay is the conclusion, and the main reason or reasons are its supporting premises. The main argument can be regarded as a brief outline that can be diagrammed using the argument structures outlined in Section 4.6. Usually the structure of the main argument can be represented by one of the three simple argument structures, although sometimes it may be somewhat more complex.

It is not always easy to distinguish the main argument from the sub-arguments of an essay, but it is important to make the attempt, for it is the main argument that contributes most to the clarity and strength of an argumentative essay. Before starting to write an essay, we should have a clear understanding of the structure of its main argument and should satisfy ourselves that it constitutes a sound argument. We should attempt to preserve this structure as we add the sub-arguments and the details of the micro-structure. Not only does this make for a better essay, it is of considerable help to the reader. Even if your thoughts aren't clear enough to lay out the entire structure of the argument before you begin writing, it is helpful to construct a rough map first; as your thoughts become clear, it should be possible to return to this rough map and improve your picture of the structural details to conform to your more considered thoughts. It is helpful to keep an eye on the structure of an argumentative essay at every stage of composition.

The MICRO-STRUCTURE consists of the details that are necessary to explain and support the main argument. It includes the sub-arguments used to defend the premises of the main argument, explanations of key terms, rebuttals of objections, and clarifications of any difficult steps in the argument. Incorporating these elements into the tree diagram of the main argument would typically make it very complex and is not usually necessary. But, when writing, we should always know precisely how they relate to the main argument.

16.2 Writing Argumentative Essays: Style

The most important criteria for style are clarity and coherence, and as long as they remain the overriding criteria there is a great deal of room for individual variation. Aesthetic criteria are relevant, but elegant and beautifully crafted writing should never be allowed to interfere with clarity and coherence. The primary purpose of an argumentative essay is to persuade our audience of the correctness of our thesis, and anything that interferes with this purpose should be avoided.

When making decisions about style, we should bear in mind the intended audience. Will they be put off by a certain style? Will they understand references to other authors? Will they understand technical terminology? What kind of footnotes are expected? What kind of examples will best illustrate for them the points we want to make? Should humour be used, or is it likely to fall flat? These questions are important because much of the success of an argumentative essay in convincing the reader depends upon how they are answered.

There are several rules of good writing that are important when writing argumentative essays:

(1) Be brief. This means that we should be able to justify every word, phrase, sentence, paragraph, and section on the ground that they contribute to the overall purpose of the essay. The negative version of this rule is: avoid padding. Generally speaking, if it isn't necessary, don't include it.

(2) Strive for simplicity. Simplicity is not the same as brevity. Simplicity is the avoidance of unnecessary complexity or obscurity. Often we can achieve simplicity by using fewer words: *Within the next ten years* ... is better than *In the period between the present and ten years from the present....* Sometimes, however, simplicity may require more words, especially when we are dealing with a complex or technical topic. A complex point that could be expressed in a single sentence may require a paragraph to express simply and clearly. We should avoid long complex sentences unless the sentence structure is relatively simple. We should also use concrete rather than abstract terms wherever possible: *pet* rather than *companion animal, touch* rather than *tactile sensation*. The passive voice should be used sparingly: *Most people regret that* ... is better than *It is regretted by most people that* ...

(3) Be specific. Using general terms instead of specific terms tends to obscure meaning and to make the reader's task more difficult. If we are discussing criminals, we should not routinely refer to them as deviants. Criminals may be social deviants, but many

deviants are not criminals, and when we use the term *deviants* we are in fact referring to both criminal and non-criminal deviants.

(4) Use examples judiciously. Examples are almost always helpful to the reader when presenting an abstract idea. But the example should be a good one; one good example is always better then several inappropriate ones. We should use more than one example only when we want to convey the range of application of an abstract idea or principle.

(5) Use quotations judiciously. If the topic requires us to talk about the views of a particular author, it is appropriate to present the author's views in his or her own words. But we should avoid quoting more than is necessary to establish the author's actual position. If the topic does not require us to talk about the views of a particular author, quotations should be used only when they contribute something to the essay. Quotations can be used to illustrate a point, to indicate the source of an idea, or to express in elegant or succinct language a point we wish to make. The danger in using quotations is that they can become a substitute for our own thinking, or can obscure the argument we are attempting to present.

(6) Always revise. We should never let anything we write reach its intended audience in an unrevised form. No one can write a perfect first draft; every essay can be improved by careful revision. It is best to set aside the draft for a few days before revising it so that we can look at it with fresh eyes.

16.3 Assessing Argumentative Essays

Assessing an argumentative essay is in principle the same as assessing a short argument. The difference is merely one of complexity; there is a great deal more to keep track of when dealing with an argumentative essay. The rules for assessing arguments that were outlined in Section 5.3 are still valid when used to assess argumentative essays but need to be applied somewhat differently. The rules are as follows:

Rule 1. Identify The Main Conclusion
Rule 2. Identify the Premises
Rule 3. Identify the Structure of the Argument
Rule 4. Check the Acceptability of the Premises
Rule 5. Check the Relevance of the Premises
Rule 6. Check the Adequacy of the Premises
Rule 7. Look for Counter-arguments

The major difference is that our assessment involves three phases: first, we conduct a provisional assessment of the main argument, second, we assess the sub-arguments, and third, we make our final assessment of the essay as a whole.

FIRST PHASE

First, we need to identify the main argument of the essay. We do this by applying the first three rules to the essay as a whole.

(1) We identify the main conclusion, by asking what is the author's main thesis, or what is the position the essay is intended to defend. If the thesis is a complex one that cannot be conveyed accurately in a single sentence, we must look for or invent a summary statement of it. For example, to be fair to the author we may need to work out our own statement of the conclusion, such as: *Under present conditions (i.e., current political opinion, the uncertainties of economic theory, and trends in world trade) the government should increase interest rates in order to control inflation.* Only when we have identified the main conclusion can we be sure that the essay constitutes an argument, that is, that it is an *argumentative essay* and not some other kind of essay. In doubtful cases, as always, we should use the principle of charity and any contextual clues to decide the question.

(2) We identify the premises by looking for the main reasons offered to support the conclusion. In an argumentative essay these premises will almost always be the conclusions of sub-arguments. If the essay is clearly written, with a clear structure, this task will be straightforward. Otherwise we will have to do some digging, especially if the conclusions of the sub-arguments have not been made explicit. The major difficulty is that we can be led astray by the sub-arguments. But if we have identified the main conclusion correctly we can avoid this difficulty by asking, *What are the main reasons the author presents as support for this conclusion?*

(3) Next, we identify the logical structure of the main argument of the essay. If we have correctly identified the premises and conclusion of the main argument, this step is quite straightforward and presents no special difficulties.

In the first phase of assessment, we provisionally apply Rules 4, 5, and 6; that is, we look to see whether the premises are acceptable, relevant, and adequate to support the conclusion. These rules must be applied provisionally at this point because we have not yet checked the sub-arguments, and the purpose of the sub-arguments is to defend the premises. But if we suspect that one or more premise is unacceptable, irrelevant, or inadequate, this provisional diagnosis tells us what to look for when we move to the second phase of assessment. Rule 7 (*Look for counter-arguments*) should be postponed until the final stage of assessment.

SECOND PHASE

Now we can turn to the sub-arguments. When identifying sub-arguments, it is helpful to identify the other elements of the micro-structure of the essay. Examples, quotations, definitions, rhetorical questions, summaries, speculation—in short, anything that is not a premise or a conclusion of an argument should be identified as such. This material is not to be ignored but should be used to interpret both the main argument of the essay and the sub-arguments. In addition, when interpreting sub-arguments, we should use the other arguments (including the main argument) as aids. The principle of charity is usually easy to follow when dealing with argumentative essays because we are given a great deal of supplementary material.

Each sub-argument should be assessed according to the normal rules for assessing arguments. The role of each sub-argument is to provide support for the premises of the main argument, so the conclusion of each sub-argument should be one of the premises of the main argument. A sub-argument may, however, contain its own sub-argument, in which case we should proceed as in the first phase: we should identify the sub-argument and make a tentative assessment of it before assessing the sub-sub-argument.

THIRD PHASE

We are now in a position to assess the essay as a whole. First, we should check to see whether our interpretation of the main argument is supported by our interpretation of the sub-arguments. If it is not, we should amend it. Next, we assess the argument by applying Rules 4, 5, and 6. Our primary concern is with the main argument, but in order to decide whether it satisfies our three criteria, we will have to examine the sub-arguments by applying our criteria to them, which will of course lead us to do the same to any sub-sub-arguments. Any weaknesses we find should now be easy to identify and describe. Finally, we should invoke Rule 7 and ask whether there are any significant counter-arguments that the essay fails to take into account.

16.4 Assessment of a Sample Argumentative Essay

To illustrate how argumentative essays should be assessed we will apply the steps outlined in 16.3 to an example. Our assessment is lengthy and thorough, not because this is necessary every time we assess an argumentative essay, but because it is important to understand what is involved in a full critical assessment. The following article has been created by drawing together a number of letters and editorials that appeared during a teachers' strike in Wellington County in 1985.

(1) Most of us have come to accept the fact that every year, somewhere in Ontario, there will be yet another teachers' strike. In a bad year there may be half a dozen strikes; in a good year there may be only one or two. Teachers' strikes have become so commonplace that normally only the local media regard them as newsworthy unless they drag on for months or involve violence.

(2) But, as anyone who has suffered through a strike knows, a strike that lasts for more than a week or two can be extremely disruptive, and a lengthy strike can have a devastating effect upon many students, especially high school students. Some decide not to return to school after the strike and thus fail to complete their education. Others cannot keep up with the accelerated pace after

the strike and become discouraged and drop out. Others find that their grades have suffered and that they cannot gain admission to the college or university program of their choice. It is becoming increasingly obvious that giving teachers the legal right to strike was a serious mistake and that the time has come to challenge that right.

(3) The fundamental dilemma we face is whether teachers are to be regarded as workers or as professionals. To understand this dilemma we need to look at the difference between workers and professionals. Workers are hired and trained by an employer to do a specific job whose details are determined by the employer: the nature and quality of the product, the materials and equipment used, the standard of workmanship, the hours of work, etc., are all determined by the employer. It is precisely because so much control lies with management that society recognizes that workers should have the right to strike, so that they can bargain effectively with their employers over pay and working conditions. Professionals, on the other hand, are not trained by their employers but by other professionals. Thus, when hired by an employer to do a specific job, they are expected and entitled to use their professional expertise to determine how they will do their work: they tell their employer how much time and what equipment and facilities they need to do their job properly. More importantly, they have professional obligations to society at large, and especially to their clients, regarding the quality of their work. It is precisely because they have a professional obligation to society and their clients that professionals should not have the right to strike. The right to strike is inconsistent with their obligations as professionals.

(4) So the question is: are teachers workers or professionals? The answer is obvious: teachers clearly fit the above description of professionals. Teachers have professional training and expertise. And they are responsible for most of what they do in the classroom: what is taught, how it is taught, how it is to be examined, and how it is to be graded. If we regarded teachers as workers, we would have to insist that these matters should be taken out of their hands on the ground that they are management prerogatives. This would be the height of absurdity.

(5) But—and this is the crux of the matter—if teachers are to be regarded as professionals then they must take their professional obligations seriously: they must recognize that their first obligation as teachers is to their students' education, and they must refuse to use their students as pawns in their quarrels with school boards. In other words, as professionals teachers should give up their right to strike. It is a sad reflection upon the teaching profession that they cannot grasp that the right to strike is inconsistent with their professional status. They want to eat their cake and have it too.

(6) Teachers sometimes argue that they only strike to achieve improvements in the educational system and that the responsibility for strikes rests with school boards, which are more concerned with dollars than with the quality of education. They claim that the goal of every teachers' strike has been to improve the quality of education. Even higher salaries, they claim, will attract

better people into the teaching profession and thus benefit students. But where is the evidence to support such claims? The fact that the teachers themselves have not put forward such evidence suggests that there is none. Indeed, such claims seem to be little more than greed masquerading as benevolence and should be rejected out of hand. Teachers who argue this way are a disgrace to what used to be an honourable profession, further proof that the teaching profession is now controlled by those who really do regard themselves merely as workers and who don't give a damn about the quality of their product.

(7) Surely the time has come to demand that the right to strike be taken away from teachers. The harmful effects of teachers' strikes are undeniable; the inconsistency between their professional status and their right to strike is clear; and the conclusion is inevitable.

FIRST PHASE

In the first phase we identify the main argument by applying the first three rules: we identify the conclusion, the main premises, and the structure of the main argument.

(1) What is the main conclusion? The final paragraph of the article presents a summary of the main argument and includes a statement of the main conclusion: *Surely the time has come to demand that the right to strike be taken away from teachers.* We shall restate it more briefly as *Teachers' right to strike should be taken away.* A check of the rest of the article ensures us that our interpretation is correct.

(2) What are the premises of the main argument? Paragraph 7 also includes a statement of two of the main premises. The first, which we will restate in the form it appears in paragraph 2, is *Teachers' strikes can have a devastating effect upon many students.* The second, which we will restate in the form it appears in paragraph 5, is *As professionals, teachers should give up the right to strike.* A check of the article as a whole supports our interpretation that these are two premises of the main argument. But we also find another premise in the rest of the article that is not included in paragraph 7. In paragraph 6 the author attempts to refute the claim made by some teachers that strikes achieve improvements in the educational system. If this claim is acceptable, it would clearly support the teachers' right to strike, so the author's attack on this claim is needed to provide additional support for the main conclusion. Hence, we need to add another premise of the main argument: *Teachers' strikes do not achieve improvements in the educational system.*

(3) What is the structure of the main argument? It is clear that each of the three premises we have identified is intended to offer independent support for the conclusion. This means that the main argument has a V structure.

As a result of the first phase of assessment we now have the following reconstruction and tree diagram of the main argument:

MAIN ARGUMENT:

P1. Teachers' strikes can have a devastating effect upon many students.
P2. As professionals, teachers should give up the right to strike.
P3. Teachers' strikes do not achieve improvements in the educational system.
C. Teachers' right to strike should be taken away.

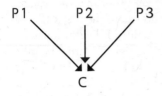

We should now make a provisional assessment of the above argument. It is clear that *if* the three premises are true, then they are relevant and adequate to provide strong support for the conclusion. So the relevancy and adequacy criteria seem to be satisfied. But are the premises acceptable? This seems much less certain, so the question we should be most concerned about in the second phase of assessment is whether the premises are acceptable.

SECOND PHASE

We now turn to the sub-arguments. There are three sub-arguments, one in support of each of the three premises of the main argument. The first sub-argument, which has P1 as its conclusion, is found in paragraph 2. Three reasons are offered in its support; they are stated below as premises P4, P5, and P6. It should be noted that they have been restated in order to express more accurately what seems to be the speaker's real meaning. These premises offer independent support for P1, which means that the first sub-argument has a V structure. Thus we have the following reconstruction and tree diagram:

FIRST SUB-ARGUMENT:

P4. Some students do not return to school after a long strike and thus fail to complete their education.
P5. After a long strike some students cannot keep up with the accelerated pace at school, become discouraged, and drop out.
P6. After a long strike some students find that their grades have suffered and that they cannot gain admission to the college or university program of their choice.
P1. Teachers' strikes can have devastating effects upon many students.

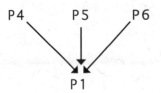

The second sub-argument, which is found in paragraphs 3, 4, and 5, is much more complex than the first. What makes it complex is that it contains three sub-sub-arguments. We shall ignore these sub-sub-arguments for the moment. In paragraph 3 the author sets up an exclusive dichotomy between workers and professionals, claiming that workers should have the right to strike but that professionals should not. In paragraph 4 the author argues that teachers are professionals and in paragraph 5 concludes that as professionals, teachers should give up the right to strike. This argument has a T structure, since the premises would all have to be true if they are to provide support for the conclusion. Thus, we have the following reconstruction and tree diagram for the second sub-argument:

SECOND SUB-ARGUMENT:

> P7. *Either teachers are workers or they are professionals.*
> P8. *Workers should have the right to strike.*
> P9. *Professionals should not have the right to strike.*
> P10. *Teachers are professionals.*
> P2. *As professionals, teachers should give up their right to strike.*

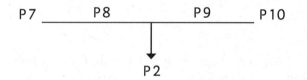

P7 _____ P8 _____ P9 _____ P10

P2

We shall now briefly examine the three sub-sub-arguments. Their role is to provide support for premises P8, P9, and P10. They have the following reconstructions and tree diagrams:

FIRST SUB-SUB-ARGUMENT:

> P11. *Workers are hired to do a specific job, all of whose details are determined by the employer.*
> P12. *Workers need to be able to bargain effectively with their employers over pay and working conditions.*
> P8. *Workers should have the right to strike.*

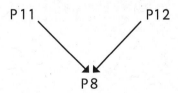

P11   P12

P8

SECOND SUB-SUB-ARGUMENT:

> P13. *Professionals have obligations to society at large, and especially to their clients, regarding the quality of their work.*

P14. *Teachers should not use their students as pawns in their quarrels with school boards.*
P9. *Professionals should not have the right to strike.*

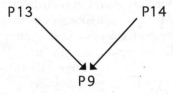

THIRD SUB-SUB-ARGUMENT:

P15. *Teachers have professional training and expertise.*
P16. *Teachers are responsible for most of what they do in the classroom.*
P10. *Teachers are professionals.*

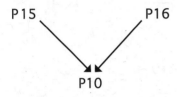

We now turn to the third sub-argument. It attempts to refute the claim that teachers' strikes have achieved improvements in the educational system by presenting two reasons. First, it argues that there is no evidence to support such a claim, since if there were evidence, teachers would have presented it, which they have not. This part of the sub-argument constitutes a sub-sub-argument. Second, it argues that the claim itself is simply based on greed. These two premises offer independent support for the conclusion. Thus, we have the following reconstruction and tree diagram:

THIRD SUB-ARGUMENT:

P17. *There is no evidence to support the claim that teachers' strikes achieve improvements in the educational system.*
P18. *The claim that teachers' strikes achieve improvements in the educational system is simply greed masquerading as benevolence.*
P3. *Teachers' strikes do not achieve improvements in the educational system.*

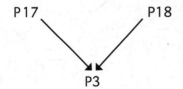

The sub-sub-argument is intended to support P17. It has the following reconstruction and tree diagram:

FOURTH SUB-SUB-ARGUMENT:

P19. If there were evidence to support the claim that teachers' strikes achieve improvements in the educational system, teachers would present it.

P20. Teachers have presented no evidence that strikes achieve improvements in the educational system.

P17. There is no evidence to support the claim that teachers' strikes achieve improvements in the educational system.

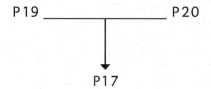

We can now present a complete reconstruction and tree diagram for the entire essay:

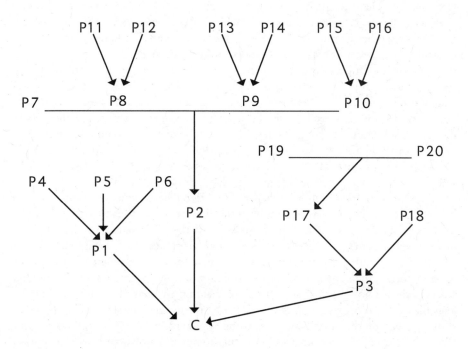

THIRD PHASE

We are now in a position to assess the essay as a whole. We will consider each sub-argument in turn.

The conclusion of the first sub-argument (i.e., P1) rests on premises that are unsupported. Each premise could only be defended by an inductive generalization, but there is no indication that the author is aware of such evidence. Possibly the author is relying upon anecdotal evidence. However, the absence of clear and specific evidence should make us cautious about accepting these premises. We cannot be sure that the premises are unacceptable, but we should at least regard their acceptability as questionable. On the other hand, the premises clearly are relevant, for they present the kind of evidence that would support the claim that lengthy teachers' strikes can have a devastating effect upon students. But are they adequate to support the conclusion? Each premise makes a claim about some students, and the vagueness of such claims makes them difficult to assess. Since the conclusion of the sub-argument is that strikes have a devastating effect upon *many* students, the premises must be regarded as inadequate. Had the conclusion been given in a weaker form, such as *Long teachers' strikes can have a harmful effect on some high-school students*, the premises of the sub-argument could be regarded as adequate, but such a conclusion would substantially weaken the main argument. The first sub-argument, therefore, must be regarded as quite weak since it only meets one of the three criteria for a sound argument.

The second sub-argument has several weaknesses. The first arises in the sub-argument itself. It relies on a dichotomy: either teachers are workers who should have the right to strike, or they are professionals who ought to reject the right to strike. But there are two other possibilities: teachers are workers who should be denied the right to strike, or they are professionals who should have the right to strike. The latter possibility is the important one that the sub-argument overlooks. There are in fact some professional groups, such as doctors and nurses, whose right to strike is now widely, if not universally, accepted. Thus, the fact that teachers are professionals does not by itself show that teachers should not have the right to strike. In other words, the second sub-argument commits the fallacy of false dichotomy and thus violates the criterion of acceptability.

But the sub-sub-arguments also have weaknesses, which we shall describe briefly. The first sub-sub-argument is designed to support one side of the false dichotomy, namely, that workers should have the right to strike. The argument is weak, however, because its premises are inadequate, since they ignore the reasons that are commonly believed to justify denying the right to strike to workers in essential services. The second sub-sub-argument is weak because the fact that professionals have obligations to society at large and to their clients is not adequate to show that these obligations are more important than any other consideration. It is also weak because the premise that teachers should not use their students as pawns in their quarrels with school boards begs the question by assuming that it is wrong for teachers to strike. The third sub-sub-argument, on the other hand, is a strong argument, although its strength is insufficient to overcome the weaknesses in the sub-argument as a whole. These weaknesses are so serious that we must regard the second sub-argument as providing no support for the conclusion of the main argument.

The third sub-argument is also very weak. Its first premise, that there is no evidence to support the claim that teachers' strikes achieve improvements in the educational system, is defended by the fourth sub-sub-argument. This is a deductive argument that is valid because it has the form of denying the consequent. Since it is a valid argument, we should accept its conclusion if we are prepared to accept its premises. It is reasonable to accept both premises, at least in the absence of contrary evidence, which means we should accept the conclusion. So the first premise of the sub-argument is acceptable. And it is clearly relevant. But it is also inadequate to support the conclusion, since it is an appeal to ignorance: the fact that there is no evidence to show that the teachers' claim is true is used to support the conclusion that the claim is false. The second premise of the sub-argument, which asserts that the teachers' claim is simply greed masquerading as benevolence, is a clear ad hominem fallacy and thus irrelevant. So the third sub-argument relies upon one premise that is acceptable and relevant, but clearly inadequate, and one premise that is clearly irrelevant. It is therefore a very weak argument.

We can now provide an assessment of the main argument. As we have seen, none of the premises is well supported. All must therefore be regarded as unacceptable. However, we have encountered nothing in our assessment of the sub-arguments that would lead us to change our provisional assessment of the premises as being relevant and adequate. Nevertheless, the argument as a whole suffers from the fatal flaw that all its premises are unacceptable, so the fact that they are relevant and adequate does nothing to provide support for the conclusion that the teachers' right to strike should be taken away.

There is, however, something that can be salvaged from the argument. We noted that the first sub-argument would have been acceptable had its conclusion been *Long teachers' strikes can have a harmful effect on some high-school students*. We also noted that the fourth sub-sub-argument was a strong argument, so we should accept its conclusion that *There is no evidence to support the claim that teachers' strikes achieve improvements in the educational system*. Although these conclusions are obviously not adequate to support the argument's main conclusion, they do suggest areas where further research and study would be useful. If we could determine precisely how much harm is caused to students by lengthy strikes, and if we knew whether or not strikes did achieve improvements in the educational system, we would be much closer to being able to make a reasonable decision on whether the right to strike should be taken away from teachers.

And finally, we must ask whether we should consider a counter-argument against the main conclusion. In fact there is one that some teachers have used when faced with demands that their legal right to strike should be taken away. Before teachers were granted the legal right to strike, and when they wanted to put pressure on a school board to secure a better contract, they would all simultaneously submit letters of resignation. The right to submit a letter of resignation is quite different from the right to strike, since forbidding individuals from resigning their jobs would be a form of slavery. Since no school board could hope to hire enough teachers to fill the mass vacancies in the middle of a school year, the teachers were able to achieve the effect of a strike without actually calling a strike. So it could be argued that if the legal right to strike were taken away from teachers, there would be no reduction in the number of "strikes," for the teachers would revert to their former practice of organizing mass resignations. The effect of this counter-argument is to show that the real issue is not the legal right of teachers to call strikes but their actual withdrawal of services either through strikes, if they are legal, or by mass resignations, if strikes are illegal. And this issue would require a rather different argument from the one we have considered.

16.5 Question for Discussion

The following argumentative essay is compiled from several discussions and articles on politics and the news media in Canada. It is worth discussing not only as an exercise in critical thinking but also because it raises an important issue.

It is clear that the Canadian media make an essential contribution to the healthy functioning of our system of government. But this does not mean that there are no grounds for complaint. Politicians, of course, regularly complain that the media fail to present news the way the government wants, or give too much coverage to the opposition, or uncover scandals they would prefer to keep buried. There is probably some substance to such complaints, but it is inevitable that there will be honest disagreements about such editorial decisions, and in any case it is the price politicians must pay for living in a democratic society. But there is a much more serious problem with the media that must be addressed, namely, the way in which they treat all politicians as fair game for any kind of sensational and unjustified attack. Many commentators have expressed concern about the irresponsibility of the news media in their treatment of politicians of all parties.

No one doubts that this kind of irresponsible journalism is very widespread. Scarcely a week goes by without the media smearing yet another politician. Reporters all seem to think of themselves as investigative reporters: if they don't dig out more dirt, they reckon they aren't doing their jobs properly. Editors feel compelled not merely to publish all the dirt, but to display it as prominently as possible. What better story to feature on the front page than an accusation of political corruption; what better film clip for television than one showing a politician losing his or her composure under the relentless questioning of a reporter? The fact is that the media can make a politician appear guilty on the basis of an accusation and can destroy a career on the basis of a few shreds of evidence that would never stand up in a court of law. Anyone who recognizes the importance of good government must view with alarm such irresponsible journalism.

We are all aware of the increase in recent years in public cynicism about politicians. Doubtless there are several factors that have contributed to this phenomenon. But one reason for it—a reason usually overlooked by the media—is the irresponsible political reporting of the news media. You cannot blame the public for its cynicism. Almost everything it knows about politicians it has learned from the news media, and since almost every story about politicians is negative, it is little wonder that the public is so cynical. The media lead the public to expect that all politicians are unsavoury characters, and consequently the public has to a great extent lost its capacity to be shocked when a truly dishonest or incompetent politician is exposed. Increasingly, the public has come to think that there are only two classes of politicians: those who have been exposed as corrupt, and those who have not yet been exposed.

Every citizen—and this includes every journalist—has certain responsibilities. One is to ensure that, as far as it is within our power, we treat our fellow citizens fairly. Another responsibility we all have is not to deliberately pursue policies that we know will deter honest and honourable people from entering public life. The news media have shown themselves to be flagrantly irresponsible on both counts. They are persistently unfair to politicians, and by driving good people out of politics they ensure political mediocrity: what could be more reprehensible?

Journalists are usually quick to respond to such complaints by invoking the freedom of the press. But the quickness of their response leads them to miss the point altogether. Freedom of the press does not mean freedom from criticism; it means the right of the media to publish whatever they want without legal interference. This is not the issue. The issue is not whether they have the legal right to attack politicians, for clearly they do, but whether they are exercising that right in a responsible manner. The mindless way in which journalists invoke freedom of the press as a defence against all criticism is yet another indication of their irresponsibility.

Some cynical journalists invoke another self-serving justification. The kind of political coverage provided by the media, they say, is what the public wants. It sells newspapers and gives the TV networks high ratings. Don't blame us, they say, blame the public that demands that kind of stuff. What nonsense! If we take this argument seriously, then we should ask how journalists differ from pimps, porn merchants, and drug dealers. The answer should be obvious, even to journalists.

The fundamental problem is that the news media have great political power but are not accountable for the way they exercise that power. We cannot take away their power without destroying them. But we can, and should, insist that they take their responsibilities seriously and exercise their power in a responsible manner.

17. Strategies for Organizing an Argumentative Essay

Among other things, Chapter 16 covered some basic points about the MACRO-STRUC-TURE of an argumentative essay. In this chapter we look at macro-structure in more detail, outlining three generic strategies for organizing the macro-structure of an argumentative essay. We call these *strategies*, since the choice of one option over the other two depends on what purpose an author has in constructing an argumentative essay. Students, in particular, can benefit from considering these options consciously when planning and writing papers in their courses.

For the sake of convenient reference, the three macro-structural strategies discussed in this chapter have been given names. These are the *Advocate's Strategy*, the *Critic's Strategy* and the *Impartial Adjudicator's Strategy*. The macro-structure associated with each name is not the exclusive domain of advocates, critics and adjudicators, but the names describe the most obvious people to use them.

To appreciate what each of these strategies entails and the need to differentiate between them, consider the type of situation in which we resort to arguments in the course of deliberating over a problem. Usually everything begins with a question that does not admit of a simple and indisputable answer upon which everyone agrees. *Should the municipality increase property taxes to finance a new building for the local arts centre?* Not everyone will agree on an answer to this question. In fact, we can expect a question such as this to generate considerable debate—some people will advocate for this finance scheme and others will criticize it in letters to the editor and submissions to the local council.

Many local artists and art lovers will answer the question with an unqualified *yes*, but in order to win broad-based support, they will need to come up with good arguments. The arguments they provide in support of this answer will *advocate* on behalf of the proposed finance scheme. Some homeowners who plan never to visit the arts centre will answer with an unqualified *no*, and they too will need good arguments to support their position. Any arguments they provide will *criticize* the proposed venture. Partisans on either side of a dispute of this sort tend to organize their arguments exclusively according to one of these two purposes or the other. People arguing on either side may respond to what the other side has said already (especially a critic) or in anticipation of what the other side might say. But, in general, it is not the responsibility of an advocate or a critic to present the other side of the dispute. An independent consultant, however, who has been hired by the city to prepare a report on the matter has to cover both sides (or, on a more complex issue, all sides). This person may answer the crucial question with a qualified *yes* or a qualified *no*. An *impartial adjudicator*, such as the consultant, must present the principal arguments in support of the proposal and the principal arguments against it. The position this person formulates must be then defined in view of the explicitly stated arguments from both sides.

In light of this example, let us clarify one detail about "point of view" and distinguish it from the problem of bias introduced in Chapter 15. As readers and audience members, we must be on the alert for biases, and media sources can be criticized for displaying biases. If we detect bias in a newspaper report, for example, then we have grounds to complain that the author and editors have imposed a one-sided interpretation of the story or distorted the facts. One thing we might say is that they have presented the story from a particular, partisan point of view *without providing an argument in favour of that point of view*. Because such stories don't defend their own point of view, they beg important questions about how the events ought to be understood. Having a point of view is not the fundamental problem in these cases. Not declaring it or not explicitly stating the reasons for taking that point of view is. Accordingly, there is nothing inherently problematic with the points of view taken by an advocate or a critic, and nothing inherently superior about the impartial adjudicator's point of view. As readers, we cannot fault an author for arguing from their point of view, especially if their explicit purpose is to defend that view; as authors, however, we must construct our arguments in ways that are appropriate to the point of view we have taken.

A second detail to clarify at this point concerns the generic function of the three strategies. All three of the strategies outlined in this chapter can be used to organize academic essays. When writing a position paper—one of the most common essay assignments in university—the author formulates a stand on a controversial issue and defends that position with evidence and arguments. It is helpful to take seriously the metaphor suggested by the label *position paper*. When we write a position paper we occupy a position within a field of options, then construct an argument that shows how or why that position is superior to the available alternatives. This task is explicit in many academic assignments. For example, in a philosophy class students may be asked to defend a position on the abortion debate, and in a history class students may be asked to defend a position on the principal causes of World War II. But the same task is implicit in many other academic essay assignments. English literature students may be asked to explain how the imagery in one poem compares with that in another poem. At first glance, this may not look like a position paper, but in essence it is. The prevalence of certain imagery in the first poem is by no means obvious, and the essay writer needs to *argue* that such imagery is present. The presence of similar imagery in the second poem also needs to be established by arguments. And whether these two poems can be related to each other by means of this imagery requires further argument. Broadly speaking, even the expository interpretation of poetry may require students to formulate and defend a position using arguments. So the strategies outlined in this chapter promise to be very useful for students in a wide range of courses.

A final point to emphasize about an argumentative essay has to do with the placement of the conclusion: the conclusion, which in many classes will be called the *thesis statement*, should be stated early in the essay, not left until the end. Too often, students take the plot of a detective story as a model for the macro-structure of an argumentative essay. In a detective mystery, about for example Sherlock Holmes investigating a murder, most of the plot follows the detective as he gathers clues and collects evidence until, at last, he can reveal the villain's identity in a climactic announcement in the final pages of the story. As events in the plot unfold, readers are invited to sift through the evidence as the detective gathers it; indeed, part of the charm of this sort of mystery lies in the benign competition between the reader and the detective to be the first to solve the crime. This adds another level of interest and suspense for the reader. Good mystery writers know this and drop clues for readers to pick up as they read, and many readers make the extra effort to piece the clues together as they go along. However, in an argumentative essay (especially in a student paper) it is inappropriate to build suspense in this way.

As a plot device in a detective story, it is appropriate to delay revealing the most important information (the identify of the criminal) in order to heighten the dramatic tension. But a long delay in stating the conclusion of an essay simply makes it harder for a reader to follow and assess the argument. A good argument can invite scrutiny, because it is strong enough to withstand critical examination. However, anything that makes scrutiny more difficult is counter-productive with careful readers who will wonder what the author is trying to hide. So an acceptable organizational principle in a detective story becomes a handicap in an argumentative essay.

Let us illustrate the three strategies concretely, with three short essays on a familiar social issue, namely, the use of active euthanasia when a patient is in the final stages of a terminal disease. (Euthanasia is the practice of facilitating a person's death when they are dying of a painful or debilitating condition. It is usually said to be active euthanasia when the person's death is hastened and passive when the person's death is allowed to happen without medical intervention to delay death.) For the purpose of illustration, let us suppose our question is, *Should active euthanasia be decriminalized for use when terminal patients are close to death?* For the sake of convenience, we shall leave aside other situations in which active euthanasia may be contemplated (e.g., accident victims and people in a persistive vegetative state, that is, a condition of irreversible loss of consciousness and responsiveness).

For the purposes of this chapter, the example essays that follow do not concentrate on some parts of the euthanasia issue that would be included in a fuller treatment of it, e.g., what exactly are the laws that would be struck from the criminal code if active euthanasia were decriminalized, and how are these laws worded? Laws are formulated differently in different jurisdictions, and we cannot explore such detailed matters here. Also, in our analysis of the essays we will not be concerned with identifying every premise in the arguments provided; rather we concentrate on those parts of the arguments that illustrate the three strategies for organizing an essay's macro-structure. Additionally, some of the empirical claims made in the example essays need to be supported with empirical evidence, and this will not be included in the essays. Since these essays are intended only to illustrate the macro-structural features of the three argument strategies, we have not provided footnotes or documented evidence for these claims. Finally, in these essays we have tried to avoid using humour, understatement, overstatement, colourful diction or any of the other wonderful rhetorical devices that authors use to make their essays more memorable or enjoyable. Again, we are trying not to divert attention from the macro-structural strategies that these essays illustrate.

17.1 Advocate's Strategy

Generally, someone who advocates for a cause is speaking in favour of a particular enterprise or policy, that is, recommending a course of action or defending a claim as true. An advocate is someone who defends a particular proposal or tenet by arguing on its behalf. If you hire a lawyer to act as your advocate in a law suit, for example, it is that person's responsibility to plead on your behalf. They must defend your interests exclusively and let opponents speak for themselves. In an academic essay, the author acts as an advocate by advancing arguments that are aimed exclusively at defending a main conclusion—or, what is usually the same thing, the thesis statement.

The following essay advocates on behalf of a proposal that has received a great deal of attention in recent years, namely, that active, voluntary euthanasia ought to be decriminalized. The main conclusion (C) is italicized for easy identification. It is found at the end of paragraph (1).

> C: *active euthanasia, in which a terminally ill person who is close to death and who requests death as a relief for their pain and suffering, ought to be decriminalized.*

The first main premise is found in the second sentence of paragraph (2), and it has to do with reducing the amount of time dying patients will have to deal with their diminished quality of life.

> P1: *active euthanasia will reduce the pain and suffering for the patients ...*

The second main premise is found in the next sentence of paragraph (2), and it has to do with the rights of these patients.

> P2: *these patients have a right to decide for themselves when their quality of life has become unbearable.*

The third main premise is found at the end of paragraph (2), and it has to do with the obligations of those who care for the dying.

P3: *if active euthanasia is decriminalized, medical professionals will be able to honour requests for euthanasia openly, without fear of prosecution.*

This argument can be diagrammed as having a T structure:

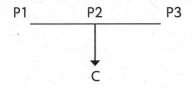

P1   P2   P3

C

There are, of course, sub-arguments that attempt to prove P1, P2, and P3, but they are not relevant to understand why the essay exemplifies the advocate's strategy. It is an exercise of advocacy, first, because C states a positive thesis, i.e., something that can be done. It is an exercise of advocacy, also, because P1, P2 and P3 together contribute positive evidence in favour of C.

Let us now read the essay as an example of the Advocate's Strategy, then we shall expand on this analysis (the paragraphs are numbered for convenient reference):

(1) Depending on the details of the situation, anyone who counsels euthanasia or hastens the death of a person who is in the final stages of a terminal disease may be prosecuted on a variety of charges, including aiding a suicide, manslaughter and murder. One reason why medical professionals are reluctant to euthanise or to help euthanise a palliative medical patient, even when it is voluntary, is a justified fear of prosecution. In many situations, active euthanasia is the only way to end a dying person's pain and suffering. So a way must be found to eliminate the need for active euthanasia or to remove the legal restrictions upon it. Since eliminating the need depends on advances in medicine that are beyond our control, we must consider why [C] *active euthanasia, in which terminally ill persons who are close to death and who request death as a relief of their pain and suffering, ought to be decriminalized.*

(2) Two fundamental reasons imply that active euthanasia should be decriminalized. First, [P1] *active euthanasia will reduce the pain and suffering for the patients* since it reduces the length of time it takes them to die, and voluntary euthanasia respects their rights to determine how they are treated. Second, [P2] *these patients have a right to decide for themselves when their quality of life has become unbearable.* Finally, [P3] *if euthanasia is decriminalized, medical professionals can honour requests for euthanasia openly, without fear of prosecution.*

(3) Palliative patients (i.e., patients who are dying and for whom medical treatment no longer promises to be therapeutic) have two interests at stake in the care they receive in their final days. First, there is their material quality of life, which we may assess by their levels of physical comfort and psychological satisfaction. People suffering through the final stages of cancer or AIDS may experience pain that can be controlled medically with morphine, and they may still be able to enjoy the pleasures of com-

panionship. However, pain control is not always effective, and sometimes the pain itself or the high doses of medication required to manage pain make it impossible to enjoy even the simplest of social pleasures. Sometimes, despite the best medical care available, patients find the pain and unhappiness too much to bear, and they make reasonable, enduring pleas to have their death hastened. In these cases, death offers the only hope to relieving their physical and psychological suffering. At this point, the quickest and most reliable way to end this suffering may be active euthanasia, i.e., euthanasia in which death is hastened by an injection of potassium chloride or some other substance that halts the heart beat or respiration.

(4) The second interest of these patients concerns their moral and political rights, in particular the rights associated with patient autonomy. Patient autonomy has become a central tenet of contemporary medical practice. This means that decisions about medical treatment must be directed as much as possible by the patients themselves rather than by the medical professionals treating them (when these decisions are made by medical professionals it is called medical paternalism). Competent patients (i.e., patients who are able to think clearly and understand the consequences of their decisions) can refuse to consent to certain forms of medical treatment, even if that treatment is necessary to sustain their life. For example, some people place a "Do Not Resuscitate" order in their medical records that instructs doctors and nurses to let them die if they should suffer a heart attack or some other life threatening condition while under medical care. In effect, a DNR order is a request for passive euthanasia (i.e., euthanasia in which the person is allowed to die without treatment from medical professionals but which is not hastened by direct intervention). Respect for patient autonomy justifies passive euthanasia, and should be extended to cover active euthanasia, too. There are many patients who would rather not leave to chance whether their lives will end in a way that is acceptable to them—namely, surrounded by family, at a time of their choosing.

(5) A request for active euthanasia imposes a serious burden upon the attending physician and everyone else connected with the patient's care, because the consequences are very serious. However, the consequences are no more serious for active euthanasia than they are for passive euthanasia. Respecting a patient's DNR order and respecting their request to hasten death are not different in kind. Still, medical professionals are permitted to withhold treatment and allow death in the first case, whereas they are subject to criminal prosecution in the second case. Just as we now acknowledge that medical professionals have a duty to respect a DNR order as a request for passive euthanasia, so should we admit that they have a similar duty to respect a request for active euthanasia. And in order for them to act on this respect, we must decriminalize the practice.

(6) Everyone directly involved in the end of a hospital patient's life would benefit from decriminalizing active euthanasia: medical professionals who care for these patients (doctors and nurses, in particular) will no longer be constrained from honouring the request made by those who feel their quality of life has irreversibly and unbear-

ably deteriorated; and the patients themselves who request euthanasia will not suffer unreasonably and will have their rights respected. The principal obstacles preventing the use of euthanasia are the laws that forbid people to assist anyone who hastens another person's death. Therefore, we must change the laws that criminalize euthanasia as a way to improve the care for palliative patients.

As we said earlier, this essay illustrates the Advocate's Strategy because the main argument is directed exclusively at defending the proposal stated in the main conclusion, that active euthanasia ought to be decriminalized. However, we must emphasize that an effective advocate does not ignore or discount alternative positions. Even if these alternatives are not stated or summarized explicitly, they can play a crucial role in shaping the argument. A good advocate is well aware of alternative positions and objections to the position being defended; accordingly, the author must define his or her own position in a way that *anticipates* these alternatives and objections. In this case, the author implicitly restricts the scope of the conclusion to voluntary euthanasia, for example (notice the wording of C: ... *and who requests death* ...). By so restricting the scope of C and the argument, the essay leaves aside related but different debates over the use of euthanasia for people who are unable to make such requests (e.g., someone in a coma).

The essay happens to have a two-paragraph introduction, but one paragraph might have sufficed in such a short paper (and, of course, a longer introduction might be necessary in a very long essay). Paragraph (1) outlines a problem and states the author's proposed solution to the problem, i.e., the conclusion [C]. Paragraph (2) then outlines the three main premises that are used to defend this conclusion, i.e., P1, P2, and P3. Paragraphs (3)–(5) constitute the body of the essay. Notice that the purpose of each of these paragraphs is to defend P1, P2 and P3 respectively. Thus, the end of paragraph (1) and all of paragraph (2) perform two functions simultaneously: (a) providing an outline of the author's main argument; and (b) providing an outline of the macro-structure of the body of the paper. The final paragraph then reiterates the conclusion (without mechanically repeating it) and makes explicit the prospect that *everyone* will benefit from decriminalizing active euthanasia.

Notice, especially, the relation in this essay between the argument outlined in the introduction and the macro-structure of the body of the paper. The T structure of the main argument is outlined above, in the analysis preceding the essay. This argument is summarized in the introduction of the essay. Turning to the body of the essay, we see that paragraph (3) defends P1, paragraph (4) defends P2, and paragraph (5) defends P3. Finally, paragraph (6) reiterates and elaborates on C. Thus, the macro-structure of the body of this essay is as follows

paragraph (3) [on P1] _____ paragraph (4) [on P2] _____ paragraph (5) [on P3]

↓

paragraph (6) [on C]

A well-structured paper is reasonably easy to summarize, and the summary provided in the introduction of this essay helps orient readers before they encounter the more complex material in the body. It is helpful to think of the entire enterprise of structuring an advocacy essay as a journey. In the introduction the author goes over the road map for readers before embarking on the journey—it announces the destination, outlines the main route, and lists major landmarks that will be passed en route. The body of the paper takes readers on the journey itself. In the conclusion, the author announces that they have arrived at the destination and may use this as an opportunity to do one of several things: (a) to extol the advantages of adopting C, (b) to suggest routes for a further journey along the same course, or (c) to indicate how they have gotten to C. In this case, the essay extols the benefits of the conclusion they have arrived at (a), but it might just as easily have suggested where the argument could go next (b), i.e., suggesting solutions to political obstacles to decriminalizing active euthanasia, or identifying methods for regulating and administering the practice. In a long essay, however, it may be necessary to review how they got to the conclusion.

17.2 Critic's Strategy

A *critic* as we are using that term is someone who argues against someone else's recommendation or claim—that is, who discourages a course of action or attempts to show that a claim is false. A criminal defence lawyer is a good example of a critic in this special, narrow sense (as distinct from the wider sense that includes a "film critic" who may find no fault with a particular film). It's the job of lawyers in criminal courts to find flaws in the prosecution's arguments. They are trying to establish that there are good reasons to doubt that the evidence points to guilt. Since the burden of proof in a criminal trial is on the prosecution, it is sufficient for the defence lawyer to criticize the prosecution's case. In an academic essay, the author acts as a critic in this sense by advancing arguments that are aimed at undermining a plausible or established claim. (Remember, we learned in 7.4.3 that arguing against a patently implausible claim, or against one that no one is likely to hold, commits the straw man fallacy.)

The following essay criticizes a common assumption about how active euthanasia would be practised, if it were to be decriminalized. As in the previous example, the main conclusion [C] is italicized. It may be found in the second sentence of paragraph (1).

> C: *the common belief [that active euthanasia would best be administered by physicians] turns out to be misconceived as an acceptable extension of current medical practice.*

The two premises that support this conclusion are found together in the next sentence, and listed as mistaken beliefs:

> P1: *It is false "that the rights possessed by a dying patient impose a duty upon the physician to provide euthanasia."*

And

P2: *It is false that "active euthanasia is consistent with the proper function of a physician."*

This argument can be diagrammed as having a V structure:

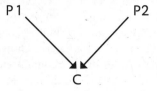

Again, as in 17.1, this map leaves out sub-arguments in support of P1 and P2; it would distract attention from the macro-structure of the Critic's Strategy to talk about them here. The argument is an exercise of criticism, first, because C is stated as a negative thesis, i.e., that a given claim is false. It is an exercise in criticism also because both P1 and P2 identify as false claims that are believed to support the mistaken belief mentioned in C.

Let us now turn to the example, after which we shall expand on this analysis:

(1) In the debate over euthanasia, it is commonly believed that active euthanasia (if accepted) would best be administered by physicians. Upon reflection, however, [C] *the common belief turns out to be misconceived as an acceptable extension of current medical practice.* There are serious reasons to resist instituting active euthanasia in practice, even if one accepts it in principle. Two mistaken assumptions stand behind the problematic popular opinion: the belief that [P1] *the rights possessed by a dying patient impose a duty upon someone responsible for their care to provide euthanasia*; and the belief that [P2] *active euthanasia is consistent with the proper function of a physician.* Both of these beliefs are problematic. Let us consider each one in order.

(2) Autonomy in general grants a person rights to govern his or her own conduct and imposes duties on other people to respect such freely chosen decisions. Autonomy means "self-rule," i.e., the ability to regulate and control one's own behaviour. Patient autonomy applies to medical patients and their special situation. Other people (medical professionals) act on behalf of patients, but they do not decide what is to be done; as much as possible, the patients decide the course of their own medical treatment. Growing concern for patient autonomy is part of a movement to recognize that people who are injured, sick or dying and in need of medical attention are still autonomous persons and deserve to retain control over their own lives. Medical professionals cannot perform tests or administer treatment on a person without that person's consent, which is why patient autonomy is so often exercised as a refusal to consent to treatment.

(3) Autonomy in general has limits, and so does patient autonomy. Just as autonomy in general does not oblige other people to do absolutely everything that a person requests of them, so does patient autonomy not oblige medical professions to satisfy every request from a patient. Those who defend voluntary euthanasia need to ask, *does patient autonomy extend so far as to oblige any other person to hasten the death of a dying person who requests it?* Such a request is, in itself, extraordinary. Whether it is morally acceptable to honour it is not answered simply by noting that the request was made voluntarily. If I request that someone torture me, no one is obliged (or even permitted) to do so simply because the request was made voluntarily. Similarly, patient autonomy does not entail that patients have a right to active euthanasia, however much the person may want it. Even if active euthanasia does bring a humane end to a person's suffering, it is such an extraordinary request that we should not say that anyone is strictly *obliged* to provide it.

(4) For the sake of the argument, let us set aside the first objection and assume that euthanasia is morally permitted (even if it is not morally obligatory). Let's also assume for the sake of argument that active euthanasia has been decriminalized. We must now consider a second question: *who is the best person to honour a patient's request and administer a lethal dose of the substance that hastens death?* The most common answer is *the patient's attending physician*. This person has the medical training to know what substances will have the desired effect without causing the patient further pain or suffering. This person knows the patient best and is in the best position to know when a request for euthanasia is being made with an adequate understanding. Finally, as the person who takes ultimate responsibility to oversee other aspects of a patient's medical care (testing, diagnosis, treatment, etc.), the attending physician ought to take responsibility for this final stage of the person's medical care. This appears to be what many defenders of active euthanasia believe.

(5) This suggestion, that a *physician* is morally permitted administer active euthanasia is, however, inconsistent with the profession's guiding purpose: that is, to heal the sick and injured. Hastening death does not contribute to this purpose; in fact, it defeats that purpose entirely. While physicians have more know-how than anyone else for administering active euthanasia in an effective and humane fashion, their sworn professional duty explicitly forbids them to put this knowledge to that purpose. The physician's oath enjoins them, *above all, do no harm*. Death, even when a person's life is painful and suffering is tremendous, is a harm. Passive euthanasia is consistent with a physician's duty, because a physician who withholds treatment—i.e., *who does nothing*—thereby avoids *doing harm*. Active euthanasia, by contrast, requires a physician to do something (e.g., administer a lethal injection).

(6) These two objections should undermine our confidence in the commonly held opinion, that, if active euthanasia is ever accepted, physicians can, and ought to be, the ones to administer it. For active euthanasia is neither consistent with the physician's duty nor required by patient autonomy.

This essay illustrates the Critic's Strategy because the main argument of the essay is directed exclusively at criticizing the popular opinion identified at the beginning, that a physician would be the best person to administer active euthanasia (should the practice ever be instituted). Unlike an advocate, a critic concentrates on existing positions on the issue in question. The critic responds explicitly to one or more of these positions. Whereas the advocate implicitly anticipates alternative positions on a contentious issue, the critic explicitly *reacts* to someone else's position. (To refute a position that no one holds—or that no reasonable person is likely to hold—is to argue against a straw man, and so we should avoid this in any case.) Finally, unlike the advocate, a critic is not obliged to actually defend an independently formulated position on the issue in question. But like the advocate, it is important for the critic to restrict the scope of the conclusion to something that can be supported by the evidence. In this case, the author concentrates on one principal assumption about how active euthanasia would be practised, leaving aside objections to other potentially problematic aspects of it.

This essay has a one-paragraph introduction. The introduction, paragraph (1), begins with a statement of the common opinion which is the focus of the essay's critique. We can call this popular opinion the critique's *target proposition*. The next four paragraphs are the body of the essay. Paragraph (2) analyses the concepts of autonomy and patient autonomy, and paragraph (3) argues that patient autonomy does not obligate anyone to perform it; we can say that paragraph (3) uses the analysis of paragraph (2) to establish P1. Paragraph (4) elaborates on details of the popular opinion that is this essay's target. Paragraph (5) argues that this opinion is misconceived. Finally, paragraph (6) briefly reiterates the main argument. The introduction of this essay performs the same two functions as those identified in our analysis of the Advocate's essay in 17.1, i.e., outlining the main argument and outlining the macrostructure of the body of the paper. Additionally, it identifies the target that gives this critique its precise focus.

Again, as with the essay in 17.1, there is a relation between the argument outlined in the introduction of the Critic's essay and the macro-structure of the body of paper. The V structure of the main argument corresponds with the macro-structure of the essay as follows:

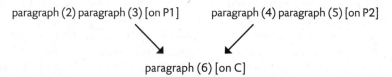

paragraph (2) paragraph (3) [on P1]   paragraph (4) paragraph (5) [on P2]

paragraph (6) [on C]

Again, we see how the macro-structure of the essay is summarized in the introduction. The only significant difference between the Critic's introduction and the Advocate's is that the Critic must clearly identify the target of the critique. In order to avoid arguing against a straw man, this targeted proposition must be stated accurately and faithfully. In the body of this Critic's essay, two elements appear that are not found in the body of the Advocate's essay: in paragraph (2) analysis is provided for the concepts of autonomy and patient autonomy; and in paragraph (4) further details are outlined as part of the targeted proposition. Not every use of the Critic's strategy will provide this additional analysis of the target proposition. But this example serves to illustrate two manoeuvres that are typical of a critique: the analysis in paragraph (2) introduces general concepts and principles that we may expect to be shared by those who accept the targeted belief and the critic; and the amplification of the targeted proposition itself in paragraph (4). In both of these paragraphs, the Critic gives the other side of the debate a chance to speak. Thus, we see that the Critic's Strategy really is explicitly dependent on rival positions, since the opponent's position must be stated in order for the critic to have a target in the first place. A good critic understands the opponent's position and is responsive to that position.

We can contrast the Critic's Strategy with the Advocate's Strategy in terms of the journey metaphor used at the end of 17.1. While the Advocate takes the reader on a journey, the Critic discourages readers from taking that journey. The Critic may do this in one of three ways: (a) by arguing that the destination is not desirable; or (b) by arguing that the route someone has recommended will not get to that destination; or (c) by arguing *both* that the destination is not desirable *and* that the route will not get there. In this essay the author has accepted active euthanasia for the sake of the argument; in other words, no objections are made about the destination. The objection is that one route to this destination, active euthanasia performed by a physician, is not acceptable, i.e., (b).

17.3 Impartial Adjudicator's Strategy

An Impartial Adjudicator has to consider and weigh the evidence from all available points of view before passing judgement. Ideally, this person will *explicitly* state or summarize all the available positions on the issue at hand. The wider and more complex the issue, the more space is required to state and assess all the available positions. This is why court judgements from the bench, consultant's reports and judicial inquiry reports are often very large documents. In academic essays, authors act as adjudicators by introducing and assessing all the principal positions, and identifying the strengths and weaknesses of each in order to define their own position. In a short paper, this requires the author to define the main thesis precisely and to state the alternatives concisely.

The following essay formulates a position on active euthanasia that gives qualified support to the proposal that we stop criminally prosecuting those who practise active, voluntary euthanasia, and uses existing objections to euthanasia to maintain that the practice must not be decriminalized entirely. Again, the main conclusion [C] is italicized. It is found at the end of paragraph (1).

> C: *[a] we should allow some use of active euthanasia but that [b] any changes should be to regulate the practice, not to decriminalize it.*

In order to show how this conclusion has been qualified in light of two alternative positions, it has been divided into two parts. Part [a] endorses the practice of active euthanasia, and part [b] states that this practice should still be limited by the threat of criminal prosecution. The first premise, which supports the first half of the conclusion [Ca] is found in the middle of paragraph (1):

P1: *caretakers should be able to honour such requests without fear of criminal prosecution.*

The second premise, which supports the second half of the conclusion [Cb], is also found in paragraph (1):

P2: *the risks that active voluntary euthanasia will be abused or used without due caution are serious and the practice must be controlled by regulation*

The argument can be diagrammed as having a T structure

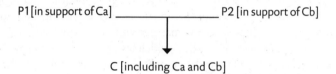

P1 [in support of Ca] _____ P2 [in support of Cb]

C [including Ca and Cb]

In this summary of the argument in the introduction, the greatest indication that this essay illustrates the Impartial Adjudicator's strategy may be found in the way the two premises are introduced. The author's *On the one hand.... On the other hand....* construction signals an attempt to incorporate evidence from two rival positions in formulating the position to be defended here.

(1) The legal attitude towards active euthanasia (in prohibitions against assisted suicide, manslaughter and murder) needs to change to accommodate situations in which patients are suffering unbearably and want to die, but any reforms need to be made without decriminalizing active euthanasia. On one hand, there are cases in which a palliative patient's quality of life has been reduced to nothing because of the pain and debilitation caused by a terminal illness such as advanced stage cancer. If a person in this state makes a clear and reasonable request to hasten death, then [P1] *caretakers should be able to honour such requests without fear of criminal prosecution.* On the other hand, [P2] *the risks that active voluntary euthanasia will be abused or used without due caution are serious and the practice must be controlled by regulation,* so we should not decriminalize the practice entirely. A brief survey of the reasons in favour of active, voluntary euthanasia and some of the principal objections to the practice suggests that [C] *we should allow some use of active euthanasia but that any changes should be to regulate the practice, not to decriminalize it.* This way we can respond humanely to people who request euthanasia without risk of undermining the integrity of palliative care.

(2) Let us first consider why the practice of active, voluntary euthanasia seems necessary. Even with advances in medicine and pain control, there are still cases in which

people die in excruciating, unmanageable and unbearable pain. Often, active euthanasia is not simply requested, it is begged for by dying patients. Until something can
be done for such people medically, we cannot ignore this suffering. In other cases,
patients' physical pain can be reduced to a tolerable level, but side effects of the medicine make it very difficult for them to enjoy a quality of life that they find acceptable.
When it is clear that their quality of life will never return to an acceptable level and
they are dying, it may be humane to honour their request to hasten death. It is because
of current limitations in medical practice that patients request active euthanasia. As
long as these limitations exist, we ought to honour requests for active euthanasia.

(3) Still, if active, voluntary euthanasia becomes acceptable medical practice, there is
a danger that it will become routine. If this occurs, then there is a further danger that
medical practitioners will become coarsened about the gravity of their roles in hastening death. Outright decriminalization of active euthanasia may reinforce these new,
coarsened views. However, if we retain the existing legal sanctions that prohibit active
euthanasia indirectly, then medical professionals get a clear message: do not engage in
this practice without due caution. This message can be sent by retaining the current
legal restrictions and establishing explicit guidelines for its use, and providing reassur-
ances that no charges will be laid if the guidelines are followed. Under the guidelines,
we could require that any use of active euthanasia be documented and reported to
ensure that it is practised openly. The introduction of regulations will allow medical
professionals to respect the requests of palliative patients and preserve the integrity
of medical practice.

(4) In the care for palliative patients, this proposal should reassure everyone: patients
should be reassured, first, that active euthanasia will be available if their quality of
life becomes unacceptable; patients should also be reassured that health care professionals will not provide euthanasia while there is still *anything else* that can be done
to make them comfortable; medical professionals should be reassured that they are
protected from aggressive prosecution; and the rest of society should be reassured the
integrity of medicine is preserved. As a model of this practice we might look at euthanasia in the Netherlands between 1984 and 2001. During this time, active, voluntary
euthanasia remained, strictly speaking, illegal, but physicians were not prosecuted if
euthanasia was reported on the death certificate and strict "carefulness guidelines"
were followed. The carefulness guidelines required the attending physician to consult another physician prior to administering euthanasia, to prove that the patient
had made an informed decision to have euthanasia, to provide documentation to the
police, etc. Euthanasia was decriminalized in the Netherlands in 2002, but there are
reports of the practice becoming over-used in recent years. Had it remained strictly
illegal, the Netherlands would have ensured a balance between humanely addressing
the needs of those palliative patients whose quality of life had become unacceptable
and remaining vigilant in protecting those patients with genuine treatment options
available.

As we said earlier, the Impartial Adjudicator's Strategy is especially useful when the conclusion of an argumentative essay must be qualified carefully. In this case, the conclusion is qualified in order to formulate a compromise position between removing current legal restrictions that apply to active euthanasia and objecting to the practice on the basis of strict principles. The position defended in this essay is defined by two alternative responses to the controversy over active euthanasia. One of the alternative positions informing the conclusion here is *similar* to that found in 17.1, and the other is *similar* to that found in 17.2. But we must be careful here not to say that these alternatives are *identical* to the positions in 17.1 and 17.2. The compromise formulated in accordance with the Impartial Adjudicator's Strategy does not explore the grounds for two alternatives in as much detail as the "partisan" strategies in 17.1 and 17.2; however, even if the alternative positions are not stated in detail, all the relevant positions are identified explicitly. It is this attempt to *include explicitly* and *incorporate* these alternatives that makes this an example of the Impartial Adjudicator's Strategy.

The essay has a one paragraph introduction, a two-paragraph body, and a conclusion paragraph. Paragraph (1) identifies both lines of argument that converge on this essay's complex conclusion. Paragraphs (2) and (3) constitute the body of the essay, with P1 being defended in paragraph (2) and P2 being defended in paragraph (3). The introduction conveys the macro-structure of the paper by two means: the complex statement of C (i.e., *regulate active euthanasia, but don't decriminalize it*), and the complex presentation of the main premises (the *on the one hand ... on the other hand ... construction*). The final paragraph then elaborates on the conclusion and identifies a precedent for the proposal being defended here. The macro-structure of the essay is as follows:

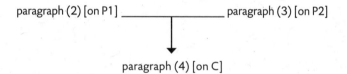

paragraph (2) [on P1]   paragraph (3) [on P2]

paragraph (4) [on C]

We can see how the Impartial Adjudicator's Strategy synthesizes the two other macro-structural patterns. Like the Advocate, the Impartial Adjudicator recommends a route to a precisely defined destination in paragraph (2); in this case, regulated, active, voluntary euthanasia is recommended for the humane treatment of terminal patients. And like the Critic, the Impartial Adjudicator discourages the reader from taking another route to the same destination in paragraph (3); in this case, the suggestion that active euthanasia be decriminalized is discouraged.

17.4 Questions for Discussion

1. Taking the essay in 17.1 as a point of departure, how might we reformulate the conclusion and premises to make it conform to the Critic's Strategy rather than the Advocate's Strategy?

2. Taking the essay in 17.2 as a point of departure, how might we reformulate the conclusion and premises to make it conform to the Advocate's Strategy rather than the Critic's Strategy?

3. Taking the essay in 17.3 as a point of departure, how might we reformulate P1 and Ca to construct an independent essay that conforms to the Advocate's Strategy?

4. Taking the essay in 17.3 as a point of departure, how might we reformulate P2 and Cb to construct an independent essay that conforms to the Critic's Strategy?

Appendix 1   Paradoxes and Puzzles

1. Logical Paradoxes

A logical paradox is any chain of reasoning that uses only meaningful and consistent premises and commits no logical errors, yet nevertheless produces contradictory conclusions. Such a result ought to be impossible, so when paradoxes arise, they present a serious challenge to our assumptions. Are the premises really meaningful? Are they really consistent with one another? Is there a hidden weakness we have failed to detect? We know that something *must* be wrong with the argument: the challenge is to find it.

The paradoxes described below have all challenged philosophers and logicians, and continue to do so, since most of them have no generally agreed-upon solution. The problem is that there are compelling reasons against rejecting any of the premises, and no one has been able to provide a plausible account of a logical error that is being committed. They can, however, also be regarded as brain-teasers for which there is as yet no *right* answer.

(1) THE BARBER PARADOX

In a certain village there lives a barber who cuts the hair of all those, and only those, inhabitants who do not cut their own hair. Does he cut his own hair? If he does not, then he is one of those who do not cut their own hair, in which case he does cut his own hair because he cuts the hair of all those who do not cut their own hair. If he does cut his own hair, then he is not one of those whose hair he cuts, because he cuts the hair only of those who do not cut their own hair. Thus, if he does, then he doesn't, and if he doesn't, then he does, which is a paradox.

This paradox, unlike those that follow, does have a solution. The first sentence makes a factual claim about the barber, namely, that he cuts the hair of all those and only those who do not cut their own hair. But why should we accept this factual claim? No one has ever suggested that such a barber actually exists, and there is no reason why anyone would ever be tempted to make such a claim. In fact, as the paradox shows, such a barber could not exist. Any barber who set out to cut the hair of all those and only those who do not cut their own hair could not possibly succeed, not as long as he was an inhabitant of the village. The paradox only arises, then, because we have made a factual claim that could not possibly be true, and the solution to the paradox is simply not to make factual assertions of this sort. Perhaps the reason the factual claim looks plausible is because we forget that the barber is himself an inhabitant of the village. If he moved away so that he was no longer an inhabitant, and visited the village regularly to cut hair, then he could cut the hair of all those and only those inhabitants who do not cut their own hair. In this case the only way to discover whether or not he cuts his own hair would be to ask him.

(2) THE SURPRISE EXAMINATION

One Friday a mathematics teacher announces to his class, *Next week there will be a test on quadratic equations. But I want the test to be a surprise when it comes, so I am not going to tell you which day it will be.* After the class, one of the students tells the teacher that she has figured out that there is not really going to be a test, at least not a surprise test. Her reasoning is as follows:

> *The test cannot be given next Friday because if we got to Thursday afternoon without having the test, we would know that it would be given the next day, and it would not be a surprise. So if it is to be a surprise, then it cannot be given on Friday. But, since Friday is ruled out, then if we got to Wednesday afternoon without having the test, we would know that it would be given the next day (i.e., on Thursday). But then it wouldn't be a surprise. So it cannot be given on Thursday. But, since both Friday and Thursday are ruled out, then if we got to Tuesday afternoon without having the test, we would know that it would be given the next day (i.e., on Wednesday). But then it wouldn't be a surprise. So the test cannot be given on Wednesday. The same argument also rules out Tuesday and Monday, so I conclude that you will be unable to give a surprise test next week.*

What is wrong with the student's reasoning? The solution to the Barber paradox won't work here, for the teacher's announcement certainly could be true. If no student was clever enough to recognize the paradox, the teacher could give the test on Tuesday, for example, and everyone would be surprised. Or, what is even more curious, the teacher could say to the student, *Your reasoning is impeccable*, and then give the test on Tuesday (or any other day), which would certainly surprise the student as well as the rest of the class.

(3) THE LIAR PARADOX

The liar paradox arises out of a feature of the following statement: *What I am now saying is a lie.* If what the speaker says is true, then it is a lie (i.e., it is false), and if what the speaker says is false, then it is not a lie (i.e., it is true). If you don't see this, consider an alternative wording: *This statement is false.* It has the same feature; if it is true, then it is false, and if it is false, then it is true.

An old objection to this paradox is that the statement refers to itself, and this, it is held, explains why the paradox arises. But the paradox can easily be reformulated in such a way as to eliminate the self-reference. Consider the following statements:

(1) Statement (2) is true.
(2) Statement (1) is false.

Since every meaningful statement must be either true or false, and since both these statements are obviously meaningful, let us suppose that (1) is true. If it is true, then (2) must be true (since that is what (1) says). But if (2) is true, then (1) must be false (since that is what (2) says). Therefore, if (1) is true, it is false, which is absurd. Therefore, (1) cannot be true. So let us suppose then that (1) is false. If it is false, then (2) must be false (since that is what the falsity of (1) means). But if (2) is false, then (1) must be true (since that is what the falsity of (2) means). Therefore, if (1) is false, it is true, which is absurd. Therefore, (1) cannot be false. But we have already shown that it cannot be true. Therefore, (1) cannot be true and it cannot be false, which is absurd, unless it is a meaningless statement. But it is not meaningless. Hence, the paradox. Note that the same result emerges if we start with statement (2): it cannot be true and it cannot be false. (An interesting variation on the two-statement version of the liar paradox was seen on a T-shirt: on the front it said, *The statement on the back of this T-shirt is true*, and on the back it said, *The statement on the front of this T-shirt is false.*)

Once again, the solution that worked for the Barber paradox won't help us here. There is nothing suspect about either statement; anyone who has ever taken a true/false quiz will use both types of statements.

(4) THE LAW STUDENT PARADOX

In ancient Athens, a student wanted to study law with the noted teacher Protagoras, but could not afford the fee. Protagoras agreed to teach him on the condition that when he completed his studies and won his first case in court, he would pay the stipulated fee. The student, however, having completed his studies, decided not to practise law at all and told Protagoras that according to their agreement he was under no obligation to pay him. Protagoras was most indignant and sued the student for his fees. He presented the following argument to the judges:

> *If I win my case, then according to the judgement of the court, the student ought to pay me the fee. But if the student wins, then according to our agreement, he ought to pay me. In either case, he ought to pay.*

The student, however, argued as follows:

If I win my case, then according to the judgement of the court, I do not have to pay the fee. And if I lose my case, then according to our agreement, I do not have to pay. In either case, I do not have to pay.

A practical solution to this paradox was once suggested by a lawyer. The judges should reject Protagoras' suit and rule that the student does not have to pay. Protagoras should then sue again, and this time the court would have to rule in his favour, since according to the agreement the student, having won his first case, would now be obliged to pay. But this practical solution does not resolve the logical paradox facing the judges at the first hearing.

(5) THE PARADOX OF OMNIPOTENCE

According to most religions, God is omnipotent. This means that there is nothing that God cannot do, if He chooses to do it. He can divide the Red Sea, cause plagues, and heal the sick. He could end disease or eliminate poverty if He chose to do so. (God's reasons for choosing not to do these things derive from His other attributes.) But could God create a stone that is too large for Him to lift? If you answer *yes*, then you have admitted that the stone is too large for Him to lift and, hence, that there is something God cannot do. If you answer *no*, then you have also admitted that there is something God cannot do. In either case, it follows that God is not omnipotent.

This paradox can, of course, easily be resolved by merely denying that God is omnipotent, but this is something that most religious believers refuse to do, for they regard omnipotence as part of God's essential nature. For these people the paradox has to be dealt with somehow. One solution is to claim that it is part of God's nature not to be bound by the laws of logic, in which case God can both create a stone that is too large for Him to lift and then lift it. After all, it is only the laws of logic that lead us to say that one cannot perform two contradictory acts. This solution, however, leaves us in a difficult situation, for if God is not bound by the laws of logic then, since our understanding of anything requires us to follow the laws of logic, there will be absolutely nothing about God that we can even begin to understand. Is there some better solution?

(6) ACHILLES AND THE TORTOISE

This is one of the paradoxes discovered by the ancient Greek mathematician Zeno.

A tortoise has challenged Achilles to a race, but Achilles, being supremely confident that he can win, allows the tortoise to get a head start. After a few minutes, Achilles sets out to overtake the tortoise. But in order to overtake the tortoise, he will first have to cover the distance the tortoise got to for his head start. Once he has done this, the tortoise will be some distance ahead again, and Achilles will then have to cover that distance. Once he has done this, he will then have to cover another distance that now separates them. And so on. He will always have to cover a distance that separates them before he will be able to pass the tortoise. But, since every time he has caught up to where the tortoise was, the tortoise has achieved another lead, he will never be able to pass the tortoise.

This is a clearly false conclusion. Where has the reasoning gone wrong?

(7) THE PRISONERS' DILEMMA

Al and Bob have been arrested and charged with several offences relating to extortion and fraud, and they are being held in prison without bail. When the prosecutor reviews the evidence, however, he realizes that although he has very strong evidence to support the less serious charges, the evidence to support the more serious charges is so weak that he is unlikely to get a conviction unless he can get at least one of them to testify against the other. He therefore approaches Al and Bob together and offers them a deal: if one of them agrees to plead guilty and testify against the other, he will be given a suspended sentence and the other one will be given a sentence of six years; but if both plead guilty, then, since neither will need to testify against the other, each will receive a sentence of four years; and if both plead not guilty, each will receive a sentence of two years. As soon as the deal has been offered, Al and Bob are taken to separate cells so that they cannot communicate with one another, and they are told that they have 24 hours to decide whether or not to accept the deal. There is no bond of loyalty or trust between Al and Bob; they each correctly assume that the other will, like himself, be motivated exclusively by self-interest. The dilemma arises when each attempts to decide, without the possibility of collaboration, whether it is in his self-interest to plead guilty. For example, Al's reasoning would be as follows:

> *I don't know if Bob will plead guilty or not. If Bob does plead guilty, then I'd get four years if I also plead guilty, and six years if I don't. So if he pleads guilty, I'd be better off pleading guilty too. If he doesn't plead guilty, then I'd get a suspended sentence if I plead guilty, and two years if I don't. So if he doesn't plead guilty, I'd be better off if I did plead guilty. So either way, whatever he decides to do, I'm better off pleading guilty.*

Of course, Bob's reasoning would lead him to the same conclusion, so both will get four years. This is a paradoxical result, for Al and Bob would each be better off if both pleaded not guilty, since in that case they would each receive two-year sentences. By seeking only their own self-interest they each receive four years, whereas a better outcome (i.e., one that serves their interests even better) eludes them. Why should self-interest lead them to a solution that is not in their self-interest?

2. Puzzles

These are just for fun, although they do require the use of various critical thinking skills for their solution. The solutions are given in Section 3 of this Appendix, but try them first before looking up the solutions.

(1) JEREMY AND HIS TWO GIRLFRIENDS

Jeremy is a rather weird fellow with two girlfriends whom he likes equally. Each Sunday afternoon he visits one of them, and in order to avoid having to decide which one to visit, he has hit upon a novel solution. Since both live on the same subway line, but in opposite directions from his subway station, he simply enters the station and takes the first train that comes in. If the northbound train arrives first, he visits Nancy, and if the southbound train arrives first, he visits Sarah. Since there is an equal number of northbound and southbound trains, Jeremy reasons that in the long run he will visit them with more or less equal frequency. But after a few months, he realizes that he is visiting Nancy four times more often than he is visiting Sarah. What is Jeremy's mistake?

(2) JONATHAN'S CLOCK

My uncle Jonathan used to teach logic at the University of Toronto. Like most logicians he was antisocial, and during the summer months he used to stay in a cabin in the woods a few miles north of Kapuskasing where he would write articles on logic. Once a week he would walk into Kapuskasing for supplies. He had no radio or television and no watch, but there was a large wind-up clock in the cabin. I asked him how he could set the clock when he first arrived in the spring, since he didn't know what the time was. He said, *Oh, I just wait until I make my first trip into Kapuskasing and figure it out from that.* I objected that he wouldn't know how long it takes to make the trip since he doesn't have a watch. *That's right*, he said, *but that's not a problem. And I don't have to lug that damn clock into Kapuskasing and back, either.* How did he figure out how to set the clock to the right time?

(3) ANNA'S ANTHROPOLOGICAL ADVENTURES, PART I

Anna was an anthropologist who was studying the inhabitants of an island in the South Pacific. The people were divided into two tribes: the Saints, who always told the truth, and the Sinners, who always lied. In all other respects, however, they were indistinguishable, a fact that would have created problems for Anna had she not taken a logic elective while at university. When she first arrived, for example, she was walking along a path through the jungle looking for the Saints' village when she came to a fork in the path. While she was wondering which way to go, she noticed a native nearby and, after a moment's reflection, put one question to the native. The answer allowed her to work out which fork to take. But since she didn't know whether the native was a Saint or a Sinner, she had to use her logical skills. What was the question?

(4) ANNA'S ANTHROPOLOGICAL ADVENTURES, PART II

When Anna had completed her anthropological research on the island of the Saints and Sinners and was about to leave, the two tribes decided to hold a celebration in her honour on the evening before her departure. There were many speeches, some of which paid tribute to her wisdom and kindness, and some of which castigated her for her stupidity and cruelty. Anna, obviously, hoped that it was the Saints who gave the former sort of speech and the Sinners who gave the latter sort. At the end, however, one chief stood up (Anna didn't know whether he was a Saint or a Sinner) and said, *Tomorrow you leave us to return to your homeland. All the members of my tribe earnestly hope that you will return to our island in the future for another visit.* He was immediately followed by the other chief, who said, *On behalf of all the members of my tribe, I say to you that you should go and never return to our island.* Anna quickly worked out whether they really wanted her to return. Did they, and how did Anna work it out?

(5) SAM AND THE SURGEON

Sam and his father had gone to a baseball game, and while driving home they were involved in a car accident. Sam's father was killed instantly, and Sam was critically injured. He was rushed to a nearby hospital where it was decided that he required immediate surgery. But when he was wheeled into the operating room, the surgeon took one look at him and said, *I can't operate on this patient. He is my son.* Sam was not adopted, and had no stepfathers or foster fathers, yet what the surgeon said was true. What is the explanation?

(6) THE WEEKLY POKER GAME

Allan, Bruce, Charles, David, and Edward are friends who meet every Tuesday evening to play poker. One of them is an accountant, one a barber, one a clergyman, one a doctor, and one an editor. The accountant's wife is Allan's sister, and Bruce's second wife is the doctor's sister. Bruce's first wife is now married to the barber. Edward and the doctor, who are brothers, are both secretly in love with the editor's wife. Charles is still unmarried. The only time they gave up their weekly poker game was when David tried to seduce the editor's wife and she complained to the doctor's wife, who told the editor. Things were a little tense for a few months, but after Allan and the doctor had a heart-to-heart talk with the editor, they agreed to start their weekly poker game again. What are the occupations of the five men?

(7) MIRANDA'S WILL

A few weeks after the death of Derwent's wealthy but eccentric aunt Miranda, the executor of her estate requested that Derwent come to his office. When Derwent arrived, the executor explained that Miranda's will directed him to give Derwent three sealed envelopes—one white, one brown, and one green—along with a letter from his late aunt. The letter said:

> *Dear Derwent,*
> *I've always thought that you were not too bright, but I am going to give you one last chance to prove me wrong. One of these three envelopes contains a*

cheque for $100,000, while the other two contain only blank pieces of paper. You get to pick one envelope, and if you fail to pick the one with the cheque, the money will be donated to the Home for Wayward Pets. On the front of each envelope is a clue, but at least one of these clues is false, and at least one of them is true. This information is sufficient to determine which envelope contains the cheque. If you cannot figure it out, it will prove that you are as stupid as I thought you were.

The clues on the envelopes were the following:

White: *The cheque is in this envelope.*
Brown: *The cheque is not in this envelope.*
Green: *The cheque is not in the brown envelope.*

Which envelope should Derwent pick?

3. Solutions to the Puzzles

(1) JEREMY AND HIS TWO GIRLFRIENDS

The crucial factor that Jeremy forgot to take into account is the spacing of the arrivals of the trains. Suppose that a northbound train arrives every ten minutes and a southbound train arrives every ten minutes. If they arrive alternately five minutes apart, then since Jeremy enters the station at random times, he will get northbound and southbound trains with more or less equal frequency. But if the southbound train always arrives two minutes after the northbound train and the next northbound train always arrives eight minutes later, then he will tend to get a northbound train 80 per cent of the time, and he will visit Nancy four times more often than he visits Sarah.

(2) JONATHAN'S CLOCK

Before Jonathan leaves to walk into Kapuskasing, he winds the clock and notes the time. He then walks at a steady pace until he reaches Kapuskasing and notes the correct time on the clock at the bank. When he finishes his business in Kapuskasing, he notes the time on the bank clock and then retraces his steps back to his cabin at the same steady pace. When he reaches the cabin, he then notes the time on his clock. He thus knows (a) how long his entire trip took (from the cabin clock) and (b) how long he spent in Kapuskasing (from the bank clock). He then subtracts (b) from (a) and divides the answer by two, and in this way knows how long it took him to walk back from Kapuskasing. He then adds this time to the time on the bank clock when he left Kapuskasing, and he can then set the cabin clock to the correct time. As long as he walked both ways at a steady pace, his cabin clock should not be more than a few minutes out.

(3) ANNA'S ANTHROPOLOGICAL ADVENTURES, PART I

The question Anna must ask is, *Which fork leads to your village?* If the native is a Saint, then he will point to the path that leads to the Saints' village, since he always tells the truth. If the native is a Sinner, then he will point to the path that leads to the Saints' village, since he always tells lies. In either case he will have to point to the path to the Saints' village. Had Anna been looking for the Sinners' village, she would still have asked the same question, but instead of taking the path the native pointed to, she would take the other path.

(4) ANNA'S ANTHROPOLOGICAL ADVENTURES, PART II

The first chief to speak must have been a Saint, because he said one thing (*Tomorrow you leave us to return to your homeland*) that you (and Anna) know to be true. So he wants Anna to return again. And, since the second chief had to be a Sinner, he must be lying and must therefore really want Anna to return. If you tried to approach this puzzle in the same way as number 3, you will have learned the importance of looking first for simple solutions and trying more complicated solutions only when the simple ones fail.

(5) SAM AND THE SURGEON

This is not really a logical puzzle, but it does illustrate the importance of paying careful attention to our assumptions. If we make assumptions that are false, it is easy to be led to accept arguments that are blatantly invalid. The assumption in this case is a sexist one, for the surgeon was Sam's mother. Until very recently most people had difficulty solving this puzzle; as sexist assumptions disappear, this "puzzle" should cease to be a puzzle.

(6) THE WEEKLY POKER GAME

Allan is the barber, Bruce is the editor, Charles is the clergyman, David is the doctor, and Edward is the accountant. The easiest way to solve puzzles of this sort is to draw up a matrix, or grid, which represents every possible combination of name and occupation.

	ALLAN	BRUCE	CHARLES	DAVID	EDWARD
Accountant					
Barber					
Clergyman					
Doctor					
Editor					

Each statement gives information that can be used to eliminate possibilities. For example, *The editor's wife is Allan's sister* means that the editor is not Allan, so an X can be put in the Editor/Allen box. It is also helpful to note the marital status of each person beside the name and occupation. Once you have eliminated four possibilities in a row (or column) you will know the occupation of one of the men, and you will also be able to eliminate the other possibilities in the appropriate column or row.

(7) MIRANDA'S WILL

The best strategy for solving this puzzle is to use the information given to eliminate possibilities. We know that at least one clue is true and at least one clue is false.

(1) So let us consider the possibility that the white clue is true. If the white clue is true, then the cheque must be in the white envelope, which means that the brown clue and the green clue are also true. But since at least one clue is false, this means that our assumption that the white clue is true must be false, that is, the white clue must be false. It also means that the cheque cannot be in the white envelope. This leaves three, but only three, other possibilities:

(2) the brown clue is true and the green clue is false.
(3) the green clue is true and the brown clue is false.
(4) both the brown and green clues are true.

(2) If the brown clue is true, then the cheque must be in the green envelope, and if the green clue is false, then the cheque must be in the brown envelope. But this is impossible, since the cheque cannot be in both envelopes, so this possibility is eliminated.

(3) If the green clue is true, then the cheque must be in the green envelope, and if the brown clue is false, then the cheque must be in the brown envelope. But this is impossible, since the cheque cannot be in both envelopes, so this possibility is also eliminated.

(4) If the brown clue is true, then the cheque must be in the green envelope, and if the green clue is true, then the cheque must be in the green envelope. And this is possible.

The last possibility is thus the only one that is consistent with the information given—that at least one clue is true and at least one is false. Therefore the cheque must be in the green envelope.

Appendix 2   Answers to Self-Tests

The self-tests are designed not to test your comprehension of concepts and principles directly, but to test the critical thinking skills that are based on them. Most of the questions are quite straightforward. If you get more than one or two wrong answers in any test, you should review the preceding material in order to discover why you are having difficulty. Usually it will be because you have misunderstood some concept or principle and not because of any difficulty in the questions themselves.

The fact that the questions are quite straightforward, however, creates a hazard that you should beware of. If you look up the answers without trying to work out an answer of your own, you will usually think that the answer given is quite obvious. This may lead you to conclude that you do not need to do the self-tests. Resist this conclusion, for it is deceptive. The answers given here should all be obvious *after* you read them, but this does not mean that they would have been obvious *before* you read them.

It may be that some of these answers are not as plausible as others that might have been given. I hope this is not the case, but my hopes are no guarantee that I have not missed some better answers. If you are occasionally convinced that your answer is better than the one you find here, you may well be correct. If your critical thinking skills have been well developed by this book, your judgement should not lead you astray.

Self-Test No. 1

I.

1. This is an argument.
PREMISE: *You promised your parents you would go home this weekend.*
CONCLUSION: *You should go home next weekend.*

2. This is probably not an argument. However, it is possible, although unlikely, that the speaker means that a reason for going home would be to have a good time. On this interpretation, the passage would be an argument.

3. This is an argument.
PREMISE 1: *Ted won the Intercollegiate 10,000 metres last year.*
PREMISE 2: *He has been training hard ever since.*
CONCLUSION: *He should win the Intercollegiate 10,000 metres this year.*

4. Most likely, this is an argument.
PREMISE 1: *The doctor told me that a second operation won't be necessary.*
PREMISE 2: *I will be able to go home this Friday.*
CONCLUSION: *I will be able to visit you next month.*

However, it is possible to interpret this passage in a way that it does not attempt to *prove* that the speaker can make the visit. Rather, it could well be an explanation of how it has become possible for the speaker to make the visit after all. Which interpretation is more plausible would depend on the context in which these things are said.

5. This is not an argument. It is merely a description of an event.

6. This is not an argument. It is merely a statement that is unsupported by any reasons or evidence.

7. This is an argument.
PREMISE: *The company's sales declined by 23 per cent in the last three months.*
CONCLUSION: *The company was justified in laying off 250 assembly line workers.*

8. This is not an argument. It is merely a claim.

9. This is not an argument. It is merely a description.

10. This is an argument, although the premises and conclusion need to be rewritten to make explicit what the argument implies.
PREMISE 1: *Last year Van and Patti both took a full course load while working 20 hours a week.*
PREMISE 2: *Last year Van and Patti both failed their semesters.*
PREMISE 3: *You are taking a full course load while working 20 hours a week.*
CONCLUSION: *You will fail your semester.*

11. This is an argument.
PREMISE 1: My purse with my cash, my watch and my necklace are missing from my hotel room.

PREMISE 2: The door of the room was locked while I was out.
PREMISE 3: There's no sign of forced entry into the room.
PREMISE 4: Only someone working in the hotel could have entered the room without breaking in.
CONCLUSION: It looks like someone on staff at the hotel stole these items.

12. This is not an argument. It is merely a narrative description of a journey.

II.

1. Sound. However, if you did not know that Winnipeg is in Manitoba, or that Manitoba is in Canada, you should have answered that it is merely a logically strong argument.

2. Merely logically strong. However, if you really thought that Beaver Creek is larger than Vancouver, you should have answered that it is a sound argument.

3. Logically strong, but if you know enough about the people named in the argument to believe that the two premises are true, then you should say that the argument is sound.

4. Merely logically strong. Even if you knew that the first premise is true, since you don't know who Katherine is, it would be incorrect to say that the argument is sound.

5. Sound, assuming that hockey is Canada's national sport. Otherwise it is a merely logically strong argument.

6. Sound. However, if you did not know that both premises are true, you should have answered that it is merely a logically strong argument.

7. Merely logically strong. Since the context indicates that the word *cat* is being used in a very broad sense, the first premise is obviously false.

8. Sound. It is not necessary to know who the Prime Minister is in order to know that he or she is a human being.

9. Merely logically strong. First, while the second premise may be true of the New York Yankees in North American major league baseball, it may well be that there is an amateur team somewhere or a professional team outside North America that has won more games. In addition, it is not true that everybody loves a winner: some people detest winners.

10. Sound. However, if you did not interpret *I* as referring to yourself, the correct answer would be that it is merely a logically strong argument.

11. Merely logically strong. All the ships named in this passage are fictional, and it's not possible to compare how fast or slow they are in relation to each other.

12. Merely logically strong. Not all dogs are excellent companions, and this claim seems to be implicit in the first premise.

Self-Test No. 2

1. Persuasive.

2. Descriptive.

3. Persuasive.

4. Emotive.

5. Descriptive.

6. Recreational.

7. Directive.

8. Performative.

9. Directive. Note, however, that although it appears to be addressed to all pedestrians, it is really a directive only for those pedestrians who want to cross the street.

10. Emotive and evocative. It is likely that the author has both purposes in mind.

11. Directive.

12. Performative.

Self-Test No. 3

1. Too narrow, because the defining phrase (*the supreme legislative body of Canada*) applies only to the Parliament of Canada, and excludes the parliaments of other countries.

2. Too broad, because the defining phrase (*art form that uses words to communicate ideas and images*) includes other art forms that use words to communicate ideas and images, such as novels and plays.

3. Too broad, because the defining phrase (*implement designed to remove snow*) includes other implements designed to remove snow, such as snow shovels and snow blowers. It is also circular, which would make the definition useless for anyone who does not know what snow is.

4. Circular.

5. Obscure. This definition would only be informative to someone who already has extensive knowledge of music theory.

6. Too broad, since the defining phrase includes several other devices that are used to fasten pages together, such as paper clips and binders. It is also too narrow, since the defining phrase excludes staplers that are designed for use in construction and for other industrial uses.

7. Too narrow, because the defining phrase excludes male nurses. It is also too broad, because it includes other health care professionals, such as doctors and chiropractors.

8. Too broad, since the defining phrase includes other kinds of one-storey buildings such as garages and shops.

9. Too broad, since the defining phrase also refers to other international organizations, such as the European Community, the Olympics, NATO, and the International Civil Aviation Organization.

10. Too broad, since the defining phrase also includes such competitive activities as operating a business, playing chess, and competing in music festivals, none of which are sports. It is also too narrow, since the defining phrase excludes such individual sports as sport fishing, surf boarding, and sky diving, which are not normally competitive.

Self-Test No. 4

1. There is a referential ambiguity here since it is unclear whether the term *his sisters* is being used collectively or distributively. If it is used distributively, the sentence means that Billy gave at least two boxes of candy, one to each sister. If it is being used collectively, the sentence means that Billy gave his sisters one box of candy to be shared between them.

2. Because *chicken* can be used metaphorically to characterize a cowardly person or literally to refer to a kind of bird, this sentence is referentially ambiguous.

3. There is a grammatical ambiguity in this sentence. Literally, the sentence means that Melissa has nothing else in the world besides her one dress. If the location of the word only is changed to make the sentence read *Melissa has only one dress*, it means that although she may have many possessions, she has only one dress. This is the more likely meaning.

4. The term *General* is referentially ambiguous. It could refer to a local hospital, in which case the sentence means that the nurses won their strike with the hospital. Or it could refer to a specific military officer, in which case the sentence means that the officer was beaten by the nurses in some kind of contest or struggle. In a town that has a local hospital that is routinely called *The General*, however, it will usually be clear which interpretation is best.

5. If the term *Conversational German* is being merely mentioned, then it refers to a textbook or a course, and the sentence means that it is a difficult book or course. If the term is being used, then the sentence means that it is difficult to learn how to speak conversational German.

6. The term *discipline* is referentially ambiguous. It could refer simply to corporal punishment, which is how some people use the term. But it could refer to a set of rules imposed by adults that children are expected to follow. It could also refer to self-discipline, that is, to a set of rules that children learn to develop for themselves. The meaning of the sentence is quite different depending upon which reference we choose.

7. Literally, the speaker has promised never to speak to the person again if he or she thinks it over and still decides to drop out of school. In most contexts, the principle of charity would require us to interpret the speaker as meaning ... *I won't say another word to you about dropping out of school.*

8. The term *instructors* is referentially ambiguous. If it is being used collectively, the sentence means that the instructors, as a group, are free to choose whatever

text they can all agree on. If the term is being used distributively, the sentence means that each instructor is free to choose whatever text he or she wishes.

9. The sentence is grammatically ambiguous. If *illegally* modifies *tested* the sentence means that the stores were illegally tested. If *illegally* modifies *sell* it means that the stores were illegally selling cigarettes.

10. This sentence is grammatically ambiguous. If *with a bright red hood* modifies *limousine* the sentence means that the limousine has a bright red hood. But if *with a bright red hood* completes *she arrived* the sentence means that she was wearing a bright red hood.

11. This sentence is grammatically ambiguous. Literally, it says that the noise the superintendent complained about was coming from *his own pyjamas*. However, the principle of charity encourages us to interpret the speaker as saying that the superintendent was wearing his pyjamas when he was complaining about noise coming from *the apartment*. The comic effect of the sentence depends on seeing the literal meaning and recognizing that the speaker intends us to interpret it as the principle of charity suggests.

12. This sentence is referentially ambiguous. The speaker could be asking about *where* on the person's body they were struck, or the speaker could be asking about *where* the person was at the time they were struck.

Self-Test No. 5

1. Analytic. If you know what a full deck of cards is, you know that it must have 52 cards. (Of course, a few card games require players to use the jokers, but this is a special case that would be cleared up by the speakers sorting out what is meant by *full deck*, not by counting cards.)

2. Analytic. Since a centimetre is defined as one-hundredth of a metre and a millimetre is defined as one-thousandth of a metre, a centimetre must, by definition, be longer than a millimetre.

3. Synthetic. There is nothing about the meanings of the words in this sentence that guarantees its truth or falsity.

4. Synthetic. The truth or falsity of this sentence can only be determined by checking a reference book on sports records. The meaning of the sentence leaves its truth or falsity an open question.

5. Synthetic. As far as we know, this is a true statement. But its truth is something we have learned and is not determined by the meaning of the sentence.

6. Contradictory. The first clause in the sentence is contradicted by the last clause.

7. Synthetic. Assuming that the speaker correctly understands the meanings of the words in this sentence, he or she could only be proven wrong by sending him or her to the southern hemisphere with a compass.

8. Synthetic. Observations would be needed to determine the truth of this statement.

9. Synthetic, on both the literal and metaphorical interpretation. In both cases, the truth of the sentence could only be determined by investigating the facts.

10. On a literal interpretation this is an analytic statement. However, it would normally be used to mean something like *You should not adopt romantic or highly speculative interpretations of ordinary things*, which is synthetic.

11. On the usual interpretation of this cliché, it is analytic. According to the analytic interpretation, *fit* is understood to mean that the peg sits snugly into the hole.

12. Contradictory. Usually, *excellent condition* means that a bicycle does not have any problems and that it does not require the kind of extensive repair work described in the second part of the sentence. (Of course, one might charitably read this sentence to mean that *after* all the repairs are completed, the bike *will be* in excellent condition, but in the present tense it is contradictory.)

Self-Test No. 6

1. The evaluative meaning is negative. Descriptively, *vicious competition* means that the usual aspects of competitiveness (such as wanting to be better than others, complaining when others do well, trying to place others at a disadvantage) are carried to extreme lengths. A good descriptive synonym would be *fierce*.

2. The evaluative meaning is negative. Descriptively, a *compulsively tidy person* is unavoidably uncomfortable with even minor untidiness, and is driven by an irresistible inner force to tidy up. A good descriptive synonym would be *extremely*.

3. The evaluative meaning is positive. Descriptively, *responsible student* means that Mark gets his homework done, submits his assignments on time, pays

attention in class, follows the school rules, and so on. Perhaps the best descriptive equivalent phrase would be hard working and thorough.

4. The evaluative meaning is negative, since a decline in moral standards means that they have changed by becoming more permissive. The descriptive meaning of *declined* in this context is that moral standards have been enforced less strictly. A good descriptive synonym is *relaxed*.

5. The evaluative meaning is negative. Descriptively, *greed* refers to a desire for money and material goods. A good descriptive equivalent would be *a substantial desire for money and material goods*.

6. The evaluative meaning is negative, because it suggests that the budget reduction has been ruthless or excessive. Descriptively, *slashed* means reduced, and *reduced substantially* is the best descriptive synonym.

7. The evaluative meaning is negative. *Very, extremely*, and *highly* all capture the descriptive meaning of *excessively* and would be good descriptive synonyms.

8. The evaluative meaning is negative. Descriptively, *suckered* means being persuaded to do something by underhanded or dishonest means. The best descriptive synonym is *persuaded*.

9. The evaluative meaning is positive since *mature* suggests the opposite of inexperienced. Descriptively, *mature years* means that he was middle-aged or older. *Old age* would be the best descriptive synonym.

10. The evaluative meaning is negative, since referring to an adult woman as a *girl* denigrates her. A better descriptive synonym is *secretary*.

Self-Test No. 7

1. A sufficient condition, since this is only one of several ways to bring down a fever. If interpreted as a necessary condition, it would mean that this is the only way of bringing down a fever, which is false.

2. The two conditions stated are jointly sufficient conditions for being required to withdraw from the university. If interpreted as a necessary condition for being required to withdraw, the statement would mean that this is the only way of being required to withdraw, which is false since one can be required to withdraw for other reasons, such as failing too many courses.

3. Almost always a necessary condition, since while no applicants will be admitted unless they meet the stated conditions, not every student who meets these conditions can expect to be admitted. If the sentence is interpreted as stating a sufficient condition it means that every student who meets these conditions will be admitted, which is a highly implausible interpretation (although not impossible).

4. Probably a necessary condition, since working hard throughout the term is not the only thing most students have to do to get an A average. If interpreted as a sufficient condition, it means that working hard will always produce an A average. This is an unlikely interpretation, since even students who work hard throughout the whole term would probably not get an A if they failed to hand in their term assignments.

5. A sufficient condition, since there are normally other defects that may lead to an essay's being returned ungraded, for example, if it is illegible or submitted late.

6. This statement gives both the necessary and sufficient conditions for winning the prize. If interpreted merely as a necessary condition, it would mean that, although every winner would have the highest average, some years the student with the highest average might not be awarded the prize. If interpreted merely as a sufficient condition, it would mean that, although each year the student with the highest average would receive the prize, another student who failed to achieve the highest average might also receive the prize, perhaps with the money divided between them.

7. A necessary condition. If interpreted as a sufficient condition, it would mean that every member of Parliament would become prime minister.

8. A necessary condition, since presumably if interest rates do not come down, the confidence of the business community will not be restored. It might also be a sufficient condition, if reducing interest rates is the only thing necessary to restore confidence in the economy, but this would only make sense if it is assumed that all the other factors necessary to restore confidence (such as stable international markets, acceptable exchange rates, reasonable taxes) are already present and are unlikely to change.

9. A necessary condition, since good physical coordination is necessary for becoming a good skier. But it is not a sufficient condition, or else anyone with good physical coordination who had never skied before would already be a good skier, which is absurd.

10. A necessary condition. If it were a sufficient condition, it would mean that everyone with a PhD would become a university professor, which is absurd.

11. Two necessary conditions, which are probably jointly sufficient. Both completing the homework and having a bath are necessary conditions for Sarah being allowed to watch television. Presumably, permission is automatically granted once these conditions are satisfied.

12. The condition is both necessary and sufficient. The *only if* means that it is a necessary condition, and the *if* means that it is also a sufficient condition.

Self-Test No. 8

1. Missing premise: *My car (van, truck, or motorcycle) doesn't have enough gas to drive you home.*

2. Missing premise: *Your car is flooded.*

3. Missing conclusion: *You should attend (or make an effort to attend) church at Easter.*

4. Missing premise: *Jennifer lives in* Chicago, *and her sister does not.*

5. Missing premise: *Students who do not attend class regularly are likely to do poorly in the course.*

6. Missing conclusion: *Todd is a teenage rebel.*

7. Missing premise: *It won't be possible to repair my hearing aid.*

8. Missing premise: *School boards have a responsibility to achieve a low drop-out rate.*

9. Missing premise: *Students who work hard on an assignment deserve a high grade.*

10. Missing premise: *Animals deserve the same kind of legal protection as humans enjoy.*

Self-Test No. 9

1. This is an explanation. The speaker is offering an explanation for his or her stage fright.

2. This is not an argument. It is a description of an event, but it includes an explanation of David's behaviour (i.e., that David was upset at what he thought was his fault and felt responsible for Michael).

3. This is an argument. It states a conclusion (*We'd better watch Mary closely for the next 24 hours*) and gives reasons to support it.

4. This is merely a general explanation of the form *X may be caused by a, b, or c*.

5. This is an explanation of why local taxes increase. By adding the comment *That is how the system works*, the speaker makes it clear that he or she is not defending (or arguing for) the system.

6. This is a report of an argument. In a context where it was clear that the speaker approved of the Supreme Court's reasoning, it could legitimately be regarded as an argument.

7. This is an argument. The conclusion is *Never turn off your computer without following the exit procedure for your software program*. The reason given in support of this conclusion consists of an explanation of what the consequences will be if the exit procedure is not followed.

8. This is probably best interpreted as an argument with a missing conclusion: *You ought to refund the entire purchase price*. The advice received from the speaker's lawyer is the reason the speaker gives for this conclusion.

9. This is an argument. It includes an explanation of why the jury system allegedly works to the advantage of criminals, but this explanation is merely a premise used to support the conclusion that the jury system should be abolished.

10. This is probably best interpreted as an explanation. In most contexts it would likely be an explanation of why Americans fail to understand how Canadian political parties operate.

Self-Test No. 10

1. [Anyone who has brains and ambition will go far in this world.](P1) [Carla has certainly got plenty of both.](P2) <u>So she will go far</u>.

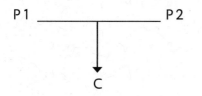

2. [I have never had any problems with the last four Fords I've bought,](P1) <u>so I don't think I'll have any problems this time</u>. Note that there is a missing premise in this argument: [A company that has made good products in the past is likely to continue to make good products.](MP2)

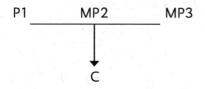

3. <u>The Expos should win the National League pennant this year</u>. [They have solid depth in their pitching staff,](P1) [their hitting has been consistently good this year,](P2) [their coaching is excellent](P3), and [there is a good team spirit.](P4)

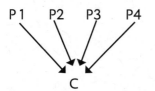

4. [A recent public opinion poll showed that more than two-thirds of Canadians believe that most politicians are dishonest.](P1) Clearly, <u>there is a crisis of confidence in Canadian politics</u>. There is a missing premise: [Widespread belief that most politicians are dishonest constitutes a crisis of confidence.](MP2)

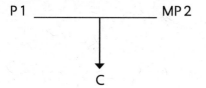

5. <u>In the last 30 years there has been a tremendous increase in the university participation rate (i.e., the percentage of population in the 18- to 22-year-old age group that attends university).</u> [In 1960, the participation rate in Canada was only 5 per cent.](P1) But [by 1990 the participation rate was over 15 per cent.](P2)

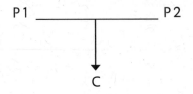

6. [Laura gets pretty good grades,](P1) [she is the best gymnast in the school,](P2) [she has a lot of friends,](P3) and [she organized the campaign last year which forced the school to start a recycling program.](P4) I think <u>she will probably win the election for president of the Students' Council.</u>

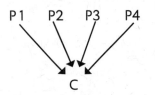

7. [If he tells his teacher he cheated, he will be punished by the principal.](P1) But [if he doesn't tell his teacher he cheated, he will be punished by his parents.](P2) Either way <u>he is going to be punished.</u>

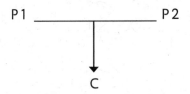

8. Since [angle CAB is 60 degrees,](P1) and [angle ACB is 40 degrees,](P2) then angle <u>ABC must be 80 degrees.</u> There are two missing premises in this argument: [Figure ABC is a triangle](MP3) and [The angles of a triangle always add up to 180 degrees.](MP4)

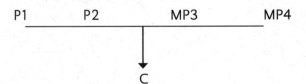

9. <u>Any reporter who says that good reporters never slant their stories but simply report the objective facts must be either stupid or dishonest</u>, since [it is obvious that one cannot write anything without an element of interpretation creeping in.](P1) There is a missing premise: [Someone who denies something that is obvious is either stupid or dishonest.](MP2)

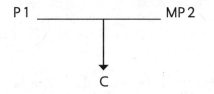

10. [That reporter is obviously not stupid.](P1) So <u>he must be dishonest</u>. There are two missing premises: [Any reporter who says that good reporters never slant their stories but simply report the objective facts must be either stupid or dishonest](MP2) and [That reporter said that good reporters never slant their stories but simply report the objective facts.](MP3)

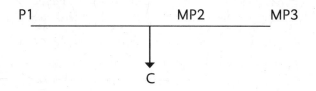

Self-Test No. 11

1. Empirical. Checking the facts about the most recent New Brunswick election will determine whether the statement is true.

2. Empirical. Checking the facts about my children's hopes regarding a white Christmas will determine whether the statement is true.

3. Non-empirical. No amount of checking empirical facts—either about St. Paul's Cathedral or about people's beliefs about it—will determine the truth or falsity of this statement. It is an evaluation.

4. Empirical. The empirical facts that will determine whether this statement is true or false are not easy to obtain, although scientists claim that there is clear and mounting evidence that it is true. But nothing other than empirical evidence could determine the truth or falsity of this claim.

5. Non-empirical. This is an analytic statement that states one of the essential features of a triangle. If you thought you could determine its truth value by measuring the angles of a triangle with a protractor, you would be treating

this as an empirical statement. But as any mathematics teacher would tell you, doing this would not get you any marks on a mathematics examination.

6. Empirical. This statement should be interpreted as meaning something like *It's certain that the Toronto Maple Leafs will not win the Stanley Cup this year*, and whether this prediction is true will be determined by what happens at the end of the season. Even if it is taken literally, however, it would still be an empirical statement whose truth would be determined by whether the speaker eats his or her hat if the team wins the Stanley Cup.

7. Empirical. This is a hypothetical statement. Some evidence right now can be obtained through complex analysis of a wide range of economic and political information; later on, if the federal government did indeed eliminate the debt, there would be more direct evidence.

8. Empirical. Despite the fact that the award is given to the best student in the school, this statement does not endorse the fact that Paula received the award. It is a simple statement of an empirical fact. In some contexts—for example, if cited as evidence that Paula is an excellent student—it could be interpreted as an evaluation.

9. Non-empirical. Although the statement includes the empirical claim that suicide rates are highest around Christmas, the primary purpose of the statement is most likely to make an evaluation of this fact.

10. Empirical. This is a claim about the effects of the policy of banning the sale of ivory. Its truth would be determined by an examination of the facts regarding the ivory market and the decline in the illegal killing of elephants in Africa.

11. Non-empirical. Because *3 out of 4 people* is arithmetically equivalent to *75% of the population* the sentence makes no empirical claim about facts.

12. Empirical. Although evaluative claims are not in themselves empirical, a report of an evaluative claim is a description of empirical fact.

13. Empirical, though not very informative. If the possibilities listed were the only logical possibilities there are—for example, if what was said was that Osama was either in Afghanistan or somewhere else or dead—then this would have been a non-empirical truth. But there are other (unlikely!) possibilities other than those listed—that he is in an international territory such as Antarctica or in international waters or in outer space.

Self-Test No. 12

1. The conclusion of the argument is:
If we want economic prosperity for Canada, we ought to be looking for wars to get involved in.
The weakness in the argument is that the premise *Every nation that has fought a major war in this century emerged from the war economically stronger than it was before* is false. Many nations, such as Britain, the USSR, Vietnam, Japan, and Iran, among others, have suffered great economic losses as a result of wars they have been involved in. This is, or should be, a matter of common knowledge.

2. The conclusion of the argument is:
The government has no right to force me and others who think the way I do to pay the GST.
The argument commits the fallacy of equivocation. The word *governed* is used collectively in the first premise but distributively in the second premise.

3. The conclusion of the argument is:
There is nothing I can do about the fact that the outboard motor I bought last year turned out to be a real lemon.
The weakness of the argument is that it relies upon a false dichotomy in the premises. The speaker assumes that there are only two possibilities open to him or her: (1) sue the company and (2) do nothing. But there are other things that could be done: for example, (3) write to the president of the company, asking for compensation, or (4) make a public stink by writing letters to the press or mounting a sign on the boat that says *Evinrudes are Lemons.*

4. The conclusion of the argument is:
Only in democracies does the human spirit flourish.
The weakness in the argument is that it begs the question. Does the human spirit flourish only in democratic societies? Yes, says the author, because undemocratic societies prevent the human spirit from flourishing. The "evidence" is just another way of stating the conclusion.

5. The conclusion of the argument is:
He should be found not guilty.
This argument commits the fallacy of inconsistency. The lawyer cannot have it both ways: if either one of the two "compelling" reasons is true, then the other must be false. They cannot consistently be asserted together.

6. The conclusion of the argument is:
People are much more interested in local issues than they are in provincial and national political issues.

The weakness in the argument is that in recent years the premise is false in Canada.

7. The conclusion of the argument is:
Scientists should accept that biblical miracles actually occurred.
The premises of the argument, however, use the word *miracle* in a quite different sense from the way the author uses it in the conclusion. The argument therefore commits the fallacy of equivocation.

8. The conclusion of the argument is:
We should adopt a non-aligned foreign policy.
The author, however, is presupposing that the two alternatives presented are the only possibilities. This is unacceptable, since it ignores the possibility of a foreign policy that does not rely upon the threat of nuclear annihilation but rejects a non-aligned foreign policy. The argument commits the fallacy of false dichotomy.

9. The conclusion of the argument is:
Professor Smith's new course will be a great course.
The weakness in the argument is that it fails to recognize the difference between being a member of a team that developed and taught a great course and developing and teaching a course by oneself. What is true of the three professors as a team may not be true of them individually. Thus, the argument relies upon a fallacy of equivocation between the collective and distributive senses of the phrase *excellent teachers*.

10. The conclusion of the argument is:
I am almost halfway through this book.
The premise *There are 13 chapters in this book* is false, as you could discover by checking the Table of Contents. Even though the conclusion is true, and the premise is relevant, the argument is weak.

Self-Test No. 13

1. There is no direct reason to think that the fact that someone's father has been convicted for fraud means that the person is completely untrustworthy. The premise is thus irrelevant. This is similar to an ad hominem, although it is the personal qualities of the speaker's father that are being attacked rather than those of the speaker. Alternatively, we could read *Like father like son* as a second premise. This might make the first premise relevant, but it's often not true.

2. Unless one is prepared to argue that the popularity of a television show is a good indicator of the quality of the show, this argument commits an irrelevant appeal to popularity.

3. This is a legitimate appeal to authority, at least if presented by someone who knows who Gödel is and knows he meets the criteria for a reliable authority. If you did not know that Gödel meets these criteria, you should refuse to accept the appeal until you have reason to believe that the criteria are satisfied.

4. This argument commits the straw man fallacy. Evolutionary theory does not claim that humans are just monkeys with less hair or that our ancestors were apes.

5. This argument commits the ad hominem fallacy. It attacks the views of feminists on the ground that feminists are selfish. It also commits the straw man fallacy, since feminists are characterized in a false way, that is, as a group that is seeking all the good jobs for women.

6. This argument appeals to *the wisdom of history* as the reason for condemning the view that mothers and fathers can be equal partners as head of the family unit. History is thus treated as a kind of authority on how the family should be organized. This is clearly an irrelevant appeal.

7. This is an example of the kind of irrelevant things we say when we are pressed to defend an irrational position. Obviously, the fact that Janine hates flying has nothing to do with whether or not the speaker is being silly.

8. This argument probably commits the straw man fallacy, since it is unlikely that the son actually believes, as his father claims he does, that everybody should be free to do whatever they want in life. Perhaps the son actually said what his father attributes to him, but in this case the father has violated the principle of charity, since the son probably meant something much more reasonable, namely, that everybody should be free to seek whatever career they want. The father's attempted rebuttal, of course, is relevant only against the unreasonable interpretation of the son's beliefs.

9. This argument commits the tu quoque fallacy, since it argues that the fact that anglophones treated francophones unfairly in the past is a good reason for the francophones to treat anglophones unfairly in the present. The only way to avoid the tu quoque charge would be to argue that revenge of this sort is morally justified.

10. This argument is a blatant ad hominem. There is not even a pretence that the schoolteacher's charges against the principal have been investigated and found to be invalid on the basis of relevant evidence.

11. This argument is both ad hominem and question begging. It is ad hominem because the cabinet minister implies that the opposition member's objection to the new program is the result of her own stubbornness rather than the government's management of the program. At the same time, it is question begging because it fails to say anything about the inefficiencies that are alleged to be responsible for the unanticipated costs.

12. This argument is a straw man. The speaker implies that infrastructure development was promoted for purposes other than stimulating the economy and improving the standard of living for the poor. But if this development was not pursued as a means to improve international trade, reduce taxes or reduce the national debt, then these are irrelevant complaints.

Self-Test No. 14

1. This is a post hoc fallacy, since the only evidence offered to show that the nuclear power plant caused the miscarriage is that the miscarriage occurred after the plant was built. There may be a causal connection, but this argument does nothing to establish it.

2. This argument probably commits the fallacy of common cause. Those who have not worked very hard during the term (a) tend to cram immediately before examinations and (b) tend to get lower marks than the average. It is more likely that both (a) and (b) are caused by not working hard during the term than that (a) causes (b).

3. This is a slippery slope fallacy. The intermediate steps in the chain of predictions are only sketched, but even if they were spelled out in detail, the final predicted outcome (complete loss of sovereignty) would probably not be well supported. Without the intermediate steps being explicitly stated, the premises are clearly inadequate.

4. There are two post hoc fallacies in this argument. (1) The stomach cramps started shortly after the fluoridation program was introduced; therefore, the fluoridation caused the cramps. (2) The stomach cramps disappeared shortly after the speaker started drinking bottled water; therefore, the bottled water cured the cramps.

5. Perhaps there is no causal relationship whatever between high school drop-out rates and the incidence of juvenile delinquency. However, there might be a common cause of the two phenomena: both might be caused by underlying social conditions. This is at least a plausible assertion. But if there is a common cause, it would not support the suggestion that increasing the drop-out rate will reduce juvenile delinquency.

6. This is a fallacious appeal to authority. The pope's scholarly credentials and undeniable concern for the welfare of the Catholic church are not adequate grounds for accepting his judgement about what *is* best for the church. His scholarly expertise on the history and traditions of the church cannot support any conclusion about admitting women into the priesthood.

7. The evidence cited by the politician is clearly inadequate to support the conclusion of the argument. There could be a number of plausible explanations for the fact that the politician has received no phone calls supporting the proposal: he or she may have a reputation for being unsympathetic to the poor; there may have been no publicity given to the proposal, so the voters may not know about it; and so on. The appeal to the absence of contrary evidence is illegitimate in this case.

8. To explain the weakness in this argument it needs to be reconstructed, for it contains a sub-argument. The reconstruction is:
P1. *All the public opinion polls for the last year have shown that the government has a lower approval rating than either of the two opposition parties.*
C1/P2. *The Premier knows that the government is not going to be re-elected.*
C2. *The Premier will postpone calling an election until the last possible moment.*
C1/P2 is not adequately supported by P1, since despite the polls it is possible that the Premier has not given up all hope of winning the election and may believe that it is possible to increase the government's approval rating before the election must be called. The strength of the sub-argument thus depends upon how much time is available before an election is required. The more time available to the Premier, the weaker the first argument is. It would have been better if, instead of C1/P2, the speaker had argued that the Premier is worried that the government may not be re-elected. C2, on the other hand, is better supported. However, it is still not a strong argument, since if the polls show an increase in the government's approval rating before the last possible moment, the Premier might call a snap election.

9. The weakness of this argument derives from the fact that most people regard the right to hold demonstrations on public property as an important democratic right, one not to be restricted unless there is a very strong reason for doing so. Clearly, the author does not agree with this view, since he or she wants demonstrations banned simply because they are an inconvenience to some people. But the argument violates the criterion of adequacy because it fails to address the reasons most people have for tolerating the inconvenience of public demonstrations.

10. This argument probably commits the slippery slope fallacy. The policy of releasing very poor countries from their debts is not refuted directly; rather, it is said that this policy entails other policies that are clearly problematic. Much of

the problem in this argument can be traced to vagueness about who the original policy applies to—that is, *some of the poorest developing nations*. What counts as being among the poorest developing nations is not specified, and this vagueness becomes more problematic because only *some* of these nations are being considered (but no criteria are provided to tell us which ones).

11. This is a fallacious appeal to authority. While the medical efficacy of marijuana is something about which a physician might have some expertise, his expertise does not include the motivation behind people who support decriminalizing it for medical purposes. Moreover, even if the doctor confined his opinions to medical matters, the therapeutic value of marijuana is not an area of medicine about which there is consensus among experts.

12. This passage commits the slippery slope fallacy. It makes *no* claim about the bill in question. Instead, it suggests without argument that, if passed, the bill will lead to inevitable, unacceptable consequences.

Self-Test No. 15

In some of the passages found in this self-test, it is possible to analyze the English sentences in more detail to uncover implied premises and sub-arguments, and in a symbolic logic course these steps would be important. However, for these exercises it is sufficient to identify the overall structure of the arguments.

1. p = You buy a new coat.
   q = You won't be able to buy your textbooks for next term.
   r = Your grades will suffer.
   If p then q.
   If q then r.
   Therefore, if p then r.
   This is a chain argument and, thus, is a valid argument.

2. p = Ellen violated the confidentiality of the committee.
   q = Ellen would have harmed herself more than anyone else.
   If p then q.
   Not-q.
   Therefore, not-p.
   This is a denial of the consequent and, thus, is a valid argument.

3. p = I will have surgery.
   q = I will have a long program of physiotherapy.
   Either p or q.
   Not-p.
   Therefore, q.
   This is a disjunctive syllogism and, thus, is a valid argument.

4. p = It will rain during the game.
    q = The team will lose.
    If p then q.
    Not-p.
    Therefore, not-q.
    This is a denial of the antecedent and, thus, is fallacious.

5. p = The Conservatives won more than 50 per cent of the votes in the
    1989 election.
    q = The Conservatives have a mandate to implement the free trade
    agreement.
    If p then q.
    Not-p.
    Therefore, not-q.
    This is a denial of the antecedent and, thus, is fallacious.

6. p = Chris wins the election.
    q = Chris is well-known to a lot of students.
    If p then q.
    Not-q.
    Therefore, not-p.
    This is a denial of the consequent and, thus, is a valid argument.

7. p = Chris is well-known to a lot of students.
    q = Chris wins the election.
    If p then q.
    Not-p.
    Therefore, not-q.
    This is a denial of the antecedent and, thus, is fallacious.
    Had we let p and q stand for the same statements as in question 6, the
    form of the argument would still be the same:
    If q then p.
    Not-q.
    Therefore, not-p.

8. p = Left-wing radicals are really committed to freedom of speech.
    q = Left-wing radicals would defend freedom of speech whenever and
    wherever it comes under attack.
    If p then q.
    Not-q.
    Therefore, not-p.
    This is a denial of the consequent and, thus, is a valid argument.

9. p = This is question 5.
    q = I am losing my mind.
    If p then q.
    Not-p.
    Therefore, not-q.
    This is a denial of the antecedent and, thus, is fallacious.

10. p = I have not lost my mind.
    q = This is question 10.
    If p then q.
    q.
    Therefore, p.
    This is an affirmation of the consequent and, thus, is fallacious. If we let
    p stand for I have lost my mind, then we have the following form:
    If not-p then q.
    q.
    Therefore, not-p.
    This is still an affirmation of the consequent. By letting p stand for the
    negative statement, it is easier to identify the form, but there is nothing
    wrong with using not-p instead of p as long as we do so consistently.

Self-Test No. 16

1. This is an inductive generalization. There is no information on the number of
questionnaires returned, so we cannot tell whether the sample is large enough.
But the sample is not a representative one, for the responses will have come
only from those who pay their municipal taxes directly, and this excludes all
tenants and almost all young people. The argument is therefore quite weak.
There is another possible weakness in the argument. Taxpayers were asked
whether they were satisfied with the recreational facilities provided by the city
at the same time as they were presented with their tax bills. It is likely that
some people who were in fact not satisfied with the current facilities would
state that they were satisfied because they were unwilling to pay higher taxes
for new facilities. This would also bias the sample and further weaken the
argument.

2. This is an analogical argument by relations. The subject case is a prospective
policy of paid leave for new fathers in Canada. The analogue case is an actual
policy of paid leave in Sweden. The relevance of the analogy depends on further details that are not included in the argument, which weakens the strength
of the argument. Most importantly, we would want to know how similar the
two policies themselves are. If the prospective Canadian policy is more gener-
ous than the present Swedish policy, then we would expect more than 12 per
cent of Canadian fathers to take paid leave, and it will cost more per father

to finance the leave. Finally, we would want to know how similar Canada and Sweden are socially. If social values are markedly different, then the program will not be received by Canadians in the same way it was received in Sweden. So while the argument is not very strong as it is stated, it is possible that it could be improved with more information.

3. This is an inductive generalization. The sample is certainly large enough, but is clearly not representative, for several reasons. (a) Canadian tourists from other provinces are under-represented, since unless they were driving home through the United States they would not be included. (b) Overseas tourists are under-represented, since most of them travel by air. (c) American non-tourists such as business people, workers, and so on are included since they were given questionnaires and may have responded even though they were not tourists. The argument is therefore weak.

4. This is a statistical syllogism. It is a weak argument because some obviously relevant information is ignored: the roommate is taking a non-specialized program, it is in arts rather than in science or engineering, and he has only a D average. All these factors make it likely that his chances of finding a job within three months of graduation are somewhat less than 90 per cent.

5. This is an analogical argument by relations. The subject case is people who oppose aid to Third World countries, and the analogue case is people who would refuse to throw a life preserver to a drowning person. This argument ignores some potentially important dissimilarities between the two cases. One can readily see how to cast a preserver to someone in the water directly in front of them, whereas few people know what programs might provide effective forms of aid. Many people oppose aid because they have legitimate concerns about the organizations that provide aid. Many other people oppose aid because they believe trade programs would be more effective. As well, this argument may commit the ad hominem fallacy, attacking the people who oppose aid rather than attempting to refute the arguments against aid.

6. This is an inductive generalization. If introductory philosophy is an elective and not a required course, it is possible that the sample may be unrepresentative, since the kind of students who choose introductory philosophy as an elective course may be more likely to expect a university education to improve their communication skills than those who would avoid philosophy as an elective. The sample in this case is self-selected, so it is difficult to know whether it might be unrepresentative.

7. This is an analogical argument by relations. The subject case is gun control legislation and the analogue case is alcohol prohibition in the United States between World War I and 1933. This is a weak analogy and, therefore, a weak argument. First, gun control legislation, unlike the prohibition of alcohol, is

not aimed at eliminating guns from society. Second, gun legislation is intended to reduce the incidence of something that is already illegal in itself, namely, murder, whereas drunkenness is not in itself illegal (even if public drunkenness, drinking under age, and drinking and driving are).

8. This is a statistical syllogism. It is weak for two reasons. It ignores the fact that the American is sufficiently interested in Canadian politics to take a course in it. It also ignores the fact that he or she is, presumably, attending a Canadian university and thus is living in Canada. Both these factors make it likely that he or she will know more about Canadian politics than the average American.

9. This is an inductive generalization. It is extremely weak, because the sample is far too small and clearly unrepresentative.

10. This passage is best interpreted as comprising two arguments. The first argument has a missing conclusion, (*Anyone who trains for six hours a day with Jim Birkin and follows his diet is likely to make the national swim team*), which also forms the premise of the second argument. The first argument is:

Last year Frances and Rhonda spent six hours a day training with Jim Birkin and followed his special diet, and made Canada's national swim team.

Therefore, anyone who trains for six hours a day with Jim Birkin and follows his diet is likely to make the national swim team.

This is a very weak inductive generalization. The sample is certainly too small, and probably biased as well. The second argument is:

Anyone who trains for six hours a day with Jim Birkin and follows his diet is likely to make the national swim team.

I am training for six hours a day with Jim Birkin and following his special diet.

Therefore, I am likely to make the national swim team.

This is a statistical syllogism. It is a strong argument as it stands, although there might be important and relevant information about the speaker that would lead us to revise this judgement. The possible strength of the second argument does not, however, compensate for the weakness of the first argument.

11. This is an inductive generalization. The sample is large enough, but it may be somewhat unrepresentative. Because the survey was conducted on a weekend, the sample probably under-represents first-year students, who are much more likely to visit their families on weekends than senior students. And senior students are probably less likely to support a fee increase to pay for new athletic facilities that may not be ready until after they graduate. In addition, perhaps those who would be most likely to support new athletic facilities are less likely to be home on a weekend because they are out training or engaged in some sporting activity. We should also want to know how the question put

to the students was framed. If the question was stated in a way that doesn't inflame student resentment about the proposed increase (*do you approve of a small fee increase as part of the school's fundraising efforts for a new athletic complex?*), then 44 per cent seems surprisingly low. But if the question was stated in a way that could inflame their resentment (*do you approve of making students pay for a new athletic complex by adding a new fee to existing fees?*), then it may be unduly biased to say that *only* 44 per cent approved of it.

12. This is an analogical argument by properties. The subject case is animal pain, and the analogue case is human pain. Human pain is associated with three features (behaviour, a central nervous system, and its evolutionary advantage), and all three of these features are evident in non-human animals. This is a strong analogy, and therefore a strong argument. Certainly, if we remain in doubt about whether non-human animals feel pain, then we have almost as much reason to doubt whether other humans feel pain too. Of course, we cannot decisively eliminate these doubts; however, this argument gives us good inductive grounds to set them aside.

Self-Test No. 17

1. Method of Agreement. The phenomenon is SARS, and the five people staying at the Metropole Hotel in Hong Kong are instances. Contact with the professor who was already infected with SARS is the common antecedent circumstance.

2. Method of Residue, used to identify an interfering factor. In ideal conditions, treating people who are young and enjoying good respiratory health, treatment procedures for SARS are almost always successful. The treatment procedures are the ordinary antecedent circumstances. Age and preestablished respiratory conditions are interfering factors.

3. Method of Concomitant Variations, uncovering an *inversely proportionate relationship* between lending rates and economic growth.

4. Joint Method of Agreement and Difference. *Method of Agreement*: All dog breeds exhibit the same capacity to respond to human cues. Therefore, dogs are able to do this because (a) they are genetically predisposed to understand these cues, or (b) they have the intellectual capacity to learn them, or (c) they developed this as part of their evolutionary heritage. *Method of Difference*: The subject case is dogs and their ability to understand human cues, and the control case is wolves and their ability to understand the same cues. Because dogs and wolves are genetically and intellectually comparable, the superior ability of dogs to understand these cues probably occurred after dogs and wolves were separated in evolution. The further comparison of dogs with primates on this ability helps rule out the possibility that dogs became more intelligent after

splitting off from wolves. If very intelligent primates are not responsive to these cues, then this possibility can be eliminated.

5. Method of Residue. The investigation into the car crash evidently began by narrowing the list of possible causes for the crash to three: weather, road conditions, or something directly connected to the driver. When weather and road conditions were ruled out, the focus narrowed further on what may have been responsible for the driver to crash the car. A list of the most likely possible causal factors associated with the driver includes all the items listed in the second sentence along with driver fatigue. When all the other factors were ruled out in the investigation, driver fatigue was the only one remaining.

6. Both Method of Difference and Method of Residues. *Method of Difference*: Twins are the subject group, and singletons are the control group. *Method of Residue, used to identify an interfering factor*: Suicidal behaviour is the phenomenon, and mental illness is the ordinary antecedent factor. If the rate of suicide amongst twins is lower than usual (while the rate of mental illness is higher), then something about being a twin interferes with the usual causal process.

7. The first argument at the beginning of this passage is best understood in terms of the Method of Concomitant Variations, as used to uncover a *proportional relationship* between stress in children and the consumption of high-fat foods and snacks. It also reveals a proportional relationship between stress in children and the frequency or size of the snacks (the newspaper account does not say whether they are the "biggest snackers" because they snack more frequently than children experiencing less stress or because they consume larger snacks). At the end of the passage, an *inversely proportional relationship* is reported between stress in children and consuming the recommended daily allowance of fruit and vegetables and eating a daily breakfast. The unstated main conclusion of the passage is that there is a *proportional relationship* between the levels of stress experienced by the children and unhealthy eating habits.

8. Joint Method of Agreement and Difference. *Method of Difference*: The subject case is the car parked in the Bronx with its licence plate removed and hood open. The control case is the car in Palo Alto with its license plate in place and hood down. Presumably, the cars were comparable looking otherwise and the neighbourhoods were also comparable, so the only difference in the antecedent circumstances is the state of the cars. When the subject car was stripped within 24 hours while the other car remained untouched, it is inferred that the principal difference in the antecedent circumstances is the cause. *Method of Agreement*: When the principal difference in the antecedent circumstances was removed by smashing in the window of the untouched car in Palo Alto, it is

inferred that it became vulnerable to attack for the same reason that the car in the Bronx was, that is, its disorderly appearance.

Self-Test No. 18

NOTE: The principles listed below are only some of those that could be invoked in an attempt to justify the particular moral judgement in question. Not all of them, of course, could be defended by an acceptable generalization argument.

1. No one who has ever been convicted of a criminal offence should hold elected public office / Only those who have a reputation for honesty and integrity should hold public office / No one with a criminal record should hold public office until at least five years after release from prison / No one who has ever cheated the government should hold public office.

2. Married women should always obey their husbands / Married women should always obey their husbands except when doing so would violate either the law or the Ten Commandments / Women with children should always obey the father of their children as long as he is supporting the children / It is wrong for parents to separate or divorce when they have children under the age of 12.

3. Citizens ought to inform the police whenever they become suspicious that a criminal offence may have been committed / Citizens of a democratic state ought to inform the police whenever they become suspicious that a criminal offence may have been committed / Citizens ought to inform the police whenever they become aware that a serious criminal offence has been committed / Citizens of a democratic state ought to inform the police when they become aware that a criminal offence has been committed, as long as they believe that the offence is morally wrong.

4. It is wrong to submit a plagiarized assignment in a course / It is wrong to submit a plagiarized assignment for credit in a course that counts towards one's degree requirements / It is always wrong to cheat / It is wrong to claim credit for work done by others.

5. Canada should give no special priority to refugees who wish to enter Canada / Canada should not accept refugees as immigrants / Prospective immigrants who attempt to jump the queue should be permanently barred from entering Canada.

Self-Test No. 19

1. To avoid complexity, we will assume that you are the student in question, that you purchased the essay, and that if you had submitted your own work it probably would have received a failing grade. Here are some of the likely good consequences:

(a) The time you would have spent working on the essay could be spent on more pleasurable activities.

(b) You will get a higher grade than you would if you wrote the essay yourself.

(c) The person you purchased the essay from will have money to spend on something that will give him or her pleasure.

The bad consequences are more complex because we have to consider some effects that are possible, although not certain, as well as the effects if you are caught cheating. Notice that (b) and (c) constitute bad effects not because they involve further cheating (since from the utilitarian's point of view cheating as such is not bad) but because the further cheating may have its own bad effects:

(a) The money you paid for the essay cannot be spent on other things you want.

(b) Your action may have a bad effect on your character, since each time you cheat it becomes a little easier to cheat the next time, and this may contribute indirectly to further bad consequences.

(c) Your action may have a bad effect on your friends if they know you cheated, since they may be encouraged to cheat by your example, and this may lead indirectly to bad consequences.

(d) If you are caught, the bad consequences to yourself would be substantial: failure in the course, possible expulsion from university, bad reputation, inability to get letters of reference for job applications.

(e) If you are caught, the reputation of the university and the value of its degrees might be adversely affected.

(f) If you are caught, the instructor will feel annoyed and/or hurt and may develop a more cynical and suspicious attitude to students generally.

2. The good consequences will consist primarily of whatever happiness results from the fact that you have more money to spend. If you use the money to buy a new coat, then the merchant, the manufacturer, and their workers will gain some benefit. If you give the money to Oxfam, then people who are starving will benefit. However, if you are caught and criminal charges are laid against you, there would also be the following good consequences:

(a) A lawyer would earn some money by defending you.

(b) Some people who might have been tempted to cheat on their income tax will probably be deterred by knowing that you were caught and prosecuted.

(c) Many people may feel a sense of satisfaction that a cheat has been caught and prosecuted.

The bad consequences will include whatever unhappiness results from the fact that you have more money to spend. If you use the money to buy illegal drugs, then you may be contributing to your own addiction. If you use the money to invest in a company that makes hard-core pornography, you may be contributing to violence against women. In addition, however, there are the following possible bad effects:

(a) The government has slightly less revenue, and there will be a very slight, but nonetheless measurable, increase in the government's deficit.

(b) Your action may have a bad effect on your character, since each time you cheat it becomes a little easier to cheat the next time, and this may contribute indirectly to further bad consequences.

(c) Your action may have a bad effect on your friends if they know you cheated, since they may be encouraged to cheat by your example, and this may lead indirectly to bad consequences.

(d) If you are caught, the bad consequences to yourself would be substantial: a fine, a criminal conviction, possible loss of your job, bad reputation.

(e) If you are caught, your family and perhaps your friends will be unhappy at your plight.

3. The good consequences will include the following:
(a) Your friend will avoid criminal charges.
(b) Your friend's insurance rates will not increase.
(c) Your friend will avoid gaining a reputation for being irresponsible.
(d) You will not lose your friend.

The bad consequences will include the following:
(a) Your friend may be encouraged to take risks while driving in the future.
(b) You may resent the fact that you had to commit a criminal offence to protect your friend.
(c) The victims of the accident will feel angry that someone got away with a crime.
(d) Your friend will not have to pay anything towards the costs of the accident, thus driving up insurance rates marginally.

4. The good consequences would include the following:
(a) Some people who would have been convicted of criminal offences will not be charged.
(b) The price would likely be reduced, thus reducing the amount of crime committed by those who steal and rob in order to get the money to buy marijuana.
(c) The government could tax marijuana and thus obtain much-needed revenue.

(d) The criminals who currently control much of the traffic in marijuana would be put out of business.

(e) Marijuana use, which is pleasurable to some people, would be more pleasurable if users and sellers did not have to worry about being charged as criminals.

The bad consequences would include the following:

(a) More people would use marijuana, thus increasing the health risks.

(b) The new marijuana users would have less money to spend on other things.

(c) Such a policy would increase pressure to legalize all illegal drugs, which would lead to an increase in their use.

5. The most important set of consequences that must be considered when dealing with this question is the impact of the ultimate victory or defeat of right-wing rebel groups in Central America. We have to compare the general happiness of the people of Central America that would result if the rebels win the struggle with the general happiness of the people that would result if the rebels lose the struggle. This question will depend upon a number of very controversial predictions concerning the kind of society that would evolve in each case. We cannot address these in any detail here, but they would force us to deal with such questions as:

» What is the probability that a victory for the rebels would produce a small wealthy elite class with most ordinary people being in abject poverty? and

» What is the probability that the defeat of the rebels would produce a Cuban-style dictatorship?

Each of these predictions would then be used as a basis for estimating the amount of happiness that would be produced for the people of Central America.

There is, however, another complicating factor that must be taken into account. This is the unhappiness that is caused by the armed struggle itself. It is possible that greater happiness would result from the victory of the rebels than by their defeat, but that, when the suffering caused by the struggle itself is included, our conclusion will have to be revised. If, for example, it is likely that the rebels can win only after a long and vicious war, but that if they do not receive arms from abroad they will suffer a quick defeat, then this additional suffering would have to be subtracted from the happiness that will result from a victory by the rebels.

In addition, we will have to consider the consequences as they affect others outside of Central America. The good consequences would include the following:

(a) Employment for workers and profits for owners and investors in the arms industry.

(b) The sense of satisfaction that people with strong right-wing sympathies will feel that the struggle against communism is being sustained.

(c) The possible beneficial diplomatic effects elsewhere in the world.

The external bad consequences might include the following:
(a) Greater distrust from Third World countries towards the nation supplying the arms.
(b) Resentment from citizens within the supplying nation against their own government for violating the sovereignty of foreign countries.
(c) The possibility that relations between the superpowers may be destabilized, thus increasing the risk of nuclear war.

Self-Test No. 20

I.

1. There are many examples of wealthy people whose lives are obviously miserable (for example, through drug addiction or alcoholism). Others, such as Kurt Cobain, Christina Onassis, and Janis Joplin, have committed suicide.

2. This certainly applies to the criminal law, but there are important areas of law in which coercion is either absent or very remote. For example, some laws lay down the conditions for making a valid will, and it is difficult to see how the function of these laws is coercive. Other examples of non-coercive laws are: laws establishing courts, various aspects of constitutional law, and laws establishing the right of an individual to run for Parliament.

3. The only real counter-example would consist of telling a joke that is not at the expense of someone else, such as a joke at one's own expense or at nobody's expense. To be effective, however, it needs to be funny.

4. The following women have become prime ministers of their countries: Angela Merkel, Margaret Thatcher, Golda Meir, Benazir Bhutto, Indira Gandhi, Kim Campbell, and Gro Harlem Brundtland. There have been numerous others.

5. The Spanish Inquisition, the Crusades, religious fanaticism in Northern Ireland, the Taliban regime in Afghanistan, Arab-Israeli hostility, and so on.

II.

1. Well, I've been a sex pervert all my life. I was raised as a sex pervert by my father, and if it was good enough for him then it is good enough for me.

2. I don't think that stealing my roommate's chemistry notes is really stealing, because he has never threatened to punish me for it.

3. And if Jim had found $20,000 lying in the street he'd be able to afford a new car; well, he has just bought a new car so he must have found $20,000 lying in the street.

4. Yes, and you shouldn't eat any salt either. It's deadly. They've proven that it kills laboratory animals when they give them a steady dose of it.

5. That's what my uncle said the day my aunt left him for good. Or, that's what the turkey said about the farmer the day before Thanksgiving.

Self-Test No. 21

1. Humour

2. Vague terms: the highest standards of craftsmanship and range of styles to suit the tastes of the modern consumer have no clear meaning. False confidence: *We are the best...*

3. If the speaker has been challenged to defend his or her earlier claim that pornography is not harmful to women, this would be a red herring. In some contexts, however, this attempt to change the topic might be legitimate.

4. Vague terms: the entire passage is vague, but *neat guy*, *laid back*, and *lots of personality* are especially vague.

5. Loaded question: The question assumes that we have been putting it off.

6. Vague terms: *got what it takes.*

7. If the speaker has been challenged to defend his or her earlier claim regarding how criminals should be treated, this would be a red herring. In other contexts, however, this statement might be legitimate.

8. Persuasive redefinition: the term *scientist* is being redefined in a way that changes its normal descriptive meaning.

9. Loaded question: the question *Is there any reason to think that this time Mulroney isn't just serving the interests of his tycoon friends in corporate boardrooms?* presupposes that normally Mulroney serves the interests of his tycoon friends. Loaded terms: *bleating, tycoon.*

10. Selectivity: focuses attention on an unrepresentative sample of events.

Glossary

(Numbers in brackets indicate section numbers where discussion of item occurs in text.)

ABSURD EXAMPLES, METHOD OF: See METHOD OF ABSURD EXAMPLES.

ACCEPTABILITY OF THE PREMISES: Premises are acceptable when they can reasonably be accepted as true. This is the first criterion for good arguments. (5.2.1)

ACCURACY OF A HYPOTHESIS: How much detail the hypothesis is able to provide as an explanation of any particular observation. (11.4)

AD HOMINEM: A fallacious argument that substitutes irrelevant information discrediting the author of a statement for genuine evidence that the statement is false. Latin for "against the man." (7.4.1)

ADEQUACY OF SUPPORT PROVIDED BY THE PREMISES: The support the premises give is strong enough for the purposes of the argument. This is the third criterion for good arguments. (5.2.1)

ADEQUACY, EXPLANATORY: See EXPLANATORY ADEQUACY.

ADVOCATE'S STRATEGY: The author defends a particular proposal or tenet by arguing on its behalf. One of the strategies for constructing an argumentative essay. (17.1)

AFFIRMING THE ANTECEDENT: An argument of the form *If p then q; p; therefore q*. Any argument of this form is formally valid. (9.4)

AFFIRMING THE CONSEQUENT: An invalid argument of the form *If p then q; q; therefore p*. Any argument of this form is formally invalid. (9.5)

AGREEMENT AND DIFFERENCE, JOINT METHOD OF: See JOINT METHOD OF AGREEMENT AND DIFFERENCE.

AGREEMENT, METHOD OF: See METHOD OF AGREEMENT.

ALTERNATIVES, EXCLUSIVE: See EXCLUSIVE ALTERNATIVES.

ALTERNATIVES, EXHAUSTIVE: See EXHAUSTIVE ALTERNATIVES.

AMBIGUITY, GRAMMATICAL: See GRAMMATICAL AMBIGUITY.

AMBIGUITY, REFERENTIAL: See REFERENTIAL AMBIGUITY.

AMBIGUOUS SENTENCE: A sentence that has two or more different but possibly quite precise meanings. (3.2.1)

ANALOGICAL ARGUMENT BY PROPERTIES: Reasoning by analogy based on a comparison of the properties of the subject case and those of the analogy case. This has the form x has A, B, C; y has A, B; It is probable, therefore, that y has C. (10.5)

ANALOGICAL ARGUMENT BY RELATIONS: Reasoning by analogue based on a comparison between relations that obtain in the subject case and those of the analogue case. This has the form x is to y as a is to b; x is R to y; It is probable, therefore, that a is R to b. (10.5)

ANALOGUE CASE: The case with which we are more familiar, which is supposed to be relevantly similar to the subject case, and which is used to draw the conclusion in an analogical argument. (10.5)

ANALOGY, REASONING BY: See REASONING BY ANALOGY.

ANALYTIC STATEMENT: A statement that is true by definition. (3.4)

ANTECEDENT CONDITION: An event connected to one that follows in a variety of ways. (3.8)

ANTECEDENT: The component p of an implication *if p then q*. Note that this may come second in an English sentence; for example, in "The picnic is off if it's raining," the antecedent is "it's raining." (9.2)

ANTECEDENT, AFFIRMING THE: See AFFIRMING THE ANTECEDENT.

ANTEDEDENT, DENYING THE: See DENYING THE ANTECEDENT.

APPEAL TO AUTHORITY: A fallacious argument which cites the (irrelevant) testimony of someone who is not a reliable authority on the matter at issue. (7.3)

APPEAL TO FORCE: A fallacious argument which substitutes an irrelevant threat of force or other kind of pressure for genuine evidence for the conclusion. (7.2)

APPEAL TO IGNORANCE: A fallacious argument which appeals to the fact that there is no evidence for a claim, to show that it is false. (8.3)

APPEAL TO PITY: A fallacious argument which substitutes an irrelevant attempt to elicit pity or sympathy for the presentation of genuine evidence for the conclusion. (7.2)

ARGUMENT: A set of statements that claims that one or more of those statements supports another. (1.1)

ARGUMENTATIVE ESSAY: A written attempt to present a coherent discussion of a subject with a view to defending a specific thesis. (16)

ARGUMENTATIVE ESSAY, THESIS OF AN: See THESIS OF AN ARGUMENTATIVE ESSAY.

AUTHORITY, APPEAL TO: See APPEAL TO AUTHORITY.

AUXILIARY HYPOTHESIS: A second hypothesis that is logically required by the hypothesis under investigation. (11.4.1)

AVERAGE, SIMPLE: See SIMPLE AVERAGE.

BEGGING THE QUESTION: The fallacy committed by an argument when its premises presuppose, directly or indirectly, the truth of its conclusion. (Also known by its Latin name, *PETITIO PRINCIPII*.) (6.7.1)

CAUSATION: What is involved when one event (the cause) is responsible for, or brings about, another event (the effect). (11.1)

CAUSE AND EFFECT, CONFUSING: See CONFUSING CAUSE AND EFFECT.

CAUSE, COMMON: See COMMON CAUSE.

CHAIN ARGUMENT: An argument of the form *If p then q; if q then r; therefore if p then r*. Any argument of this form is formally valid. (9.4)

CHARITY, PRINCIPLE OF: See PRINCIPLE OF CHARITY.

CIRCULAR DEFINITION: A definition that includes the term being defined (or its cognate) in the definition. (2.9.4)

COHERENCE THEORY OF TRUTH: A theory that holds that a particular statement is true when it is part of a coherent set of mutually supporting statements. (6.1.2)

COLLECTIVE USE OF A TERM: Occurs in a statement that says something about the class as a whole. (3.2.2)

COMMON CAUSE: A fallacy committed when it is claimed that there is a causal relation between A and B when in fact both A and B are caused by a third factor, C. (8.5.3)

COMPLEX QUESTION: See LOADED QUESTION.

COMPLEX STATEMENT: A statement that contains one or more other statements as component parts. (9.2)

CONCLUSION: The statement in an argument that its premises are supposed to support. (1.1)

CONCOMITANT VARIATION, METHOD OF: See METHOD OF CONCOMITANT VARIATION.

CONFIRMATION, INDUCTION BY: See INDUCTION BY CONFIRMATION.

CONFIRMING INSTANCE: An actual observation showing that an observation statement is true. (10.4)

CONFUSING CAUSE AND EFFECT: Fallacious reasoning in which an effect is identified as a cause and the cause is identified as the effect. (8.5.2)

CONJUNCT: Each of the two components of a conjunction. (9.2)

CONJUNCTION: A truth-functional statement (written *p and q*) with two components (*p, q*); its logical operator corresponds to the English *and*. The statement is true only when *p* is true and *q* is true; it is false when *p* is false, or when *q* is false, or when both *p* and *q* are false. (9.2)

CONNOTATION: See SENSE OF A WORD.

CONSEQUENT: The component q of an implication *if p then q*. Note that this may come first in an English sentence; for example, in "The picnic is off if it's raining," the consequent is "the picnic is off." (9.2)

CONSEQUENT: The event that follows an antecedent condition. (3.8)

CONSEQUENT, AFFIRMING THE: See AFFIRMING THE CONSEQUENT.

CONSEQUENT, DENYING THE: See DENYING THE CONSEQUENT.

CONSEQUENTIALIST MORAL THEORIES: See TELEOLOGICAL MORAL THEORIES.

CONTEXTUAL DEFINITION: Definition that conveys the meaning by using the word in a standard context and by providing a different sentence with the same meaning but without the word. (2.8)

CONTRADICTORY STATEMENT: A statement that is false by definition. (3.4)

CONTROL GROUP: One of two divisions of a group to be studied in a scientific investigation: the division into which a change (or EXPERIMENTAL VARIABLE) is not introduced. (11.2.2)

CORRELATION: A regular co-occurrence of two events, occurring at the same time or in the same sequence. (11.1)

CORRELATION, SIGNIFICANT: See SIGNIFICANT CORRELATION.

CORRESPONDENCE THEORY OF TRUTH: A theory that holds that the truth of a statement is its correspondence to a fact. (6.1.1)

COUNTER-ARGUMENT, METHOD OF: See METHOD OF COUNTER-ARGUMENT.

COUNTER-EXAMPLE: A particular exception to a generalization, used to show that the generalization relied upon in the argument is not universally true. (13.2)

COUNTER-EXAMPLES, METHOD OF: See METHOD OF COUNTER-EXAMPLES.

COUNTERFACTUAL ARGUMENT: An argument whose premises are known or assumed to be false. Used to explore the consequences of these premises. (1.3)

CRITERIA: Standards. (5.2)

CRITERIAL APPROACH: An approach to the theory of argument assessment which proceeds mainly by examination of the standards that a good argument must meet. This is the central approach of this text. (5.2)

CRITIC'S STRATEGY: The author argues against someone else's recommendation or claim. One of the strategies for constructing an argumentative essay. (17.2)

CRUCIAL EXPERIMENT: An experiment designed to resolve an impasse between rival, equally adequate, hypotheses. (11.4)

DEDUCTIVE ARGUMENT: An argument whose premises, if true, guarantee the truth of the conclusion. (1.2)

DEFINITION BY SYNONYM: Defining a word by providing a precise synonym. (2.8)

DEFINITION, CIRCULAR: See CIRCULAR DEFINITION.

DEFINITION, CONTEXTUAL: See CONTEXTUAL DEFINITION.

DEFINITION, ESSENTIALIST: See ESSENTIALIST DEFINITION.

DEFINITION, GENUS-SPECIES: See GENUS-SPECIES DEFINITION.

DEFINITION, OPERATIONAL: See OPERATIONAL DEFINITION.

DEFINITION, OSTENSIVE: See OSTENSIVE DEFINITION.

DEFINITION, REPORTIVE: See REPORTIVE DEFINITION.

DEFINITION, STIPULATIVE: See STIPULATIVE DEFINITION.

DENOTATION: See REFERENCE OF A WORD.

DENYING THE ANTECEDENT: An invalid argument of the form *If p then q; not-p; therefore not-q*. Any argument of this form is formally invalid. (9.5)

DENYING THE CONSEQUENT: An argument of the form *If p then q; not-q; therefore not-p*. Any argument of this form is formally valid. (9.4)

DEONTOLOGICAL MORAL THEORIES: Theories that hold that the rightness or wrongness of an action is to be determined by appeal to an objective moral principle, according to which actions of that type are right or wrong. (12.2)

DESCRIPTIVE FUNCTION OF LANGUAGE: Language's use to convey factual information. (2.3)

DESCRIPTIVE MEANING: The information communicated by a term. (3.6)

DIAGRAM, TREE: See TREE DIAGRAM.

DICHOTOMY, FALSE: See FALSE DICHOTOMY.

DIFFERENCE, METHOD OF: See METHOD OF DIFFERENCE.

DIRECTIVE USE OF LANGUAGE: Language's use to command others to do something or to provide advice. (2.3)

DISCONFIRMING INSTANCE: An actual observation showing that an observation statement is false. (10.4)

DISJUNCT: Each of the two components of a disjunction. (9.2)

DISJUNCTION: A truth-functional statement (written *either p or q*) with two components (*p, q*); its logical operator corresponds (roughly) to the English *either ... or*. The statement is false only when *p* and *q* are both false; it is true otherwise—that is, when one or both of the components are true. (9.2)

DISJUNCTIVE SYLLOGISM: An argument of the form *either p or q; not-p; therefore q*. Any argument of this form is formally valid. (9.4)

DISTRIBUTIVE USE OF A TERM: This occurs in a statement that says something about each and every member of the class named by that term. (3.2.2)

EMOTIVE FUNCTION OF LANGUAGE: Language's use to express feelings or emotions. (2.3)

EMPIRICAL FACT: A fact that is observable in principle—that is, if one were in the right place at the right time, under the right conditions. (6.1.1)

EMPIRICAL STATEMENT: A statement that asserts an empirical fact, or a set of empirical facts. (6.1.1)

EQUIVOCATION: The fallacy committed by an argument when a premise has two interpretations, one acceptable and one unacceptable, and when it is the unacceptable interpretation that is required by the conclusion. (6.7.3)

ESSAY, ARGUMENTATIVE: See ARGUMENTATIVE ESSAY.

ESSENTIALIST DEFINITION: A definition that attempts to report the real nature of what is being defined. (2.7.3)

EVALUATIVE FUNCTION OF LANGUAGE: Language's use to make value judgements—to evaluate things. (2.3)

EVALUATIVE MEANING: The positive or negative value judgement communicated by a term. (3.6)

EVOCATIVE FUNCTION OF LANGUAGE: Language's use to evoke feelings or emotions in an audience. (2.3)

EXCLUSIVE ALTERNATIVES: Alternatives that cannot both (or all) be true: when one is true, the other(s) must be false. (6.7.4)

EXHAUSTIVE ALTERNATIVES: Alternatives that cover all the possibilities. (6.7.4)

EXPERIMENT, CRUCIAL: See CRUCIAL EXPERIMENT.

EXPERIMENTAL VARIABLE: A change introduced into the subject group. This variable is hypothesized to be the cause of any subsequent difference between the subject and control groups. (11.2.2)

EXPLANATION: An attempt to show why or how something happens (or has happened). It is taken for granted that the event happened—which is in contrast to an argument attempting to prove that some event happened. (4.4.2)

EXPLANATORY ADEQUACY: A hypothesis is explanatorily adequate in proportion to its scope and accuracy. (11.4)

EXTENSION: See REFERENCE OF A WORD.

FACT, EMPIRICAL: See EMPIRICAL FACT.

FALLACIES APPROACH: An approach to the theory of argument assessment which proceeds mainly by attempting to describe the main types of fallacious argument—the common mistakes one must guard against. (5.1)

FALLACY: An error or weakness in an argument that detracts from its soundness, but is disguised so that it may look like the conclusion is supported. (5.1)

FALSE CONFIDENCE: When a questionable claim is presented with great confidence, attempting to mislead the audience into thinking it cannot seriously be questioned. Another irrational technique of persuasion. (14.4)

FALSE DICHOTOMY: The fallacy committed by an argument when a premise presents us with a choice between two alternatives and assumes that they are exhaustive or exclusive or both, when in fact they are not. (6.7.4)

FALSIFIED TRUTH-CLAIM: A truth-claim that has been shown to be false. (6.2)

FORCE, APPEAL TO: See APPEAL TO FORCE.

FORMAL INVALIDITY: Describes an argument that is not formally valid; that is, it is such that if its premises are true, then its conclusion may nevertheless be false. (9.5)

FORMAL VALIDITY: Describes an argument such that if its premises are true, then its conclusion must also be true. (9.3)

FRAMEWORK, INTERPRETIVE, OF A NEWS STORY: See INTERPRETATIVE FRAMEWORK OF A NEWS STORY.

GENERALIZATION ARGUMENT: A moral argument that applies the generalization principle. (12.3)

GENERALIZATION PRINCIPLE: A right action is one that is entailed by a principle that is acceptable when applied generally (that is, to everyone in similar circumstances), and a wrong action is one that is entailed by a principle that is unacceptable when applied generally. (12.3)

GENUS-SPECIES DEFINITION: A definition that mentions a larger category (a genus) to which that kind of thing belongs, and then specifies what makes that particular kind (that species) different from the other species in that genus. (2.8.1)

GRAMMATICAL AMBIGUITY: An ambiguity that arises when the grammatical structure of a sentence allows two interpretations, each of which gives rise to a different meaning. (3.2.3)

GUILT BY ASSOCIATION: The technique of attacking an opponent or an opponent's position by suggesting a similarity with another person or position that the audience regards in an unfavourable light. This is a technique of irrational persuasion when this is a faulty analogy. (14.9)

HYPOTHESIS: A principle or statement that, if true, would explain the event(s) or situation(s) to which it applies. (10.4)

HYPOTHESIS, ACCURACY OF: See ACCURACY OF A HYPOTHESIS.

HYPOTHESIS, AUXILIARY: See AUXILIARY HYPOTHESIS.

HYPOTHESIS, SCOPE OF: See SCOPE OF A HYPOTHESIS.

HYPOTHESIS, SCOPE RESTRICTION OF: See SCOPE RESTRICTION OF A HYPOTHESIS.

IDEA THEORY OF MEANING: The view that the meaning of a word consists of the idea or mental image that is associated with the word. (2.2.2)

IGNORANCE, APPEAL TO: See APPEAL TO IGNORANCE.

IMPARTIAL ADJUDICATOR'S STRATEGY: An impartial adjudicator considers and weighs the evidence from all available points of view before passing judgement. In academic essays, authors act as adjudicators by introducing and assessing all the principal positions, and identifying the strengths and weaknesses of each in order to define their own position. (17.3)

IMPLICATION: A truth-functional statement (written *if p then q*) with two components (*p, q*); its logical operator corresponds (roughly) to the English *if ... then*. The statement is false only when *p* is true and *q* is false; it is true otherwise—that is, when *p* is false, or when *q* is true, or both. (9.2)

INCOMMENSURABILITY OF THEORIES: Theories are incommensurable when there is no available standard that is independent of both theories and by which we can test to determine which theory is better. (11.4.1)

INCONSISTENCY: The fallacy committed by an argument when it contains, implicitly or explicitly, a contradiction, usually between two premises. (6.7.2)

INDUCTION BY CONFIRMATION: A form of inductive reasoning in which confirming instances, and the lack of disconfirming instances, are used as evidence to support a hypothesis. (10.4)

INDUCTIVE ARGUMENT: An argument whose premises, if true, make it reasonable to conclude that the conclusion is true, but do not provide an absolute guarantee. (1.2)

INFERENCE INDICATORS: Words that indicate that one thought is intended to support (i.e., to justify, provide a reason for, provide evidence for, or entail) another thought. Examples include *therefore, since, thus, implies, consequently, because, it follows that, given that.* (1.1)

INFERENCE: The process of reasoning from one thought A, to another, B, when we believe that A *supports* or *justifies* or *makes it reasonable to believe* in the truth of B. (1.1)

INTENSION: See SENSE OF A WORD.

INTEREST, VARIABLE OF: See VARIABLE OF INTEREST.

INTERPRETIVE FRAMEWORK OF A NEWS STORY: The general pattern of beliefs,

attitudes, and biases that lie behind particular examples of news coverage. (15.3.2)

INTERROGATIVE USE OF LANGUAGE: Language's use to elicit information. (2.3)

INVALIDITY, FORMAL: See FORMAL INVALIDITY.

JOINT METHOD OF AGREEMENT AND DIFFERENCE: Justification of a causal conclusion by use of both methods— Agreement and Difference—at once. One of Mill's methods. (11.2.3)

JOINTLY SUFFICIENT CONDITIONS: A collection of conditions which are not individually sufficient, but which are sufficient as a group when all occur. (3.8)

LOADED QUESTION (also called COMPLEX QUESTION): A question containing an assumption that any possible answer would confirm. These are used as an irrational technique of persuasion. (14.3)

LOADED TERM: A term with a clear descriptive meaning and a positive or negative evaluative meaning, which is used in an attempt to persuade us to accept the evaluation conveyed by the term. This is an irrational technique of persuasion. (13.4)

LOGICAL OPERATOR: An element of a truth-functional statement connecting (or, in the case of negation, modifying) the component sentences and determining how the truth or falsity of the whole statement is related to the truth or falsity of the components. (9.2)

LOGICAL PARADOX: Any chain of reasoning that uses only meaningful and consistent premises and commits no logical errors, yet nevertheless produces contradictory conclusions. (Appendix I)

LOGICAL STRENGTH: An argument is said to have logical strength when its premises, *if true*, actually provide support for its conclusion. (1.2)

MACRO-STRUCTURE: The large-scale, overall structure of an argumentative essay. (16.1)

MATCHING: Ensuring that the subject and control groups initially have identical proportions of people with a certain trait. (11.2.2)

MEAN: See SIMPLE AVERAGE.

MEANING AS USE: The approach that explains meaning of linguistic items—primarily sentences, but, derivatively, words—in terms of their use. (2.2.3)

MEANING, DESCRIPTIVE: See DESCRIPTIVE MEANING.

MEANING, EVALUATIVE: See EVALUATIVE MEANING.

MEANING, THEORIES OF: See REFERENCE THEORY OF MEANING, IDEA THEORY OF MEANING, MEANING AS USE.

MEDIAN: The middle point in a range of values: half the cases in the range are above this point, and half below. (14.6)

MENTION: See USE VS. MENTION

METHOD OF ABSURD EXAMPLES: A method for arguing back by constructing an argument with a closely parallel structure to the one being criticised, with true

premises, and with an obviously false or absurd conclusion. (13.3)

METHOD OF AGREEMENT: The observation that the same antecedent circumstances occur in all instances of the same phenomenon provides justification for the conclusion that the antecedent circumstances cause the phenomenon. One of Mill's methods. (11.2.1)

METHOD OF CONCOMITANT VARIATIONS: The observation that an antecedent circumstance varies proportionately to a phenomenon provides justification that the antecedent circumstance is the cause of the phenomenon. (An inverse relation between the two variations shows that the first is a negative causal factor.) One of Mill's methods. (11.2.4)

METHOD OF COUNTER-ARGUMENT: A method for arguing back by constructing a different argument attempting to show that the conclusion under criticism is false or problematic. (13.4)

METHOD OF COUNTER-EXAMPLES: A method for arguing back involving presentation of a counter-example showing that the generalization cannot be relied on the way the argument does. (13.2)

METHOD OF DIFFERENCE: The observation that the antecedent circumstances in two instances of a phenomenon are all the same except one provides justification that one is the cause of the phenomenon. One of Mill's methods. (11.2.2)

METHOD OF RESIDUE: When we have a complex phenomenon, the cause of which is partly explained by one or more antecedent circumstances, then we have reason to believe that any unexplained aspect of the phenomenon is caused by the remaining antecedent circumstances. One of Mill's methods. (11.2.5)

MICRO-STRUCTURE: The small-scale structure of each sub-argument and its parts, in an argumentative essay. (16.2)

MILL'S METHODS: A set of five procedures for systematically and methodically extrapolating from the observable temporal order of things to the causal order which is not directly observable. These are: the Method of Agreement, the Method of Difference, the Joint Method of Agreement and Difference, the Method of Concomitant Variations, and the Method of Residue. (11.2)

MODE: The particular value that occurs most frequently in a range of values. (14.6)

MORAL SCEPTICISM, RADICAL: See RADICAL MORAL SCEPTICISM.

MORAL THEORIES: See DEONTOLOGICAL MORAL THEORIES and TELEOLOGICAL MORAL THEORIES.

NECESSARY CONDITION: An antecedent condition without which the consequent wouldn't happen. In other words, X is a necessary condition for Y if, and only if, when X is false Y must also be false (or, when X is absent Y cannot occur). (3.8)

NEGATION: A truth-functional statement (written *not-p*) with one component (*p*), its logical operator corresponds to the English "not" or "it is false that." The statement is true when the component is false, and false when the component is true. (9.2)

NON SEQUITUR: An argument with irrelevant premises. Latin for *it does not follow*. (7.2)

OBSERVATION STATEMENT: An empirical prediction deduced from a hypothesis. (10.4)

OPERATIONAL DEFINITION: Definition made by specifying a rule or operation. (2.8.4)

OPERATOR, LOGICAL: See LOGICAL OPERATOR.

OSTENSIVE DEFINITION: A definition that conveys the meaning by giving examples. (2.8)

PARADOX, LOGICAL: See LOGICAL PARADOX.

PERFORMATIVE USE OF LANGUAGE: Language's use to perform actions, such as can be performed merely by saying a sentence; for example, when one says "I hereby promise / find the accused guilty / christen this boat / resign." (2.3)

PERSUASIVE REDEFINITION: The redefinition of a familiar term or phrase that has both a descriptive and an evaluative meaning in such a way as to change its descriptive meaning while keeping its evaluative meaning the same. (14.10)

PERSUASIVE USE OF LANGUAGE: Language's use to persuade people to accept something or to act in a certain way. (2.3)

PETITIO PRINCIPII: See BEGGING THE QUESTION.

PITY, APPEAL TO: See APPEAL TO PITY.

POST HOC: The fallacious argument that because something comes before an event, it must therefore be the cause of that event. Short for the Latin *post hoc ergo propter hoc*, which means "after this therefore because of this." (8.5.1)

PRAGMATIC THEORY OF TRUTH: A theory that holds that the truth of a statement consists in the fact that it leads to the successful solution of a real problem. (6.1.3)

PREMISE (plural: PREMISES): The statement in an argument that is supposed to provide support for the conclusion. (1.1)

PREMISES, ACCEPTABILITY OF: See ACCEPTABILITY OF THE PREMISES.

PREMISES, ADEQUACY OF SUPPORT PROVIDED BY: See ADEQUACY OF SUPPORT PROVIDED BY THE PREMISES.

PREMISES, RELEVANCE OF: See RELEVANCE OF THE PREMISES.

PRESUPPOSITION: A premise that is a general principle the speaker takes to be important in the connection between the other premises and the conclusion, but that is missing (unstated) in the argument. (4.2)

PRINCIPLE OF CHARITY: A principle for interpreting someone's words according to which one should, when faced with various possible interpretations, always adopt the one that interprets those words as expressing views that are as reasonable, plausible, or defensible as possible. (3.1)

PRINCIPLE OF UTILITY (also called THE GREATEST HAPPINESS PRINCIPLE): We ought always to choose, from among the actions open to us, the action that will produce the greatest happiness of the greatest number of people affected by it. (12.6)

PRINCIPLE, GENERALIZATION: See GENERALIZATION PRINCIPLE.

PRINCIPLE, GREATEST HAPPINESS: See PRINCIPLE OF UTILITY.

PROPERTIES, ANALOGICAL ARGUMENT BY: See ANALOGICAL ARGUMENT BY PROPERTIES.

PROPERTY: A feature that is attributable to a thing considered on its own. (10.5)

PROPOSITION, TARGET: See TARGET PROPOSITION.

QUESTION, COMPLEX: See LOADED QUESTION.

QUESTION, LOADED: See LOADED QUESTION.

RADICAL MORAL SCEPTICISM: The denial that basic moral principles are objective facts, capable of rational proof, and the belief that acceptance of such principles can only be explained by reference to some deep psychological need or to our social and cultural history. (12.2)

RANDOMIZING: Ensuring that the subject and control groups initially have identical distributions of all relevant traits by assigning members to groups randomly—that is, without regard for specific relevant traits. (11.2.2)

REASONING BY ANALOGY: A form of inductive reasoning in which there is an attempt to support a conclusion by pointing to a separate case supposed to be similar. (10.5)

RECONSTRUCTING AN ARGUMENT: The process of identifying and extracting the premises and conclusion (including spelling them out when they are unstated but implied), and making explicit the connection between them (i.e., the structure of the argument). (4.1)

RECREATIONAL USE OF LANGUAGE: Language's use merely to amuse ourselves and others: puns, word-games, songs, etc. (2.3)

RED HERRING: An irrelevant issue introduced to distract hearers and shift the topic to one about which the speaker is on firmer ground. An irrational technique of persuasion. (14.8)

REDEFINITION, PERSUASIVE: See PERSUASIVE REDEFINITION.

REDUCTIO AD ABSURDUM: An argument in which a statement is proven to be true by assuming it to be false and then deriving a contradiction from that assumption. A species of counterfactual argument. (1.3)

REFERENCE OF A WORD: The class of things to which the word refers (also known as its DENOTATION or EXTENSION). (2.6)

REFERENCE THEORY OF MEANING: The view that the meaning of a word consists in what it refers to. (2.2.1)

REFERENTIAL AMBIGUITY: An ambiguity that arises when a word or phrase could, in the context of a particular sentence, refer to two or more properties or things. (3.2.2)

RELATION: A feature that is attributable to the relationship between two or more things. (10.5)

RELATIONS, ANALOGICAL ARGUMENT BY: See ANALOGICAL ARGUMENT BY RELATIONS.

RELEVANCE OF THE PREMISES: Premises are relevant when they provide support for the conclusion. Relevance of the premises is the second criterion for good arguments. (5.2.1)

REPORT OF AN ARGUMENT: The attribution of an argument to somebody other than the speaker; the speaker does not necessarily endorse the argument. (4.4.1)

REPORTIVE DEFINITION: A definition intended to convey the information needed to use a word correctly in its standard use. (2.7.1)

RESIDUE, METHOD OF: See METHOD OF RESIDUE.

SAMPLING: A form of inductive reasoning in which observations of a portion of a group are used to justify a conclusion about the whole group. (10.2)

SCEPTICISM, RADICAL MORAL: See RADICAL MORAL SCEPTICISM.

SCOPE OF A HYPOTHESIS: The number of instances of a phenomenon that the hypothesis explains. (11.4)

SCOPE RESTRICTION OF A HYPOTHESIS: A hypothesis is restricted in scope when it purports to explain only some of the relevant observations. Otherwise, it is unrestricted, universal. (11.4)

SELECTIVITY: An irrational technique of persuasion which attempts to mislead an audience into a generalization by producing an unrepresentative sample. (14.5)

SENSE OF A WORD: What we understand when we understand its meaning (also known as its CONNOTATION or INTENSION). (2.6)

SENTENCE, VAGUE: See VAGUE SENTENCE.

SIGNIFICANT CORRELATION: A correlation that justifies a causal conclusion because the antecedent circumstance is the only one that correlates with the phenomenon. (11.2.1)

SIMPLE ARGUMENT: An argument with a single premise and a single conclusion. (4.6.1)

SIMPLE AVERAGE (also called MEAN): The value obtained by adding all the values in a range, and dividing the sum by the number of values. (14.6)

SIMPLE STATEMENT: A statement that does not contain any other statement as a part. (9.2)

SLIPPERY SLOPE: A fallacious argument which attempts to justify a negative assessment of a policy by appealing to a chain of consequences, each one causing the next, ending with an undesirable result. This is fallacious when it is not likely that the policy will really result in this outcome. (8.4)

SOUND ARGUMENT: An argument that has both logical strength and true premises. (1.3)

STATEMENT: A sentence (i.e., a set of words) that is used to make a claim that is capable of being true or false. (1.1)

STATEMENT, ANALYTIC: See ANALYTIC STATEMENT.

STATEMENT, COMPLEX: See COMPLEX STATEMENT.

STATEMENT, CONTRADICTORY: See CONTRADICTORY STATEMENT.

STATEMENT, EMPIRICAL: See EMPIRICAL STATEMENT.

STATEMENT, OBSERVATION: See OBSERVATION STATEMENT.

STATEMENT, SIMPLE: See SIMPLE STATEMENT.

STATEMENT, SYNTHETIC: See SYNTHETIC STATEMENT.

STATEMENT, TRUTH-FUNCTIONAL: See TRUTH-FUNCTIONAL STATEMENT.

STATISTICAL SYLLOGISM: A form of inductive reasoning in which a generalization stating that a percentage Z of a group has a certain property is used to justify a conclusion that it is probable to degree Z that a particular item in that group has that property. (10.3)

STIPULATIVE DEFINITION: A definition that creates a new precise meaning. (2.7.2)

STRATEGY, ADVOCATE'S: See ADVOCATE'S STRATEGY.

STRATEGY, CRITIC'S: See CRITIC'S STRATEGY.

STRATEGY, IMPARTIAL ADJUDICATOR'S: See IMPARTIAL ADJUDICATOR'S STRATEGY.

STRAW MAN: A fallacious argument that irrelevantly attacks a position that appears similar to, but is actually different from, an opponent's position, and concludes that the opponent's real position has thereby been refuted. (7.4.3)

SUBJECT CASE: The case about which one is trying to draw a conclusion in an analogical argument. (10.5)

SUBJECT GROUP: One division of a group to be studied in a scientific investigation: the division into which a change (or EXPERIMENTAL VARIABLE) is introduced. (11.2.2)

SUFFICIENT CONDITION: An antecedent condition such that if it happens, the consequent will follow. In other words, X is a sufficient condition for Y if, and only if, when X is true Y must also be true (or, when X is present Y must occur). (3.8)

SYLLOGISM, DISJUNCTIVE: See DISJUNCTIVE SYLLOGISM.

SYLLOGISM, STATISTICAL: See STATISTICAL SYLLOGISM.

SYNONYM, DEFINITION BY: See DEFINITION BY SYNONYM.

SYNTHETIC STATEMENT: A statement whose truth or falsity is not solely dependent upon the definitions—the meanings—of the words involved. (3.4)

T ARGUMENT: An argument with two or more premises, none of which offers significant support for the conclusion by itself; but all the premises do support the conclusion when working together, in combination. This argument is so-called because the lines in the tree diagram joining the premises to the conclusion form a T. (4.6.2)

TARGET FEATURE: The feature of the subject case in an analogue argument about which the conclusion is being drawn. (10.5)

TARGET PROPOSITION: The position against which the author of an essay argues; the focus of an essay's critique. (17.2)

TELEOLOGICAL MORAL THEORIES (also called CONSEQUENTIALIST MORAL THEORIES): Moral theories that hold that the rightness or wrongness of an action is to be determined by appeal to the goodness and badness of the consequences of all the actions open to the agent: the right action is the one which will have the best overall consequences. (12.2)

THEORY: A systematically integrated set of general principles, methods of investigation, and concepts whose function is to explain a wide array of phenomena. (11.4.2)

THESIS OF AN ARGUMENTATIVE ESSAY: The main conclusion of an argumentative essay; this is usually a position or point of view, but may be merely a simple statement. (16)

TREE DIAGRAM: A schematic representation of the structure of an argument using letters (P1, P2, MP3, C, etc.) to represent the premises and conclusion, and an arrow to represent *therefore*. (4.6)

TRUTH, COHERENCE THEORY OF: See COHERENCE THEORY OF TRUTH.

TRUTH, CORRESPONDENCE THEORY OF: See CORRESPONDENCE THEORY OF TRUTH.

TRUTH, PRAGMATIC THEORY OF: See PRAGMATIC THEORY OF TRUTH.

TRUTH-CLAIM, FALSIFIED: See FALSIFIED TRUTH-CLAIM.

TRUTH-CLAIM, UNDETERMINED: See UNDETERMINED TRUTH-CLAIM.

TRUTH-CLAIM, VERIFIED: See VERIFIED TRUTH-CLAIM.

TRUTH-FUNCTIONAL STATEMENT: A complex statement whose truth or falsity is entirely determined by the truth or falsity of the component statements. (9.2)

TU QUOQUE: A fallacious argument which attempts to show that a criticism directed at the speaker is irrelevant by claiming that the accuser is open to the same criticism. Latin for "you too." (7.4.2)

UNDETERMINED TRUTH-CLAIM: A truth-claim that has been neither shown to be true nor shown to be false. (6.2)

USE VS. MENTION: Usually, sentences use words, referring to their reference. But sentences may merely mention words, referring to the word itself. (Careful writers put words intended this way inside quotation marks, or in italics.) (3.2.4)

UTILITARIANISM: The moral theory whose central principle is that the best action is the one that generates the most happiness. (12.6)

UTILITY: Fitness for a practical purpose. (12.6)

UTILITY, PRINCIPLE OF: See PRINCIPLE OF UTILITY.

V ARGUMENT: An argument with two or more premises, each of which offers some support for the conclusion by itself; in combination, the support of each is added. This argument is so-called because the lines in a tree diagram joining two premises to the conclusion form a V (though not when there are more than two). (4.6.3)

VAGUE SENTENCE: A sentence that lacks a precise meaning. (3.2.1)

VALIDITY, FORMAL: See FORMAL VALIDITY.

VARIABLE OF INTEREST: A subsequent difference in the members of the subject group. (11.2.2)

VARIABLE, EXPERIMENTAL: See EXPERIMENTAL VARIABLE.

VERIFICATION: The process of determining whether a truth-claim is true. (6.2)

VERIFIED TRUTH-CLAIM: A truth-claim that has been shown to be true. (6.2)

Index

absurd examples, 240–41

abusing the person. *See* ad hominem fallacy

acceptability, 126, 129, 161

   criterion of, 97–98, 110, 113, 145, 304

   of premises, 97, 99, 114–15, 204, 295–96

   of truth claims, 110–13, 263

Achilles and the tortoise, 328

ad hominem fallacy, 131–32

adequacy, 161–62

   criterion of, 139–41, 174–75, 177

   of hypotheses, 177, 207–08, 210, 212, 214

   of premises, 97–98, 139, 141, 295–96

Advocate's Strategy, 309, 312–15, 320

aesthetic statements, 108

affirming the antecedent, 162

affirming the consequent, 166, 177

agreement

   joint method of agreement and difference, 194, 199–202

   jointly necessary and sufficient causes, 196

ambiguity, 56–60, 66. *See also* vagueness

   fallacy of equivocation and, 120

   grammatical, 59

   referential, 58–59

   use and mention, 60

analogical reasoning, 179–83

analogy (in guilt by association), 257

analytic statements, 62, 108

Anna's anthropological adventures, 330

antecedent, 66, 159, 193

   affirming the, 162

   denying the, 166

appeal to authority, 129–30, 142–43, 238–39, 353, 355–56

appeal to consequences, 227–30. *See also* greatest happiness principle; utilitarian arguments

appeal to force, 128

appeal to ignorance, 143, 305

appeal to pity, 96, 127–28

appeal to popularity, 128–29

appeal to principles of right and wrong, 222–25, 228

arguing back, 237–43

argument, 18, 95

   analogical (*See* analogical reasoning)

   chain, 162, 164–65

   complex, 86–88

   counter-arguments, 100, 242–43, 295, 297

   counterfactual, 21–22

   deductive (*See* deductive reasoning)

   explanatory, 79–81

   inductive (*See* inductive reasoning)

   joint method of agreement and difference, 194, 199–202

   jointly necessary and sufficient causes, 196

   main, 293, 296

   method of agreement, 194–96

   method of concomitant variations, 194, 202–03

   method of difference, 194, 197–200

   method of residue, 194, 203–04

   premises (*See* premises)

   reconstructing, 73–88, 163–64, 299–303

   reductio ad absurdum, 22, 146

   reports of, 78–79

   simple structure, 83

   sound, 21, 97–98, 114–15, 139, 161–62

   strategies for assessing, 95–100

   sub-arguments, 293, 295–97

   T structure, 84, 86, 144, 163

   V structure, 85–86, 88, 99, 299–300, 317, 319

   valid argument forms, 162–63

argument to the best explanation, 207

argumentative essays, 295–306

   intended audience, 291, 294

   strategies for organizing, 309–23

   structure, 291–93, 295–96, 309

   style, 291, 294–95

use of examples in, 295–96
use of quotations in, 296
argumentum ad hominem. See ad hominem fallacy
Aristotle, 192
    logic, 24–25
    reference theory of meaning, 33
artificial intelligence, 24
artificial language, 24
audience, 291, 294
Austin, John, 34–35
authority. *See* appeal to authority
auxiliary hypothesis, 210
average, 253. *See also* mean

barber paradox, 325
begging the question, 115–17, 310
beliefs, 103
    problem-solving function of, 104
bias, 173, 263–64, 267, 271, 273, 310

causal agent, 196
causal claims, 193–94
causal explanations, 80
causal factors, 147, 192–93
causal fallacies, 147–50, 192
causal relations, 192–94
Causality, Law of, 109–10
chain argument, 162, 164–65
chain of predictions *vs.* chained predictions, 144–46
charity, principle of, 55–56, 75–77, 81, 90, 134
Charter of Rights and Freedoms, 263
circular definitions, 48
coherence theory of truth, 102–03, 108
collective use of term, 59
common cause fallacy, 149, 192
common knowledge, 111–12, 115
common sense, 111
complete causal account, 192
complex arguments, 86–88
complex questions, 249–50
complex statement, 157
computer science, 24
conclusion, 18
    adequate support for, 97–98
    of argumentative essay, 293, 311
    identifying, 98, 295–96
    jumping to, 139, 141
    missing, 73–74, 77, 90, 99
confirmation
    induction by, 175–79
confirming instances, 175–77
confusing cause and effect, 148–49
conjunction, 158, 160
consequences, appeals to, 227–30. *See also* utilitarian
    arguments
consequent, 66, 159
    affirming the, 166

denying the, 162
context, 35, 81, 111, 126
    for proof of truth claims, 112
contextual method of definition, 46
contradictory statements, 62, 108
correlation, 192–94
    significant, 195–96
correspondence theory of truth, 101–02
counter-arguments, 100, 242–43, 295, 297
counter-examples, 238–39
counterfactual arguments, 21–22
counterfactual statements, 192
creationism, 211, 213–14
Criminal Code of Canada, 69
criteria of a sound argument, 97–98, 114–15, 139, 161–62
criterial approach, 95–100
critical thinking skills, 22–23, 269, 273
    moral questions, 24
Critic's Strategy, 309, 316–20
crucial experiment, 207

deductive reasoning, 20, 141, 155–66
    weaknesses, 171–72
definition, 42, 296
    circular, 48
    essentialist, 44, 49–51
    genus-species method, 44
    obscure, 49
    operational method of, 46
    ostensive method of, 45
    purposes of, 43–44
    reportive, 43, 46–49
    stipulative, 49–51
    too broad, 47, 50
    too broad and narrow, 47
    too narrow, 47, 50
denying the antecedent, 166
denying the consequent, 162, 177
deontological theories, 222
descriptive function of language, 36, 64
descriptive meaning, 64, 248, 257–58
directive function of language, 38
discarded "truths," 113
disconfirmed hypothesis, 207, 212
disconfirming instances, 177–78
disjunction, 158, 160
disjunctive syllogism, 163
distributive use of term, 59
domino effect. *See* slippery slope fallacy

emotive function of language, 37
empirical fact, 102–03, 105, 107–09
empirical predictions, 144, 175
empirical proof, 110
empirical statements, 102, 106–10, 192
empirical truth-claims, 106–07

in news reporting, 270–71
equivocation, 115, 120
essentialist definitions, 44, 49–51
Ethical Discussion in the Classroom (Ethics Research
    Group), 232
ethical statements, 108
evaluative function of language, 36, 64
evaluative meaning, 64–65, 248, 257–58
evocative function of language, 37
evolution/creation debate, 211, 213
evolutionism, 213–14
exclusive alternatives, 121
exhaustive alternatives, 121
experimental variable, 197
experts, 233. *See also* appeal to authority
explanations (explanatory arguments), 79–81
explanatory adequacy of hypothesis, 207–8, 210, 212,
    214
extended argument. *See* argumentative essays

facts, 102–03, 233
factual claims. *See* empirical truth-claims
fallacies, 25, 95–96
    ad hominem, 131–32
    affirming the consequent, 166, 177
    begging the question, 115–17
    causal, 147–50, 192
    common cause, 149, 192
    confusing cause and effect, 148–49
    denying the antecedent, 166
    equivocation, 115, 120
    false dichotomy, 115, 121–22, 227
    inconsistency, 115, 117–19
    post hoc, 147–48
    slippery slope fallacy, 144–46
    straw man, 133–34
    tu quoque, 132
fallibility
    recognition of, 233
false confidence, 251
false dichotomy, 115, 121–22, 227
falsification, 105, 107
formal validity, 161–62, 165–66
foundational principles, 109–10
freedom of the media, 263–64

general empirical statements, 106
generalization argument, 223–26, 231
    inductive, 107, 172–74
generalization of moral judgements, 232
genus-species method of definition, 44
getting the facts straight, 233
Golden Rule. *See* generalization argument
goodness, criterion of, 228
grammatical ambiguity, 59
greatest happiness principle, 227–28. *See also* appeal to
    consequences; utilitarian arguments

guilt-by-association, 257

hasty conclusion. *See* jumping to conclusions
Holmes, Oliver Wendell, 217
humour, 255
Huygens, Christian, 208–10
hypocrisy, 119
hypotheses, 175–76, 178, 180
    accuracy of, 207–08
    explanatory adequacy of, 207–08, 210, 212, 214
    rival, 207–08, 210–11

idea theory of meaning, 34
impartial adjudicator's strategy, 309, 320–23
implication, 159
incommensurability, 213
inconsistency, 115, 117–19
induction by confirmation, 175–79, 207
    non-scientific contexts, 176, 178–79
induction by hypothesis, 207
inductive generalization, 107, 172–74
inductive reasoning, 20, 141, 155, 171–83, 198, 203
inference, 17–21, 23, 78, 98, 139–41, 148, 194, 196,
    198, 204
inference indicators, 18
interpretation, 212
interpretation (in news reports), 267–68, 270
interpretive frameworks (media), 271–73
interpretive skills, 23
interrogative function of language, 38
introduction (to argumentative essay), 292
invalidity, formal, 165–66
inversely proportional variations, 202
irrational techniques of persuasion, 247–58, 263
irrelevant premises, 126–29, 139

Jeremy and his two girlfriends, 330
joint method of agreement and difference, 194,
    199–202
jointly necessary and sufficient causes, 196
jointly sufficient conditions, 69
Jonathan's clock, 330
jumping to conclusions, 139, 141

knowledge
    body of, 203
    common, 111–12, 115
    new, 172, 191

language, 33, 35. *See also* meaning
    complexity of, 31–32
    descriptive function of, 36, 64
    emotive, 37
    evaluative, 36, 64
    evocative function of, 37
    interrogative function of, 38

natural, 24
  performative function of, 38
  recreational function of, 39
  relationship to thinking, 31–32
  spoken, 32
  written, 32
Law of Causality, 109–10
law student paradox, 327
liar paradox, 326
light as a particle. *See* wave/particle debate
Lister, Joseph, 217
loaded questions, 249–50
loaded terms, 247–48, 264–65
Locke, John
  idea theory of meaning, 34
logic, 25
  mathematical, 25
  science of, 24–25
  truth-functional, 162
  use in natural language, 24
logical operator, 158, 163
logical paradoxes. *See* paradoxes
logical strength, 19–21, 75–77, 155–56, 161, 172
logical structure, 296

macro-structure, 292
macro-structure of argumentative essay, 309, 312, 323
matching, 198
mathematics, 24–25, 111
mean, 253
meaning, 31–52, 55–92. *See also* language
  context, 35
  descriptive, 64, 248, 257–58
  evaluative, 64–65, 248, 257–58
  idea theory of, 34
  reference theory of, 33
meaning as use, 34–35, 42
mechanistic theory, 213
media, 252, 263–64
  assessing news reports, 270–73
  bias, 264–66, 309
  conflicting news reports, 267–68
  interpretive frameworks, 271, 273
  loaded terms, 265
  objectivity, 266–67
  political perspective, 271
  role in democratic societies, 263–64
  special protection, 263–64
median, 253
method of agreement, 194–95
  limitations, 196
method of concomitant variations, 194, 202–03
method of difference, 194, 197–200
method of residue, 194, 203–04
Michelson, Albert, 210
Michelson-Morley experiment, 210
Mill, John Stuart, 194, 202–04

Miranda's will, 331
misleading statistics, 243–54
  graphs, 254
  selectivity, 253
missing conclusion, 73–74, 77, 90, 99
missing premises, 73–77, 80, 90, 99, 119, 129, 145, 238–39
mode, 253
moral judgements, 219
  generalizability, 220
  vs. judgements of taste, 219–20
moral justification, 221
moral maturity, 232–34
moral reasoning, 219–34
moral theories, 222
Morley, Edward, 210

natural language, 24
necessary and sufficient conditions, 66–68, 147, 192
negation, 158, 160
negative results, 178
new knowledge, 171–72
news media. *See* media
newspapers. *See* media
Newton, Isaac, 208–09
non-empirical proof, 110–11
non-empirical statements, 103, 108–09
non-empirical truth-claims, 108–10
non-sequitur, 126–27. *See also* irrelevant premises

objectivity (news media), 266–67
obscure definitions, 48
observation statements, 175, 177
observed variable of interest, 197
operational method of definition, 46
ostensive method of definition, 45

paradox of omnipotence, 328
paradoxes, 325–29
particle hypothesis. *See* wave/particle debate
particular empirical statements, 106
passive voice, 294
Pasteur, Louis, 214, 217
performative function of language, 38
persuasion
  irrational techniques of, 247–58, 263
persuasive function of language, 37
persuasive redefinition, 257–58
petitio principii. See begging the question
"point of view" *vs.* bias, 267, 310
position paper, 310
post hoc, 147–48
pragmatic theory of truth, 104–05
predictions
  empirical, 144, 175
premises, 18
  acceptability, 97, 99, 114–15, 139, 295–96

adequacy, 100, 295–96
adequate, 97
identifying, 99, 295–96
missing, 73–77, 80, 90, 99, 119, 129, 145, 238–39
relevance, 97, 99, 125–29, 295–96
truth or falsity, 19–21
presuppositions, 75–77, 80, 110, 113
principle of charity, 55–56, 75–77, 81, 90, 134
principle of utility, 228–29, 231
prisoners' dilemma, 328
probability, 144, 172, 174, 180, 186, 194, 200
probative arguments, 80–81
proof, 20, 97, 104, 108, 110–13, 221, 231
properties
analogical argument by, 181–82
proportional relations, 202
public opinion polls, 107
puzzles, 329–34

quantum theory, 210
quotations
use in argumentative essays, 295–96

radical sceptics, 221
randomizing, 198
rational agreement, 231
reasoning, 17–18
analogical, 179–83
deductive, 155–66, 171–72
inductive, 141, 171–83, 198, 203
reasoning skills, 23
reconstructing the argument, 73–88, 163–64, 299–303
recreational function of language, 39
red herring, 256
reductio ad absurdum, 22, 146
reference (denotation or extension), 43
reference theory of meaning, 33
referential ambiguity, 58–59
relations
analogical argument by, 181–82
proportional, 202
relevance, 161–62
criterion of, 125–26
of premises, 97, 99, 295–96
religious statements, 108–09
reportive definitions, 43, 46–49
assessing, 46–49
restricted hypotheses, 207–08, 210
rhetorical questions, 296
rival hypotheses, 207–08, 210–11
rival restricted hypotheses, 210
rival unrestricted hypotheses, 211
rules in assessing arguments, 98–100
rules of good writing. See style

Sam and the surgeon, 331
sampling, 173

bias in, 173
selectivity, 252
science of logic, 24
sciences, 46, 90, 110, 123, 171
computer science, 24
scientific reasoning, 176, 178, 191–204, 207–12
selectivity, 252, 264–65, 273. See also bias
in use of statistics, 253
Semmelweis, Ignaz, 214–17
sense (connotation or intension), 43
significant correlation, 195–96
simple argument structure, 83
simple statement, 157
slippery slope fallacy, 144–46
sound arguments, 21, 115, 125, 129, 139, 155, 161, 180,
292–93
speculation, 296
standard usage, 43–44, 46, 49–51
statements, 18
aesthetic, 108
analytic, 62, 108
complex, 157
contradictory, 62, 108
counterfactual, 192
empirical, 102, 106–10, 192
non-empirical, 103, 108–09
observation, 175, 177
religious, 108–09
simple, 157
synthetic, 62
thesis, 311
truth-functional, 157–58, 160, 163
statistical empirical statements, 106
statistical syllogism, 174–75
stipulative definitions, 43, 49–51
straw man fallacy, 133–34
style, 291, 294–95
subject case, 181
subject group, 197
sufficient conditions. See necessary and sufficient
conditions
summaries, 296
surprise examination, 326
symbolic logic, 24
synonyms, 45
synthetic statements, 62

T arguments, 84, 86, 144, 163
target feature, 181
teleological or consequentialist theories, 222
theory
definition of, 212
interpretive role, 213
thesis, 292–93
thesis statement, 311
thin edge of the wedge. See slippery slope fallacy
tolerance, 233

tree diagram, 83, 86, 299
truth
    coherence theory of, 102–3, 108
    correspondence theory, 101–02
    pragmatic theory of, 104–5
    truth or falsity of premises, 19–21, 23
truth-claims, 101–23
    acceptability, 263
    non-empirical, 108–10
    undetermined, 105
    verification, 105, 107
truth-functional logic, 162
truth-functional statements, 157–58, 160, 163
tu quoque fallacy, 132–33
Two Wrongs fallacy. *See* tu quoque fallacy

universal empirical statements, 107
unobserved factors, 199

unrestricted hypotheses, 208
utilitarian arguments, 228–29, 231

V arguments, 85–86, 88, 99, 299–300, 317, 319
vagueness, 56–57, 248–49. *See also* ambiguity
valid argument forms, 162–64
validity
    deductive, 141
    formal, 161–62, 165–66
verification, 105, 107
verification skills, 23

wave/particle debate, 208–11, 213
weekly poker game, 331
Why... ? question, 193–94, 213
Wittgenstein, Ludwig, 34–35

Young, Thomas, 210